YOUR ASTROLOGY GUIDE 2012

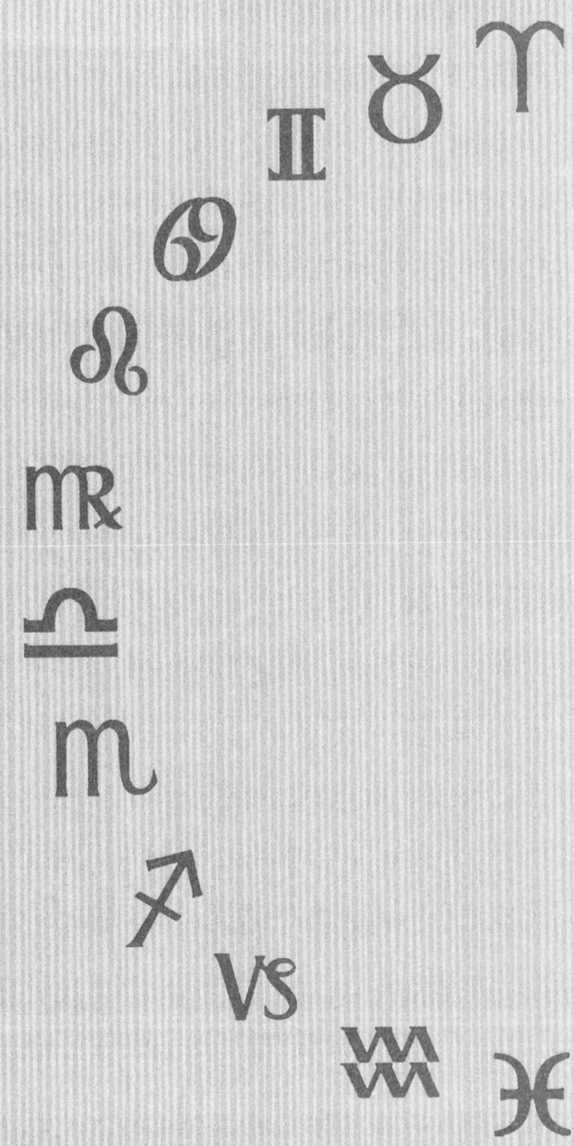

YOUR ASTROLOGY GUIDE 2012

RICK LEVINE & **JEFF** JAWER

STERLING ETHOS
New York

New York

An Imprint of Sterling Publishing
387 Park Avenue South
New York, NY 10016

ISBN 978-1-4027-7939-8

Distributed in Canada by Sterling Publishing
c/o Canadian Manda Group, 165 Dufferin Street
Toronto, Ontario, Canada M6K 3H6
Distributed in the United Kingdom by GMC Distribution Services
Castle Place, 166 High Street, Lewes, East Sussex, England BN7 1XU
Distributed in Australia by Capricorn Link (Australia) Pty. Ltd.
P.O. Box 704, Windsor, NSW 2756, Australia

For information about custom editions, special sales, and premium and corporate purchases, please contact Sterling Special Sales at 800-805-5489 or specialsales@sterlingpublishing.com.

Manufactured in the United States of America

2 4 6 8 10 9 7 5 3 1

TABLE OF CONTENTS

ACKNOWLEDGMENTS

Many people continue to contribute to this annual book, both in conception and in production. Some have been with us from the start; some have only recently joined the team. First of all, our heartfelt thanks to Paul O'Brien, whose creative genius behind Tarot.com led us to this project. Paul is our agent, our friend, and his vision opened the doors to make this book possible. On the production side, we are grateful for our editor, Gail Goldberg. Her ability to clarify concepts, untangle sentences, and sharpen our words is matched by her commitment to presenting astrology in an intelligent light. We appreciate her energetic Mars in efficient Virgo; her persistent attention to detail continues to challenge us to write better books. Of course we are very grateful to Michael Fragnito, editorial director at Sterling Publishing, for his initial vision of what this book could be, his tireless support for the project, and his trust in our work. Barbara Berger, Sterling's supervising editor on this book, has shepherded the project with Taurean persistence and good humor under the ongoing pressures of very tight deadlines. We thank Laura Jorstad for her refinement of the text, and project editor Mary Hern for her careful guidance. We are thankful to Marcus Leaver, Jason Prince, Karen Nelson, Elizabeth Mihaltse, Rebecca Maines, and Gavin Motnyk at Sterling. Thanks go to Bob Wietrak and Jules Herbert at Barnes & Noble, and whoever said yes in the beginning. We appreciate 3+Co and Asami Matsushima for the original design; and thanks for the art and ideas from Jessica Abel and the rest of the Tarot.com team. Thanks, as well, to Tara Gimmer and company for the author photo.

Rick: I am indebted to a truly great writing partner. Thank you, Jeff, for showing up with a combination of unwavering reliability, solid astrology, and the willingness to keep pushing the envelope of creativity. My deep appreciation also goes to Gail Goldberg, editor extraordinaire, who doesn't ever let us take the easy way out. Her steadfast commitment to making a difference through what we say in these annuals has made each of them better. And, of course, we are blessed with readers who are hungry for valid astrology information that is based on hope rather than fear. We are here because of you.

Jeff: Thanks, Rick, for the consistently high quality of your astrology, your writing, and the great gift of your friendship. I have special thanks for Gail Goldberg who served this book and its readers with uncommon dedication and skill. Thanks, too, to my live-in inspirations: my wife, Danick, whose music fills our home with creativity, and my daughters, Laura and Lyana, whose joyous discoveries of life fill me with hope for the future.

INTRODUCTION

YOU ARE THE STAR OF YOUR LIFE

The more you learn about yourself, the better able you are to wisely use the energies in your life. For more than 3,000 years, astrology has been the sharpest tool in the box for describing the human condition. Used by virtually every culture on the planet, astrology continues to illuminate the link between individual lives and planetary energies and cycles.

The purpose of this book is to help you take a more active role in creating your present and, by extension, your future by showing you how to apply astrology's ancient wisdom to today's world. Our aim is to facilitate your day-to-day journey by revealing the turns in the road of life and describing the best ways for you to navigate them.

Astrology's highest use is to enable you to gain knowledge of yourself and perspective of your surroundings. It is common to go through life feeling blown about by forces beyond your control. Astrology can help you see the changing tides within and outside you. By allowing you to recognize the shifting patterns of mood and circumstance at work in your life, it helps you to stay centered and empowered. As you follow along in this book, you will grow to better understand your own needs as well as the challenges and opportunities you encounter.

In *Your Astrology Guide: 2012*, we describe the patterns of your life as they are reflected in the great cycles of the sky above. We do not simply predict events, although we give examples of them throughout the book. Rather, we are reporting the planetary energies—the cosmic weather in which you are living—so that you understand these conditions and know how to use them effectively. The power, though, is not in the stars, of course, but in your mind, your heart, and the choices that you make every day. Regardless of how strongly you are buffeted by the winds of change or bored by stagnation, your mind has many ways to see any situation. Learning about the energies of the Sun, Moon, and planets will both sharpen and widen your perspective. Thousands of years of human experience have proven astrology's value; our purpose is to show you how to enrich your life with it.

The language of astrology gives the gift of awareness, not a rigid set of rules. It works best when blended with common sense, intuition, and self-trust. This is your life, and no one knows how to live it as well as you. Take what you need from this book and leave the rest. Think of the planets as setting the stage for the year ahead, but it is you who are the writer, director, and star of your life.

ABOUT US

We were practicing astrology independently when we joined forces in 1999 to launch StarIQ.com. Our shared interest in making intelligent astrology available to as wide an audience as possible led to StarIQ, as well as a relationship with Tarot.com and the creation of this book. While we have continued to work independently as well, our collaboration has been a success and a joy as we've made our shared goals a reality, and we plan for it to continue long into the future.

RICK LEVINE

I've always wanted to know the answers to unanswerable questions. As a youth, I studied science and mathematics because I believed that they offered concrete answers to complex questions. I learned about the amazing conceptual breakthroughs made by modern man due to the developing technologies that allowed us to peer into the deep reaches of outer space and also into the tiniest subatomic realms. But as I encountered imaginary numbers in higher mathematics, along with the uncertainty of quantum physics, I began to realize that our modern sciences, as advanced as they are, would never satisfy my longing to understand my own individual life or the world around me. I learned that our basic assumptions of time and space fall apart at both ends of the spectrum—the very big and the very small. I became obsessed with solving the puzzle of the cosmos and discovering its hidden secrets.

As a college student at the State University of New York at Stony Brook in the late sixties, I studied psychology and philosophy, and participated in those times as a student of the universe. I read voraciously and found myself more interested in the unexplainable than in what was already known. As a psychology student, I was less concerned with running rats through mazes than with understanding how the human mind worked. I naturally gravitated to the depth psychologies of Sigmund Freud and Carl Jung. Additionally, the life-altering information coming from the humanistic psychology movement presented me with an academic framework with which to better understand how human potential could be further developed. I knew then and there that human consciousness was expanding and that I wanted to be a part of this evolutionary process. In this environment, I first encountered the writings of R. Buckminster Fuller. He appealed to my scientific mind-set, but blessed me with new ways to view my world. In the early 20th century, Albert Einstein had clearly demonstrated that energy is simply the transformation of light into mass and mass into light—but that was just an intellectual concept to me.

Bucky Fuller, however, went on to establish a scientific language to describe the relationships between mass and light, particles and waves. His incredible geodesic domes are merely representations of what he discovered. I began to understand that what we can see is but a faint shadow of the knowable universe. I learned that everything vibrates. There are no things out there, just different frequencies of vibration—many of which are so fast that they give us the illusion of a solid world. Even something as basic as the color green or red is merely a label for certain frequencies of light vibration.

This was my world when I first discovered that astrology was more than just a parlor game. Already acquainted with the signs of the zodiac, I knew that I was an impulsive Aries, a pioneer, and an independent thinker. I noticed how my friends and professors fit their sun signs. Then, I was astounded to learn that Jung's *Analytical Psychology of Four Types* was based upon the astrological elements of fire, earth, air, and water. And I was amazed to discover that a great scientist, such as Johannes Kepler—the Father of Modern Astronomy—was himself a renowned astrologer. The more I read, the more I realized that I had to become an astrologer myself. I needed to know more about astrology and how it works. Now, nearly 40 years later, I know more about astrology—a lot more—with still so much to learn.

Astronomers have their telescopes, enabling them to see things tele, or far away. Biologists have microscopes to see what is *micro*, or small. We astrologers have the horoscope, extending our view of the *horo*, or hour. For more than three decades, I have calculated horoscopes—first by hand, later with computer—and have observed the movement of time in its relationship to the heavenly bodies. I have watched the timing of the transitions in my own life and in the lives of my family, friends, and clients. I have been privileged to see, again and again, the unquestionable harmony between the planetary cycles and our individual lives. I am proud to be a part of an astrological renaissance. Astrology has become increasingly popular because it fulfills our need to know that we are a part of the cosmos, even though modern culture has separated us from nature. It is not man versus nature. We are nature—and our survival as a species may depend on humanity relearning this concept. I take my role as an astrologer very seriously as I use what I have learned to help people expand their awareness, offer them choices, and educate them on how to cooperate with the cosmos instead of fight against it. I contributed to reestablishing astrology in academia as a founding trustee of the Kepler College of Astrological Arts and Science (Lynnwood, Washington). I maintain an active role in the international community of astrologers as a member of the International Society for Astrological Research (ISAR), the National Council for Geocosmic Research (NCGR), the Association for Astrological Networking (AFAN), and the Organization for Professional Astrology (OPA).

In 1999, I partnered with Jeff Jawer to create StarIQ.com, an innovative astrology website. Since then Jeff and I have been working together to raise the quality of astrology available to the public, first through StarIQ.com and, later, through our partnership with Tarot.com. It continues to be a real privilege and thrill to work with Jeff and to now offer the fruits of our labors to you.

JEFF JAWER

I've been a professional astrologer for more than 30 years. Astrology is my career, my art, and my passion. The excitement that I felt when I first began is still with me today. My first encounter with real astrology was in 1973 when I was going through a painful marriage breakup. All I knew about astrology at the time was that I was a Taurus, which didn't sound very exciting to me. "The reliable Bull is steadfast and consistent," I read. "Not given to risk taking or dramatic self-expression, Taurus prefers peace and comfort above all." Boring. Fortunately, I quickly discovered that there was more to astrology—much more.

An amateur astrologer read my chart for me on my 27th birthday, and I was hooked. I bought the biggest astrology book I could find, began intensive study, found a teacher, and started reading charts for people. Within a few months, I changed my major at the University of Massachusetts at Amherst from communications to astrology under the Bachelor's Degree with Individual Concentration program. There were no astrology classes at the university, but I was able to combine courses in astronomy, mythology, and psychology, with two special seminars on the history of astrology, to graduate in 1975 with a B.A. in the history and science of astrology. In 1976, I moved to Atlanta, Georgia, the only city in the United States with a mandatory examination for professional astrologers. I passed it, as well as the American Federation of Astrologers' professional exam, and served twice as president of the Metro Atlanta Astrological Society and as chairman of the City of Atlanta Board of Astrology Examiners.

For several years, I was the corporate astrologer for International Horizons, Inc., a company that sold courses on English as a second language in Japan. The owner had me research the founding dates of banks he was interested in acquiring so that I could advise him based on their charts. Later, he and I created Astro, the world's first electronic astrology calculator. In 1982, I was one of the founding members of the Association for Astrological Networking (AFAN), an organization that plays a major role in defending the legal rights of astrologers. AFAN joined with two other organizations, the International Society for Astrological Research (ISAR) and the National Council for Geocosmic Research (NCGR), to present the first United Astrology Congress (UAC) in 1986. UAC conferences were the largest astrology events in North America for more than a decade. I served on the UAC board for four years.

I began teaching at astrology conferences in the late 1970s, and there I met many of the world's leading astrologers, many of whom are my friends to this day. I have taught at dozens of conferences and local astrology groups around the United States. I have lectured at the World Astrology Congress in Switzerland four times, as well as in Holland, France, England, Belgium, Spain, Germany, Canada, Brazil, and Australia. However, the most important time for me personally was the two years I spent teaching for the Network of Humanistic Astrologers based in France. There I met my wife, Danick, in 1988. Her double-Pisces sensitivity has added to my work and my life immeasurably.

Counseling individual clients is the core of my professional life, as it is for most astrologers, but writing about astrology has always been important to me. I've written hundreds of articles for journals, magazines, books, websites, and newspapers ranging from the monthly calendar for *The Mountain Astrologer* to sun-sign forecasts for *CosmoGIRL!* magazine. Currently, I write "LoveScopes" (a weekly sun-sign romance horoscope), the "New Moon Report," and other specialized material for Tarot.com, AOL, and StarIQ.com. I've also been employed in the astrology industry as director of public relations for Matrix Software and vice president of Astro Communication Services, two of the field's oldest companies. Rick and I founded StarIQ in 1999, the beginning of our professional collaboration. We produce a daily audio forecast called *Planet Pulse*, and *StarTalkers*, a weekly radio broadcast. Early in my career, I contributed to pioneering the field of experiential astrology, also called astrodrama. It's been a great adventure to combine theater games, psychodrama, Gestalt techniques, visualization, movement, art, and sound to bring astrology to life in workshops around the world. To experience astrology through emotions and in the body, rather than by the intellect alone, can ground one's understanding of the planets and signs in a very useful way.

Think about Venus, for example. She's the goddess of love, the planet of beauty and attraction. What if you need more sweetness in your life? Imagine how Venus walks. Now, get up and do your own Venus walk to the kitchen. Feel in balance and graceful as your feet embrace the floor and as your hips sway. Be Venus; invite her presence to you. Glide, slide, and be suave; you're so beautiful. Remember this walk if you're feeling unloved and, the next thing you know, Venus will arrive. Each planet is different, of course, according to its unique character. You'll learn another dance from responsible Saturn—a slower march across the floor, head upright, shoulders back—steady and straight, but not too stiff. Try that one for self-discipline.

Astrology describes the energy of time, how the quality of Tuesday afternoon is different from Wednesday morning. Seeing when and where patterns arise in your life gives you clearer vision and a better understanding of the choices that are open to you. The rich language of astrology makes a cosmic connection that empowers you and rewards the rest of us as you fulfill more and more of your potential.

AUTHOR'S NOTE:

Your Astrology Guide uses the Tropical zodiac based on the seasons, not the constellations. This method of determining signs has been and continues to be the practice of Western astrologers for over 2,000 years. Aries, the beginning of the Tropical zodiac, starts on the first day of spring every year. Contrary to what you may have heard, no one's sign has changed, regardless of when you were born and the addition of a thirteenth sign is not relevant to Western astrology.

Measuring and recording the apparent movement of the Sun, the Moon, and the planets against the backdrop of the heavens is a complex task because nothing is stationary. Even the location of the constellations with respect to the seasons gradually changes from year to year. Since astrologers are concerned with human behavior here on Earth, they created a twelve-fold zodiac that is anchored to four seasons as their primary frame of reference. Obviously, astrologers fully understand that there are eighty-eight official constellations and that the moving planets travel through many of them (including Ophiuchus and Orion), but these are not—and never have been—part of the Tropical zodiac created by astrologers.

ASTROLOGY'S ORIGINS

Astrology is as old as time. It began when events in the sky were first observed to affect events here on Earth. The turning of day into night, the rising and falling of the tides with the Moon's cycles, and the changing seasons were watched by humanity long before written history, even at the very dawn of human civilization. Ancient Egyptians tracked the star Sirius to predict the flooding of the Nile River, which was essential to their agriculture. Babylonians, Mayans, Hindus, Chinese, and virtually every other group of people on the planet have practiced a form of astrology. Part science, part religion, calendar, mythology, and almanac, astrology remains the most comprehensive and coherent system for understanding life on this planet.

In the 2nd century AD, Claudius Ptolemy codified astrology, based on its origins in Mesopotamia and development in classical Greece. Astrology was an essential part of the scientific and philosophical evolution that gave birth to Western civilization. Another major path of development occurred in India, where Vedic astrology remains an integral part of the culture. Astrology was originally used to address collective concerns such as climate and warfare. It was rarely applied to the lives of individuals, except for rulers whose fates were considered tied to those of the nation. Astrology is still applied to public concerns, especially in the burgeoning field of financial astrology, which is used for stock-market forecasting. Today, however, the vast majority of astrology is applied to the lives of individuals through personal consultations, computer-generated reports, horoscope columns, books, and the Internet.

The importance of astrology has risen, fallen, and risen again in the Western world. Through the Renaissance and the Elizabethan period, astrology was part and parcel of daily life. Shakespeare's numerous references to it are just one indicator of its wide acceptance and popularity in his time. However, the rationalism of René Descartes and his followers took hold in philosophical circles and demanded that modern science exclude anything that cannot be proven according to its methods. Astrology was banished from academia in 1666, and it remained outside the intellectual mainstream for almost 300 years. Modern astrology began its rebirth in the early part of the 20th century largely due to the work of Alan Leo, the father of sun-sign astrology. A second, and larger, wave of interest grew out of the counterculture movement of the 1960s when interest in metaphysics and Eastern religions also gained momentum. The brilliant works of the Swiss psychologist Carl Jung and French-American astrologer Dane Rudhyar inspired a new generation of astrologers, including the authors of this book.

ASTROLOGY TODAY: EMPOWERMENT

Thanks to Jung, Rudhyar, and many other brilliant minds, modern astrology has largely separated itself from the fatalism of the past when, for example, the sighting of an approaching comet meant the king would die and nothing more. Today's astrology is, as Rudhyar wrote, "person-centered," with the focus on individual choice and personal growth rather than the simple prediction of events. In fact, while we do write about events in this book, we spend more time describing energy patterns and emotions for several reasons.

First, you're a unique individual. You may share characteristics and tendencies with fellow members of your sun sign, but you will experience them in your own way. In addition, you have a personal birth chart in which the positions of the Moon, planets, and other factors distinguish you from the other members of your sun- sign clan. Analyzing how all the planets and signs interact in a person's chart is the foundation of a personal consultation with a professional astrologer or a detailed custom report like those available at http://www.tarot.com/astrology/astroprofile.

ENERGY, EVENTS, AND EMOTION

At its essence, astrology describes energy. Energy can take many forms; it can be an event, emotion, or attitude. We suggest the possible outcomes of astrological events in this book, but they are examples or models of how the planetary energies might be expressed. Each person is going to experience these patterns in his or her own unique way. We have learned that it is more helpful to understand the underlying energy patterns of events than it is to describe them. You may not be able to change the world outside you, but you have an enormous range of choice when it comes to your thoughts and attitudes.

We are here to assist you with ideas and information rooted in history and woven into the cloth of our culture. We recognize and honor you as the center of your life. This book is not a collection of ideas that are foreign to your nature, but a recollection of human experiences that exist within all of us. Whether you know their meanings or not, all the signs and planets live within you. They are part of your human heritage, a gift of awareness, a language not meant to label you and stick you in a box, but a treasure map to yourself and the cosmos beyond. It is a glorious journey we all share. May your way be filled with light this year and in the years to come.

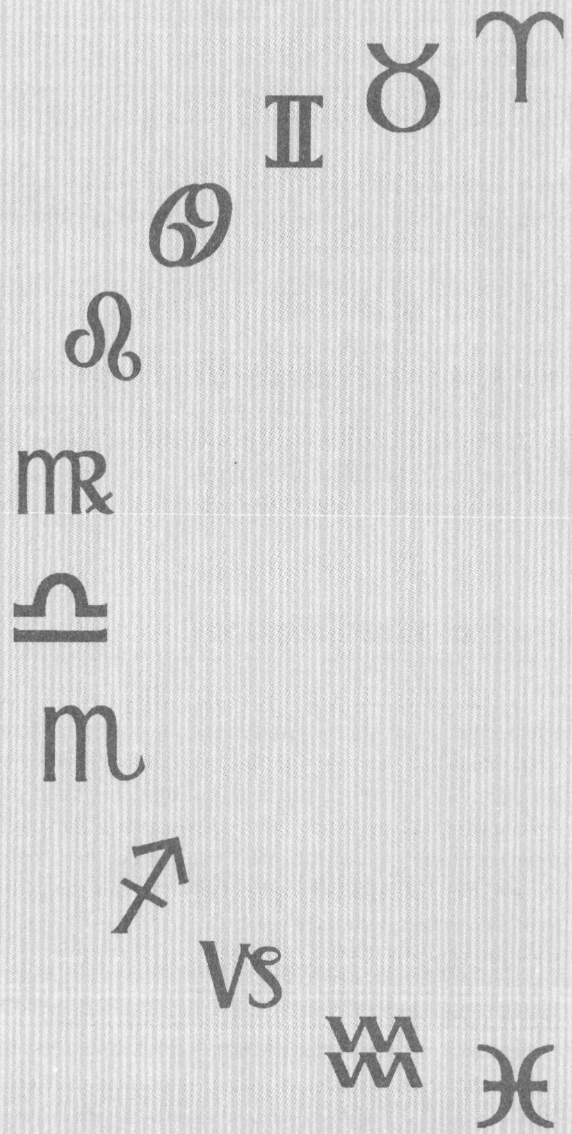

PART 1

2012 ASTROLOGY & YOU

HOW TO USE THIS BOOK

ASTROLOGY BASICS

WHAT'S YOUR SIGN?

In this book, we present a view of the year ahead for each sun sign. Your sign is based on the Sun's position at the moment of your birth. As most people know, the Sun travels through the twelve signs of the zodiac over the course of a year. However, the Sun doesn't change signs at the exact moment on the same date every year. If you were born within two days of the cusp (the end or beginning) of a sign, a more exact calculation may be required to determine your sun sign. So, if you are uncertain about your sign, consult an astrologer or get a free copy of your birth chart from http://www.tarot.com/astrology/astroprofile to determine the correct one. In addition to giving you the exact position of the Sun at the moment of your birth, an individual birth or natal chart includes the positions of the Moon and planets as well, which provides a much more detailed astrological view of your life. This information is used in private consultations and computer-generated astrology reports. The sun sign does not tell your entire astrological story. But it is powerful enough to light up your consciousness with ideas that can change your life.

For those of you who have your astrology chart, in addition to reading the chapter in this book on your sun sign, you will also want to read about your moon and rising signs as well. Your intuition will guide you as you integrate the information.

TRANSITS

The information presented in this book is based on the relationship of the planets, including the Sun and the Moon, to the twelve signs of the zodiac in 2012. The movement of the planets in their cycles and their geometric relationship to one another as they interact are called **transits**; they are the primary forecasting tool for astrologers.

As planets enter into specific relationships with one another, astrologers consider the astrological events that occur. For example, when the Sun and the Moon align in a certain way, an event called an **eclipse** occurs. As you read this book, many of you will study more than one sign, whether you are checking up on someone you know or on your own moon or rising sign. You will notice that certain dates are often mentioned repeatedly from sign to sign. This is because major planetary events affect everyone, but some more than others, and in different ways.

For example, in 2012, there is a Full Moon Eclipse in Sagittarius on June 4. Everyone will feel the power of the eclipse, but individual reactions will vary. Its effects will be most obvious for Sagittarius and its opposite sign Gemini. Since this particular eclipse is stressed by Mars, it will also be challenging for Aries, the sign ruled by this planet. The cosmic weather rains on all of us; the water can be parted in twelve ways, each a door to a sign that will experience it differently.

RULING OR KEY PLANETS

Every sign is associated with a key or ruling planet. There is an affinity between signs and their planetary rulers—a common purpose that connects them, like lungs with breathing or feet with walking. In astrology's early days, the Sun (Leo) and the Moon (Cancer) ruled one sign each, and the rest of the known planets—Mercury, Venus, Mars, Jupiter, and Saturn—ruled two. However, in the modern era, new planets have been discovered and astrology has evolved to reflect this. The discovery of Uranus in the late eighteenth century coincided with revolutions in the United States and France, triggered a technological revolution that's still going on today, and transformed astrology's traditional rulership system. Radical Uranus was assigned to rule inventive Aquarius, while its old ruler, Saturn, took a step back. Neptune, discovered with photography sixty-five years later, became the ruler of Pisces, nudging Jupiter into the background. And if Pluto hasn't purged Mars from Scorpio, it's certainly taken the dominant role in expressing this sign's energy. We mention ruling planets quite a bit in the book as we track the cycles of a given sign. The sign Aries, named for the Greek god of war, is ruled by Mars, the Roman name for the same god. Transits of Mars, then, play a leading role in the forecasts for Aries. Venus is used in the same way in the forecasts for Taurus. For double-ruled Scorpio, Aquarius, and Pisces, we take the traditional and modern planetary rulers into account. The planets and the signs they rule are further discussed later in this section.

ELEMENTS

The four astrological elements are fire, earth, air, and water. The action-oriented fire signs—Aries, Leo, and Sagittarius—are warm and dynamic. The sense-oriented earth signs—Taurus, Virgo, and Capricorn—are practical and realistic. The thought-oriented air signs—Gemini, Libra, and Aquarius—are logical and sociable. The emotion-oriented water signs—Cancer, Scorpio, and Pisces—are intuitive and instinctual. Signs of the same element work harmoniously together. In addition, fire and air signs work well together, as do earth and water.

INGRESSES

An **ingress** is the entry of a planet into a new sign. The activities and concerns of the planet will be colored by that sign's energy. For example, when the communication planet Mercury enters Leo, the expressive qualities of that sign tend to make for more dramatic speech than in the previous sign, self-protective Cancer. When Mercury leaves Leo for detail-oriented Virgo, thoughts and words become more precise. Each planet has its own unique rhythm and cycle in terms of how long it takes that planet to move through all the signs. This determines how long it stays in one sign. The Moon, for example, flies through a sign in two and a half days, while Uranus takes seven years.

HOUSES

Your natal chart is divided into twelve astrological houses that correspond to different areas of your life. This book uses solar houses that place your sun sign in the 1st

House. In this system, when a planet enters a new sign, it also enters a new house. Thus, the effect of a planet's ingress into a particular sign depends also on which house of the sign in question it's entering. For example, for a Gemini sun sign, Gemini is its own 1st House, followed by Cancer for the 2nd, Leo for the 3rd House, and so on. If you are a Taurus, your 4th House is Leo. As a Scorpio, your 8th House is Gemini. If this is confusing, don't worry about counting houses; we do it for you. The influence of an astrological event differs considerably based on which house of a sign it falls in.

You'll notice that there are many different, but related, terms used to describe each house, sign, and planet. For example, Mars is called feisty, assertive, impatient, or aggressive at different times throughout the book. Also, we use different house names depending on the emphasis we perceive. You'll find the 4th House described as the 4th House of Home and Family, the 4th House of Security, and the 4th House of Roots—all are valid. We change the descriptions to broaden your understanding, rather than repeat the same limited interpretation over and over. Later in this section is a brief description of all the houses.

ASPECTS

Aspects are geometrically significant angles between planets and a key feature of any astrological forecast. A fast-moving body like the Moon will form every possible aspect to every degree of the zodiac during its monthly orbit around the Earth. The Sun will do the same in a year, Mars in two years, Jupiter in twelve. The slower a planet moves, the less common its aspects, which makes them more significant because their effect is longer. A lunar aspect lasts only a few hours, and one from Mercury a day or two, but a transit like the Jupiter-Neptune square that occurs three times this year can last for a week or two or more.

The qualities of the two planets involved in an aspect are important to its meaning, but so is the angle between them. Soft aspects like **sextiles** and **trines** grease the cosmic wheels, while hard ones like **squares** and **oppositions** often reflect bumps in the road. **Conjunctions**, when two planets are conjoined, are arguably the most powerful aspect and can be easy or difficult according to the nature of the planets involved. To learn more about the nature of the aspects, turn to the next chapter.

The effect of an aspect on each sun sign is modified according to the houses of that sign where the planets fall. A Venus-Mars trine from Cancer to Scorpio is the harmonious expression of Venus's desire for security with Mars's instinct to protect. They are both in water signs, thus compatible. And if you are a Pisces, Venus in Cancer is in your 5th House and Mars in Scorpio is in your 9th, stirring romance and adventure. Alternatively, if you are a Gemini, Venus in Cancer is in your 2nd House and Mars in Scorpio is in the 6th. Applying the cozy relationship of a trine to Gemini's chart gives the interpretation that there will be a comfortable flow in the practical realms of money and work.

RETROGRADES

All true planets (i.e., excluding the Sun and Moon) turn **retrograde** from time to time. This means that the planet appears to go backward in the zodiac, revisiting recently traveled territory. As with other planetary phenomena, astrologers have observed specific effects from retrogrades. The days when planets turn from direct, or forward, motion to retrograde and back again are called **stations** (because the planet appears to be stationary). These are significant periods that emphasize the energy of the stationing planet.

A retrograde station, when backward motion begins, indicates the beginning of a relatively introspective cycle for that planet's energy. At a direct station, the energy that has been turned inward during the retrograde period begins to express itself more overtly in the outer world once again. Retrogrades can cause certain aspects to occur three times—first forward, then retrograde, then forward again. These triple events can be like a play that unfolds in three acts. The first aspect often raises an issue that's reconsidered or adjusted during the second transit and completed during the third.

LUNATIONS AND ECLIPSES

New Moons, Full Moons, and eclipses are important astrological events. These aspects involving the Moon are called **lunations**. Every month the Sun and Moon join together at the New Moon, seeding a fresh lunar cycle that affects us each in a personal way. The New Moon in the partnership sign of Libra sparks relationships, while the New Moon in the resource sign of Taurus brings attention to money. Two weeks later, the Moon opposes the Sun at the Full Moon. This is often an intense time due to the pull of the Moon in one direction and the Sun in another. The Full Moon in Cancer, for example, pits the need (Moon) for inner security (Cancer) against the Sun in Capricorn's urge for worldly recognition. The Full Moon can be stressful, but it is also a time of illumination that can give rise to greater consciousness. At the Full Moon, instead of seeing yourself pulled apart by opposing forces, it helps to imagine that you're the meeting point where the opposition is resolved by a breakthrough in awareness.

Planets that form significant aspects with the New or Full Moon play a key role in shaping their character. A New Moon square Jupiter is challenged by a tendency to be overexpansive, a negative quality of that planet. A Full Moon conjunct Saturn is bound in seriousness, duty, or doubt symbolized by this planet of necessity.

Eclipses are a special class of New and Full Moons where the Sun and Moon are so close to their line of intersection with the Earth that the light of one of them is darkened. The shadow of the Moon on the Sun at a Solar Eclipse (New Moon) or of the Earth on the Moon at a Lunar Eclipse (Full Moon) makes them memorable. They work, in effect, like super New or Full Moons, extending the normal two- to four-week period of these lunations to an influence up to six months before or after the eclipse. An eclipse will affect each person differently, depending on where it falls in a chart. But they can be unsettling because they usually mark the ends of chapters in one's life.

HOW THIS BOOK IS ORGANIZED

In this book, we take a look at what 2012 holds in store for each of the twelve signs. We evaluate each sign according to the transits to it, its ruler, and its solar houses. The chapter on each sign begins with an overview of the year for the sign. Here we suggest some of the key themes that the sign will encounter in 2012 in general as well as in specific areas of life: love, career, money, health, home, travel, and spirituality. Each of these areas is identified with an icon, as shown at the top of the next page, for easy reference.

The overview is followed by a month-by-month analysis of all of the most important astrological events for that sign. This will enable you to look at where you are as well as what may be coming up for you, so that you can best make choices about how you'd like to deal with the planetary energies at work.

KEY TO ICONS IN OVERVIEW SECTIONS FOR EACH SIGN

LOVE AND RELATIONSHIPS

CAREER AND PUBLIC LIFE

MONEY AND FINANCES

HEALTH AND VITALITY

HOME AND FAMILY

TRAVEL AND HIGHER EDUCATION

SPIRITUALITY AND PERSONAL GROWTH

TIMING, KEY DATES, AND SUPER NOVA DAYS

The monthly forecast for each sign includes a description of several Key Dates that month. (Eastern time is used throughout the book.) We provide some likely scenarios of what may happen or how someone born under the sign might experience the planetary effects at the time of the Key Dates. It is wise to pay closer attention to your own thoughts, feelings, and actions during these times. Certain Key Dates are called Super Nova Days because they are the most intense energetic periods, positive or negative, of the month.

Note that the exact timing of events, and your awareness of their effects, can vary from person to person, sometimes coming a day or two earlier or arriving a day or two later than the Key Dates given.

The period of influence of a transit from the Sun, Mercury, or Venus is a day before and a day after the exact aspect. A transit of Mars is in effect for about two days coming and going; Jupiter and Saturn lasts for a week or more; and Uranus, Neptune, and Pluto can be two weeks.

Although the Key Dates are the days when a particular alignment is exact, some people are so ready for an event that they'll act on a transit a day or two before. And some of us are so entrenched in the status quo or unwilling to change that it may take a day or two for the effect to manifest. Give yourself an extra day around each Key Date to utilize the energy, maximize the potential, and feel the impact of the event. If you find astrological events consistently unfold in your life earlier or later than predicted, adjust the dates accordingly.

Our goal is to help you understand what is operating within you, below the surface, rather than simply to tell you what's going to happen. This is where you have control so that, to a large degree, what happens is up to you. We describe which buttons are being pushed so that you can see your own patterns and have greater power to change them if you want. Every astrological event has a potential for gain or loss. Fat, juicy, easy ones can make us lazy, while tough ones can temper the will and make us stronger. It usually takes time and hindsight to measure the true value of an experience.

THE PLANETS, THE HOUSES, AND ASPECTS

THE PLANETS

The planets are the basic building blocks of astrology. As our ancestors observed the cycles of these wandering stars, they attributed characteristics to them. Each of these richly symbolic archetypes represents a particular spectrum of meaning. Their intimate relationship to the Greek and Roman myths helps us tell stories about them that are still relevant to our lives today. No matter what your sun sign is, every planet impacts your life according to its symbolism and its placement.

 THE SUN

Rules Leo
Keywords: *Consciousness, Will, Vitality*
The Sun is our home star, the glowing filament in the center of our local system, and is associated with the sign Leo. Our ancestors equated it with God, for it is the source of energy and is what animates us. In fact, we base our entire calendar system on the Earth's relationship to the Sun. It represents the core of individual identity and consciousness. The masculine Sun has dignity, courage, and willpower. We feel the Sun's role as our main purpose in life; it fuels our furnace to fulfill our mission. We recognize its brightness in anyone who has a "sunny" personality. It is charismatic, creative, and generous of heart. But it can also be proud, have too much pride, and turn arrogant or self-centered. When the Sun is shining, we can see the world around us; it gives us a world of "things" that we can name and describe. It could be said that the Sun symbolizes objective reality.

 THE MOON

Rules Cancer

Keywords: *Subconscious, Emotions, Habits*

We've all seen how the Moon goes through its phases, reflecting the light of the Sun, and have felt the power of the Full Moon. Lunations are important astrological markers. The Moon changes signs every two and a half days and reflects the mood of the public in general. Although our year calendar is based upon the Sun, each month (comes from "moon"—moonth) closely approximates the cycle of the Moon. The Moon is closer to Earth than anything else in the heavens. Astrologically, it represents how we reflect the world around us through our feelings. The Moon symbolizes emotions, instincts, habits, and routine. It describes how we nurture others and need to be cared for ourselves. The feminine power of the Moon is also connected with the fertility cycle of women. Because it is the source of security and familial intimacy, our Moon sign is where we feel at home. The Moon is associated with the sign Cancer and with concerns about our home and family.

 MERCURY

Rules Gemini and Virgo

Keywords: *Communication, Thoughts, Transportation*

Mercury, the Heavenly Messenger, races around the Sun four times each year. Its nearly ninety-day cycle corresponds with the seasons of the calendar. Mercury, our intellectual antenna, is the planet of perception, communication, rational thought, mobility, and commerce. It is the mental traveler, able to move effortlessly through the realms of thought and imagination. Mercury organizes language, allows us to grasp ideas, enables us to analyze and integrate data, and assists us in all forms of communication. Cars, bicycles, telephones, delivery services, paperwork, and the mind itself are all manifestations of quicksilver Mercury, the fastest of the true planets. However, Mercury also has a trickster side and can cleverly con us into believing something that just isn't true. Mercury is associated with curious Gemini in its information-gathering mode, and with discerning Virgo when it is analytically sorting through the data.

VENUS

Rules Taurus and Libra

Keywords: *Desire, Love, Money, Values*

Venus is the goddess of love, our relationship antenna, associated with the spectrum of how we experience what is beautiful and pleasurable to us. With Venus, we attach desire to our perceptions. On one end, Venus can indicate romantic and sensual love. On the other end, Venus is about money and all things of value—financial and emotional. This manifests as our attraction to art, music, and even good food. Every beautiful flower and every act of love contains the essence of sweet Venus. We look to Venus to describe what we like—an important key to understanding partnerships, particularly personal ones. To a certain extent, our chemistry with other people is affected by Venus. Although Venus is traditionally associated with femininity, both women and men are impacted by its rhythms. A morning star, Venus rules Taurus and is associated with the simple and sensual side of physical reality. As an evening star, it rules Libra, where it represents the more intellectual side of love and harmony.

MARS

Rules Aries, co-rules Scorpio

Keywords: *Action, Physical Energy, Drive*

Mars, the god of war, is the planet of action, physical energy, initiative, and aggression. It is the first planet beyond Earth's orbit, and its role is to take what we have and extend it to the outer world. Mars represents the masculine force of individuality that helps define the ego and our sense of unique identity. It represents how we move forward in life and propels us toward new experiences and into the future. Mars drives us to assert ourselves in healthy ways, but the angry red planet can also be impatient and insensitive, engendering violence and destruction. When insecure, it turns offensive and can attack others. Mars can also express erotic passion, the male counterpart of the female Venus; together they are the cosmic lovers. As the pioneering risk taker, Mars rules fiery Aries. As a volcanic force of power, it is the traditional ruler of Scorpio.

♃ JUPITER

Rules Sagittarius, co-rules Pisces

Keywords: *Expansion, Growth, Optimism*

Jupiter is the largest of the true planets. It represents expansion, growth, and optimism. It was called the Greater Benefic by ancient astrologers due to its association with good fortune. Today, modern astrologers understand that too much of a good thing is not necessarily beneficial. Jupiter rules the excesses of life; undoubtedly, it's the planet of bigger, better, and more. Wherever there's too much, you're apt to find Jupiter. Often called the lucky planet, Jupiter symbolizes where opportunity knocks. Yet it is still up to us to open the door and walk through. Jupiterian people are jovial, but this gassy giant is also associated with humor, philosophy, enthusiasm, and enterprise. In its adventurous mode, Jupiter rules globetrotting Sagittarius, but as the planet of religion and belief systems, it has a traditional connection to Pisces.

♄ SATURN

Rules Capricorn, co-rules Aquarius

Keywords: *Contraction, Maturity, Responsibility*

Saturn is the outermost planet visible to the naked eye, and as such represented the end of the road for our sky-watching ancestors. In premodern times, Saturn was the limit of our human awareness; beyond it were only the fixed stars. Now, even with our telescopic capability to peer farther into the vastness of space and time, Saturn still symbolizes the limits of perception. It is about structure, order, necessity, commitment, and hard-earned accomplishments. It's the stabilizing voice of reality and governs rules, regulations, discipline, and patience. Saturn is Father Time, and represents the ultimate judgment that you get what you deserve. But Saturn isn't only stern or rigid; it is also the teacher and the wise old sage. When we embrace Saturn's discipline, we mature and learn from our experiences. As the serious taskmaster, Saturn is the ruler of ambitious Capricorn. As the co-ruler of Aquarius, Saturn reminds us that rigid rules may need to be broken in order to express our individuality.

CHIRON

(Does not rule a sign)

Keywords: *Healing, Pain, Subversion*

Chiron is the mythological Wounded Healer, and although not a true planet in the traditional sense, it has become a useful tool for modern astrologers. Chiron is a relative newcomer to the planetary lineup and was discovered in 1977 between the orbits of Saturn and Uranus. It describes where we can turn our wounds into wisdom to assist others. It is associated with the story of the wounded Fisher King, who, in medieval tales about the Holy Grail, fished (for souls) in order to salve his incurable suffering. Chiron not only symbolizes where and how we hurt, but also how our words and actions can soothe the pain of others. It doesn't, however, always play by the rules and can work against the status quo. Its rhythms can stir up old memories of emotional discomfort that can lead to increased understanding, vulnerability, and the transformation of heartache and grief into the gifts of love and forgiveness.

URANUS

Rules Aquarius

Keywords: *Awakening, Unpredictable, Inventive*

Uranus is the first planet discovered with technology (the telescope). Its discovery broke through the limitations imposed by our five senses. It symbolizes innovation, originality, revolution, and delighting in unexpected surprises. Uranus operates suddenly, often to release tensions, no matter how hidden. Its action is like lightning—instantaneous and exciting, upsetting and exhilarating. Uranus provokes and instigates change; its restless and rebellious energy hungers for freedom. Its high frequency and electrical nature stimulate the nervous system. This highly original planet abhors the status quo and is known to turn normal things upside down and inside out. As the patron planet of the strange and unusual, it is the ruler of eccentric Aquarius.

 NEPTUNE

Rules Pisces

Keywords: *Imagination, Intuition, Spirituality*

Neptune is god of the seas, from which all life arises and is eventually returned. Imaginative Neptune lures us into the foggy mists where reality becomes so hazy that we can lose our way. It is the planet of dreams, illusions, and spirituality. It dissolves boundaries and barriers, leading us into higher awareness, compassion, confusion, or escapism. Grasping the meaning of Neptune is like trying to hold water in our hands. No matter how hard we try, it slips through our fingers—for Neptune is ultimately elusive and unknowable. It rules all things related to fantasy and delusion. A highly spiritual energy, the magic of Neptune encourages artistic vision, intuitive insight, compassion, and the tendency to idealize. Neptune governs the mystic's urge to merge with the divine and is associated with the spiritual sign Pisces.

♇ PLUTO

Rules Scorpio

Keywords: *Passion, Intensity, Regeneration*

Pluto, lord of the underworld, is the planet of death, rebirth, and transformation. As the most distant of the planets, Pluto moves us inexorably toward a deeper understanding of life's cycles. Under Pluto's influence, it often seems as though the apparently solid ground has disintegrated, forcing us to morph in ways we cannot intellectually understand. Pluto is the mythological phoenix, a magical bird that rises from the ashes of its own destruction by fire. It contains the shadow parts of ourselves that we would prefer to keep hidden, but healing and empowerment come from facing the unfathomable darkness and turning it into light. Manipulation and control are often issues with Pluto. A healthy relationship with Pluto adds psychological understanding and clarity about our motivations. As the ruler of magnetic Scorpio, it is associated with power and emotional intensity.

☊ ☋ NODES OF THE MOON

(Do not rule a sign)
Keywords: *Karma, Soul, Past Lives*
The Nodes of the Moon are opposing points where the Moon's orbit around the Earth intersects the Earth's orbit around the Sun. Although not real planets, these powerful points have an astrological influence in that they describe the ways we connect with others. They are useful in understanding the challenges and opportunities we face in our soul's journey through its lifetime here on Earth. For many astrologers, the Lunar Nodes are symbolic of past lives and future existences. The South Node, at one end of the nodal axis, represents the past—the unconscious patterns of our ancestral heritage or those brought into this life from previous incarnations. These are often talents that can easily be overused and become a no-growth path of least resistance. At the other end, the North Node represents the future—a new direction for growth, development, and integration.

THE HOUSES

Every astrology chart is divided into twelve houses, each ruling different areas of life and colored by a different sign. Just as planets move through the zodiac signs, they also move through the houses in an individual chart. The twelve houses have a correspondence to the twelve signs, but in an individualized chart, the signs in each house will vary based on the sign on the cusp of the 1st House, called a rising sign or ascendant. The rising sign is determined by the exact time of your birth. We use solar houses, which place the sun sign as your 1st House, or rising sign.

1ST HOUSE

Corresponding Sign: Aries
Keywords: *Self, Appearance, Personality*
A primary point of self-identification: When planets move through this sector, the emphasis is on your individuality and surface appearances. It is often associated with how we interact with others when we first meet them. Planets here tend to take on great importance and become more integrated into your personality.

2ND HOUSE

Corresponding Sign: Taurus
Keywords: *Possessions, Values, Self-Worth*
Associated with values, resources, income, and self-esteem: When planets move through the 2nd House, they can modify your attitudes about money and earning. This is a concrete and practical area of the chart, and although it is linked to possessions, the 2nd House typically does not include things you cannot easily move, such as real estate or what you share with someone else.

3RD HOUSE

Corresponding Sign: Gemini
Keywords: *Communication, Siblings, Short Trips*
Relates to how you gather information from your immediate environment: It's associated with the day-to-day comings and goings of your life. Siblings can be found here, for this is where we first learn to build intimacy when we're young. Planets moving through this house can affect the pace and quality of your day and how you communicate with those around you.

4TH HOUSE

Corresponding Sign: Cancer
Keywords: *Home, Family, Roots*
Associated with the earliest imprints of childhood, your family roots, and how you're connected to your own feelings: This is your emotional foundation and describes what you need to feel at home. This is where you are nurtured, so when planets travel through this sector, they stir up issues of security and safety. As the deepest place in your chart, it is sometimes only you who knows about it.

5TH HOUSE

Corresponding Sign: Leo
Keywords: *Love, Romance, Children, Play*
Associated with fun, but also represents self-expression, creativity, love affairs, and children: The 5th House is about the discovery of self through play, and includes sports, games, and gambling. When planets move through your 5th House, they can excite you to take risks and connect with the innocence of your inner child.

6TH HOUSE

Corresponding Sign: Virgo
Keywords: *Work, Health, Daily Routines*
Related to service and working conditions: Like the 3rd House, it describes your daily life, but the consistency of it rather than the noisy distractions—it's where you strive for efficiency and effectiveness. Planets here modify your habits, diet, and exercise. Although considered the house of health and hygiene, transits here don't always indicate illness; they can also increase our concern for healthier lifestyles.

7TH HOUSE

Corresponding Sign: Libra
Keywords: *Marriage, Relationships, Business Partners*
Encompasses one-to-one relationships: Its cusp is called the descendant and is the western end of the horizon. It's where and how we meet other people, both personally and professionally. In a larger sense, this is how you project who you are onto others. Planets moving through here can stimulate intimate relationships, but can also increase the intensity of all of your interactions with the outside world.

8TH HOUSE

Corresponding Sign: Scorpio
Keywords: *Intimacy, Transformation, Shared Resources*
A mysterious and powerful place, associated with shared experiences, including the most intimate: Traditionally the house of sex, death, and taxes, it's the place where you gain the deepest levels of relationships, personally and professionally. When planets move through your 8th House, perspectives can intensify, intimacy issues are stimulated, and compelling transformations are undertaken.

9TH HOUSE

Corresponding Sign: Sagittarius
Keywords: *Travel, Higher Education, Philosophy*
Associated with philosophy, religion, higher education of all kinds, and long-distance travel: It's where you seek knowledge and truth—both within and without. Planets moving through this house open portals to inner journeys and outer adventures, stretching your mind in ways that expand your perspectives about the world.

10TH HOUSE

Corresponding Sign: Capricorn

Keywords: *Career, Community, Ambition*

The most elevated sector of your chart; its cusp is called the midheaven: This is the career house, opposite to the home-based 4th House. When planets move through your 10th House, they activate your ambition, drive you to achieve professional excellence, and push you up the ladder of success. This is where your public reputation is important and hard work is acknowledged.

11TH HOUSE

Corresponding Sign: Aquarius

Keywords: *Friends, Groups, Associations, Social Ideals*

Traditionally called the house of friends, hopes, and wishes: It's where you go to be with like-minded people. The 11th House draws you out of your individual career aspirations and into the ideals of humanity. Planets traveling here can activate dreams of the future, so spending time with friends is a natural theme.

12TH HOUSE

Corresponding Sign: Pisces

Keywords: *Imagination, Spirituality, Secret Activities*

Complex, representing the ending of one cycle and the beginning of the next: It is connected with mysteries and places outside ordinary reality. When planets move through this house, they stimulate your deepest subconscious feelings and activate fantasies. It's a private space that can seem like a prison or a sanctuary.

ASPECTS

As the planets move through the sky in their various cycles, they form ever-changing angles with one another. Certain angles create significant geometric shapes. For example, when two planets are 90 degrees apart, they conform to a square. A sextile, or 60 degrees of separation, conforms to a six-pointed star. Planets create aspects to one another when they are at these special angles. All aspects are divisions of the 360-degree circle. Aspects explain how the individual symbolism of a pair of planets combines into an energetic pattern.

CONJUNCTION

0 degrees ★ **Keywords:** *Compression, Blending, Focus*
A conjunction is a blending of the separate planetary energies involved. When two planets conjoin, your job is to integrate the different influences—which in some cases is easier than others. For example, a conjunction of the Moon and Venus is likely to be a smooth blending of energy because of the similarity of the planets. But a conjunction between the Moon and Uranus is likely to be challenging because the Moon needs security, while Uranus prefers risk.

SEMISQUARE AND SESQUISQUARE

45 and 135 degrees ★ **Keywords:** *Annoyance, Mild Resistance*
Semisquares and sesquisquares are minor aspects that act like milder squares. They're one-eighth and three-eighths of a circle, respectively. Like the other hard aspects (conjunctions, oppositions, and squares) they can create dynamic situations that require immediate attention and resolution. Although they are not usually as severe as the other hard aspects, they remind us that healthy stress is important for the process of growth.

SEXTILE

60 degrees ★ Keywords: *Supportive, Intelligent, Activating*
Sextiles are supportive and intelligent, combining complementary signs—fire and air, earth and water. There's an even energetic distribution between the planets involved. Sextiles often indicate opportunities based on our willingness to take action in smart ways. Like trines, sextiles are considered easy: The good fortune they offer can pass unless you consciously take an active interest in making something positive happen.

QUINTILE

72 and 144 degrees ★ Keywords: *Creativity, Metaphysics, Magic*
Quintiles are powerful nontraditional aspects based on dividing the zodiac circle into five, resulting in a five-pointed star. Related to ancient goddess-based religious traditions, quintiles activate the imagination, intuition, and latent artistic talents. They're clever, intelligent, and even brilliant as they stimulate humor to relieve repressed tensions.

SQUARE

90 degrees ★ Keywords: *Resistance, Stress, Dynamic Conflict*
A square is an aspect of resistance, signifying energies at odds. Traditionally, they were considered negative, but their dynamic instability demands attention, so they're often catalysts for change. When differences in two planetary perspectives are integrated, squares can build enduring structures. Harnessing a square's power by managing contradictions creates opportunities for personal growth.

TRINE

120 degrees ★ **Keywords:** *Harmony, Free-Flowing, Ease*
A trine is the most harmonious of aspects because it connects signs of the same element. In the past, trines were considered positive, but modern astrologers realize they are so easy that they can create a rut that is difficult to break out of. When two planets are one-third of a circle apart, they won't necessarily stimulate change, but they can often help build on the status quo. With trines, you must stay alert, for complacency can weaken your chances for success.

QUINCUNX

150 degrees ★ **Keywords:** *Irritation, Adjustment*
A quincunx is almost like a nonaspect, for the two planets involved have a difficult time staying aware of each other. As such, this aspect often acts as an irritant, requiring that you make constant adjustments without actually resolving the underlying problem. This is a challenging aspect because it can be more annoying than a full-fledged crisis. Quincunxes are a bit like oil and water—the planets are not in direct conflict, but they have difficulty mixing with each another.

OPPOSITION

180 degrees ★ **Keywords:** *Tension, Awareness, Balance*
When two planets are in opposition, they are like two forces pulling at either end of a rope. The tension is irresolvable, unless you are willing to hold both divergent perspectives without suppressing one or the other. More often than not, we favor one side of the opposition over the other and, in doing so, project the unexpressed side onto others or situations. For this reason, oppositions usually manifest as relationship issues.

ASTROLOGY

WORLD REPORT 2012

Astrology works for individuals, groups, and humanity as a whole. You will have your own story in 2012, but it will unfold along with seven billion other tales of human experience. We are each unique, yet our lives touch one another; our destinies are woven together by weather and war, by the economy, science, music, politics, religion, and all the other threads of life on planet Earth. We make personal choices every day, yet great events usually appear to be beyond the control of any one of us. When a town is flooded, it affects everyone who lives there, yet individual astrology patterns describe the specific response of each person.

We are living in a time when sources of self-awareness fill books, TV and radio shows, websites, podcasts, newspapers, and DVDs, and we benefit greatly from them. Yet despite all this wisdom, conflicting ideas, desires, and values cause enormous suffering every day. Understanding personal issues is a powerful means for increasing happiness, but knowledge of our collective concerns is equally important for our safety, sanity, and well-being. This astrological look at the major trends and planetary patterns for 2012 provides a framework for comprehending the potentials and challenges we face together, so that we can move forward with tolerance and respect as a community as we also fulfill our potential as individuals.

The astrological events used in this World Report are the transits of the outer planets, Chiron, and the Moon's Nodes, as well as the retrograde cycles of Mercury and eclipses of the Sun and Moon.

MAJOR PLANETARY EVENTS

JUPITER IN TAURUS: SUSTAINABLE GROWTH

June 4, 2011–June 11, 2012

New visions sparked by Jupiter in fiery Aries are now in the process of being tested by reality. Bright ideas come down to earth in sensible Taurus, where we can gain material benefits from recent discoveries. A practical approach to progress enables us to make incremental improvements that will endure. Viable sources of cheaper and cleaner energy reflect the gifts of generous Jupiter in this resource-rich sign. However, we may be more stubborn and resistant to unfamiliar ideas this year. A selfish desire for wealth can close minds to inspiring concepts if they take time to turn a profit. Philosophical Jupiter in fixed Taurus narrows our intellectual comfort zone, so we may not be inclined to ask provocative questions that challenge our core beliefs. This transit can also decrease our interest in any opportunity unless we're assured of tangible results. Knowing the difference between a personal truth that works individually and a universal truth that applies to everyone makes it possible to feel secure while remaining open to learning more.

JUPITER IN GEMINI: INFORMATION OVERLOAD

June 11, 2012–June 25, 2013

Astrological tradition considers multifaceted Gemini an awkward place for truth-seeking Jupiter. We can be inundated with so much information that it's nearly impossible to see the forest for the trees. Jupiter's long-range vision may be obscured by a million-and-one ideas that scatter attention, diffusing the focus we need to achieve long-term goals. However, this is a mind-opening transit that stirs curiosity about a wide variety of subjects. Still, a tendency to skim the surface makes it difficult to concentrate and gain in-depth knowledge in any one area. Expansive Jupiter in communicative Gemini can also be quite verbose—the volume of information is valued more than its substance. Nevertheless, we are able to assimilate large amounts of data and make interesting connections between previously unrelated points. Philosophical flexibility and mental versatility are gifts of this transit, while inconsistency of beliefs and careless planning are some of its less desirable qualities.

JUPITER'S ASPECTS

Jupiter forms a cooperative sextile with healer Chiron on February 14, opening the door to a major discovery in medicine or a breakthrough within a personal relationship. Lucky Jupiter's fortuitous trine on March 13 with Pluto, the planet of hidden treasures, is especially rewarding for those willing to dig more deeply for the answers they seek. Irritating quincunxes between confident Jupiter and doubting Saturn on May 16 and December 22 can make it difficult to decide on a course of action when obstacles frustrate our forward progress. Although a solution may seem to be elusive, gentle persistence will likely bring positive results. Jupiter's dynamic square with dreamy Neptune on June 25 lifts us with inspiration, although wishful thinking creates fantasies that are out of reach. Jupiter runs the gauntlet as it creates uncomfortable aspects with Pluto, Saturn, and Chiron on July 18–24. We see opportunities for growth all around us, yet might not be able to put our plans into action. However, a calculated risk could bring the rewards we seek with help from an inventive Jupiter-Uranus sextile on July 22.

SATURN IN LIBRA: JUSTICE FOR ALL

October 29, 2009–April 7, 2010
July 21, 2010–October 5, 2012

Stern Saturn's shift into peace-seeking Libra marked a new chapter in our relationships, but we still have some tough challenges to face before we can fully achieve the harmony it symbolizes. When Saturn in Libra functions at its highest potential, cooperation and civility allow diplomacy to flourish as reason replaces force. The need to weigh both sides of any argument can slow personal and public dialogue, yet it's worth the price to build bridges over seemingly impassable chasms. Saturn is "exalted" in Libra according to astrological tradition, suggesting a highly positive link between the planet's principle of integrity and Libra's sense of fair play. The negative side of Saturn, though, is its potential for rigidity, which can manifest now as a stubborn unwillingness to listen. Resistance to opposing points of view is simply an opportunity to test their worth; only with careful consideration can they be properly evaluated. Responsible individuals and leaders recognize the importance of treating others as equals as the foundation for any healthy relationship.

Karmic Saturn is judgmental and known to deliver exactly what we deserve. When it's in Libra the Scales, justice becomes one way of restoring balance. Accordingly, legal systems around the world may take steps to correct social inequities and governmental and corporate abuses of power. In the United States, we will see ongoing political attempts to establish harmony between historically divided camps with polarized views about individual rights on such fundamental issues as abortion, euthanasia, and immigration. The courts will be expected to adjudicate these differences, even when there seems to be no common ground. Since Libra is the sign of relationships, we can anticipate more cases that address the growing acceptance of same-sex marriage. It's also likely that we'll see significant legal battles that recognize the imbalance between individuals and corporations, and rulings that reevaluate humanity's relationship with the environment.

Saturn began a series of clever quintiles with regenerative Pluto on November 11, 2011, that recur this year on March 28 and August 19. This brilliant alignment of these planetary heavyweights can reveal solutions to the stickiest problems, especially when power and authority are involved.

SATURN IN SCORPIO: LOOKING INTO THE SHADOWS

October 5, 2012–December 23, 2014
June 14, 2015–September 16, 2015

Responsible Saturn in formidable Scorpio is a test of resolve. We are challenged to look into the dark corners of our psyches where fears about love, money, and mortality hide. It's tempting to turn away from these complicated subjects, yet the price of doing so is high because we are then controlled by unconscious impulses. Power struggles and relationship disappointments are common when we fail to face emotional issues, no matter how intense they may seem. Saturn in Scorpio is a reminder that no one is entirely pure and simple. The complexities of giving and receiving affection, dealing with hidden desires, and working with manipulative people are numerous. However, for those who are willing to show up and do the work, Saturn also offers clarity and authority, enabling us to address these complicated matters. Taking responsibility for dark feelings doesn't mean that we must suppress them; it's a signal to engage them with patience rather than punishment. Discovering what we truly desire (and detest) is a powerful step toward creating healthier relationships. We may not get all our needs met, yet acknowledging them makes it possible to have an honest discussion and to negotiate in good faith. Personal and professional alliances work more effectively when we stop keeping secrets from ourselves. Consolidation of financial institutions as a result of bad loans could be even more common with Saturn in Scorpio. Thankfully, the planet's sweet trines with spiritual Neptune on October 10, June 11, 2013, and July 19, 2013, combine unrelenting faith and commitment that can turn dreams into reality.

URANUS IN ARIES: FAST FORWARD

May 27, 2010–August 13, 2010
March 11, 2011–May 15, 2018

Radical Uranus's visit to pioneering Aries fires up engines of change. We can expect that the rapid acceleration of technological discoveries will continue. We get the sense that things will never be quite the same again during the Awakener's seven-year visit to this first sign of the zodiac: Both planet and sign favor innovation. When electrical Uranus was in Aries from 1843 to 1850, the first telegraph broke through the limitations of geography, enabling instantaneous communication over great distances. Uranus was again in Aries from 1927 to 1934, giving us the first transatlantic flight, the discovery of penicillin, the first television broadcasts, and significant developments in quantum physics. Exciting breakthroughs in a variety of scientific fields can be expected again this time around, including discoveries that alter our understanding of the origins of the solar system and the development of life on Earth. We may make major strides in recognizing the nature of matter at more primal levels. It's also likely that we'll see significant advancements in the transmission of information and tap new sources of energy that can finally reduce our dependence on petroleum products.

Individual rights—a primary concern of both Aries and Uranus—will take on greater importance as we balance the influences of excessive government and corporate power with humanitarian concerns and populist political movements. Perhaps a new model of human potential will begin to emerge as we explore our creative powers along with evolutionary concepts that alter the very nature of our identity. The process of merging man and machine should continue to accelerate as a new generation of prosthetic devices becomes commonplace. Uranus is associated with artificial intelligence, so we'll likely see microchip implants that extend our sensory mechanisms, an upsurge in robotics technologies, and another explosion in the ubiquity of computers. Nevertheless, something is missing. We are not satisfied with our modern world or with the kinds of work and consumerism that have replaced a more organic and soulful way of living. Yet it is in the awakening of an entirely new view of humanity and of human consciousness that futuristic Uranus in Aries will have the most impact. In 1931, when Uranus was last in Aries, Aldous Huxley wrote his prophetic novel *Brave New World*. Now, as this surprising planet is back in the first sign of the zodiac, we are truly standing at the edge of a brave new world of our own creation. As we step into an uncertain and unknowable future, we can expect some unusual experiments, discoveries, and inventions that are likely to dramatically alter the image that we have of ourselves and our world.

NEPTUNE IN AQUARIUS: ENVISIONING THE FUTURE

January 28, 1998–April 4, 2011
August 4, 2011–February 3, 2012

Aquarius is an air sign that symbolizes intelligence, while Neptune is a planet associated with faith. It has been tricky to blend Neptune's nonmaterial reality with the technological realms of Aquarius, because imagination exists beyond the limits of language. Nevertheless, Neptune in Aquarius has shown us how to integrate science with spirituality. Doubting the wisdom of organized religions continues to be prominent as logic replaces unquestioning beliefs. Increasing numbers of people have grown disillusioned with overzealous religious leaders who preach one thing and do another. We have seen much deception in the last decade from governments, banks, corporations, and churches—and this could rise again in a crescendo during the final weeks of Neptune's fourteen-year visit to Aquarius. However, the more metaphysically inclined are likely to continue the popularization of technology as a way to better understand our spirituality. On an individual level, Neptune in Aquarius helps us acknowledge the close relationship between intuition and thoughts as new theories of quantum consciousness reveal that the mind is not separate from the rest of the body. Neptune-related activities such as meditation and yoga continue to gain popularity for calming our jangled nervous systems and integrating mind, body, and spirit in a peaceful and holistic manner.

NEPTUNE IN PISCES: COLLECTIVE CONSCIOUSNESS

April 4, 2011–August 4, 2011
February 3, 2012–March 30, 2025

Imaginative Neptune's entry into its watery home sign signals a spiritual awakening that transcends the threshold of our individual differences to reconnect all humanity in an integrative web of common awareness. Compassion shifts from an idealistic concept to an active energy that puts us directly in touch with one another in a more emotional way. The last time Neptune was in Pisces—from 1847 through 1862—concern for others was reflected in the abolitionist movement to end slavery in the United States and to free the serfs in Russia. It's very likely that this transit of Neptune will again put issues of injustice and inequality in the spotlight.

Dissolving boundaries on a personal level is both inspiring and confusing. As the great tide of humanity rises and falls, we can feel that we are being swept away by invisible forces beyond our control. These may, in fact, relax borders among nations in a long-term process that puts common concerns above separatist national interests, although a fear-driven backlash is also likely. It's possible that religious differences also become less problematic as the faithful focus more on flexibility of spirit than rigidity of ritual. We may grow more psychically attuned with one another and with nature. The unifying forces of Neptune and Pisces remind us that *All is one* is not an abstraction, but the way the world really works.

The value of water is likely to increase, along with investments in conservation and desalinization. However, the effects of pollution will also grow painfully evident, leading to a scarcity of fresh, clean water. Neptune, the god of the seas, is the planetary ruler of oil. In fact, in 1859 when Neptune was last in Pisces, the very first oil well was drilled in Pennsylvania. Now the search for new fuel sources continues to grow in its urgency as the catastrophic ecological impact of the oil industry becomes inescapable. Neptune in Pisces increases sensitivity to toxins, requiring more thorough cleanup of existing waste and a more cautious approach to introducing new products into the environment. These may be the last days of environmentally disastrous plastics as we know them, with current chemical formulas replaced by biodegradable substitutes. The negative effects of prescription drugs—both personally and environmentally—become more obvious, precipitating radical changes in the manufacture and use of pharmaceuticals while increasing the demand for natural medicine and organic food.

PLUTO IN CAPRICORN: STRUCTURAL REALIGNMENT

January 25, 2008–June 14, 2008
November 26, 2008–March 23, 2023

Pluto takes about 245 years to complete one journey around the zodiac, but observations of its movement after its discovery in 1930 quickly revealed its power. This tiny but potent planet entered no-nonsense Capricorn in 2008, signaling a turn toward major changes in the architecture of society. Capricorn is associated with established institutions such as government and business, so regenerative Pluto's visit indicates a drawn-out process that will ultimately alter the most fundamental organizational structures supporting our culture, including a major restructuring of the economy. While the short-term suffering of financial contraction is already apparent, this painful process is a necessary step in the total overhaul of our overextended, hyper-consumerist society into one in which humans and nature will ultimately exist in greater harmony.

Capricorn is a practical earth sign, so we can expect growing urgency in the serious environmental crises we face. Global warming, for instance, will intensify pressures on corporations, governments, and individuals, forcing inevitable upheavals that will radically impact our modern way of life. Since Pluto is associated with the process of elimination, the accumulated effects

of dumping toxins into the air, water, and soil will continue to become more evident during its long transit of this sign. All waste falls under Pluto's dominion, so we will likely continue our battles with the harmful fallout from oil spills, radioactive by-products, and other industrial garbage. Obviously, this could overpower all other issues and require a degree of change not seen since Pluto last transited Capricorn from 1762 to 1778. Democracy, like the mythological Phoenix bird that flew from the ashes of ruins, arose from the destructive American and French Revolutions that ended monarchy. The same transit that gave birth to the individual freedoms we take for granted is now reenergizing a modern-day struggle to keep them.

The good news is that evolutionary events of this magnitude do not occur overnight. The corruption of existing institutions takes time—enough for those capable of adapting to begin the necessary process of reform. Since Capricorn has to do with hierarchical rule from the top, this Pluto transit will continue to knock down those who have traditionally pulled the levers of power. Yet regardless of where state, church, banks, education, and industry go, there is constructive work we each can and must do as individuals at this time. Both Pluto and Capricorn are associated with power, so the application of personal will is a critical issue and can make the difference between utopia and oblivion. Instead of merely relying on someone else to maintain and advance civilization, we each have the capacity—and, ultimately, the responsibility—to increase our own tangible contribution to the world.

The first step may be a personal reexamination of our career ambitions and individual life goals. For some, this could grow out of dissatisfaction or a sense of impotence in life that's not limited to Pluto's transit this year. Although this journey is likely to be the result of many interrelated events, for some it may be catalyzed by an economic downturn, the loss of a job, or a natural disaster. Of course, this can feel like an overwhelming challenge; meeting our increasing responsibilities can be a daunting task. Thus it's best to address small but important issues as they surface, where it's possible to see results more quickly and gain the confidence we need to continue moving forward. But we must remember that we won't necessarily be able to notice the changes day to day because Pluto moves so slowly. Although we cannot see a glacier moving, its relentless power relocates mountains that stand in its way. We are living at a special moment in history; this is a significant crossroads. Humanity has an unprecedented opportunity to become more empowered, allowing us to consciously create the future rather than unconsciously repeating mistakes of the past.

CHIRON IN PISCES: GLOBAL HEALING

April 20, 2010–July 20, 2010
February 8, 2011–April 17, 2018

Chiron's first foray into metaphysical Pisces since its discovery in 1977 increases the popularity of holistic forms of health care and subtle healing modalities. Although the interest in mind-body medicine has been steadily growing for many years, it will receive a significant boost from breakthroughs in harnessing nonphysical energies that can positively impact our well-being. Alternative retirement homes and wellness communities will be in higher demand to address the growing needs of aging baby boomers. Since Chiron travels between the orbits of rational Saturn and radical Uranus, it ferries between the known and the unknown, working as a maverick outside traditional models. Its association with forgiveness while in spiritual Pisces reminds us that blame is never part of the solution; it merely perpetuates our problems. This isn't about avoiding the truth; it's about the power of unconditional love as a healing force that releases us from the pain of past wounds. The physical and mental well-being of individuals may be recognized as part of collective patterns, rather than separate experiences.

Ultimately we are more aware than ever of the human suffering all around the world. The role of spirituality in global healing will continue to grow more significant as we see more shortcomings of organized religions—each one staking its claim as the only path to salvation. Although we are limited in what we can do on a personal level, it is no longer an option to leave the work for someone else. The pain of standing by and doing nothing is greater than the frustration of not being able to fix everything.

THE MOON'S NODES

MOON'S NORTH NODE IN SAGITTARIUS, SOUTH NODE IN GEMINI: EXPLORING THE EDGE

March 3, 2011–August 29, 2012

The North Node in Sagittarius symbolizes the benefits of seeking answers that are beyond the cozy confines of our familiar world. We spin our wheels and fail to advance when we repeat South Node in Gemini patterns of rambling on endlessly about small things while ignoring the larger issues that drive the human spirit. Gemini's motivation is to keep conversations going without worrying about what's being said, even when their content is trivial. Surrendering the need to give equal value to every idea and observation frees us to ride the North Node in Sagittarius to the outer edges of a new vision that addresses who we are and what life means. Adventurous Sagittarius encourages risky behavior while reminding us that it's better to aim high and fall short than to keep turning in circles within the limited world that we already know.

MOON'S NORTH NODE IN SCORPIO, SOUTH NODE IN TAURUS: SWIMMING IN THE DARK

August 29, 2012–February 18, 2014

The Moon's North Node in Scorpio points us in a direction for growth and integration that comes from encountering intense feelings and unfulfilled desires. It is tempting, though, to withdraw into the pleasurable comfort of the habit-driven South Node in Taurus that tends to avoid complications and heavy emotions. Yet passion, not pacification, is the road to personal fulfillment now. A willingness to push beyond the boundaries of politeness can ruffle feathers, yet it will ultimately solve more problems than it creates. The key is to wed intensity with kindness so that this deeper level of connecting is done with sensitivity to everyone's needs.

MERCURY RETROGRADES

All true planets appear to move backward from time to time, because we view them from the moving platform of Earth. The most noticeable and regular retrograde periods are those of Mercury, the communication planet. Occurring three or four times a year for roughly three weeks at a time, these are periods when difficulties with details, travel, communication, and technical matters are more common than usual.

Mercury's retrograde is often perceived as negative, but you can make this cycle work for you. Because personal and commercial interactions are emphasized, you can actually accomplish more than usual, especially if you stay focused on what you need to complete instead of initiating new projects. Still, you may feel as if you're treading water—or worse, being carried backward in an undertow of unfinished business. Worry less about making progress than about the quality of your work. Pay extra attention to all your communication exchanges. Avoiding misunderstandings and omissions is the ideal way to minimize complications. Retrograde Mercury is best used to tie up loose ends as you review, redo, reconsider, and, in general, revisit the past.

MARCH 12 IN ARIES, DIRECT APRIL 4 IN PISCES: CAUTIONARY TALE

The desire to think and act quickly is strong with Mercury in impulsive Aries, yet its backward turn is a warning to avoid hasty words and actions. Our instincts tell us to push ahead as fast as we can, yet we are being asked to slow down and integrate what we already know. Our minds can feel like they're exploding when Mercury backs over shocking Uranus on March 18, but it's best to let fresh ideas ripen before exposing them to the world. The Mercury-Uranus combo triggers sudden disturbances in electrical systems or creates unexpected misunderstandings if we gloss over seemingly unimportant details. The messenger planet retreats into impressionable Pisces on March 23, seasoning thoughts with sensitivity and imagination before we share them openly after Mercury turns direct.

JULY 14–AUGUST 8 IN LEO: ALL THE WORLD'S A STAGE

Enthusiasm and insecurity promote exaggeration with Mercury in proud Leo. Excitement about creative concepts could push new messages or original concepts into the spotlight prematurely. We know what we want to say and can be overdramatic in our presentation because we're so eager to be acknowledged. This retrograde cycle can be highly creative because it begins with clever Mercury forming a supportive sextile to artistic Venus. This period is ideal for refining a pitch, product, or process before taking it public. Don't be too forceful on July 22–24, when Mercury connects with assertive Mars and exuberant Jupiter. There's no need to oversell an idea; the brilliant Mercury-Uranus trine on July 25 can indicate an innovative breakthrough, but it will still take time for our plans to mature. Confidence is the key to finding the right pace because its presence ensures patience, while its absence can lead us to jump the gun or come across as overly aggressive.

NOVEMBER 6 IN SAGITTARIUS, DIRECT NOVEMBER 26 IN SCORPIO: THE WAITING IS THE HARDEST PART

Mercury in Sagittarius is like an unbridled horse that races ahead without restraint. Its tendency for outspokenness is often refreshing yet becomes problematic as this chatty planet turns retrograde. Frustration runs high because Mercury turns retrograde just before reaching a harmonious trine with brilliant Uranus, making us wait until the aspect is exact on December 14 before we're able to reap the benefits of a new idea. In the meantime, Sagittarian good humor darkens as Mercury returns to suspicious Scorpio on November 14. Innocent remarks may be interpreted negatively, signaling a need to temper truth with tenderness. Mercury's anxious semisquare with domineering Pluto on November 19 can create conflict that increases through November 22 when the Winged Messenger forms stressful aspects with both Mars and Uranus. A power struggle could turn nasty unless we pay extra attention to what's going on. Fortunately, a benefit of retrograde Mercury in Scorpio is that greater attention to details can reveal previously unseen solutions or uncover underused resources.

ECLIPSES

Solar and Lunar Eclipses are special New and Full Moons that indicate significant changes for individuals and groups. They are powerful markers of events, with influences that can appear up to three months in advance and last up to six months afterward. Eclipses occur when the New or Full Moon is conjunct one of the Moon's Nodes. Solar Eclipses occur at the New Moon and are visible in narrow paths, but not everywhere that the Sun is visible. Locations where the eclipse can be seen are more strongly influenced by it. Lunar Eclipses occur during Full Moons and are visible wherever the Moon is seen.

MAY 20, SOLAR ECLIPSE IN GEMINI: LOST IN SPACE

This annular Solar Eclipse in Gemini is stressfully squared by nebulous Neptune, suggesting confusion, scandals, and floods. Its trajectory stretches from the coast of China to the western United States, but its central path through Tokyo makes Japan the likeliest locale for a major event. Individually, it's a reminder that too much information can be just as disorienting as a lack of data. Neptune encourages idealism and spiritual pursuits, but we must exercise intelligent discrimination to avoid falling prey to a fantasy.

JUNE 4, LUNAR ECLIPSE IN SAGITTARIUS: CHECK THE FACTS

Relationships could be rocky with the eclipsed Moon opposing loving Venus and tensely squared by aggressive Mars. We can feel forced to make a decision before we're ready, yet the cavalier Sagittarius Moon encourages us to jump ahead before thinking about the consequences of our actions. Vital information may be missing, or communications could be so vague that coming to a rational conclusion is difficult. Back up, think things through carefully, ask more questions, and review recent conversations before making any serious commitments.

NOVEMBER 13, SOLAR ECLIPSE IN SCORPIO: RESISTANCE IS FUTILE

This total eclipse of the Sun in resolute Scorpio is excellent for letting go of unhealthy habits. Deeply rooted obsessions can reach a critical point where it becomes evident that it's time to relinquish control. Financial and emotional pressures create a need to reassess priorities. This New Moon Eclipse is in an anxious semisquare to ruthless Pluto, increasing the stakes and decreasing our willingness to compromise. Stubbornly resisting change becomes detrimental and even destructive, reminding us to step back and measure the costs of our behavior with a much-needed dose of detachment.

NOVEMBER 28, LUNAR ECLIPSE IN GEMINI: BABY STEPS

Optimistic Jupiter's conjunction to the eclipsed Full Moon represents high hopes, yet a lack of resources might push them out of reach. Tight-fisted conjunctions of Venus and Saturn and Mars and Pluto demand fiscal restraint and careful time management. Meanwhile, maverick Chiron squares the restless Gemini Moon, provoking risky behavior in order to avoid a painful issue. It's wise to avoid making big promises that might be difficult to deliver. We can either aim lower in our aspirations for the time being or prepare to work harder and longer to get where we want to go.

THE BOTTOM LINE: BE THE CHANGE

The mainstream media have been sending fearful apocalyptic messages that 2012 is a year of monumental change because of the shift in the Mayan calendar on December 21. End-of-the-world predictions are nothing new and this one, like the others, is premature. In fact, there are several Mayan calendars, ranging from one of 260 days to the Long Count Calendar of 5,126 years that turns over in December. It does not mark the end of time; it simply indicates the end of one cycle and the beginning of the next. While there are significant astrological patterns this year, the Mayan calendar doesn't correspond with them. Nevertheless, a general perception of dramatic change could contribute to making it a reality.

A major astrological pattern starts this year that won't finish until January 2015, indicating that we are in a period of significant transformation. Uranus, the planet of surprises and breakthroughs, forms seven disruptive squares with provocative Pluto during a three-year period. They occur on June 24 and September 19, 2012, May 20 and November 1, 2013, April 21 and December 15, 2014, and March 16, 2015. This long-lasting connection between revolutionary Uranus and volcanic Pluto will foment change on a grand scale. The last time these two planets were squared to each other was in 1932–1934, when the United States was suffering from an economic depression and fascism was altering the political landscape of the world. Hopefully we won't have to relive the hardships of the 1930s if we learned anything from the 1960s, when Uranus and Pluto were again stirring unrest. This pair of change agents formed conjunctions in 1965 and 1966 that gave rise to the hopeful social movements around the globe that characterized this most memorable decade.

The Uranus-Pluto squares that start this year are, in essence, the next step in the process that began nearly fifty years ago. Issues that arose then will spring back into collective awareness with a renewed sense of urgency that will again wake the masses and inspire radical action.

Uranus in innovative Aries is pushing against entrenched power represented by Pluto in Capricorn. But this is not simply a response to external authorities; it signals a significant shift in the sense of who we are. The mix of technology and medicine with rapid advances in genetic research makes it possible to alter the human body and redirect our evolutionary path. The 1960s gave birth to liberation movements based on race, gender, and sexual preference that have gone a long way toward ending the old models of family and community. It was, like all revolutionary periods, marked by creativity and chaos, as well as freedom and fear. As we launch ourselves into a future of our own making, resistance is to be expected. Traditional institutions will condemn experimentation, and our own psyches will recoil against the forward thrust of history. Yet major changes are coming whether we accept them or not. Clearly, the powerful tides of time cannot be stopped. The wisest path is to participate with a spirit of innovation and the flexibility to adapt to unexpected events, as we lead humanity to the next stage of adventure and discovery.

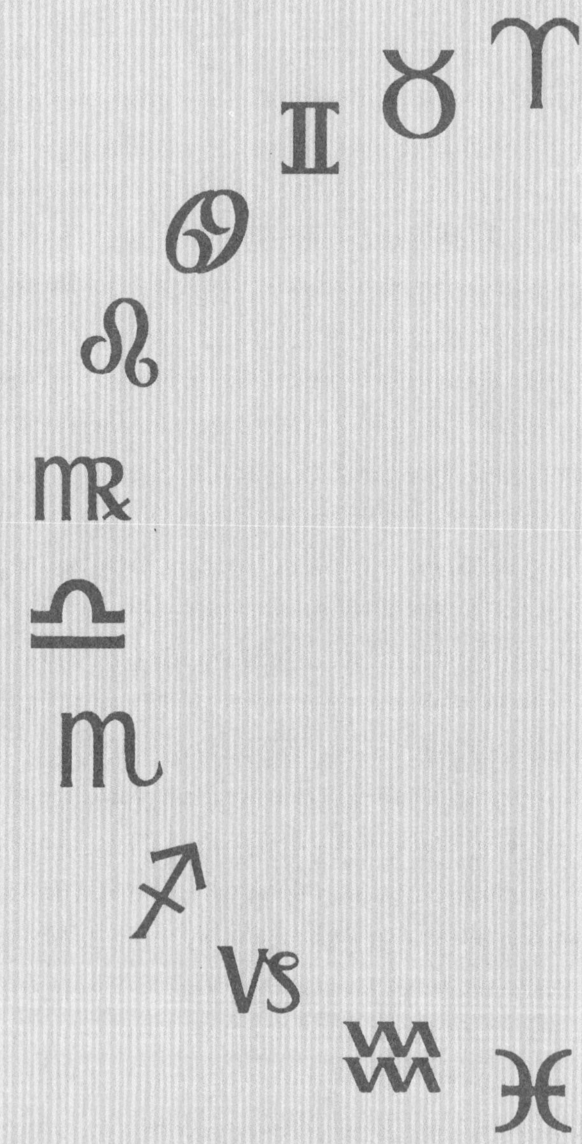

PART 2

AUGUST–DECEMBER 2011 OVERVIEW 2012 ASTROLOGICAL FORECASTS

ARIES

MARCH 21–APRIL 19

ARIES

2011 SUMMARY

The winds of change are blowing in your direction this year, bringing unparalleled opportunities for growth, innovation, and discovery. Confidence, courage, and, perhaps, recklessness can drive you forward to aim higher and move faster than ever before. Open your mind and let your imagination carry you to visions of freedom and excitement that will satisfy your deep need for adventure. Finding a creative outlet for your current intensity will direct this innovative force in a positive direction.

AUGUST—*restoration and renovation*

Attending to all your tasks with careful attention to the little things will clear the way for bigger things to happen.

SEPTEMBER—*reigniting the flame*

Be patient and persistent as you deal with your obligations. Eventually the clouds of drudgery will disperse so that playtime can return.

OCTOBER—*fair rate of exchange*

Instead of fixating on what you're missing in a relationship, appreciating whatever benefits you receive can pave the way to greater satisfaction.

NOVEMBER—*dreams on hold*

Finding brief moments of freedom every day provides the fresh air you need to keep going when you can't get away from it all.

DECEMBER—*as above, so below*

Think globally and act locally is more than a political slogan; it's the way you bring your highest aspirations down to earth and make them real.

2011 CALENDAR

AUGUST

WED 3–THU 4 ★	Discuss delicate matters with discretion
TUE 9–THU 11 ★	Claim your power and a positive breakthrough can happen
TUE 16–THU 18 ★	**SUPER NOVA DAYS** The challenge is to find a safe place within yourself
THU 25 ★	Keep your schedule light to allow time for both work and rest
SUN 28–TUE 30 ★	Explore the potential of your untapped talents and resources

SEPTEMBER

TUE 6 ★	Step outside the system and make a little magic
SUN 11 ★	Don't give too much, spend too much, or expect too much today
SAT 17–SUN 18 ★	**SUPER NOVA DAYS** Letting go of what you don't need frees up your energy
FRI 23 ★	Connect with new people to bring more pleasure and prestige
THU 29–FRI 30 ★	Your quick thinking can help you escape a sticky situation

OCTOBER

MON 3 ★	Channel your extra energy into a healthy physical outlet
TUE 11 ★	Face the facts and feelings, and make a difficult decision
MON 17 ★	Create something new instead of stirring up trouble
SUN 23 ★	You may react strongly to any attempts to influence you today
WED 26–FRI 28 ★	**SUPER NOVA DAYS** You can get a lot done when left to your own devices

NOVEMBER

WED 2–THU 3 ★	New pleasures and brilliant ideas make life entertaining
MON 7 ★	A gentle touch today will do more good than a hard shove
WED 16 ★	You can be extremely convincing when making a powerful point
WED 23 ★	**SUPER NOVA DAY** Keep your excitement under wraps for the best results
FRI 25 ★	The road to adventure appears to be beckoning

DECEMBER

FRI 2–MON 5 ★	**SUPER NOVA DAYS** Conflict with an authority figure is possible now
SAT 10 ★	Take small persistent steps of self-improvement
THU 22 ★	Your spirits lift with new hopes and bright ideas
THU 29 ★	Be careful; you could feel vulnerable to pressure today

ARIES OVERVIEW

You have been swept up by the fast pace of your life since Uranus the Awakener entered independent Aries on March 11, 2011. **This year reveals even more changes that will rattle your windows and shake the foundations of your life.** And although you may have concerns about the road ahead, your appetite for new experiences will overcome your worry. Fortunately, you Rams rise to the challenge when placed in unfamiliar situations and look forward to exploring uncharted lands. Throughout the year, unpredictable Uranus continues to expose buried tensions—physical, emotional, and spiritual—bringing opportunities for you to make the radical changes that align with your shifting perspectives.

Expanding your awareness isn't necessarily easy, especially around June 24 and September 19, when Uranus runs into the first two of seven harsh squares with Pluto that recur through 2015. Intense Pluto entered your 10th House of Career in 2008, beginning a long-term change in your direction in life that will, until 2023, gradually transform how you relate to the world. **Now, however, your professional ambitions are suddenly electrified by the squares from high-voltage Uranus. Unexpected developments require you to alter the course you thought would carry you into the future.**

Be patient as you move steadily toward your goals, even if you are tempted to bolt ahead without any second thoughts. Opportunistic Jupiter in determined Taurus visits your 2nd House of Self-Worth through June 11, bolstering your confidence and rewarding pragmatism more than idealism. Meanwhile, your key planet, Mars, remains in efficient Virgo and your 6th House of Work until July 3. His retrograde period from January 23 through April 13 can stall your progress on the job, but gives you another chance to focus on the details and sharpen your skills so you have everything in order once it's time to push ahead. Jupiter's entry into your 3rd House of Communication on June 11 opens the way for you to interact with others on a more positive basis. This can push you to take a significant project to the next level as long as you don't scatter your energy by trying to accomplish too much too fast.

Relationships continue to teach you important lessons this year as taskmaster Saturn completes its two-year visit to your 7th House of Others. But old assumptions about partnerships come up for reconsideration, and you may be required to reaffirm a recent commitment or make a new one when Saturn enters your 8th House of Intimacy on October 5. Fortunately, you are able to infuse common sense into your vision of the possibilities that lay ahead. **Although the challenges you face now are likely to continue well into 2013, hard-earned stability begins to return by the end of this year if you can resist the temptation to aim higher than you can reach.**

LET'S TALK ABOUT LOVE

You struggle to balance your desire for companionship with your need for independence. Your preconceived notions about love have already come up for review and will continue to evolve in ways you might not expect. Even if you're sure that security is more important than stimulation, romantic Venus's extended stay in restless Gemini from April 3 until August 7 revives your taste for adventure. Talking about your attractions uncovers unexplored issues, especially when Venus is retrograde on May 15–June 27 in your 3rd House of Communication. Be cautious around June 4 when the cavalier Sagittarius Lunar Eclipse opposes Venus and harshly squares Mars. Luckily, your love life picks up when Venus visits your 5th House of Romance on September 6–October 3 and your 7th House of Partnerships on October 28–November 21.

THE POWER OF NOW

Following your ambitions is hard work this year as individualistic Uranus in your 1st House of Personality squares incisive Pluto in your 10th House of Career. Brilliant flashes of awareness become part of your everyday life, and it can be tricky managing your high level of intuition in a way that doesn't threaten order and authorities. Fortunately, since responsible Saturn entered relationship-oriented Libra in the fall of 2009, you have acquired expertise that enables you to work more effectively with others. It's now up to you to use your new skills to create stable partnerships prior to Saturn's entry into Scorpio on October 5. When Saturn begins its two-year visit to your 8th House of Shared Resources, you'll find it easier to take on financial commitments or make investments that involve others.

MAKE YOUR OWN LUCK

Jupiter continues its moneymaking magic, having entered your 2nd House of Income on June 11, 2011, for a one-year stay. Venus adds her glitter to the mix when she visits your 2nd House on March 5–April 3. Arguably your best opportunity to bank some extra cash, get a long-awaited raise, or win in a game of chance is on March 13–14, when a prosperous Venus-Jupiter conjunction forms a fortuitous Grand Earth Trine with Mars in your 6th House of Work and Pluto in your 10th House of Status. Remember, successful timing isn't just about picking the ripe cherries; you'll have more fruit to harvest if you cultivate opportunities by meeting obligations along the way. Don't blow a windfall; put some money aside for tighter times, such as on November 26 when Venus conjuncts austere Saturn.

PREVENTION IS THE BEST MEDICINE

Your key planet, Mars, tells the story of your health this year. Normally, this planet of physicality spends about six weeks in each sign, but now its every-other-year retrograde keeps it in health-conscious Virgo from November 10, 2011, until July 3. This extended visit to your 6th House of Self-Improvement is a great time to enhance your fitness by paying more attention to your diet and exercise regimen. Mars is retrograde on January 23–April 13, giving you a second chance to improve your health if you missed the opportunity at the New Year. Review your progress and then develop a more holistic approach to your well-being when the Sun and Mercury are in your 6th House on August 22–September 16 and when Venus visits on October 3–28.

EASY DOES IT

You're challenged to settle down at home for most of the year because so much continues to draw you into the world. Instead of just relaxing with your family, you want your residence to be a place where you can express your individuality without being judged. You could be fussier than usual, but practice the art of compromise before turning trivial whims into open conflicts. The summer brings you more time to hang around the house with loved ones; Mercury visits your 4th House of Home and Family on June 7–25, followed by the Sun's transit on June 20–July 22 and Venus's appearance on August 7–September 6.

CHANGE OF PLANS

It's not a great year for globetrotting, but you're still likely to do your fair share of traveling. When journeying Jupiter enters your 3rd House of Short Trips on June 11 for a yearlong stay, expect more quick business jaunts and weekend getaways. The Gemini Solar Eclipse on May 20 and the Gemini Lunar Eclipse on November 28 both rattle your 3rd House, indicating unforeseen excursions that suddenly make so much sense you cannot avoid them. But a real adventure may be in store for you on June 4, when the Sagittarius Full Moon Eclipse illuminates your 9th House of Faraway Places and when Mars transits your 9th House on October 6–November 16.

MAKE IT REAL

Your spiritual growth comes in subtle ways. Metaphysical Neptune is working its magic in your karmic 12th House of Soul Consciousness, where it will inspire your dreams for years to come. Visionary Jupiter forms an imaginative quintile with Neptune on April 4, opening your mind to new ways of seeing the cosmos and possibly bringing you a teacher who helps you discover a new worldview. You might have to rework this evolving perspective when Jupiter squares Neptune on June 25. Continued study and practice ensures pragmatic results around October 10, when serious Saturn harmoniously trines insightful Neptune to bring your dreams down to earth.

RICK & JEFF'S TIP FOR THE YEAR:
Face Your Fears

Fear can be a sign of wisdom, especially for you Rams who often jump into a new situation before you consider whether or not it's a smart idea. Succumbing to your apprehension, however, can be crippling. Sometimes all that's needed is careful consideration before you charge ahead. Fortunately, practicing patience can transform your doubt into true confidence, but you'll still need to muster up the courage to stand up to those things that scare you the most.

JANUARY

FALSE START

Your year begins with fireworks; opinionated Mercury dynamically squares impetuous Mars on **January 1**, inciting animated discussions or even an open conflict. Nevertheless, you look forward to the possibilities ahead with eager anticipation. Unfortunately, you may quickly grow frustrated if a project at work doesn't take off as quickly as you expect, because your key planet, Mars, is slowly crawling along in your 6th House of Routine until it turns retrograde on **January 23**. Instead of adding more tasks to your schedule, you'd be wise to go back and methodically complete projects you've already started; put off any major new endeavor until after **April 13**, when Mars resumes direct motion. If you aren't accomplishing as much as you want, remember that you'll achieve more later if you cautiously build momentum instead of fearfully rushing ahead. You have an opportunity now to review and eliminate worn-out habits that no longer serve your purposes. This extended visit by Mars to your health-related 6th House is also a chance to enhance your immune system through proper nutrition and a regular exercise program.

You enjoy spending time with your family when the security-conscious Cancer Full Moon on **January 9** lights up your 4th House of Domestic Conditions. Still, you're reminded to return to work with an industrious trine from energetic Mars in the 6th House of Employment to the ambitious Capricorn Sun in the 10th House of Career on **January 12**. The intellectual Aquarius New Moon on **January 23** activates your 11th House of Long-Term Goals, but your plans will likely run into detours and delays as Mars turns retrograde. Even if your thoughts are clear, cut yourself some slack and allow extra time to complete your work.

KEEP IN MIND THIS MONTH

Over-optimistic commitments can get you into trouble if circumstances beyond your control delay your progress.

KEY DATES

JANUARY 1 ★ *give peace a chance*

You have a lot of facts at your disposal today, but watch out for your tendency to fall back on an old pattern and start an argument. Instead of fighting to prove that you're right, acknowledge that there are multiple points of view. Luckily, a creative quintile between the willful Sun and restraining Saturn enables you to make a sensible choice and move beyond the current stress of warrior Mars.

JANUARY 7–9 ★ *time to talk*

You run through a gamut of emotions that begins with irritation triggered from the bickering between graceful Venus and impatient Mars on **January 7**. Your annoyance builds because the cosmic lovers cannot agree on a single course of action, but communicator Mercury's easy aspects indicate that you can make everything better by discussing your differences. You are cautiously optimistic about your career when Mercury enters practical Capricorn and harmoniously trines buoyant Jupiter on **January 8**, but then excitement can turn into anxiety as Mercury squares jumpy Uranus. Nevertheless, colleagues might not even realize that you are worried, for the Full Moon in hard-shelled Cancer on **January 9** allows you to hide your moods behind a wall of stoicism.

SUPER NOVA DAYS

JANUARY 12–14 ★ *the force is with you*

You have an air of invincibility on **January 12** thanks to the Sun's bright trine to energetic Mars, while loving Venus's trine to reliable Saturn the next day gives you uncharacteristic patience. Make the most of the cosmic momentum as an intense Mercury-Pluto conjunction in your public 10th House announces to the world that you are a force to be reckoned with. Fortunately, you can get away with pushing toward your goals now because your drive is softened by gentle Venus as she bumps into compassionate Neptune, dives into the healing waters of Pisces, and happily harmonizes with lucky Jupiter on **January 13–14.**

JANUARY 19–23 ★ *not so fast*

These are tricky days for you, because the Sun's stressful square to taskmaster Saturn on **January 19** asks you to choose between a professional and a personal goal. Your decision seems final, and the Sun's shift into your social 11th House on **January 20**, along with its square to opportunistic Jupiter on the **22nd**, suggests that the tide really is changing. But the quirky Aquarius New Moon on **January 23**—usually the beginning of a new cycle—is accompanied by Mars turning retrograde, a sure sign that you will soon be reconsidering your options before starting anything new.

FEBRUARY

MARCHING IN PLACE

This month is all about methodically showing up for the daily grind. Your key planet, Mars, tells the story as he stalls in your 6th House of Routine, emphasizing the regularity of your life. Mars just turned retrograde on **January 23**, so you'll need time to accept the fact that you aren't able to make as much progress as you want. But don't let panic trick you into thinking that you're doing something wrong. Instead, settle into steady patterns that work for you and enable you to hold on to the ground you've already gained. You'll have opportunities to make up for lost time after Mars turns direct on **April 13**. Be careful on **February 1** when the cosmic lovers, Venus and Mars, stand off in a tug-of-war. If the sweet satisfaction of love seems far away, open your heart to the pleasures around you rather than allowing your discouragement to turn into anger. On **February 3**, dreamy Neptune's shift into compassionate Pisces begins a gradual process that softens your antagonistic approach and increases your patience with others. The fiery Leo Full Moon on **February 7** activates your 5th House of Love while romantic Venus enters your ardent sign on **February 8**, increasing your desires as well as your charm.

Fantasy leaks into the real world on **February 13** when Mercury enters surreal Pisces and then hooks up with Neptune on Valentine's Day. Luckily, your serious attitude, coupled with hard work, can stabilize a relationship as the Sun trines karmic Saturn on **February 18**. Although you may still be experiencing frustration because of a general lack of momentum, the psychic Pisces New Moon on **February 21** can offer you encouraging glimpses of where you're heading in the future.

KEEP IN MIND THIS MONTH

Don't be discouraged by your lack of progress; a setback may be a blessing in disguise that gives you more time to solidify your plans.

KEY DATES

FEBRUARY 1 ★ *opposites attract*

Although you may think that you know what you want, it's not easy to put it into words when messenger Mercury forms an anxious sesquisquare with aggressive Mars. Meanwhile, the relationship tension associated with the Venus-Mars opposition can distract you from what you should be doing today. There's a fine line between flirting and fighting. Talking about the stress doesn't seem to alleviate it, but you may be able to find a playful way to transform unease into excitement.

FEBRUARY 7–10 ★ *expect the unexpected*

The dramatic Leo Full Moon on **February 7** triggers your creative instincts as she brightens your 5th House of Self-Expression. Clever Mercury's conjunction with the Sun in emotionally detached Aquarius encourages logic over emotions, while Venus's entry in impetuous Aries on **February 8** inspires you to share your feelings. This paradox is further complicated by an irritating quincunx between affectionate Venus and unforgiving Saturn. Additional quincunxes to cantankerous Mars from Mercury on **February 9** and the Sun on **February 10** leave you less than satisfied. Luckily, an electric Venus-Uranus conjunction on the **9th** can suddenly blast through all the static and bring a surprising resolution to a delicate situation.

SUPER NOVA DAYS

FEBRUARY 13–15 ★ *stranger than fiction*

It's easy for you to get your point across on **February 13**, when messenger Mercury harmoniously trines practical Saturn. But just as you think your ideas are solid, Mercury slips into illusory Pisces, weaving facts into fantasies. Mercury conjoins spiritual Neptune on **February 14**, setting the stage for a higher form of expression—and right now music and art can capture realities that remain elusive in words. Still a cooperative sextile between optimistic Jupiter and healer Chiron can show you how to learn from your dreams. A complex Venus-Pluto square on **February 15** acts as a carrot on a stick, luring you into emotional involvement as you seek to balance the current intensity with the possibility of happiness.

FEBRUARY 21–25 ★ *light at the end of the tunnel*

The Pisces New Moon on **February 21** falls in your 12th House of Endings and is a significant turning point in ways that aren't immediately obvious to you. This lunation's conjunction with nebulous Neptune makes it even tougher to put your life into perspective. Uncomfortable aspects to Mars on **February 22–23** remind you that you still have much to accomplish before things settle back into place and make sense again. Luckily, the Sun's focused conjunction with restorative Chiron on **February 24**, and its supportive sextile with auspicious Jupiter on the **25th**, are harbingers of the growth and opportunity that lie ahead.

MARCH

BUILDING MOMENTUM

This month kicks off to a noisy start. Although your key planet, Mars, remains in reverse gear until **April 13**, Mercury the Communicator drives into enterprising Aries on **March 2** and conjuncts explosive Uranus on **March 5**. But the Sun's tense opposition to retrograde Mars on **March 3** is frustrating because familiar conflicts thwart your progress, forcing you into a holding pattern. A similar message arrives when diplomatic Venus opposes restrictive Saturn on **March 4** and then enters sensible Taurus on **March 5**, rewarding a slow and steady style. Even fleet-footed Mercury flying through Aries begins to throw obstacles in your way as it heads toward turning retrograde on **March 12**, returning briefly to supersensitive Pisces on **March 23**.

Paradoxically, this can be an awesome month for you as you stand in the center of your world and gather strength and courage. It's not about reaching your goals now; it's about accepting your place in the bigger scheme of things. You can improve your lifestyle when the discriminating Virgo Full Moon illuminates your 6th House of Health and Habits on **March 8**. But this Full Moon also activates a long-lasting trine between confident Jupiter and compelling Pluto that's exact on **March 13**. Your potential for finding satisfaction seems unlimited as Venus, the money planet, joins Jupiter on **March 14** and Mars trines Venus, Jupiter, and Pluto on the same day! Together these planets create a solid Grand Earth Trine that can be the firm foundation on which you build throughout the rest of the year. Still, don't rush blindly ahead, even as the Sun's return to your sign on the Spring Equinox on **March 20**, coupled with the Aries New Moon on **March 22**, announces the beginning of the next phase of your life.

KEEP IN MIND THIS MONTH

You can easily complicate the moment by impulsively pushing ahead too soon. However, patience builds character and improves your chances for success.

KEY DATES

MARCH 3–6 ★ *let it be*

Someone is making your life more difficult now, and you're ready to fight for your beliefs when the Sun in your 12th House of Spirituality opposes militant Mars on **March 3**. But engaging in conflict could backfire and leave you isolated during an emotionally cool Venus-Saturn opposition on **March 4**. Although you're tempted to raise the stakes by forcing immediate resolution when quicksilver Mercury joins volatile Uranus on **March 5**, uneasy feelings will settle down on their own as Venus forms a cooperative sextile with forgiving Neptune on **March 6**.

SUPER NOVA DAYS

MARCH 12–14 ★ *make it happen*

Mercury's backward turn on **March 12** in your 1st House of Self can rattle your world if you let your impatience get the better of your determination. But even the retrogrades of Mars and Mercury now won't be enough to prevent you from planting the seeds for later success. Get ready to ride an impressive wave created by resourceful Venus and expansive Jupiter as they trine evolutionary Pluto in your 10th House of Career and energetic Mars in your 6th House of Self-Improvement on **March 13–14**. But try not to focus on short-term gratification. This grand trine in practical earth signs suggests good fortune if you are willing to put in the hard work after the initial excitement wears off.

MARCH 18–22 ★ *spontaneous combustion*

It's easy to say something you'll regret later as chatty Mercury backs over shocking Uranus on **March 18**, possibly reigniting an unresolved issue from their prior conjunction on **March 5**. This time, however, you can create more problems than you realize; things move quickly as the Sun enters imprudent Aries on **March 20**, joins Mercury on the **21st**, and hooks up with the New Moon on the **22nd**. This cosmic party in your sign can provoke a sudden release of pent-up tension that allows you to break through previous resistance and make a fresh start.

MARCH 28–29 ★ *tipping point*

You must balance your goals against those of your partner on **March 28**, due to a transformative quintile between hardworking Saturn in your 7th House of Relationships and turbulent Pluto in your 10th House of Public Responsibility. The situation can reach an impasse on **March 29** when the Sun squares Pluto, possibly forcing a confrontation. Luckily, an easygoing Mercury-Venus sextile allows you to talk about your feelings without blaming anyone else for your current predicament.

APRIL

READY, SET, GO!

You've had your fair share of delays since your key planet, Mars, turned retrograde on **January 23**. Prepare yourself, though; your life is now about to take off, because the action planet turns direct on **April 13**. Projects that have met obstacles in the past will begin to gain momentum as you are finally cleared for takeoff. Your creativity is stimulated when artistic Venus enters witty Gemini on **April 3**, and you're already on the move when messenger Mercury ends its retrograde period on **April 4**. Instead of being forced to go over the details again or to rethink your strategy one more time, you can look ahead and start putting your plan into motion. The amicable Libra Full Moon on **April 6** activates your 7th House of Partners, making this a smart time to work with someone you trust to further your goals.

Although **April 13** is a pivotal point because energetic Mars starts moving forward, it will take time for you to build up speed. Don't get discouraged when the Sun in impatient Aries opposes constrictive Saturn on **April 15**. Acknowledge where your resistance shows up and find a way to let it go because you'll have plenty of new ideas once clever Mercury enters Aries on **April 16**. The Sun's entry to practical Taurus and your 2nd House of Self-Esteem on **April 19**, combined with its empowering trines with Mars and Pluto on **April 23** and **April 29**, respectively, gives you solid footing to take the next step in your work. Additionally, the Taurus New Moon on **April 21** harmonizes with both Mars and imaginative Neptune, validating your dreams and providing you with the resources and determination to make them come true.

KEEP IN MIND THIS MONTH

You get so excited when things go your way that you may take on too much. Pace yourself so you don't burn out.

KEY DATES

APRIL 3–6 ★ *hope springs eternal*

You don't have to contain your enthusiasm on **April 6**, when the sociable Libra Full Moon brings someone into your life who encourages you to charge ahead with your bold plans. But your anticipation is already off the charts because lovely Venus dances into your 3rd House of Information on **April 3**, increasing your desire to step up the pace. No matter how busy you are, you'll eagerly find time to squeeze more into your days when interactive Mercury turns direct on **April 4**. Fortunately, all this activity is further supported by creative aspects to intuitive Neptune from visionary

Jupiter and Venus on **April 4–5**. Don't be afraid to take definitive action during this powerful period of growth.

APRIL 7–9 ★ *keep your cool*

Conflicts are likely on **April 7** with a dynamic square between flirty Venus in fickle Gemini and feisty Mars in critical Virgo. Then the brilliant Sun clashes with Mars the next day, stirring up trouble for no good reason. Be aware of your edginess and take responsibility for your feelings so you can channel all this anxiety creatively. An unexpected breakthrough on **April 9** can lead to short-lived pleasure when a thrilling Venus-Uranus sextile sparks your desire for immediate gratification.

SUPER NOVA DAYS

APRIL 13–16 ★ *reclaim your power*

Superhero Mars begins to restore your confidence when he turns direct on **April 13**, but you could quickly grow discouraged if you expect that everything will change overnight. Yes, you can finally see the potential rewards for all of the hard work you've done over the last few months. But you may become so intoxicated with the possibilities that you'll need a serious attitude adjustment by **April 15**, when sobering Saturn opposes the Sun. Although your enthusiasm may be premature, logical Mercury enters your 1st House of Self on **April 16**, enhancing your ability to express your intentions so clearly that others rally to your support.

APRIL 21–23 ★ *let freedom ring*

Seize new opportunities to make money on **April 21**, when the Taurus New Moon occurs in your 2nd House of Income. The Sun's supportive sextile with psychic Neptune on **April 22** and trine with instinctive Mars on **April 23** gives you an uncanny ability to know how pushy to be when negotiating for what you want. But its mental Mercury's conjunction with independent Uranus on the **22nd** that tells you how a current promotion can bring you increased autonomy on the job and new options for your discretionary spending.

A FAMILIAR TUNE

You can make steady progress this month now that action-hero Mars is moving direct. But you may also need to make choices about your lifestyle that you thought you had already handled as Mars revisits familiar territory in your 6th House of Self-Improvement. These déjà vu experiences can become more bothersome as needy Venus in scattered Gemini slows down to retrograde in your 3rd House of Communication on **May 15**, delaying satisfaction and requiring you to repeatedly rehash conversations that you can't seem to bring to an agreeable conclusion. The emotional Scorpio Full Moon on **May 5** falls in your 8th House of Shared Resources, possibly leading to a disagreement over who owns what. Keeping an open mind about community property is crucial, especially when expressive Mercury enters simplistic Taurus on **May 9**, prompting stubbornness, no matter what the cost.

Fortunately, you receive a burst of motivational energy and support for your ideas around **May 13–16**, when Mars forms a stabilizing Grand Earth Trine with Mercury and formidable Pluto, allowing you to accomplish more than you thought possible. But peace of mind eludes you, because Venus's retrograde turn combines with frustrating aspects from hopeful Jupiter to cynical Saturn on **May 16** and resentful Pluto on **May 17**. Let go of negative feelings; a New Moon Eclipse on **May 20**—just hours after the Sun enters flexible Gemini on **May 20**—indicates that you can change your mind in an instant to make life easier for yourself. Luckily, getting others to follow your lead is more feasible when Mercury joins optimistic Jupiter on **May 22**, enters your busy 3rd House of Communication on **May 24**, and aligns with the Sun on **May 27**.

KEEP IN MIND THIS MONTH

Having information doesn't mean that you'll use it effectively. Less talk and more action produce the best results.

KEY DATES

MAY 5–8 ★ *reversal of fortune*

Interactions with others are complicated on **May 5** when the intense Scorpio Full Moon activates your 8th House of Deep Sharing. Although you long for more passion in relationships, messenger Mercury opposes somber Saturn to filter out much of the emotional content of your conversations. However, dynamic aspects from surprising Uranus to buoyant Jupiter on **May 7** and to active Mars on **May 8** may turn you from feeling sad about what you've lost to being excited about what's to come. Instead of looking back, focus your attention on what you can do now to create a happier future.

SUPER NOVA DAYS

MAY 13–16 ★ *build for the future*

These exciting days lift your spirits, yet your current optimism doesn't tell the whole story. The Sun's annual conjunction with euphoric Jupiter on **May 13** is enough to make your world seem brighter. Then it gets even better on **May 13–16**, when Mercury, Mars, and Pluto form a practical grand trine. What you create now has lasting value. However, Venus turns retrograde on **May 15**, reminding you that you probably won't find love or wealth overnight. Be patient, since Jupiter's irritating quincunx to Saturn from your 2nd House of Self-Worth on **May 16** brings uncertainty into the equation. Ultimately, your hard work will bring a reward, so hold your present course despite any self-doubt.

MAY 20–22 ★ *flights of fancy*

The truth eludes you on **May 21** when trickster Mercury awkwardly aspects rational and reasonable Saturn, messing with your basic perceptions of reality. Your ability to think critically is already compromised, for the fickle Gemini Solar Eclipse on **May 20** allows your thoughts to fly on any breeze that comes along. Be careful, for the gentle wind of belief gains power and persistence on **May 22** as Mercury joins boundless Jupiter. You may find it tough to change your mind.

MAY 27–30 ★ *laughter is the best medicine*

The willful Sun joins brainy Mercury on **May 27** to focus your concentration, but together they sextile experimental Uranus on **May 27–28** to spark innovative ideas that are out of the ordinary. Still, your thinking might be convoluted, for dark Pluto quincunxes Mercury and the Sun on **May 28–29**. If others misunderstand you, Mercury's square to combative Mars on **May 30** triggers an argument that you're unlikely to resolve. It's smarter now to express your anger with humor than by direct confrontation.

JUNE

POINT OF NO RETURN

This is a month of dramatic transitions that foreshadow larger changes ahead. The farsighted Sagittarius Full Moon Eclipse on **June 4** falls in your 9th House of Future Vision, shaking things up at work enough to cause you to rethink your long-term plans. Although this eclipse reveals tensions on the job, the real pressure comes from a shocking square between rebellious Uranus in your 1st House of Self and powerful Pluto in your 10th House of Public Responsibility that's exact on **June 24**. This is the first of seven such alignments that recur through **2015**, in a series that's bound to pit your need for freedom of personal expression against the demands of the world. Fortunately, Jupiter begins its yearlong visit to your 3rd House of Communication on **June 11**, empowering your words with a sense of purpose so others will take you more seriously. Although your friends may encourage you to explore a wide variety of options, you must focus your attention where you have the most impact instead of trying to change things beyond your control.

Information is power on **June 19**, when the curious Gemini New Moon plants a seed of hope in your 3rd House of Data Collection. But you may not have enough time to assimilate what you already know before the Summer Solstice on **June 20**, when the Sun slips into security-conscious Cancer and you withdraw into the safety and familiarity of your personal life. You could lose track of what's important when indulgent Jupiter squares misleading Neptune on **June 25**. Effusive Mercury enters your 5th House of Self-Expression on the same day, so beware going overboard talking about yourself.

KEEP IN MIND THIS MONTH

Although you can count on support from your family and friends, your final choices must be your own.

KEY DATES

SUPER NOVA DAYS

JUNE 3–7 ★ *turbulence ahead*

You're already in a serious frame of mind on **June 3** when thoughtful Mercury trines solemn Saturn. The Full Moon Eclipse in philosophical Sagittarius on **June 4** deepens your contemplative mood as you wonder whether or not you are on the right path. Unfortunately, glamorous Venus squares reckless Mars in the 6th House of Details, highlighting your annoyance with the routine of your job. Although you might try to smooth over the rough spots when Venus joins the Sun on **June 5**, anger management may be in order as the Sun squares Mars on **June 7**. Even if you use your extra energy constructively, Mercury's entry into passive Cancer challenges you to express your feelings without stirring up unnecessary conflict.

JUNE 11–13 ★ *window of opportunity*

More people seem to be coming in and out of your life now on a daily basis. All the activity is due to Jupiter's entry into your 3rd House of Immediate Environment on **June 11**, which is a long-lasting transit. This increased contact with friends and acquaintances is good news that can open your mind to new possibilities. But it's challenging to think straight as rational Mercury aspects erratic Uranus and demanding Pluto, arousing anxious thoughts and self-doubt. Avoid overreacting, for the issues being stirred will take time to resolve. Fortunately, the Sun's trine to sensible Saturn in your 7th House of Partners on **June 13** indicates that you'll get the sound advice you need.

JUNE 19–21 ★ *learning to fly*

Your life is more unstable than you realize on **June 19**, when the flighty Gemini New Moon scatters your attention prior to mental Mercury's run-in with dogmatic Saturn the next day. Although the Sun's entry into tenacious Cancer blesses you with uncharacteristic patience, your nervous system is also stimulated by an exciting sextile from sensual Venus to outrageous Uranus in your 1st House of Personality. Observe your extreme mood swings instead of acting on any one impulse. Your emotions should settle down on **June 21**, when Mercury's cooperative sextile to Mars enables you to successfully walk your talk.

JUNE 29 ★ *between a rock and a hard place*

Changes at work leave you tense at home as the Sun challenges the lingering Uranus-Pluto square. It's hard to be cheerful when you feel as if you're stuck, with nowhere to go. Nevertheless, avoid striking out in anger. Instead, consciously use the positive Mercury-Jupiter sextile to talk about your frustrations in a way that eases the stress and creates a better future.

JULY

THE THINGS WE DO FOR LOVE

Now that magnetic Venus is moving direct in your sign, you're caught in a tug-of-war that pits your intense desire for success against your need to retreat from the world to enjoy time with loved ones. The recent waves of high intensity continue as the ambitious Capricorn Full Moon conjuncts impassioned Pluto on **July 3** in your 10th House of Career. Although you know what you want and have a plan to get it, your energy is drawn toward family relationships now, delaying your success. You cannot rush off and do things your way, for energetic Mars enters diplomatic Libra on the **3rd** and remains in your 7th House of Partnerships until **August 23**, forcing you to balance your desires with the needs of those close to you. Although supportive aspects to unconventional Uranus are indicative of unusual events on **July 4**, your life may quiet down a bit as communicator Mercury grinds to a halt to enter its retrograde phase, which lasts from **July 14** to **August 8**.

Meanwhile, Mars brews up trouble as it trines Jupiter, squares Pluto, and opposes Uranus on **July 17–18**. An annoying quincunx from indulgent Jupiter in your interactive 3rd House to controlling Pluto on **July 18** further challenges you to balance your interpersonal distractions with your responsibilities. The nurturing Cancer New Moon on **July 19** activates your 4th House of Foundations, reminding you that there's no substitute for the emotional support of friends and family. The Sun's entry into demonstrative Leo and your fun-loving 5th House on **July 22** offers you opportunities to get out and enjoy yourself, tempting you through the end of the month to leave more serious matters for later consideration.

KEEP IN MIND THIS MONTH

Set yourself fewer goals right now. You'll still feel a sense of accomplishment—but also have more time to enjoy what matters most.

KEY DATES

JULY 3–4 ★ *healthy dialogue*

Your personality sparkles when irrepressible Mercury forms easy aspects to irresistible Venus and intelligent Uranus on **July 4**. Yet you can't shake your anxiety, because Mercury and Venus create stressful quincunxes with Pluto and the self-restrained Capricorn Full Moon on **July 3**. Be careful about projecting your frustration onto a close friend or partner, for cranky Mars enters relationship-oriented Libra on the **3rd**. Although you'd prefer not to confront someone who's trying to usurp your authority, a difficult conversation may be your only way to maintain control.

JULY 8–9 ★ *tell the truth*

You're feeling spacey when confusing Neptune is aspected by Mars on **July 8** and the Sun on the **9th**. You might believe that your actions are speaking louder than your words, but others can misinterpret your behavior unless you take the time to clearly explain your motives. Don't expect anyone to guess at your intentions. Be specific and say exactly what's on your mind.

JULY 14–15 ★ *reality check*

Witty Mercury is playing the role of trickster when, on **July 14**, it apparently stops and turns backward in your 5th House of Creativity. A disarming Mercury-Venus sextile the same day increases your ability to cleverly convince others of the merits of your ideas. But your logic may not withstand scrutiny, and the Sun's harsh square to judgmental Saturn on **July 15** can break the magic spell of your words. You may need to improve your plan before it can work.

SUPER NOVA DAYS

JULY 19–22 ★ *crisis and emergence*

You experience a dark night of the soul when the emotionally sensitive Cancer New Moon on **July 19** falls in your 4th House of Security, luring you down a path of introspection. Your confidence will rebound by **July 22** when the Sun enters proud Leo, but not before you question the purpose of your life. Luckily, you receive an additional cosmic boost from a pair of uplifting sextiles, indicating that this is an excellent time to share your ideas with others and push your agenda forward.

JULY 30–31 ★ *sweet smell of success*

You can't tell the difference between assertion and aggression on **July 30**, thanks to an aggravating quincunx between the Sun and domineering Pluto. However, your persistence is rewarded on **July 31** when the Sun's harmonious trine to progressive Uranus in your sign blasts you into the future. Additionally, satisfaction is all but assured by lovely Venus's trine to unwavering Saturn the same day.

AUGUST

A CHANGE WILL DO YOU GOOD

You may feel overwhelmed at times this month, but holding onto the status quo is not a viable option. You'll be better served if you actively work toward radical transformation rather than attempting to prevent it. On **August 1**, your optimism can lift your spirits when the futuristic Aquarius Full Moon harmonizes with jovial Jupiter. The Sun's cooperative sextile with Jupiter on **August 2** encourages your spontaneity, but you would be wise to fine-tune your plans prior to **August 8** while cerebral Mercury is still retrograde. Nevertheless, this is not a great time to make decisions about love, for Mercury in your 5th House of Romance forms an uncertain quincunx with deceptive Neptune on **August 4–11**.

Your frustration runs high in the middle of the month. Although the second occurrence of the intense Uranus-Pluto square isn't exact until **September 19**—the first was on **June 24**—the Sun's harsh rays stress this long-lasting configuration on **August 14–15**, illuminating troublesome issues. You might feel as if you're facing insurmountable resistance—and it's further agitated by contentious Mars conjuncting naysayer Saturn on the **15th**. The creative Leo New Moon on **August 17** cooperates with Saturn and Mars, however, enabling you to settle down, channel your energy, and regain control of your current situation. There is no easy escape from your responsibilities when the Sun enters hardworking Virgo and your 6th House of Employment on **August 22**, followed by Mars moving into intense Scorpio and your 8th House of Deep Sharing on **August 23**. Fortunately, you are able to draw energy from a deep reserve when powerful Pluto supports the Pisces Full Moon in your 12th House of Inner Peace on **August 31**.

KEEP IN MIND THIS MONTH

Although you may feel stuck, it's crucial to keep your life in motion as the pressure for change mounts.

KEY DATES

AUGUST 1–3 ★ *leap of faith*

Happy-go-lucky Jupiter boldly tells you to say yes to friends and groups as it forms a superconductive trine with the brilliant Aquarius Full Moon that illuminates your sociable 11th House on **August 1**. It's challenging to put an opportunity into proper perspective when courageous Mars aspects intuitive Neptune on **August 3**. You can't do it all just because your dreams seem so real. However, you won't know what's possible unless you try.

AUGUST 8–11 ★ *free your mind*

Think about what's next on **August 8**, when analytical Mercury turns direct in your 5th House of Romance and Self-Expression to unleash your creative instincts and help you accomplish more in the weeks ahead. Let your feelings guide you as emotional Venus aligns with spiritual Neptune on **August 9**. But don't spend too much time pondering what you want until after Mercury's bothersome quincunx to Neptune on **August 11**.

SUPER NOVA DAYS

AUGUST 15–17 ★ *against all odds*

Edgy Mars conjoins restrictive Saturn in your 7th House of Others on the **15th**, dampening your enthusiasm about relationships. You may question your recent progress in the days leading up to the lively Leo New Moon on **August 17**. You're willing to put on your best face, but it's still challenging to keep your spirits up when vulnerable Venus in your 4th House of Security opposes domineering Pluto on **August 15** and then squares unstable Uranus on **August 16**. Domestic tensions feel unmanageable and you don't know what will happen next. Fortunately, the New Moon activates your 5th House of Creativity while also being stabilized by Saturn. Your commitment to honest communication should lead to success if you can remain calm in the face of turmoil.

AUGUST 19–20 ★ *power play*

Expect a subtle yet profound shift in authority when ambitious Saturn forms a dynamic quintile with fierce Pluto in your 10th House of Status on **August 19**. You can take control as the Sun sextiles your key planet Mars on **August 20**—but be on guard against your own arrogance, because rash Mars aspects self-righteous Jupiter the same day.

AUGUST 29–31 ★ *face the music*

You're ready to do whatever is necessary at work on **August 29** when the Sun in your 6th House of Details trines unstoppable Pluto. But there may be unexpected consequences to your actions as unruly Uranus enters the scene on **August 30**. The dreamy Pisces Full Moon on **August 31** tempts you to escape reality, but Mercury's entry into rational Virgo tells you it's wiser to listen to logic.

SEPTEMBER

THE COST OF FREEDOM

You're tested this month when circumstances beyond your control thwart your pursuit of your heart's desire. With eclectic Uranus in your 1st House of Personality, you're in a long-term process of reclaiming your individuality. You could push so hard this month that you inadvertently become a threat to someone whom you really want as an ally. Your key planet, Mars the Warrior, is in passionate Scorpio and your 8th House of Transformation throughout the month, and he urges you to beat the drums of rebellion on **September 3–4** when he aspects Pluto and Uranus. The second of seven squares between Uranus and dark Pluto in your 10th House of Career is exact on **September 19**. The first one, on **June 24**, may have triggered your discontent, but the issues you face are complex and may not reach final resolution until the last Uranus-Pluto square on **March 16, 2015**.

The Virgo New Moon on **September 15** falls in your 6th House of Details, making this an ideal time to take small strategic steps on your great journey. Instead of making grandiose plans without substance, do something manageable that has lasting impact. But it becomes more challenging to maintain your composure on **September 20**, when communicator Mercury adds to the dynamic Uranus-Pluto tension. The Sun's entry into socially astute Libra on **September 22** is the Fall Equinox and a time to balance your personal ambitions with those of a partner or workmate. The heat is on as intense aspects fuel the relationship pressure cooker right up through the fiery Aries Full Moon on the **29th**.

KEEP IN MIND THIS MONTH

Everything seems to be in a state of change, yet taking your time before reacting will work to your ultimate advantage.

KEY DATES

SEPTEMBER 3–5 ★ *singing the blues*

You feel left out on **September 3** when tender Venus in emotional Cancer squares stern Saturn in your 7th House of Partners. It might seem as if others are holding back their support or even avoiding your friendly overtures. However, you won't likely be deterred because fearless Mars is teaming up with relentless Pluto to help you press your point. But there could be unexpected repercussions when Mars forms an unstable quincunx with surprising Uranus on **September 4**. Clear and direct communication is your best bet, since messenger Mercury connects with Pluto on the **4th** and Mars on the **5th**.

SEPTEMBER 7–10 ★ *tone it down*

Your ability to say exactly what you mean is your greatest strength on the **10th**, when analytical Mercury joins the willful Sun in your 6th House of Details. Although your enthusiasm can be contagious, you must be extra-careful not to exaggerate, because the Sun and Mercury form overzealous squares with jubilant Jupiter on **September 7–8**. You'll accomplish more if you can rein in your exuberance.

SEPTEMBER 12–16 ★ *all fired up*

You're ready to try something completely different as the Moon and Venus in attention-seeking Leo harmoniously trine unorthodox Uranus on **September 12–13**. But you could draw the ire of someone who is intimidated by your defiant behavior. The careful Virgo New Moon on **September 15** may be a chance for you to clarify your intentions and skillfully retreat just enough to put the situation into perspective. But you'll still be fighting against your own tendency to make a mountain out of a molehill when overeager Mars aspects unrestrained Jupiter on **September 16**.

SEPTEMBER 18–20 ★ *now or never*

You're more urgent than ever about finding your direction in life when profound Pluto ends its retrograde phase on **September 18**. It feels as if your whole future depends on what you do now as the wobbly square between reckless Uranus and Pluto becomes exact on **September 19**. Don't shoot off at the mouth before considering the impact of your words when mischievous Mercury in your 7th House of Partners opposes Uranus and squares Pluto on **September 20**.

SUPER NOVA DAYS

SEPTEMBER 25–29 ★ *unstable ground*

Your patience is tested in the tempestuous few days before the Aries Full Moon on **September 29**. This wild lunation is conjunct with electrifying Uranus in your 1st House of Personality and square transformational Pluto in your 10th House of Status. But the waves are already overwhelming you when the cosmic lovers, Mars and Venus, create stressful aspects to the Uranus-Pluto square on **September 25–26**. Instead of trying to control your environment, pay attention to your feelings and change the way you react.

OCTOBER

DREAM THE POSSIBLE DREAM

Recent relationship tensions and work pressures begin to ease as you distance yourself from last month's intensity and begin to let go of the past. Four planets change signs on **October 3–6**, focusing your intentions, intensifying your emotions, and encouraging you to look ahead rather than in the rearview mirror. Messenger Mercury delivers a much-needed reality check as it runs into authoritative Saturn on **October 5**, prior to both planets entering passionate Scorpio and your 8th House of Intimacy and Transformation. Your mind is churning with unfulfilled dreams when your ruling planet, Mars, enters inspirational Sagittarius and your 9th House of Faraway Places on **October 6**. Fortunately, several helpful aspects culminate with realistic Saturn smoothly trining wishful Neptune on **October 10**, allowing you to define the most significant themes of your fantasies and begin a manifestation cycle that continues as this aspect recurs through **July 19, 2013**.

By midmonth you're caught between two extremes and your frustration could tempt you to act without thinking. Don't be tricked into believing you can solve a complex problem with one quick move. Yes, the fair-minded Libra New Moon falls in your 7th House of Relationships on **October 15**, but you aren't feeling all that balanced because expansive Jupiter forms a stressful aspect with restrictive Saturn as well. Your enthusiasm for life grows when just-do-it Mars opposes farsighted Jupiter on **October 28** and intelligent Mercury enters your adventurous 9th House on **October 29**. This is a smart time to study a new subject or plan a trip, for the determined Taurus Full Moon, also on the **29th**, helps you bring your ideas to fruition.

KEEP IN MIND THIS MONTH

Give yourself permission to rest, but don't get too comfortable—you still have plenty to do while the cosmic tides are in your favor.

KEY DATES

OCTOBER 5–7 ★ *better safe than sorry*

Although serious relationship issues require your attention on **October 5**, you won't be overwhelmed by the drama because everyone involved is doing their best to be rational. Nevertheless, an illusory Mercury-Neptune trine stimulates your fantasies, inspiring action by **October 6** when enterprising Mars enters your 9th House of Big Ideas. Even if you're intending intended to remain practical, Mars's conflicted square with mystical Neptune on **October 7** tempts you to throw caution to the wind.

OCTOBER 9–10 ★ *smooth sailing*
Listen carefully to a friend who encourages you to follow your dreams on the **9th**, when the Sun in your 7th House of Others trines wise Jupiter. You are ready to do whatever it takes to reach your professional goals as ruthless Pluto in your 10th House of Career aspects Venus in your detail-oriented 6th House. Don't doubt your decision; a Mercury-Pluto sextile on **October 10** all but guarantees that your logic is sound. Disciplined Saturn's balancing act with magical Neptune makes whatever you imagine possible.

SUPER NOVA DAYS
OCTOBER 14–16 ★ *enough is enough*
Although the objective Libra New Moon on **October 15** shows you both sides of a dilemma, you won't have trouble making a decision, because assertive Mars creates a free-flowing trine with brilliant Uranus that inspires you with intuition. Reckless action may temporarily clear the air of tension, but it won't address the deeper questions you now face. What you do may be less important than how far you take it, because sweet Venus's square to overindulgent Jupiter on **October 16** challenges you to observe sensible limits.

OCTOBER 25 ★ *observe the stop sign*
If it feels like your life has been running out of control, the Sun's annual conjunction with bossy Saturn may force you to stop, look, and listen before you proceed any farther. Don't try to power your way through the emotional resistance. Pay attention to the cues that you receive from others and from yourself.

OCTOBER 28–29 ★ *make it last*
You're challenged to act with self-discipline, since you won't get any complaints from others when generous Jupiter opposes spontaneous Mars on **October 28**. This cosmic green light boosts your enthusiasm and your energy. Mercury's square to uncertain Neptune can fog your thinking on **October 29**, but luckily the steady Taurus Full Moon is in your 2nd House of Personal Resources. Acting with common sense will assure you have enough time, money, and determination to complete what you start.

NOVEMBER

ANYTHING CAN HAPPEN

While the pressures of your business and personal relationships are unrelenting, intense cosmic forces this month have the power to turn coal into diamonds. The choice is yours. You can either sell yourself short and give up before you reach your goal, or dig deeply into the shadows of your soul and reaffirm your commitment to growth, excellence, and positive change. Until **November 16**, your key planet, Mars, is in hopeful Sagittarius and your 9th House of Big Ideas. Venus in your 7th House of Others attracts unstable relationships on **November 1–3** as she activates the epic Uranus-Pluto square that lingers into next year. Meanwhile bold Mars stirs up a bit of magic as he forms creative quintiles with ethereal Neptune and lovable Venus. It feels as if your fantasies can overtake reality, but your adventurous plans can unravel during trickster Mercury's retrograde phase **November 6–26**. Additionally, an intense Scorpio New Moon Eclipse in your 8th House of Transformation on **November 13** is a further indication that you must let go of self-limiting assumptions if you truly want to succeed.

It's even more difficult to manage the current tension between your need for security and your restlessness after an awkward quincunx between conservative Saturn and uninhibited Uranus on the **15th**. You grow increasingly ambitious once Mars enters industrious Capricorn and your 10th House of Career on the **16th**, but might face unexpected reactions to your rash behavior on **November 23–27** when Mars aspects Uranus, Saturn, and Pluto. If you stand up for your beliefs, the transitional Gemini Full Moon Eclipse on the **28th** marks a finish to your hard work and brings signs of welcome relief.

KEEP IN MIND THIS MONTH

You cannot judge your success by external events. It's more important to consider your emotional and spiritual growth than what's occurring in the material world.

KEY DATES

NOVEMBER 1–4 ★ *the love game*

You may be frustrated when someone interferes with your plans as Mars semi-squares Saturn in your 8th House of Deep Sharing on the **1st**. But a sudden twist on the partnership path creates excitement and angst as desirable Venus opposes unpredictable Uranus on the same day before dynamically squaring passionate Pluto on the **3rd**. Fortunately, the outcome could be wonderful as the cosmic lovers, Venus and Mars, hook up in a creative quintile on **November 4**.

NOVEMBER 9 ★ *beautiful dreamer*

Delicious Venus is the main story today as she aligns with enchanting Neptune to blur the edges between reality and fantasy. Venus also forms a free-flowing trine with joyful Jupiter—one of the loveliest planetary combos—suggesting that pleasure is within your reach.

SUPER NOVA DAYS

NOVEMBER 13–17 ★ *dark side of the moon*

You reach a turning point when the powerful Scorpio New Moon Eclipse on **November 13** sets the stage for dramatic changes. Retrograde Mercury in your 9th House of Future Vision is arguing with confused Neptune, making it difficult to solidify plans. Clarity returns when the communication planet backs into perceptive Scorpio on **November 14**. Unfortunately, having accurate data doesn't mean that you'll choose a sensible course of action because authoritative Saturn forms a shaky quincunx with unruly Uranus on the **15th**. Luckily, you gain objectivity and direction when energetic Mars enters calculating Capricorn the next day. A supportive Mars-Neptune sextile on **November 17** allows you to be practical without losing touch with your dreams.

NOVEMBER 21–23 ★ *strike when the iron is hot*

Everything changes on **November 21**, when the Sun enters cavalier Sagittarius and your 9th House of Adventure. You're eager to begin your new journey, yet a complicated emotional connection can force you to set aside your plans as Venus enters impassioned Scorpio and your 8th House of Intimacy on the same day. Although sorting through feelings is a struggle, a decisive action settles the matter on **November 23** when a combustible Mars-Uranus square blasts you with an incredible sense of urgency.

NOVEMBER 26–29 ★ *instant karma*

An odd mixture of strategic planning, impulsive reactions, and unfolding melodrama can affect your job and your pocketbook as Mercury turns direct on **November 26**, Mars joins suspicious Pluto on **November 27**, and the Gemini Full Moon Eclipse rattles your 3rd House of Communication on **November 28**. Stand firm in your convictions; if you face reality when resourceful Venus conjuncts Saturn on the **26th**, you'll be supported when she sextiles Mars and Pluto on **November 28–29**.

DECEMBER

INTO THE WILD BLUE YONDER

Your challenge this month is to maintain a practical perspective on the opportunities that come your way. Propitious Jupiter continues its yearlong visit to your 3rd House of Information, presenting you with an endless stream of data—some vitally significant, some just noise. Jupiter becomes the focus of uncomfortable quincunxes from lover Venus and warrior Mars on the **December 1**, warping your perceptions and making it difficult to know how much confidence to place in your point of view. Everything seems bigger and better than it actually is when the Sun in extravagant Sagittarius opposes Jupiter from your 9th House of Big Ideas on **December 2**. Although the Sagittarius New Moon on **December 13** encourages you to take bold steps on your personal journey, its bothersome semisquare to doubting Saturn can put obstacles in your path.

It's tempting to tell a tall tale when messenger Mercury opposes Jupiter on **December 17**, followed by charming Venus on **December 22**. Jupiter forms additional quincunxes with Pluto and Saturn on **December 20–22**, this time revealing your tendency to be over-optimistic in your definition of success. Fortunately, responsible Saturn forms a cooperative sextile with manipulative Pluto on **December 26**, enabling you to manage your resources and effectively work toward completing your mission. The nurturing Cancer Full Moon on **December 28** brightens your 4th House of Home and Family, yet the magnetic Sun-Pluto conjunction on **December 30** indicates that your year won't end on a quiet note. But even when Venus and Mars, the cosmic lovers, quarrel on **December 31**, a brilliant Mars-Uranus sextile offers innovative solutions that accelerate the speed of change.

KEEP IN MIND THIS MONTH

Instead of trying to make major decisions that change the direction of your life, focus on doing whatever you can to make minor improvements day by day.

KEY DATES

SUPER NOVA DAYS

DECEMBER 1–2 ★ *out of bounds*

You're convinced you can't control the chaotic pace of your life these days. However, captivating Venus in your 8th House of Intimacy forms a distorting quincunx with giant Jupiter on **December 1**, throwing off your judgment. You'll likely err on the side of excess, because excitable Mars is also quincunx with Jupiter. Don't rely on others to tell you when you've reached your limit, either. Boundless Jupiter opposes the Sun on **December 2**, suggesting that your friends will be nodding in approval even when you've gone too far.

DECEMBER 10–13 ★ *the illusion of logic*

Communicator Mercury's entry into your 9th House of Philosophy on **December 10** and subsequent square to disorienting Neptune on the **11th** leaves you confused, because you're more interested in abstract concepts now than practical realities. Although you do get a burst of pragmatism from a Mars-Saturn quintile on the **12th**, the idealistic Sagittarius New Moon on **December 13** can still entice you to fire the arrows of your intentions before you consider what makes the most sense.

DECEMBER 16–18 ★ *yes you can*

You're overwhelmed with mixed emotions when confusing Neptune squares loving Venus in your 9th House of Higher Truth on **December 16**. But your enthusiasm can successfully carry you through this stressful period if you don't take on more than you should when gregarious Mercury and active Mars dynamically aspect jovial Jupiter on the **17th** and **18th**.

DECEMBER 21–22 ★ *catch a falling star*

The Sun's shift into serious Capricorn marks the Winter Solstice in the Northern Hemisphere. Although this longest night is a time for inner reflection, the Sun shines in your 10th House of Status, awakening your ambitions. Luckily, the Sun's cooperative sextile with metaphysical Neptune on the **22nd** reminds you to incorporate the magic of your dreams into your plans.

DECEMBER 28–31 ★ *go big or go home*

You may be afraid to exercise your power to its fullest extent, but you can still save the day if you're willing to take everyone's feelings into consideration before you act. The tenacious Cancer Full Moon on **December 28** raises the stakes and makes negotiation difficult, while the Sun's conjunction with extreme Pluto on the **30th** can put everyone on edge from the heightened emotional intensity. But this is no time to hold back; superhero Mars connects with electrifying Uranus on **December 31**, giving you something to party about if you trust your instincts.

TAURUS

APRIL 20–MAY 20

TAURUS

2011 SUMMARY

For you, Taurus, 2011 is a powerful time of endings and beginnings. You are completing a twelve-year opportunity cycle, making this a very significant year. Instead of racing ahead, do what you Bulls do best: Carefully create new goals, start slowly, and build momentum as you gain clarity and confidence. Taking shortcuts will be frowned upon; the best results will come from your dogged persistence. You now begin to understand the benefits of global thinking and become less attached to your worldly aspirations.

AUGUST—*it's complicated*

Don't take yourself so seriously. Any stress that comes to the surface now is likely connected to larger issues that will take more time to fully resolve.

SEPTEMBER—*work in progress*

Your stubborn determination is both a blessing and a curse. You might make some progress, but changing your strategy could be much more effective.

OCTOBER—*sensory overload*

When life seems easy, danger lurks in the form of overindulgence and laziness. However, focusing on specific goals can help you to continue to grow.

NOVEMBER—*building to a crescendo*

If you fall short of a goal, don't waste energy on feeling discouraged. Instead, pick up the pieces and get ready to try again when the time is right.

DECEMBER—*don't look back*

Financial independence won't buy you any additional security now. Real stability will come from aligning your life with your heart.

2011 CALENDAR

AUGUST

MON 1–FRI 5 ★	**SUPER NOVA DAYS** Your positive attitude rubs off on others
MON 8–THU 11 ★	Avoid conflict; focus on your long-term goals instead
THU 18 ★	You have the dogged determination necessary for success
SUN 21–THU 25 ★	You could suddenly fall in and out of love now
SUN 28–TUE 30 ★	Your confidence returns as pleasures overcome difficulties

SEPTEMBER

FR I2 ★	Luck is on your side today and things work out in your favor
SUN 11–WED 14 ★	**SUPER NOVA DAYS** Widen your spiritual horizons
SAT 17–SUN 18 ★	The price of emotional freedom is higher than you expect
SUN 25–WED 28 ★	You may feel trapped now; fight for what you want
THU 29 ★	In your quest for security, you could also isolate yourself

OCTOBER

SAT 1–MON 3 ★	Blind optimism could land you in a heap of trouble
THU 6–FRI 7 ★	Improving your attitude tilts the scales in your favor
MON 10–FRI 14 ★	**SUPER NOVA DAYS** Don't bother trying to hide your intentions
SUN 23–WED 26 ★	Prepare for emotional fireworks; look for creative solutions
FRI 28–MON 31 ★	You may receive assistance from a secret ally

NOVEMBER

WED 2–THU 3 ★	Your perceptions are colored by your desires
SAT 5–MON 7 ★	Wait and see what happens before making your next move
WED 16 ★	Your enthusiasm rocks, but all that glitters is not gold
THU 24–SUN 27 ★	**SUPER NOVA DAYS** Check your list twice

DECEMBER

THU 1–MON 5 ★	Powerful emotional undercurrents are brewing
SAT 10–TUE 13 ★	**SUPER NOVA DAYS** Seek radical solutions to increase your income
SUN 18–MON 19 ★	Don't withdraw just because you are afraid of disappointment
TUE 20–SAT 24 ★	Set aside past worries and get ready for fun

TAURUS OVERVIEW

You start the year with vision and enthusiasm that's filled with promise for the future. Lucky Jupiter spent the second half of 2011 in your sign, planting seeds of hope in your personal life. But progress likely slowed on August 30, 2011, when Jupiter turned retrograde. Then, on December 25, 2011, Jupiter began moving forward again, and it now welcomes the New Year with a wave of optimism that's ready to expand your reality. This fresh start, though, runs into a speed bump on January 23 when Mars, the planet of initiation, turns backward in your 5th House of Self-Expression. Creative projects may encounter delays and romantic impulses could be blocked, and you must backtrack and tie up loose ends before Mars starts moving forward again on April 13. Don't allow impatience to frustrate you, because the adjustments you make will produce even better results in the long run. Even when you're sure that you're right on track for love, fame, or fortune, this detour can lead you to a more rewarding path. Faith in yourself is all that's required to recognize that "not right now" doesn't mean "never." **Like a fine wine, you and your concepts will increase in value when you don't rush the process.**

Jupiter skips into buoyant Gemini and your 2nd House of Resources on June 11. There it will spend the following twelve months, peppering you with ideas about how to increase your income. **One secret to cashing in on this transit is to develop additional skills and seek extra revenue streams.** A few bucks earned on the side may not seem like much at first, but it can add up when it keeps coming in on a regular basis. Another key to financial growth is your willingness to take on tasks even if you question your competence. You don't have to be an expert to make more money this year; using a wide range of skills may be worth more than concentrating your efforts on deepening just one talent.

You've been working to refine your relationship skills thanks to stately Saturn's presence in accommodating Libra and your 6th House of Adjustments since the summer of 2010. Saturn the Tester shifts into steamy Scorpio and your 7th House of Partnerships on October 5, however, announcing a new era in personal and professional alliances. **Your apprenticeship is over and it's time to face your allies and your adversaries from a position of greater authority.** Yes, it's nice to be nice, and compromise will never go out of style when you're dealing with others. Still, this transit signals a more powerful degree of emotional engagement. Negatively, Saturn may bring up old doubts and fears that undermine your confidence in your ability to get what you want from others. Positively, you become more aware of your unspoken needs and desires, and you can address them more openly.

RUNNING HOT AND COLD

You alternate between risk taking and retreat this year, leaving matters of the heart in a volatile state. Retrograde Mars in your romantic 5th House from January 23 until April 13 gives you a second chance to repair a damaged relationship or to reconnect with a loved one from your past. A Sagittarius Lunar Eclipse in your 8th House of Deep Sharing on June 4 opposes artistic Venus and squares active Mars to arouse a desire for new sources of emotional and physical fulfillment. Conflict with a current partner could produce stress that's meant to pull your partnership out of a rut. Taking chances to revivify it or seeking someone new if you're single is probably a safer bet than denying discomfort and avoiding change. Serious Saturn's entry into your 7th House of Partners on October 5 is followed by an intense Scorpio Solar Eclipse on November 13 that increases your appetite for intimacy. Trust your desires instead of trying to rationalize your feelings away.

FIGHT-OR-FLIGHT REFLEX

Keeping yourself on an even keel is essential to maintaining harmonious relationships on the job, which can make a major difference in your professional life this year. Pay careful attention to those around you to sense when it's smart to stand up for yourself and when avoiding confrontation is best. A critical period starts on July 3, when enterprising Mars enters your 6th House of Work. You may find yourself fighting to stay cool when dealing with unreliable colleagues or impatient customers. Yet this is the right time to consider a change of task or employment if you're not satisfied in your current position. Mars's conjunction with Saturn on August 15 will let you know if it's better to stay put or to seek new challenges.

A STRONG FINISH

Financially, the second half of 2012 is likely to be better for you than the first. Generous Jupiter's move into your 2nd House of Resources on June 11 is a strong indicator of economic advances to come. However, your ruling planet Venus's retrograde turn in your 2nd House on May 15 may cause some delays or backtracking in money matters. Work on reducing debt and cutting expenses during this period. Venus turns direct on June 27, which will start to loosen the purse strings. You will probably need to spend more to make more; invest in upgrading equipment and picking up new work skills. Pursue prosperity in two different ways this year; take a slow and methodical approach until mid-June, and a more relaxed and exploratory one after that.

PRACTICE SELF-RESTRAINT

Expansive Jupiter in your 1st House of Self brings a sense of physical well-being until June 11. However, you're also tempted to overindulge yourself while this hungry planet is in your sensual sign. One way to satisfy your desires without packing on extra pounds is to seek quality over quantity. Spending more money on nutritious and organic foods so that you are eating a well-balanced diet on a regular basis, for example, will save you dollars in the long run by cutting health care costs. Strict Saturn spends most of 2012 in your 6th House of Habits, where it demands strong willpower and discipline if you want to maintain a high level of energy. Creative quintiles from responsible Saturn in Libra to purging Pluto on March 28 and August 19 mark optimum periods for coming up with original ways to break your unhealthy habits.

WORK IN PROGRESS

Complications with kids can require extra time and effort when Mars is retrograde in your 5th House of Children from January 23 until April 13. Try to focus on one specific issue at a time with a constructive attitude. Communication issues could arise with family members when tongue-tied Mercury slips into reverse gear in your 4th House of Roots on July 14. Shoring up shaky relationships and making home repairs are excellent ways to solidify your emotional and physical foundation through Mercury's direct turn on August 8.

SOMEWHERE OVER THE RAINBOW

You're a bit of a homebody, because security-conscious Saturn is the planetary ruler of your 9th House of Travel. Yet there's a chance that you could take the trip of a lifetime this year. Saturn's long-lasting trine with dream-catching Neptune—it's exact on October 10—can take you on a voyage that frees you from the dullness of your daily routine. Even if you don't visit exotic places, your mind is opening to studying an inspiring subject in a serious way. Exploring a metaphysical interest or furthering your artistic education are opportunities you might want to pursue later this year.

LETTING GO TO GROW

Your spiritual life has been rocking and rolling ever since dynamic Uranus entered your 12th House of Divinity in 2010. A series of potent squares between Uranus and transformational Pluto that will peak in 2015 begins on June 24 and September 19, kicking your metaphysical education into a higher gear. This process of inner growth involves surprising revelations and the sudden release of old, deeply held beliefs. Messenger Mercury's retrograde turn in your reclusive 12th House on March 12 instigates a three-week period of reflection and review. Your tendency to cling to outmoded ideas could lead to struggles with others; you might even find yourself arguing just to be stubborn. Enlightenment comes from letting go of what you knew in the past and embracing a brave new vision of what's to come.

RICK & JEFF'S TIP FOR THE YEAR: Heed the Call

Defending the status quo is a common reaction to pressure. Yet fighting the forces of change will not keep them from affecting your life. When you sense a rising tide of movement within you or get pushed around by external events, resist the temptation to freeze. Instead, pick up the pace by quickening the rhythm of your thoughts and actions to get ahead of the wave, becoming a bold leader instead of being a reluctant follower.

JANUARY

CLIMB THE LADDER TO SUCCESS

Take a strategic view of your life, especially your career, this month. The warming rays of the Sun fall in your 9th House of Travel and Higher Education until the **20th**, drawing your attention to faraway places and intellectual development. These aren't vague dreams or wishes; with the Sun in practical Capricorn, long-distance connections and serious studies can raise your professional ceiling and make room for advancement. Brainy Mercury's move into Capricorn on **January 8** brings ideas into focus, clarifies goals, and shows you the steps you need to take to get ahead. It can be tempting to withdraw to safer territory with the Full Moon in self-protective Cancer on **January 9**. Attending to personal matters is important, of course, but don't use that as an excuse to retreat and settle for less.

You pick up support and inspiration from friends and groups when your ruling planet, Venus, enters sympathetic Pisces and your 11th House of Teamwork on **January 14.** But this is a two-way street so that giving selflessly will get you back even more. The New Moon in innovative Aquarius sows seeds of awareness in your 10th House of Career on **January 23**. A dynamic square from expansive Jupiter to this Sun-Moon conjunction is meant to motivate you to take risks. Expressing yourself more openly may rock the boat at work, yet inventive Uranus's favorable sextile to the New Moon carries you through rough waters and lands you in a better place. Still, patience is essential when energetic Mars turns retrograde in your 5th House of Self-Expression later on the **23rd**. Romantic overtures and artistic endeavors encounter complications if you're in a hurry. Going slower will get you there faster in the long run.

KEEP IN MIND THIS MONTH

This is an appropriate moment to aim for greater recognition—but remember that the road to success is full of twists and turns that require more skill than speed.

KEY DATES

JANUARY 7 ★ *building a mystery*

You sense that your professional and personal relationships are off balance as yearning Venus forms two challenging aspects. The contrast between your need for freedom and your sense of service is reflected in an awkward quincunx between Venus in Aquarius and Mars in Virgo. You must distinguish when to stick to the rules and when it's time to break them if you hope to dance around potential conflicts. Jealousy, greed, and mistrust could provoke obsessive behavior with a tense Venus-Pluto semisquare. Go for quality instead of quantity and you'll have a much better chance to get what you need, even if you have to look hard to find it.

SUPER NOVA DAYS

JANUARY 13–14 ★ *the audacity of hope*

Your imagination is inspired and your heart is stirred by divine daydreams of love and pleasure. Venus joins whimsical Neptune on **January 13**, blurring the boundaries between fantasy and reality. While you could misread someone or make a financial miscalculation, don't withdraw in fear. It's healthier to move forward with the assurance that only a stabilizing Venus-Saturn trine can give you. On the **14th**, Venus sails into forgiving Pisces, where she sextiles magnanimous Jupiter. Love and approval come easily if you stop struggling and allow yourself to openly receive what's offered. There's no need to keep score when you're with people you trust. Drop your defenses, and there's no limit to the joy you can experience.

JANUARY 20–22 ★ *genius at work*

Creative ideas and financial savvy combine to make this a very rewarding period for you. The Sun's entry into intellectual Aquarius on **January 20** provides a fresh perspective on your professional life. A slick solar alignment with ingenious Uranus on the **21st** and a square with ambitious Jupiter on the **22nd** motivate you to look outside the box in search of more meaningful work. Your expectations may be high, but they are within reach on the **20th** when a shrewd Venus-Pluto sextile gives you an honest assessment of your talent. Even if you come up short somewhere, you instinctively know how to make the most of what you have and find the additional resources you need.

JANUARY 27–28 ★ *the more the merrier*

Objective analysis and stimulating conversations widen your horizons when Mercury enters Aquarius and your professional 10th House on **January 27**. Heavy thinking, though, will not get in the way of good times on the **28th** when a fat Venus-Jupiter semisquare expands your appetite for fun. You may go too far or say too much, perhaps shocking someone with your words. Yet your sense of humor allows you to stretch the social limits without breaking any meaningful bonds.

FEBRUARY

PARALLEL UNIVERSES

Two contrasting trends this month make your life very interesting . . . and somewhat complicated. First, a softening cycle starts when spiritual Neptune leads a trio of planets into its home sign, Pisces, on **February 3**. This is a very long wave of increased sensitivity that will ebb and flow in the background during Neptune's thirteen-year stay in this sign. However, you begin to feel the effects quickly with perceptive Mercury's shift into empathetic Pisces on the **13th** and conjunction with Neptune in your 11th House of Groups on the **14th**. Imaginative friends and co-workers cook up ideas that inspire your dreams or confuse you with cloudy concepts and inaccurate information. The Sun follows suit on **February 19** to deepen your sense of compassion and encourage greater participation in altruistic organizations. You can be a charismatic leader or fall under the spell of a charming charlatan. Apply some good old Taurus common sense to temper fantasy with reality.

The dualistic nature of the month also leaves you managing urgent desires for love, pleasure, and approval that are triggered when Venus leaps into reckless Aries on **February 8** and joins spontaneous Uranus on the **9th**. A sudden attraction to people and things that are usually out of bounds could provoke irresponsible behavior. These transits are in your 12th House of Secrets, stimulating forbidden desires that can lock you in a hidden world of shame or liberate you to enjoy unconventional forms of pleasure. Responsible Saturn's retrograde turn on **February 7** is a key factor in managing the spiritual and erotic influences pervasive this month. Rely on your inner guidance rather than on external rules to navigate the twisty roads between these very different places.

KEEP IN MIND THIS MONTH

Recognizing the difference between a passing fancy and a deeply held need will simplify the complex choices you're facing now.

KEY DATES

FEBRUARY 1 ★ *age of innocence*

The mood around you might be playful or petulant with today's spicy, sassy Venus-Mars opposition. The vulnerability of Venus in Pisces intensifies the power of any personal judgments, while hyperactive Mars in your 5th House of Fun could put you in a teasing mood. However, you find it a lot tougher to take it than to give it, which heightens tension in relationships. Still, there's something sexy in the air if the mood isn't spoiled by callous comments. When you play the game of love with a light touch, you're much more likely to end up feeling like a winner.

SUPER NOVA DAYS

FEBRUARY 7–9 ★ *destination unknown*

This is a "stop, go, don't go so fast" few days as tempting Venus arouses a range of emotions that can shake up your personal circumstances. A testy quincunx with curmudgeonly Saturn on **February 7** may leave you feeling underappreciated. Hurdles lie between you and your object of desire that could undercut your self-confidence despite the spotlight of the proud Leo Full Moon. On **February 8**, Venus fires into restless Aries, inciting a quick change of perspective that cools interest in the past while inflaming new desires. Venus's conjunction with revolutionary Uranus on the **9th** is like a lightning bolt out of the blue that marks a breakthrough in relationship or self-worth issues. Unexpected news could catch you off guard yet suddenly reveal different ways to experience pleasure and demonstrate your worth.

FEBRUARY 15–18 ★ *out of the shadows*

Secrets may surface on **February 15** as Venus squares suspicious Pluto. It can be tough to trust others when feelings of betrayal arise. Still, this is more about digging deeply within yourself than being manipulated by others. An honest assessment of your wants and talents will show what you need to eliminate and where you have to work harder to achieve satisfaction. An over-the-top Mars-Jupiter aspect infuses you with energy that can explode in anger if you don't have a creative or physical outlet for it. Happily, a comforting trine between the Sun and trustworthy Saturn in your 7th House of Partners puts relationships on more solid ground on the **18th** when reason and cooperation overcome conflict.

FEBRUARY 21–22 ★ *heart of gold*

The New Moon in compassionate Pisces on the **21st** is joined by idealistic Neptune in your team-oriented 11th House. Committing to a worthy cause or trying to save a friend is a noble endeavor. Yet jumping in without a clearly defined role might cost more than you expect. A Venus-Mars quincunx on **February 22** is a further reminder that successful collaboration requires adjustments, so negotiate the fine details before agreeing to anything.

MARCH

DELICIOUS DISTRACTIONS

Your heart opens to love this month—and your mind wanders off into dreamland. The gifts of joy and attraction come from alluring Venus's entry into Taurus on **March 5**. Her four-week stay in your sign is a time to indulge yourself in pleasure, soak up sensual delights, and earn more appreciation from others. Yet while you slow down to sip the sweetness of life, inquisitive Mercury races into brash Aries on the **2nd** to provoke impulsive thinking. Communications can be especially complicated since Mercury turns retrograde on **March 12** and slips back into surreal Pisces on **March 23**, helping you revive old dreams, before turning forward again on **April 4**. While you're enjoying the taste of life's most delectable fruits, you could also be missing messages or messing up data that requires more careful attention.

The Virgo Full Moon lights up your 5th House of Play on **March 8**, reinforcing your desire for fun and your yearning for creative self-expression. You'll find the balance between supporting others and fulfilling your own needs shifting. Pleasure, though, is not a privilege; it's an essential key to your happiness and well-being. You are blessed by a trine between beneficent Jupiter in Taurus and powerful Pluto in Capricorn on **March 13**. This favorable alignment helps you stretch your resources, including time and energy, allowing you to have plenty of recreation but still get your work done. The Spring Equinox on **March 20** is when the Sun enters Aries, starting the astrological year in your 12th House of Endings. Be sure to clean up unfinished business before you tackle anything new.

KEEP IN MIND THIS MONTH

Even if pleasing yourself is a priority, don't become so preoccupied that you fail to meet your other responsibilities.

KEY DATES

MARCH 3–4 ★ *not so fast*

Passions escalate with a hot Sun-Mars opposition on **March 3**—but if you act on your emotions, it may create a multitude of complications. Covetous Venus crosses swords with contentious Mars on the **3rd** and opposes restrictive Saturn on the **4th**. It's like seeing exactly what you want and being told that you can't have it. Fortunately, this isn't a *no*, it's just a *not yet*. Think of it as a testing period when commitment and patience are required in your relationships. However, you must acknowledge the price of getting what you want before you can move forward.

SUPER NOVA DAYS

MARCH 13–14 ★ *the force is with you*

Luck is on your side as propitious Jupiter and your key planet, Venus, unearth hidden resources with their happy trines to resourceful Pluto on the **13th**. You're able to transform losses into gains on **March 14**, when magnetic Venus makes her annual conjunction with Jupiter. This good-fortune union is enhanced by favorable trines to dynamic Mars that complete a stabilizing Grand Earth Trine, giving you the drive and graciousness to showcase your talents and increase your desirability. Taking on seemingly impossible tasks makes sense as you tap into a deep well of power with enough confidence to overcome nearly any obstacle.

MARCH 22–24 ★ *surprise wake-up call*

The Aries New Moon on **March 22** sends waves of electricity through your system. Shocking events or perhaps your own longing for change could force you out of familiar patterns. You might not understand the strange things you're feeling, but it's wise not to make any sudden moves. Ideally, the Sun's conjunction with catalytic Uranus on **March 24** wakes you up and exposes a fresh perspective that leads you out of a rut. Real change may be ignited in an instant, but requires time to take root. You may be feeling disconnected from others, but it's your chance to obtain some distance to reassess your relationships. Making minor alterations to your daily routine is an easy way to invite change without rocking your world. If you're hungry for more radical shifts, lay a proper foundation before taking a courageous leap.

MARCH 28–29 ★ *love is a battlefield*

A tense aspect between innocent Venus and dark Pluto could force you to make a tough choice on **March 28**. You might prefer to avoid confrontation and keep your options open; however, it's better to cut out someone or something you don't need than to hold on for dear life. A smart sextile between Mercury and Venus on the **29th** occurs just in the nick of time to restore some peace and harmony to your life.

APRIL

BRIGHT AND SHINY FUTURE

April is always special, because it's the month that the Sun enters your sweet and sensual sign. This planetary changing of the guard occurs on **April 19**, when you step out of the shadows into the light of a fresh cycle of growth and change. Your momentum gets an extra injection of fuel when energetic Mars turns direct on **April 13**, ending a lethargic retrograde period that began on **January 23**. Your initiative was impeded while Mars marched backward in your 5th House of Love and Creativity, forcing you to retreat, reevaluate your current situation, and then make new plans. Now a freer flow of feelings and self-expression empowers you to put your ideas into action as Mars starts pushing ahead again.

A more flexible attitude could get money moving more easily when Venus enters adaptable Gemini and your 2nd House of Income on **April 3**. Revelations about work can arise during the Libra Full Moon in your 6th House of Employment on **April 6**. If frustration tempts you to flee from responsibility, this lunation is a reminder to keep your options open. Continue to engage in discussions that can pacify an unpleasant situation or lead to a new job. The New Moon in Taurus on **April 21** supplies you with another shot of energy. It harmonizes with Mars in efficient Virgo and idealistic Neptune, combining imagination and application to help you turn dreams into reality. Even petulant Pluto lends a hand with a precise trine to the New Moon, providing focus and resourcefulness to maximize the return on your efforts.

KEEP IN MIND THIS MONTH

Holding on to the past for no reason is useless, but investing new energy in old projects or love affairs can give them fresh life.

KEY DATES

APRIL 5–7 ★ *the art of seduction*

You could lose touch with reality and be cheated in financial matters or a relationship when evaluative Venus and the Sun form stressful aspects with dreamy Neptune on **April 5–6**. It's fine to fantasize about love and money as long as you don't make decisions based more on hope than reality. Do your best to be bold without being foolish on the **7th** as an edgy Venus-Mars square stirs your libido and spices up your personality. Knowing when to push and when to back off is essential for managing both personal and professional partnerships.

APRIL 9–10 ★ *seek diversity*

A slick sextile between vivacious Venus and spontaneous Uranus make **April 9** an exciting and innovative day. You are more adventurous than usual, willing to let go of old tastes and open to exploring new and surprising forms of fun. However, your tendency to talk too much or second-guess yourself may complicate connections on **April 10**. If you know what you want and tell the whole truth (and nothing but), you'll avoid sending mixed messages that create confusion and waste time.

APRIL 15–16 ★ *the price of pleasure*

Stern Saturn rears up and challenges the Sun on **April 15** and Venus on the **16th**, possibly throwing up roadblocks of rejection, delay, or devaluation. These are not insurmountable barriers; they are signals to step back and take a longer-term view of relationships and the consequences of seeking pleasure. If you're mature, patient, and responsible, you can earn respect, repair relationships, and still have a good time without overdoing it.

SUPER NOVA DAYS

APRIL 19–21 ★ *invest in your future*

Doors of opportunity open with the expressive Sun's entry into practical Taurus on **April 19**. It's up to you, though, to walk through them confidently and competently if you want to find the rewards you're seeking. Mastering details could make all the difference; don't try to get by on charm or good looks when hard work is the true key to success. The Taurus New Moon on **April 21** points the way to talents and assets that you aren't fully exploiting. It doesn't matter how gifted you are if you don't apply yourself with a growing sense of purpose.

APRIL 29 ★ *never say never*

A transformative Sun-Pluto trine renews your hopes for travel, education, or adventure that you may have given up as a lost cause. The enthusiastic Leo Moon illuminates your 4th House of Roots, revealing latent creative talents and an itch for excitement. Being playful now is more than a simple diversion; it can provide a spark of inspiration that arouses new ambitions and motivates you to fulfill them.

MAY

BACK TO THE FUTURE

Reconsidering the past may be just as important for you as looking forward this month. Your ruling planet, Venus, slips into retrograde on **May 15** and travels backward in your 2nd House of Income until **June 27**. This challenges you to put your financial house in order, reduce your debt, and manage your resources more effectively. The love planet's reversal can revive romantic memories, provoking nostalgia and a desire to reconnect with someone from your past. This retrograde cycle also stirs your interest in talents and abilities that you may not have fully developed, yet a little remedial work can sharpen these skills faster than you think. The Full Moon in mysterious Scorpio on **May 5** shines its powerful light in your 7th House of Partners and could bring simmering relationship issues to a boil. This is an emotionally charged time when resentment or jealousy may erupt. However, it's also an opportunity to gain a deeper understanding of your personal and professional relationships so you can clarify what you need and then concentrate on getting it.

You receive a major boost to your self-esteem and your hopes for the future on **May 13** when the Sun joins lucky Jupiter in dependable Taurus. Still, no matter how certain you are about what you want and where you're going, you may have to adjust and make some compromises to reach your destination. The Sun's entry into multitasking Gemini on the **20th** occurs in your 2nd House, keeping fiscal issues on the front burner. Just a few hours later, the Gemini New Moon Eclipse allows innovative moneymaking ideas to take root if you weed impractical dreams and schemes from your garden of prosperity.

KEEP IN MIND THIS MONTH

Revisiting your past may create regrets. Still, the useful insights you gain make remembering worthwhile.

KEY DATES

MAY 3–5 ★ *true confessions*

Conversations flow easily on **May 3** when verbose Mercury forms a slick sextile with agreeable Venus. Tackle tough subjects before the **5th**, though, because Mercury's opposition to strict Saturn presents a less welcoming picture. You must address your finances with clarity and a mastery of the facts if you want to be taken seriously. The intense Scorpio Full Moon—also on **May 5**—has a powerful emotional undertow that can dredge up issues from the past, especially in relationships. Expressing feelings of discontent will rock the boat, yet bringing them out into the open can revive an ongoing partnership or clear out obstacles to finding a new one.

SUPER NOVA DAYS

MAY 13–16 ★ *in the zone*

Your horizons are stretched and hopes are raised by an enriching Sun-Jupiter conjunction on **May 13**. The bridge you're building between the realities of the present and your dreams for the future can carry you to new heights. You see yourself in such a positive light that doubt melts in the warmth of growing self-confidence. Patience and persistence, which you know well, are key ingredients to making magic happen. Active Mars's stressful semisquare with Saturn on the **15th** could present difficulties on the job or reveal the limits of your skills. However, a potent Mars-Pluto trine on **May 16** strengthens your determination to overcome any barriers by cutting out distractions and focusing on achieving your goals.

MAY 21–23 ★ *out with the old, in with the new*

Toss out old ideas on **May 21** to make room for new and better ones when Mercury joins promising Jupiter on **May 22**. Indeed, your ability to convince others right now is so impressive that you could get them to believe just about anything. Not so on the **23rd**, when your logically sound presentation could be entirely misconstrued as illusory Neptune squares the stubborn Taurus Sun. However, the upside of this journey from fact to fantasy is that it helps you organize information in ways that make an impossible dream come true.

MAY 25–27 ★ *stroke of genius*

Data-driven Mercury slips on a square with squishy Neptune on **May 25** that can cause confusion in money matters. What you're seeing is not what you get and what you're saying may not be what others hear. Imagination is served at the expense of precision, which can certainly be useful for creative activities. Thankfully, even the fuzziest images may come into focus when Mercury joins the Sun on **May 27** and forms a lucky sextile to inventive Uranus. Lightning strikes of insight appear to come out of the blue and suddenly make sense of previously puzzling contradictions.

JUNE

DOLLARS MAKE SENSE

This busy month lets you clean up clutter, make your life more efficient, and enhance your sense of self-worth. The action starts with the Sagittarius Full Moon Eclipse on **June 4**, which could force you to make an important relationship decision. This Lunar Eclipse in a tense square with do-it-now Mars rattles your 8th House of Deep Sharing and can drive a wedge into a current partnership or propel you toward a new emotional or financial alliance. Playing it safe by making minor modifications is not enough to resolve a critical issue. Sometimes it's better to risk going too far than doing nothing at all. On **June 11**, enterprising Jupiter enters diversifying Gemini, where it will spend a year expanding economic opportunities in your 2nd House of Resources. You can enhance your cash flow during this time by developing new skills, practicing more flexible thinking, and exploring additional ways to earn money.

The New Moon in Gemini on **June 19** brings even more emphasis to your financial 2nd House. Uranus makes the first of seven squares to Pluto on **June 24** in a series that ends on **March 16, 2015**. You feel an irrational urge to run away from it all that clashes with your fear of being judged negatively for abandoning your responsibilities. Yet a totally revamped look at your life will reveal surprising ways to find slices of freedom. Saturn turns direct on the **25th**, slowly opening a loving message from your ruling planet, telling you that you're worth more than you think.

KEEP IN MIND THIS MONTH

Instead of pushing hard against obstacles, go around them. You'll get you to your destination more quickly.

KEY DATES

JUNE 1 ★ *clever conquests*

You may finally hear back from someone who has been slow to respond to you as friendly Mercury connects with flirty Venus. This easygoing pair enables you to stay cool during an intense discussion, stimulating fresh ideas that appeal to a hard-to-please person. You don't have to lose sight of your purpose, even if switching tactics is what it takes to get what you want.

SUPER NOVA DAYS

JUNE 4–5 ★ *a smile is your umbrella*

You stumble socially on **June 4**, when attractive Venus forms a stressful square to active Mars. You might be casual when someone else is being formal or vice versa, making it hard to find a comfortable rhythm with others. Keeping a cheerful attitude is the antidote to anger on this intense Sagittarius Full Moon day. Fortunately, beautiful Venus conjuncts the Sun on the **5th**, making it easier for you to see the sunny side of life. Turning on the charm can melt someone's cold heart and remind you that being playful is sometimes the most effective way to get things done.

JUNE 11 ★ *bite your tongue*

Tensions are high and nerves pulled taut today due to Mercury's harsh square with shocking Uranus and opposition to polarizing Pluto. You find your thoughts veering from stark fear to flights of fancy, which can provoke explosive conversations. If you feel attacked by unfair criticism, it's best to avoid a snappy comeback. Scoring a point with a pungent remark might also alienate a potential ally. Save your unusual ideas for your own projects rather than expressing them in potentially destructive ways.

JUNE 20 ★ *unconventional methods*

The Sun swims into Cancer today, marking the Summer Solstice and heating up your 3rd House of Communication. A quirky Venus-Uranus sextile reveals a fresh perspective that can untangle a sticky relationship issue or unblock a financial problem. While emotions can drown you in doubt, you'll find answers where you least expect to find them when you remember to think ahead instead of looking back.

JUNE 29 ★ *surprise metamorphosis*

You're torn between your urge to hold on tight and your impulse to break free today. The Sun's hard aspects with penetrating Pluto and radical Uranus can make you feel queasy with uncertainty. Simple statements can trigger strong reactions and trusting others is difficult when you're not sure where you stand yourself. This is a better time to tear down barriers than to build supportive structures. Taking a risk and inventing new ways to express yourself is more rewarding than trying to change someone else's behavior.

JULY

RIDE THE WAVE

Staying cool is your key to navigating through the churning planetary waters this month. You will be pushed out of your comfort zone more than once, and being proactive about how you react is more important than simply trying to enforce your will on others. Mars, the planet of action, enters diplomatic Libra and your 6th House of Self-Improvement on **July 3**. A soft touch and a willingness to compromise will allow you to maintain tranquility. The Capricorn Full Moon on the same day is an intense event given provocative Pluto's conjunction to this otherwise orderly Moon. Erratic Uranus's challenging square to the Sun-Moon opposition signals sudden changes ahead. Trying to stand your ground could be a recipe for disaster, while jumping on an unexpected chance to travel or further your education can dramatically expand your horizons. Messenger Mercury begins its three-week retrograde cycle on **July 14**, giving you even more reason to be as flexible as possible. Mercury retrogrades in your 4th House of Home and Family—an area where you'll need to make renovations and readjustments.

Practicing patience is paramount with the cautious Cancer New Moon on **July 19**. Observe more and say less, because serious Saturn's square to this lunation requires emotional restraint; careless words can undermine trust. Financial issues grab your attention as excessive Jupiter, in your 2nd House of Money, clashes with Saturn on the **20th** and flows smoothly with futuristic Uranus on the **22nd**. Any stabs of fear or doubt you experience are quickly followed by bright new ideas for maximizing your resources. The Sun's shift into dramatic Leo on **July 22** adds to the wave of creativity pulling you to success.

KEEP IN MIND THIS MONTH

When circumstances call for an immediate response, slowing down to think things through is essential for making the best decisions.

KEY DATES

JULY 3–4 ★ *catch your balance*

If you're feeling awkward and uncertain in relationships or about money on **July 3**, wait it out and you'll likely find quick relief. An unstable Venus-Pluto quincunx easily wounds feelings and prompts fears of loss. On the **4th**, however, Mercury and Venus align with unpredictable Uranus to provide solutions when you least expect them. A charming Mercury-Venus sextile shows you at your entertaining best.

JULY 8–9 ★ *sixth sense*

Use sensitivity instead of strength on **July 8** as muscular Mars skids into a slippery quincunx with empathic Neptune. Forcing an issue will only push you off target, wasting time and energy, while using your intuition can show the way around obstacles. You could receive misleading information from a usually reliable source on the **9th** due to the Sun's anxious aspect with spacey Neptune. Take time to sort it all out rather than jumping to conclusions.

SUPER NOVA DAYS

JULY 17–18 ★ *hazardous work conditions*

You struggle to maintain harmonious relationships on the job while Mars is charged up in your 6th House of Employment. His friction-free trine with boundless Jupiter on the **17th** gets the day off to a high-energy start that encourages big plans. However, you're quickly pulled back down to earth as a forceful Mars-Pluto square demands that you concentrate on one task. Conflict may ensue, especially with an irresolvable quincunx between philosophical Jupiter and extreme Pluto on the **18th** that widens the gap between contrasting belief systems. An edgy opposition from Mars to volatile Uranus could cap things off with an outburst of anger. If everyone involved can remain tolerant, unusual ways of addressing issues can produce rapid results.

JULY 28 ★ *no more drama*

Don't take what you hear too personally today, and be extra careful about what you say to others; words are readily misinterpreted when retrograde Mercury forms an irritating semisquare with likable Venus. Trivial remarks could expand into major issues, yet if you're able to trust the other person, an awkward moment of truth can clear the air and put your relationship back on track.

JULY 31 ★ *surprise development*

Innovation and common sense work well together today. The Sun's trine with Uranus triggers sudden insights that could untangle knots or raise your awareness. All your brilliant concepts, though, are useless if you don't have the means to make them real. Luckily, a well-balanced trine between pragmatic Saturn and Venus reflects your good judgment about people. This favorable alignment also indicates a clear sense of values that helps you accurately measure the cost of achieving your goals and the ability to find the resources you need.

AUGUST

STEP UP TO THE PLATE

It pays to act boldly this month, because the confident Leo Sun is lighting up your 4th House of Foundations until **August 22**. Use your creativity to kick up your cash flow when prosperous Jupiter in your 2nd House of Income forms a supportive trine with the ingenious Aquarius Full Moon on **August 1**. Another signal for pushing ahead comes on **August 8**, when communicative Mercury turns direct in your 5th House of Self-Expression. The ideas that you've been turning over in your mind are ready to be shared. Active Mars conjuncts sobering Saturn in your 6th House of Work on **August 15**, enlightening you with a clear picture of how much effort is required to manage your ongoing tasks. If you can dig in with renewed passion and discipline, staying in your current position makes sense. But if you're facing insurmountable obstacles and continuing frustration at your current place of employment, this is a good time to reassess your options.

You enjoy an ideal balance of enthusiasm and skill on **August 17**, when the Leo New Moon forms supportive sextiles to reliable Saturn and energetic Mars. Refining techniques, developing new systems, or getting additional training will provide you with the tools you need to give substance to your clever concepts. The Sun's entry into productive Virgo and your outgoing 5th House on **August 22** is another reminder of the creative potential available to you now. Mars dives into watery Scorpio and your 7th House of Others on the **23rd**, challenging you with competitive individuals or prodding you to take the lead in your relationships. On **August 31**, the compassionate Pisces Full Moon in your 11th House of Friends conjuncts healing Chiron to reveal how forgiveness can deepen the bonds between you and others.

KEEP IN MIND THIS MONTH

Your future is not limited to the world you see around you. Drawing from a deep well of imagination expands your vision beyond your current horizons.

KEY DATES

AUGUST 2 ★ *brush it off*

A Sun-Jupiter sextile opens up your perspective on personal matters today, especially related to home and family. The anxious Sun-Venus semisquare—the only hard aspect possible between them—recurs on **August 31**. Uncertainty about self-worth can arouse strong reactions that make a simple comment feel like a harsh criticism. Be kind in your own judgments of others and take what you hear with a grain of salt.

AUGUST 7–9 ★ *picnic in the park*

Venus sidles into caring Cancer and your 3rd House of Communication on **August 7** to initiate more intimate conversations. Closeness grows when you listen with real concern for someone else's well-being and share your needs in a safe, appropriate environment. Mercury's direct turn on **August 8** also opens the way to new discussions or gets interrupted exchanges back on track, especially when the subjects are creativity, family, or matters of the heart. Romantic feelings and daydreams of love are welcomed on **August 9** by a mesmerizing Venus-Neptune trine. The sensual Taurus Moon sweetens the atmosphere, so make sure to set aside some time to taste the delights of good company, fine food, music, art, or nature.

SUPER NOVA DAYS

AUGUST 15–16 ★ *groundbreaking news*

Everyone's nerves are on edge when tender Venus in Cancer opposes domineering Pluto on **August 15** and squares jumpy Uranus on the **16th**. Secrets may surface that rock relationships, yet tapping into a deeper level of truth can also wipe away illusion to get a clearer view of real issues. A demanding Mars-Saturn conjunction on the **15th** could pile on pressure at work as well. It's wise to avoid making any sudden moves on the job or at home until the emotional ground you're standing on stops shaking. Meanwhile, managing routine tasks provides a sense of purpose until you figure out the bigger issues related to love and money that are being revealed now.

AUGUST 22–23 ★ *work in progress*

The Sun's entry into industrious Virgo on **August 22** encourages you to take the lead in romantic matters and creative projects. Refining your style of presentation makes you more compelling to others. Don't expect to be accepted as you are; you would have so much more to offer if you just give it a little more effort. Settling for less is not a viable option with competitive Mars moving into transformative Scorpio and your 7th House of Companions on the **23rd**. You may encounter more demanding people, yet your ability to connect with greater concentration and commitment weeds out unworthy partners and makes way for more rewarding relationships.

SEPTEMBER

IT'S SHOWTIME

It's time to step up and express yourself more openly now. The Sun may be in shy Virgo, but it's shining in your showy 5th House of Love and Creativity until **September 22**. This is your chance to enter the spotlight and profess your heart's desires or demonstrate your skills as a performer. If you don't think you're ready to reveal yourself in this way, start practicing to develop the confidence needed to put on a good show. Venus, your seductive ruling planet, dances into charismatic Leo on **September 6** to encourage even more dramatic behavior. This transit happens in your domestic 4th House, which may produce passionate melodramas on the home front or just motivate you to lavishly redecorate. The Virgo New Moon on **September 15** spurs you to discover new ways to play and to refine your presentation skills. Be gentle and generous with yourself; self-criticism could undermine your efforts.

On-the-job relationships improve when communicative Mercury glides into gracious Libra and your 6th House of Work and Service on **September 16**. Your ability to negotiate strengthens as long as you truly listen to what others have to say and are honestly willing to meet them halfway. The deep rumbling you're sensing is a reawakening of transformational Pluto, which turns direct on **September 18** and makes its second of seven squares with revolutionary Uranus on the **19th**. One little surprise could make you think the world is falling apart, but it isn't. The Autumn Equinox, marked by the Sun's entry into harmonious Libra on **September 22**, is a turning point that helps you regain your balance and meet challenges in a more positive way.

KEEP IN MIND THIS MONTH

Acting more boldly in pursuit of your interests not only attracts attention but also keeps you from worrying too much about the little things.

KEY DATES

SEPTEMBER 3 ★ *room for improvement*

Frustration due to a lack of recognition is possible with a demanding Venus-Saturn square today. Yet if you can take a little advice, you might gain clarity about what you need to do to earn some respect. A powerful sextile from regenerative Pluto to pushy Mars in your 7th House of Partners could bring an astute individual who motivates you to be more efficient.

SEPTEMBER 5–7 ★ *know your limits*

A joyous trine between Venus and the connective Moon's North Node attracts supportive people and sweetens your relationships on **September 5**. The love planet's move into Leo on the **6th** tempts you with excess as Venus forms a semisquare with bountiful Jupiter. The risk that you'll go too far or overestimate someone grows on the **7th** with an over-the-top Sun-Jupiter square and a vague Venus-Neptune quincunx. It's wonderful to open your heart and mind to wider fields of happiness as long as you don't break the bank—or your heart.

SEPTEMBER 13 ★ *flavor of the month*

You're in the mood to experiment with pleasurable Venus's cozy trine to unorthodox Uranus. Delightful events could arise unexpectedly, especially when you're willing to stretch your limits. Trying out new experiences can be invigorating and could even bring new life to a relationship that's lost some of its spice.

SEPTEMBER 20–21 ★ *shock and awe*

Mental Mercury's opposition to weird Uranus and square to manipulative Pluto on **September 20** can stir up strange ideas and disturbing conversations. Fortunately, good humor and generous feelings from a gregarious Venus-Jupiter sextile should keep tension from getting out of hand. But even if stress at work is shaking your trust, a socially adept quintile between Venus and unflappable Saturn should restore order on the **21st**.

SUPER NOVA DAYS

SEPTEMBER 25–29 ★ *the heat is on*

Relationships get rocky when Venus and Mars make hard aspects with Uranus and Pluto on **September 25–26**. Important issues that you haven't faced could explode in an unexpected moment of anger or, preferably, in a sudden urge for frankness. This could be a great opportunity to initiate an honest dialogue. But beware overreaction, because your volatile emotions can leave you excited at an unexpected attraction, or cause a blowup with a colleague, lover, or friend. Venus in prideful Leo squares Mars in Scorpio on the **27th**, which intensifies almost every interaction. The impudent Aries Full Moon on the **29th** activates your 12th House of Destiny, conjuncting Uranus and opposing Pluto to further agitate your emotions. Thankfully, courage and kindness can transform conflict into a more desirable form of passion.

OCTOBER

HEART-TO-HEART

The always-interesting subject of love and relationships comes into the foreground this month. Magnetic Venus, your charming ruling planet, enters refined Virgo and your 5th House of Romance on **October 3**, where she is likely to enhance your image until the **28th**. Knowing what you want from others yet being willing to make reasonable compromises around those expectations is the key to opening love's door. Focusing on solutions instead of problems puts you in a positive place where people can respond to you more favorably. On **October 5**, Mercury and Saturn enter transformational Scorpio and your 7th House of Partnerships. The communication planet's twenty-four-day passage through your relationship house initiates contacts and intensifies conversations. However, serious Saturn's transit lasts more than two years, demanding higher levels of accountability in your alliances but heightening the potential for more rewarding returns.

Pushing past your usual limits is appropriate with energizing Mars's move into adventurous Sagittarius and your 8th House of Transformation on **October 6**. Boundaries will be stretched; it's better for you to take calculated risks of your own choosing than have to react to challenges thrust upon you. An optimistic trine from Jupiter to the Libra New Moon on **October 15** brightens your 6th House of Work, planting seeds of hope for your career. This is an especially good time to make fresh contacts and expand your skill set. The Sun enters sizzling Scorpio on the **22nd**, adding fuel to the fires of change in your 7th House of Relationships, building toward a breakthrough at the Taurus Full Moon on the **29th**.

KEEP IN MIND THIS MONTH

It's okay to expect more from your relationships as long as you're willing to make the personal commitment necessary to reach common ground.

KEY DATES

OCTOBER 2–3 ★ *vacillating values*

Your realistic attitude helps you evaluate people, projects, and purchases accurately on the **2nd**. Venus's savvy sextile with practical Saturn just before her entry into Virgo on the **3rd** is excellent for making long-term decisions. But the situation changes rapidly when Venus opposes Neptune and fantasy may become too alluring to resist. Use your imagination, along with a touch of romance—as long as you don't float off into dreamland and lose touch with common sense.

OCTOBER 8–10 ★ *great expectations*

You're edgy on **October 8** with a socially awkward Venus-Uranus quincunx lingering in the air. But a generous Sun-Jupiter trine and a perceptive Venus-Pluto trine on the **9th** enable you to be very astute about people and money, especially related to your job. A series of slow-moving Saturn-Neptune trines that begins on **October 10** and ends on **July 19, 2013**, can help make your dreams come true. These creative aspects in your sociable 7th and 11th Houses blend Saturn's clear sense of purpose with Neptune's compassion and idealism.

OCTOBER 16–17 ★ *more is not always better*

It's terrific to be optimistic, but a challenging square from extravagant Jupiter to Venus could raise your hopes beyond reason on **October 16**. Widening your field of interests and tastes is fine as long as you don't make a serious commitment that can cost you too much time, money, or trust. Sobering Saturn's hard-nosed semi-square with Venus on the **17th** quickly brings a dose of reality that can be disappointing if you've gone too far.

SUPER NOVA DAYS

OCTOBER 22–25 ★ *keeping it real*

The Sun's entry into your 7th House on **October 22** starts a new cycle of connections that can reshape your personal and professional relationships. The Sun's aspects with visionary Jupiter and Neptune on the **23rd** widen your net to pull in more people and increase your public influence. It's vital to avoid making promises you can't keep or blindly accepting someone else's big ideas. The Sun's conjunction with fact-checking Saturn on the **25th** rewards responsibility and realism. Although facing limits or delays can be discouraging, knowing exactly where you stand with partners is a powerful foundation for building enduring alliances.

OCTOBER 28–29 ★ *bull in a china shop*

A passionate Mars-Jupiter opposition on **October 28** fires you up with enthusiasm for a moneymaking idea or an erotic connection. Venus shifts into objective Libra the same day, providing some balance that can help you avoid going to extremes. Speak up if you feel that you're not being treated fairly on your job, but don't cause a scene. The Taurus Full Moon and quicksilver Mercury's entry into outspoken Sagittarius on the **29th** pack your words with more punch than you realize.

NOVEMBER

LIFE IN THE BALANCE

Reviewing relationships is a priority on your planetary calendar this month. Communicative Mercury goes retrograde in your 8th House of Intimacy on **November 6** and backpedals into your 7th House of Partners before turning direct on the **26th**. Expect three weeks of reassessing agreements and making adjustments in personal and financial matters. You might also reconnect with someone from the past or see the reemergence of an issue you thought was resolved, altering the tone of a current alliance or reviving interest in an old one. A Scorpio New Moon Eclipse on **November 13** rattles your 7th House and is a key factor in altering how and with whom you connect. If tense issues arise, face them with as much clarity about your desires as you can. When you share truth with kindness, trust follows.

Energetic Mars boosts your ability to organize, plan, and manage projects when he enters industrious Capricorn and your 9th House of Big Ideas on **November 16**. Travel is likely, especially for business and educational reasons, during this busy time that lasts through **December 25**. The Sun shoots into enthusiastic Sagittarius and your 8th House on **November 21**, promoting risk-taking in relationships, the same day that desirable Venus enters possessive Scorpio and your 7th House to increase awareness of control issues that you might prefer to overlook. The Gemini Full Moon on **November 28** is a Lunar Eclipse in your 2nd House of Personal Resources. If you've stretched yourself too thin, this is a not-so-gentle reminder to rein in spending and focus all your attention on increasing your primary source of income.

KEEP IN MIND THIS MONTH

Changing your mind after serious reflection is a viable option right now. Admitting your mistakes is a sign of strength rather than weakness.

KEY DATES

NOVEMBER 1–4 ★ *the trouble with love*

Venus's opposition to unconventional Uranus on **November 1** may thrill you with sudden attractions to unusual people and things but can also spring financial surprises. Opening your mind to fresh experiences is fine as long as you don't leap without looking. Venus encounters exigent Pluto on **November 3** and presents you with the bill for any inappropriate behavior. But if you discover that you can't live without some amazing new object or an irresistible individual, you'll figure out what you must do to make it happen.

NOVEMBER 9 ★ *sweet as honey*
This is a great day to play, show off your personality, and pursue romance as captivating Venus forms an inviting trine with exuberant Jupiter. Your ability to impress others can also benefit you professionally now. People are ready to buy whatever you have to sell. Honor your integrity and don't promise more than you can deliver.

NOVEMBER 17–18 ★ *blessing in disguise*
Conversations reveal hidden desires and secrets that challenge you to rethink a relationship when retrograde Mercury joins the Sun in your 7th House of Partnerships and Public Life on **November 17**. Yet even if uncomfortable truths are exposed, you have the cleverness to turn potential losses into positive gain on the **18th** when your resourceful ruling planet, Venus, makes a magical quintile to transformative Pluto.

NOVEMBER 21–22 ★ *incurable romantic*
Passion grows when sultry Venus and the radiant Sun enter the partnering 7th and 8th Houses of your chart on **November 21**. Be careful how you use your powers of seduction—and watch out for falling under the charm of someone else—because desires can move beyond the bounds of reason as both the Sun and Venus connect with deceptive Neptune on the **22nd**. It's healthy to have moments of escape when imagination and beauty lift your spirit and love opens your heart as long as you return to reality afterward.

SUPER NOVA DAYS
NOVEMBER 26–29 ★ *face your fears*
A chilly Venus-Saturn conjunction on **November 26** could put you face-to-face with harsh realities in partnerships. If you set the agenda with a clear statement of your expectations, however, you can build trust. Mercury turns direct that same day, releasing information that's been on hold since it went retrograde on **November 6**. A punchy and potent Mars-Pluto conjunction on the **27th** gives you the willpower to overcome struggles as long as you concentrate on your goal. Venus sextiles Pluto on the **28th**, the same day as the Gemini Lunar Eclipse, deepening personal connections and making you a more astute judge of character. Then, on **November 29**, a sassy Venus-Mars sextile helps you motivate others to get the results you want.

DECEMBER

BEYOND THE HORIZON

Carve out some quiet time this month to examine your goals for the future and how you can achieve them. Curious Mercury peers into the distance to see where relationships are going when it enters farseeing Sagittarius and your 8th House of Deep Sharing on **December 10**. The Sagittarius New Moon on **December 13** inspires you to spread your wings to fly farther with your current partner, or to seek more rewarding connections elsewhere. You're uncharacteristically willing to take risks when electrifying Uranus turns direct on the same day and desirable Venus moves into cavalier Sagittarius on the **15th**.

Three outer planet transits challenge you to adjust your expectations but can also lead you to a well of untapped resources. Jupiter in agile Gemini in your 2nd House of Income forms awkward quincunxes with unrelenting Pluto and unyielding Saturn on **December 20–22**, repeating patterns that began last spring on **May 16** and finish on **March 29, 2013**. These aspects point you toward alternative ways to earn money and increase your sense of self-worth. Stepping around disapproving individuals is wiser than confronting them directly now. Unexpected events could shake up a holiday gathering when the Sun squares irrepressible Uranus on **December 25**. Fortunately, a smart Saturn-Pluto sextile the next day empowers you to be more successful by aligning with positive people. Although the nurturing Cancer Full Moon on the **28th** in your 3rd House of Communication invites cozy sharing with friends and family, the Sun's conjunction with Pluto on the **30th** ends the year with great intensity. It's time to cut out the small talk and get to the core of the matter.

KEEP IN MIND THIS MONTH

You'll be much better off making thoughtful decisions based on where they will take you in the years ahead rather than shortsighted, random moves.

KEY DATES

DECEMBER 1–2 ★ *on the road to excess*

It's tempting to overdo just about everything on **December 1** when Venus and Mars both quincunx extravagant Jupiter. The key to finding balance is to favor quality over quantity. Don't go for someone or something that's not healthy for you just because emotional insecurity is blurring your judgment. The Sun-Jupiter opposition on the **2nd** amplifies this wave of optimism, which is terrific as long as you're doing the selling instead of the buying. Make your points in a convincing manner but don't take what others have to say too much to heart.

SUPER NOVA DAYS

DECEMBER 10–12 ★ *rogue tactics*

You could be in for some heavy-duty negotiations on **December 10** when Venus forms a tense semisquare with Pluto. It's better to be tough and walk away from an agreement than to act like a weakling who is overly eager to compromise. Determine what you need and then do exactly what it takes to get it. **December 12** is an excellent day to attract a magnetic individual when sexy Venus in Scorpio hooks up with the Moon's North Node in your 7th House of Relationships. Scary as it is to engage someone who evokes such strong feelings, you'll find it well worth the effort. Bravely following your heart adds excitement to a current alliance or helps initiate an intriguing new connection.

DECEMBER 15–16 ★ *on the wings of love*

Unrestrained enthusiasm, faith, and imagination can take you into uncharted waters now. Venus's move into effusive Sagittarius on **December 15** is followed by her square with surreal Neptune on the **16th**. This combination could tempt you to make impractical choices about love or money. Yet even if you do allow fantasy to overcome reason, the inspiration you receive from stretching your boundaries can make it all worthwhile.

DECEMBER 21–22 ★ *sensory overload*

The Sun's entry into ambitious Capricorn marks the Winter Solstice on the **21st**. You have a new, more serious sense of purpose that motivates you to aim higher in the year ahead. Your keys to success are discipline and a commitment to do the hard work necessary to advance your career and gain more satisfaction in your personal life. It's also essential that you manage your expectations by finding the right balance between hope and realism. Lovable Venus's opposition to joyful Jupiter on **December 22** stimulates your appetite for more approval, affection, and fun. Yet it's possible to become overindulgent and allow immediate needs for gratification to blind you to the consequences of your actions. Knowing how to truly enjoy life's delights is a blessing of being a Taurus . . . as long as you don't take it too far.

GEMINI

MAY 21–JUNE 20

GEMINI

2011 SUMMARY

Your fertile mind is spinning out more ideas than ever this year, and your challenge is to focus your attention on turning the best ones into reality. Two key elements are purpose and practice, so set goals and work diligently on reaching them. Cutting out concepts that sound good on paper but fail the test of reality could look like a setback, but it's another reminder to take yourself seriously enough to concentrate on the best and let go of the rest.

AUGUST—*practice makes perfect*

The river of wisdom flows deeply in you, but you may have to stop talking long enough to hear its subtle message.

SEPTEMBER—*duties and delights*

Doing the hard work of addressing your stickiest personal problems first will make the pleasure that follows even more delicious.

OCTOBER—*the art of regeneration*

Taking the easy way out may seem like a shortcut on the road to success, but in the long run it will only slow your progress.

NOVEMBER—*traffic management*

Turning down an offer that sounds too good to be true will keep you from exhausting yourself chasing rainbows.

DECEMBER—*say good-bye to yesterday*

It's better to stretch yourself and take risks than to allow excuses and distractions to keep you from reaching for the stars.

2011 CALENDAR

AUGUST

TUE 2–THU 4 ★	Pay attention to the tone of your words
MON 8 ★	Use this time creatively instead of forcing clarity
SAT 13–WED 17 ★	**SUPER NOVA DAYS** Try saying no before going too far
SUN 21–TUE 23 ★	Attend to your own needs before those of others
WED 24–SAT 27 ★	Financial frustration leads to being fiscally resourceful

SEPTEMBER

THU 8–FRI 9 ★	Objectivity chases away illusions
MON 12–WED 14 ★	**SUPER NOVA DAYS** Ask your colleagues for help
THU 22–SUN 25 ★	Mixed messages throw off your perceptions
TUE 27–WED 28 ★	You can't control other people's thoughts

OCTOBER

THU 6 ★	Find the information you need and commit it to memory
TUE 11–THU 13 ★	Follow your own star
SUN 16–MON 17 ★	Be alert to an overdose of optimism
SUN 23–MON 24 ★	Apply unconventional ideas to your work
WED 26–FRI 28 ★	**SUPER NOVA DAYS** Transform your fear into passion

NOVEMBER

TUE 1–THU 3 ★	Your dreams can inspire others
THU 10 ★	Be practical without losing touch with your soul's needs
WED 16–FRI 18 ★	Don't let logic get in the way of your instincts
WED 23–FRI 25 ★	**SUPER NOVA DAYS** Delays can feel like major setbacks

DECEMBER

THU 1–SUN 4 ★	Impatience could lead to harsh words
SAT 10–SUN 11 ★	**SUPER NOVA DAYS** Acting decisively creates momentum
TUE 13 ★	Move ahead with potential new contacts
THU 22 ★	Toss caution to the wind
WED 28–THU 29 ★	Too much information stretches your nerves

GEMINI OVERVIEW

This could be a great year for you because bountiful Jupiter returns to your sign on June 11 for its once-every-twelve-year visit. You might grow impatient waiting for Jupiter to enter clever Gemini, but there's much to do in preparation for the opportunities awaiting you. **It would be wise to use the first part of the year to finish up old business** while Jupiter moves through your 12th House of Endings. You are being given a chance to see how previous successes and failures are connected to recurring patterns in your life. You can fine-tune your current ambitions with the insights you gain, empowering you to plan for the future with newfound confidence.

Once the giant planet reaches your 1st House of Self on June 11, it's important to take your own counsel and trust yourself, rather than allowing the opinions of others to carry too much weight. Jupiter is astrology's most fortunate planet, and its yearlong visit to your sign is a harbinger of the significant personal growth in front of you. **This is not about achieving overnight success; nevertheless, a positive attitude can lead to advancement in business and growing public recognition.** Even if a decision turns out to be a mistake, you are able to quickly learn from it and adjust your course accordingly. This is not a time to stand still, but rather a calling to set high goals in all areas of your life and then reach for the stars.

Although you can make a lot of progress this year, it becomes more challenging to be realistic about your life purpose when spiritual Neptune enters your 10th House of Public Responsibility on February 3. This long-lasting transit can inspire you to seek more meaning from your work, yet it also complicates your professional aspirations if being of service becomes more important than making money. A lack of clarity about your goals could tempt you to stretch too far or miss your mark entirely when boundless Jupiter squares confusing Neptune on June 25. But uncertainty will likely be swept away by the opening act of a larger-than-life drama activated by the first of seven Uranus-Pluto squares on June 24. This dynamic conflict between independent Uranus in your 11th House of Long-Term Goals and intense Pluto in your 8th House of Intimacy can raise questions about who's in control of your life. **You may need to reevaluate your priorities and take bold action to establish new objectives.** Personal and professional relationships are stressed when you make sudden changes that profoundly impact others as well as yourself. Fortunately, the issues emphasized this year won't require a final resolution until the last Uranus-Pluto square in 2015. Still, it's wise to start working on a major overhaul of your goals now, while the planets are still working in your favor.

KEEP IT REAL

Karmic Saturn in relationship-oriented Libra and your 5th House of Love anchors you to the status quo until October 5, and it's important that you continue to work on existing issues. On June 4, the cavalier Sagittarius Full Moon Eclipse rattles your 7th House of Partnerships. Its opposition to sweet Venus and square to combative Mars can reignite painful feelings. If you don't face serious matters of contention with a loved one, the restless Gemini New Moon Eclipse on June 19 could lead to foolish actions that you might later regret. Your relationship houses are activated again by the Gemini Full Moon Eclipse on November 28, but its conjunction with beneficial Jupiter suggests a positive outcome as long as you keep channels of communication open throughout the year.

WHAT DREAMS ARE MADE OF

It's difficult to maintain a balanced perspective about your professional life when giant Jupiter clashes with fuzzy Neptune on June 25 and maverick Chiron on July 24. However, if you don't over-inflate your expectations, your dreams can inspire you to great heights. With compassionate Neptune camped out in your 10th House of Career until 2025, you'll need to realign your objectives with a higher calling. You should receive much-needed assistance from dependable Saturn's entry into your 6th House of Employment on October 5. Turn your fantasies into reality and overcome self-imposed limitations when stabilizing Saturn trines Neptune and Chiron on October 10 and November 16.

UPS AND DOWNS

Your income and spending patterns fluctuate with your emotions throughout the year. Applying yourself with steady determination could bring rewards, however, especially on March 13–14 as Venus joins Jupiter and trines Pluto and Mars to create a beneficial Grand Earth Trine. Don't throw away your gains when Venus turns retrograde in your sign on May 15–June 27. Be especially careful about making a risky investment around the Full Moon Eclipse on June 4. Money matters generally improve when Venus visits your 2nd House of Income on August 7–September 6, with the exception of a rough spot on August 15–16. Be confident about a financial decision on October 9, but don't overextend yourself. Unexpected financial wrinkles on November 1–3 should smooth out by November 9.

PROACTIVE MEASURES

Unexpressed emotions can have a significant impact on your physical condition this year as Pluto squares Uranus on June 24 and September 19. Make healthy lifestyle changes early in the year, for the South Lunar Node is in Gemini through August 29, encouraging your tendency to adapt to stress by dancing around its edges rather than dealing with the real issues. Fortunately, Mars in your 6th House of Health on August 23–October 6 boosts your vitality, but you must express excess energy rather than turning it inward. Strict Saturn points out your physical weak spots; only extra effort on your part will protect your health when it enters your 6th House on October 5 for a two-year visit. The mysterious Scorpio Solar Eclipse on November 13 brings a secret out into the open. This should ultimately have a positive effect on your health by releasing detrimental tension.

HOME IS WHERE YOUR HEART IS

A change of address isn't out of the question this year, but you'll experience an intense focus on domestic affairs even if you don't move anywhere. Assertive Mars in your 4th House of Home and Family until July 3 motivates you to take a stand for what you want. But Mars is retrograde on January 23–April 13, provoking irritability and even conflict. Burn off excess heat now by undertaking physically demanding projects around the house or in the garden. Your family is in the spotlight when the Sun and Mercury make their yearly visits to your 4th House on August 22–September 22. Finally, domestic issues settle down on October 3–28 when lovely Venus passes through your 4th House.

WANDERLUST

Turning big plans for traveling into reality could take time this year. Although your 9th House of Voyages is activated by Venus until January 14, her conjunction with imaginative Neptune on the 13th is what stimulates your dreams of faraway lands. The Sun and Mercury further illuminate your travel plans on January 20–February 19, but you are wiser to wait until after journeying Jupiter enters Gemini on June 11. Pay extra attention to details and confirm your reservations twice if you need to travel when Mercury is retrograde on March 12–April 4, July 14–August 8, and November 6–26.

SPIRITUAL WARRIOR

You began a quest to rediscover the purpose of your life when philosophical Jupiter entered Taurus and your 12th House of Soul Consciousness on June 11, 2011. Jupiter remains in this mysterious house until June 11, 2012, motivating you to continue your metaphysical studies or to find a spiritual teacher or guru. It's time to project your inner experiences onto the outer world—and fortunately metaphysical Neptune enters your 10th House of Public Responsibility on February 3 for a fourteen-year stay to help with this process.

RICK & JEFF'S TIP FOR THE YEAR:
Maintain a Healthy Perspective

The rate of change is escalating and you may feel pressure to make decisions that will have a lasting impact. Blind optimism and extreme pessimism are not helpful, yet may be the result from having no clear frame of reference. Unquestionably, these are times of great transition, but they, too, will fade into the past. Avoid the shortsighted desperation that comes from fear by remembering to look out beyond the present moment and toward the distant horizon.

JANUARY

ON THE THRESHOLD OF A DREAM

The future seems so close this month that you might just want to reach out to grab it. Unfortunately, even if you're sure a goal is right around the corner, you might actually need all year to reach it. That's because hardworking Saturn edges closer all year to a harmonious trine with inspirational Neptune in your 11th House of Dreams, but doesn't actually get there until **October 10**. On **January 7**, your key planet, Mercury, forms supportive sextiles to both Saturn and Neptune, coaxing you to believe that your fantasies are real. Mental Mercury's entry into calculating Capricorn and your 8th House of Shared Resources on **January 8** enables you to be more practical by involving others in your plans. Although you can incorporate their ambitions into your overall strategy, the tenacious Cancer Full Moon on **January 9** illuminates your 2nd House of Personal Resources, shifting the focus back to your individual needs.

You may find the recognition that you seek with Venus's move into your 10th House of Career on **January 14**—if you remain focused on your objectives. You'll need self-discipline when the ambitious Capricorn Sun squares scrupulous Saturn on **January 19**. But resistance falls away as the Sun enters experimental Aquarius and your 9th House of Big Ideas on **January 20** and squares expansive Jupiter on **January 22**. Your progress could slow as energetic Mars turns retrograde on **January 23**, the same day as the futuristic Aquarius New Moon. Even if your tactics are sound and your execution is skillful, you still might feel as if you're losing ground. Don't panic; Mercury enters Aquarius and your visionary 9th House on **January 27**, stimulating innovative thinking as you reformulate your plans.

KEEP IN MIND THIS MONTH

Success doesn't necessarily look the way you expect. Although you might be disappointed, what you do now can be instrumental in what you accomplish later on in the year.

KEY DATES

JANUARY 1 ★ *ears wide open*

You'd like to enjoy this day off with your friends and family, but you might become irritable if holiday festivities don't meet your expectations. You think that you're being reasonable, but if others don't agree they will tell you exactly where your logic has gone astray. Instead of reacting defensively, listen to the feedback you receive now because it could help you in the days ahead.

SUPER NOVA DAYS

JANUARY 7–9 ★ *trust your intuition*

Your thinking is sound on **January 7** when intelligent Mercury connects with authoritative Saturn and psychic Neptune. Be prepared to make your plans even more concrete when Mercury enters earthy Capricorn the next day. But if Mercury's easy trine to opinionated Jupiter encourages false assumptions, its harsh square to electric Uranus can shock you with the truth. Ultimately, what you choose is not as important as honoring your own feelings, for the sensitive Cancer Full Moon on **January 9** falls in your 2nd House of Values, gently reminding you not to abandon your core beliefs.

JANUARY 12–13 ★ *in the zone*

Harmonious aspects to uncontainable Mars on the **12th** and taskmaster Saturn on the **13th** motivate you to roll up your sleeves and work extra-hard. Fortunately, your efforts should be rewarded, because you know what you want and are willing to be patient in order to achieve the desired results. But clever Mercury joins potent Pluto in your 8th House of Transformation, enticing you to believe that you have superpowers and can get whatever you want. Be careful about pushing your agenda too hard or you could undo your recent gains.

JANUARY 21–23 ★ *slow down; you're moving too fast*

You may not be very efficient in the days prior to the intelligent Aquarius New Moon in your 9th House of Journeys on **January 23** as you think about the great adventures ahead. The Aquarius Sun is zapped by Uranus the Awakener on **January 21**, blasting your brain with inventive ideas. The Sun's dynamic square to global Jupiter on the **22nd** extends your vision even farther. But the winged messenger Mercury trines Mars just as the warrior planet turns retrograde on the **23rd**. Although this could unravel your plans, it also can extend a deadline, giving you more time to get everything in order.

JANUARY 27–28 ★ *blue skies ahead*

A somber Mercury-Saturn square on **January 27** can bring discouragement as a setback reveals a flaw in your plan. Fortunately, Mercury combines with brilliant Uranus and broad-minded Jupiter on the **28th**, enabling you to come up with bright ideas to overcome almost any obstacle in your path.

FEBRUARY

VISION QUEST

This month gets off to a bumpy start with relationship issues affecting your ability to concentrate at work, but the overall outlook is still relatively smooth. Angry words may slip off your tongue too easily on **February 1**, when communicator Mercury forms an anxious aspect with argumentative Mars. But if you're careful about what you say when Mercury creates tension on **February 6, 9–10, and 23–25,** the little flare-ups that might occur won't be obstacles to your happiness or success. You may sense a subtle yet profound shift of energy when slow-moving Neptune the Dreamer swims into watery Pisces and your 10th House of Career on **February 3** for a thirteen-year stay. You could become disillusioned with your chosen life path, dreaming about changing your occupation to a more meaningful pursuit. Talking about your dissatisfaction can lead to constructive feedback when Mercury trines trustworthy Saturn on **February 13**. Your dreams inspire you to reach beyond the ordinary as Mercury conjuncts Neptune on the **14th**, followed by the Sun on the **19th**.

You may feel a powerful urge to share an original idea on **February 7**, when the expressive Leo Full Moon brightens your 3rd House of Information and Education. Eloquent Mercury is aligned with the Sun in intellectual Aquarius, allowing the words to flow like quicksilver. But your aspirations may take longer to reach fruition than you realize, because Saturn the Tester turns retrograde in your 5th House of Self-Expression just hours prior to the Full Moon. Harsh criticism or stubborn resistance to your professional plans won't deter you on **February 21**, when the imaginative Pisces New Moon joins visionary Neptune in your 10th House of Responsibility.

KEEP IN MIND THIS MONTH

Even if you have to handle one concern after another, minor interruptions won't get in the way of your long-term progress.

KEY DATES

FEBRUARY 1 ★ *cosmic tug-of-war*

You can feel the dissension in the air as the cosmic lovers, Venus and Mars, pull in opposite directions. Enticing Venus in your professional 10th House can turn the workplace into a playground, luring you away from home. You may already be short-tempered with cranky Mars now retrograde in your 4th House of Domestic Conditions, so quarrelsome Mercury could incite conflict as it stressfully aspects Mars. Although the tension is palpable, don't succumb to your frustration and start an unnecessary fight.

SUPER NOVA DAYS

FEBRUARY 7–10 ★ *call of the wild*

You are inspired to do things differently this week, and the demonstrative Leo Full Moon on **February 7** can bring your ideas into bloom. The Sun's alignment with persuasive Mercury in your 9th House of Future Vision gives you the passion you need to convince others that you are speaking the truth. But needy Venus forms an annoying quincunx with doubting Saturn, possibly inhibiting others from fully supporting you. Luckily, Venus enters pioneering Aries on the **8th** and joins explosive Uranus on the **9th**, creating the breakthrough you desire. Nevertheless, your excitement still may be tempered by a controlling Mercury-Pluto aspect on **February 10**, indicating that a powerful person might resist your suggestion and hinder your progress.

FEBRUARY 14–18 ★ *dare to believe*

Your Valentine's Day expectations are high thanks to Mercury's dreamy conjunction with wistful Neptune on **February 14**, but if the power equation is out of balance you may see the darker side of love with a tough square between romantic Venus and passionate Pluto the next day. A struggle for control could get out of hand, but calm communication should smooth ruffled feathers when messenger Mercury cooperatively sextiles cheerful Jupiter on **February 16** and Pluto on the **18th**. Fortunately, the Sun's superconductive trine to responsible Saturn assures that your good judgment will prevail.

FEBRUARY 21–23 ★ *account for your actions*

The Pisces New Moon on **February 21** affirms the current emphasis on your 10th House of Public Responsibility, yet you may struggle to see your objectives due to the presence of misleading Neptune. If the awkward Venus-Mars quincunx on **February 22** tricks you into making a social faux pas, apologize and move on. Defending bad behavior, even if inadvertent, will just escalate the problem when Mercury opposes impertinent Mars on **February 23**.

FEBRUARY 28 ★ *all's well that ends well*

You are at the top of your game today as the Sun in your 10th House of Status sextiles insightful Pluto. Instead of spending time reviewing the past, concentrate on the present moment; your well-intended actions should have positive results.

MARCH

BUILDING A FOUNDATION

It's hard to relax because you're so excited about what's ahead, and your impatience is nearly unbearable with Mercury blasting into impetuous Aries on **March 2**. But a series of tense aspects to Mars in your 4th House of Family and Saturn in your 5th House of Spontaneity on **March 2–4** can block your progress by weighing you down with personal matters or parental responsibilities. Although fleet-footed Mercury usually speeds up your thought process while in Aries, you may feel mentally sluggish as the messenger planet slows to enter its retrograde phase on **March 12**. Now that both Mars and Mercury are traveling backward, you may find that these two planets can place a hold on an important project or indicate unexpected delays, especially if you feel pressure to make something happen right now. Paradoxically, when your momentum is interrupted or a deadline is postponed, you may actually feel a sense of relief—as if you've been graced with additional time to get your plans in order.

You find much-needed calm amid a sea of change when the analytical Virgo Full Moon on **March 8** highlights your domestic 4th House and activates a practical Grand Earth Trine. Although this grand trine peaks on **March 13–14**, giving you an overall sense of well-being, it is no time to be lazy. What you do now can have a profound and lasting impact, even if success seems postponed. Another wave of enthusiasm ensues at the Spring Equinox on **March 20** when the Sun enters fiery Aries to light up your 11th House of Goals. But even if you have accepted the lingering constraints to progress, the enterprising Aries New Moon on **March 22** kicks off the next cycle and focuses your attention on the future.

KEEP IN MIND THIS MONTH

Don't expect too much too soon from your current investments of time or money. Frustration and disappointment could get in the way of your success.

KEY DATES

MARCH 1–3 ★ *shoulder to the wheel*

You feel like a pinball being bounced around when your words run into a judgmental Mercury-Saturn quincunx on **March 1**. But you aren't willing to take no for an answer when quicksilver Mercury enters excitable Aries on **March 2**. You may be surprised that your enthusiasm doesn't carry you farther, but ambitious Saturn's harsh aspects to Mars and the Sun will demand more hard work from you before you can achieve success. The Sun in your 10th House of Status tensely opposes militant Mars on the **3rd**, indicating that you may need to fight for what you deserve. Pick your battles wisely or you'll lose ground by alienating those who can help you reach your goals.

MARCH 5 ★ *stroke of genius*

You're hit with lightning bolts of original ideas and out-of-the-blue solutions to irresolvable problems today thanks to quick-witted Mercury's conjunction with electrifying Uranus. It can be difficult for you to remember your thoughts, they come and go so fast. Normally, this cerebral activation occurs annually, but Mercury's retrograde will reactivate this innovative aspect on **March 18**, so you have a second chance this month to turn your brainstorm into reality.

SUPER NOVA DAYS

MARCH 12–14 ★ *lucky break*

Although Mercury turns retrograde on **March 12**, its three-week reversal is softened by a Grand Earth Trine that stabilizes your life against the uncontrollable changing tides. This grand trine rests upon the powerful connection between confident Jupiter and fierce Pluto that is exact on **March 13**. Unfortunately, the sweet presence of delicious Venus can be so comforting that you don't take advantage of the energy now at your disposal. The auspicious Venus-Jupiter conjunction on **March 14** falls in your 12th House of Destiny, indicating a possible financial windfall or luck in love. The third point of this magical grand trine is held by retrograde Mars in your 4th House of Security, reinforcing your drive for satisfaction in your personal, rather than professional, life.

MARCH 26–29 ★ *navigating rough waters*

Mischievous Mercury retrogrades through tricky territory in your 10th House of Career. On **March 26** you may be reminded of Murphy's Law: "If anything can go wrong, it will." Fortunately, the Winged Messenger aspects buoyant Jupiter soon after restrictive Saturn, so snafus at work shouldn't last long. Meanwhile, a transformative Saturn-Pluto quintile on the **28th** requires you to reconsider your entire strategy, and an intensifying Sun-Pluto square on **March 29** fuels a conflict if you aren't willing to modify your long-term goals.

APRIL

ON THE MOVE

This month, your recent efforts begin to bring you the acknowledgment and financial rewards you seek. Venus, the planet of love and money, enters your sign on **April 3,** initiating a feel-good period when you find it easier to attract positive attention. Normally, this phase lasts for only a few weeks, but Venus turns retrograde on **May 15**, extending her visit until **August 7**. Although the overall effects of this transit should be pleasurable, Venus squares whimsical Neptune on **April 5** and physical Mars on **April 7**, creating stress associated with your unfulfilled desires. Fortunately, unexpected gratification is possible when Venus sextiles surprising Uranus on **April 9.** Meanwhile, communicator Mercury—retrograding since **March 12**—turns direct in your 10th House of Career on **April 4** to free up blockages in your professional plans. Pent-up tensions begin to dissipate on **April 13** when Mars finishes his retrograde phase, which started on **January 23**. An additional boost of energy increases your momentum, although it may take a few days for you to notice the effect.

You'll likely feel overwhelmed when the sociable Libra Full Moon shines the spotlight on your 5th House of Love on **April 6,** forming harsh aspects with Venus, Mars, and Neptune and further intensifying a relationship dilemma. The steadfast Taurus New Moon in your 12th House of Inner Peace on **April 21** is a welcome relief from the hectic pace of life. Its harmonious aspects to Mars and Neptune come to the rescue and give you an opportunity to put your feet up, indulge your senses, and relax. Enjoy yourself now while you have the chance.

KEEP IN MIND THIS MONTH

It's smart to recharge your batteries as the stress subsides—but be sure you don't frivolously waste an opportunity to improve your life.

KEY DATES

APRIL 4–7 ★ *green light*

Be ready to jump if you receive the go-ahead on a work project that recently encountered delays as your ruling planet, Mercury, turns direct on **April 4**. Luckily, a powerful quintile between flamboyant Jupiter and fanciful Neptune enables you to be even more creative than usual. But be careful, because flirty Venus in fickle Gemini squares deceptive Neptune on **April 5**; you're so convincing, you could even fool yourself. The lovely Libra Full Moon on **April 6** increases your ability to please others, but a Venus-Mars square on **April 7** leads to trouble if you aren't being completely honest with everyone involved.

APRIL 12–16 ★ *uphill climb*

Witty Mercury cannot help you talk your way out of a tight spot on **April 12** when it forms an uncomfortable quincunx to severe Saturn. Unfortunately, the Sun's tense opposition to Saturn on **April 15** is even more judgmental and less forgiving. But you're not eager to succumb to the voice of authority when sizzling Mars turns up the heat by going direct on **April 13**, followed by Mercury's entry into red-hot Aries on the **16th**. Hard work, rather than clever words, is your current key to success.

SUPER NOVA DAYS

APRIL 20–23 ★ *irreconcilable differences*

You can't anticipate the impact of what you say when loquacious Mercury in Aries quincunxes insistent Mars on **April 20**. Your crazy ideas may trigger unexpected anger, especially when Mercury hooks up with unstable Uranus on **April 22**. Fortunately, Mars is sweetly trined by the sensible Taurus New Moon on the **21st** and by the Sun on the **23rd**, enabling you to defend your innovative ideas against an unreasonable attack.

APRIL 25 ★ *the truth shall set you free*

You are being challenged today to dig beneath the surface until you know the score, and then you must share what you learn. Paradoxically, expressive Mercury's square to ruthless Pluto demonstrates the messenger planet's power to overcome dark forces by exposing hidden information. Your openness and integrity prove that fear is no match for the truth.

APRIL 29 ★ *destiny's calling*

An unstoppable wave of change washes through your life now as the solidifying Taurus Sun in your 12th House of Spirituality forms a superconductive trine to transformational Pluto. Normally, you would be tempted to avoid this level of intensity, but you intuitively know there's no way around it. There are aspects of your life that aren't working, yet you've been unable to let them go. Rather than being frightened by the unknown territory ahead, you are eager to explore it, for you know this is your chance to advance and evolve.

MAY

SLOW DOWN AND SMELL THE ROSES

Conflicting cosmic messages rev up your communication engine while also tempting you with the peace and quiet of increased isolation. Paradoxically, your friends are even more important to you than usual, as this month begins with chatty Mercury in excitable Aries in your 11th House Social Networking. But your quick wit isn't a substitute for real understanding, and Mercury's worried opposition to judgmental Saturn on **May 5**—the same day as the intense Scorpio Full Moon—reminds you that others may not be entertained by your lighthearted humor. Mercury's entry into easygoing Taurus and your 12th House of Privacy on **May 9** is another sign that you need to slow down and maybe even retreat into a more relaxed lifestyle for a while. Fewer distractions are in order while three planets—Mercury, the Sun, and Jupiter—travel through your secretive 12th House.

> **KEEP IN MIND THIS MONTH**
>
> *Although your life is settling into a steady rhythm, be prepared to revise your plans when the tempo shifts.*

Pleasure-seeking Venus turns retrograde in your sign on **May 15**, highlighting your need for reflection and solitude. Nevertheless, she remains in your 1st House of Personality for an extended stay until **August 7**, offering her blessings of love and money to those who are patient. But waiting isn't your forte, and the Sun's entry into flighty Gemini on **May 20**, just a few hours prior to a Solar Eclipse, can make you anxious. However, this New Moon Eclipse is also a start of a fresh cycle if you're willing to let go of your old expectations. The pace of your life quickens when your ruling planet, Mercury, flies into noisy Gemini on **May 24**.

KEY DATES

MAY 5–7 ★ *bigger is better*

You seek ways to better yourself on **May 5**, when the complex Scorpio Full Moon illuminates your 6th House of Self-Improvement. However, you may be overwhelmed by how much you want to change; it's hard to know where to start. You have no shortage of good ideas, but they are dismissed by people who question your ability as your key planet, Mercury, opposes stern Saturn. Baby steps won't work now. Take a leap of faith; grandiose Jupiter aspects radical Uranus on **May 7**, rewarding bold and innovative action.

MAY 13–16 ★ *beyond the horizon*

The Sun's annual conjunction with jaunty Jupiter on **May 13** fills you with confidence. Luckily, you intuitively know how to translate an opportunity into reality now as articulate Mercury in reliable Taurus forms a solid Grand Earth Trine with courageous Mars and formidable Pluto on **May 13–16**. You can draw on deep reserves of energy to accomplish your goals, but you still may fall short of your own high expectations because Jupiter forms an irritating quincunx with pessimistic Saturn on **May 16**. Additionally, Venus begins her six-week retrograde phase on **May 15**, tempting you with the promise of satisfaction while placing it just beyond your reach. Don't let frustration get the best of you; use your time wisely by preparing for what's ahead.

SUPER NOVA DAYS

MAY 20–22 ★ *let the new times roll*

You know better than to hold on to your past when the Sun and Moon enter restless Gemini on **May 20** and the New Moon Eclipse pushes the restart button in your 1st House of Self. This Solar Eclipse forms an imaginative biquintile to productive Saturn in your 5th House of Self-Expression, enabling you to tap into a creative flow. But managing the intensity can challenge you, especially with verbal Mercury forming uneasy aspects with Saturn and Pluto on **May 21**. Although you may think that an idea is not worth pursuing, Mercury's conjunction with promising Jupiter on the **22nd** restores your confidence in your plan and encourages you to take it to the next level.

MAY 27–30 ★ *hot under the collar*

Your innovative thoughts are not restrained by social etiquette when expressive Mercury joins the Sun in curious Gemini. Together, on **May 27–28**, this pair creates a cooperative sextile with unorthodox Uranus in your 11th House of Groups, inviting you to share your radical ideas with friends. Unfortunately, they may not be as supportive as you wish. Be cautious; Mercury's square to competitive Mars on **May 30** can reveal differences of opinion that escalate into an unnecessary argument.

JUNE

OPPORTUNITY KNOCKS

Every twelve years, expansive Jupiter visits your sign for a year, bearing good news and initiating another cycle of opportunity. Your self-confidence soars as this gassy giant begins pumping up your 1st House of Self on **June 11**. But this month becomes a dance between optimistic hopes and unrealistic dreams, because Jupiter slowly moves toward a disquieting square with mythical Neptune that culminates on **June 25**, challenging you to keep your expectations in perspective. Meanwhile, an unexpected clash over money could erupt between you and your friends or associates when volatile Uranus in your 11th House of Groups squares relentless Pluto in your 8th House of Shared Resources on **June 24**. Someone may exert power over you through manipulative behavior such as withholding money or love, precipitating unexpected events that are beyond your control. Fortunately, this is only the opening volley; you have time to figure out how to handle the next round of conflict, as the Uranus-Pluto square recurs seven times through **March 16, 2015**.

A business or personal relationship brings excitement into your life on **June 4**, when the Sagittarius Full Moon Eclipse falls in your 7th House of Partnerships. Step back and contemplate your feelings when your key planet, Mercury, slips out of your sign and into introspective Cancer on **June 7**. The Gemini New Moon on **June 19** is your time to make a fresh start, yet it's so close to the Summer Solstice on **June 20** that you may lack objectivity as you move closer to the great changes ahead. Luckily, you are able to express yourself more decisively when cerebral Mercury enters lively Leo and your 3rd House of Information on **June 25**.

KEEP IN MIND THIS MONTH

This is a bellwether month that can give you a glimpse of the dynamic landscape you'll be traversing over the next few years.

KEY DATES

JUNE 3–5 ★ *fairy-tale ending*

You're finally ready to settle down and take yourself seriously when thoughtful Mercury forms a productive trine to sobering Saturn on **June 3**. However, it's nearly impossible to maintain a rational approach to your responsibilities while also responding to the stresses of a personal relationship. The adventurous Sagittarius Lunar Eclipse on **June 4** distracts you with visions of distant horizons. But its alignment with retrograde Venus in flirtatious Gemini and square to aggressive Mars can turn the heat up on love too much and too fast unless you pay close attention to your emotions. Fortunately, Venus conjoins the Sun on **June 5**, indicating a pleasant outcome to a challenging series of events.

JUNE 11–13 ★ *patience, grasshopper*

Although you may be inspired by the arrival of jolly Jupiter in your sign on **June 11**, you're also distracted as nervous Mercury squares erratic Uranus and opposes Pluto, foreshadowing the Uranus-Pluto square that's exact on **June 24**. An unexpected change in your financial condition is possible with Mercury in your 2nd House of Self-Worth, but the current tension might also stem from a power play in a complicated relationship. Self-restraint is advised; wait to make your move until clarity returns when the Sun trines stabilizing Saturn on **June 13**.

JUNE 19–21 ★ *start from scratch*

Your current restlessness reaches a tipping point at the Gemini New Moon on **June 19**. However, it's unlikely that you'll make any significant changes yet because the Sun slips into passive Cancer on **June 20**, turning your energy inward and slowing your pace. Additionally, you may need to confront the shortcomings of your escape plan as the frustrating Mercury-Saturn square unravels your dreams, crashing them down to earth. But all is not lost, for a thrilling Venus-Uranus sextile dangles new carrots of desire in front of you and you receive an energetic boost on **June 21**, when Mercury forms an opportunistic sextile with go-getter Mars.

SUPER NOVA DAYS

JUNE 27–29 ★ *stormy weather*

Changes are coming fast and furious now. If you made good use of Venus's retrograde period—it began on **May 15**—her direct turn on **June 27** begins a process that can bring greater freedom of expression and financial rewards for your efforts. But first you must navigate through the troubled waters stirred by the Sun's opposition to secretive Pluto and square to rebellious Uranus on **June 29**. Remember, issues around money, control, and personal relationships may be overwhelming you in the moment, but they're tied to longer-lasting cycles that will continue to have significant impact.

JULY

ADJUSTING TO A NEW REALITY

Although the changes that began recently could take months, even years, to play through to their conclusions, there's no doubt that you have entered a new phase of your life. But instead of recklessly pushing ahead on your journey, take a few deep breaths, assimilate what has already happened, and reevaluate your plans for what comes next. You may be more inclined to seek out some summertime festivities once physical Mars enters your 5th House of Love and Play on **July 3**, where he remains until **August 23**. But all is not fun and games, as indicated by the serious Capricorn Full Moon—also on **July 3**—that conjuncts extreme Pluto in your 8th House of Transformation. Additionally, trickster Mercury's retrograde phase on **July 14–August 8** occurs in your 3rd House of Immediate Environment, delaying further progress and requiring you to reassess your priorities. Use this time to improve your strategy for following through on the transitions already under way.

Your renewed sense of faith is a reflection of the positive effects of Jupiter, now firmly entrenched in your sign until next summer. But your positive thinking alone isn't enough to overcome powerful forces that pull you away from your goals when Jupiter forms a quincunx with domineering Pluto on the **18th**. Although the cautious Cancer New Moon on the **19th** restrains impulsive tendencies, your nerves are on edge and a feeling that anything can happen is in the air. Thankfully an exciting Jupiter-Uranus sextile on the **22nd**, followed by a series of supportive aspects, indicates smoother sailing through the end of the month as long as you balance your need for immediate results with the wisdom of long-term planning.

KEEP IN MIND THIS MONTH

You may feel a great sense of urgency to push issues to the next level, but forcing change is not the smartest move now. You have more time than you think.

KEY DATES

JULY 3–4 ★ *balancing act*

You're ready to risk your comfort by confronting a deep emotional issue on **July 3**, when the ambitious Capricorn Full Moon illuminates your 8th House of Intimacy. Unfortunately, affectionate Venus is more irritating than soothing as she forms an uneasy quincunx with penetrating Pluto. But the current intensity is tempered by the entry of Mars into graceful Libra and your 5th House of Self-Expression. Honest communication should bring positive results as talkative Mercury aspects surprising Uranus and amicable Venus on **July 4**.

JULY 8–9 ★ *who's on first?*

Curious Mercury's skillful quintile to strategic Saturn on **July 8** encourages you to ask smart questions, but a confusing Mars-Neptune quincunx distorts the truth and makes it nearly impossible for you to get your bearings. Your loss of certainty is further exacerbated by the Sun's anxious aspect to nebulous Neptune on the **9th**. Specific answers may not be forthcoming, but your imagination can fuel a creative process that doesn't need facts.

SUPER NOVA DAYS

JULY 14–17 ★ *no free lunch*

You can sweet-talk your way through a sticky situation on **July 14**, when your key planet, Mercury, turns retrograde as it forms a sexy sextile with enchanting Venus. But the Sun's resistant square to constrictive Saturn the next day won't let you sidestep your responsibilities to have a good time or avoid future consequences of your current actions. Impulsive Mars, in your playful 5th House, amplifies your confidence and your energy as he harmoniously trines indulgent Jupiter on **July 17**. Nevertheless, think before you act; an unforgiving Mars-Pluto square on the same day can extract a severe price if you aimlessly pursue a passing pleasure.

JULY 18–22 ★ *larger than life*

Everything seems bigger and more important on **July 18–22** when inflationary Jupiter aspects Pluto, Saturn, and Uranus, blowing problems out of proportion and presenting solutions that seem better than they actually are. But no single answer appears to resolve a current relationship dilemma. However, anxiety and frustration can catalyze a sudden energetic shift as Mars opposes Uranus on **July 18**. Meanwhile, the nurturing Cancer New Moon on **July 19** in your 2nd House of Self-Worth reminds you that respecting others is easier if you value your own feelings, too.

JULY 31 ★ *carpe diem*

The Sun's easy trine to spontaneous Uranus spurs you to seize the moment, while a stabilizing Venus-Saturn trine allows you to patiently wait for gratification. Fortunately, a magical quintile between clever Mercury and action-hero Mars shows you a sensible balance between these two extreme approaches to success.

AUGUST

FLYING BY THE SEAT OF YOUR PANTS

This month is full of change and is bound to bring a few surprises along the way. The action starts immediately as the quirky Aquarius Full Moon on **August 1** falls in your 9th House of Adventure, tempting you to dream about the future rather than take care of business in the present moment. But messenger Mercury is still retrograde in your 3rd House of Communication, so it's tough to make progress if you're dealing with delays caused by misunderstandings, incorrect assumptions, or lack of preparation. Fortunately, your efforts should begin to pay off soon after Mercury turns direct on **August 8**, while gracious Venus's entry into nurturing Cancer on **August 7** encourages you to consider other people's feelings before speaking your mind.

Your frustration builds through **August 15**, when hot Mars joins cold Saturn in your 5th House of Romance and Self-Expression, confronting you with unavoidable consequences of recent behavior. Issues about love and money could become more troublesome, yet the dramatic Leo New Moon on **August 17** is a turning point that empowers you to take direct action to resolve recent difficulties. The Sun's entry into efficient Virgo on **August 22** helps you to focus on your intentions. Set specific goals, for little will stand in your way once Mars enters passionate Scorpio and your 6th House of Work on **August 23**. A second Full Moon this month on **August 31** shines in your 10th House of Career in psychic Pisces, strengthening your intuition about the outcome of an important professional decision. Analytical Mercury sharpens your perceptions and fine-tunes your logic as it slips into precise Virgo, also on the **31st**.

KEEP IN MIND THIS MONTH

Although you can see that you're making progress again, you still must handle day-to-day situations as they arise before you think about what comes next.

KEY DATES

AUGUST 1–4 ★ *spellbound*

You catch glimpses of what's around the next bend when the brilliant Aquarius Full Moon on **August 1** illuminates your 9th House of Future Vision. But your optimism may be blinded by the zealous Jupiter-Moon trine that encourages you to expect too much. On **August 2**, the outgoing Leo Sun aspects excessive Jupiter and bewitching Venus, further enticing you with a variety of potentially pleasurable distractions. You could waste time and energy as dreamy Neptune's influence on **August 3–4** has you chasing elusive satisfaction. Show some self-restraint before you suffer the consequences of overindulgence.

AUGUST 8–9 ★ *it's getting better all the time*

You've struggled to keep your life in order since **July 14**, when your key planet, Mercury, turned retrograde. Fortunately, it becomes easier for you to maintain the hectic pace when expressive Mercury turns direct in generous Leo on **August 8.** Others may notice a positive change in your attitude, too, with your words reflecting a new sense of optimism. But don't fool yourself about love or money, because attractive Venus in your 2nd House of Self-Worth trines imaginative Neptune on **August 9**. Visualize the best possible outcome by letting your dreams be your guide, but anchor your logic to reality.

SUPER NOVA DAYS

AUGUST 14–17 ★ *shadow dancing*

You can exhaust yourself trying to avoid a difficult lesson about love now—or you can stop rationalizing and delve deeply into your emotions. The Leo Sun's anxious sesquisquares to potent Pluto and shaky Uranus on **August 14–15** put you on notice that there is no stable place to stand as shifting circumstances test your resolve. Additionally, needy Venus in emotional Cancer opposes Pluto and squares Uranus on **August 15–16**, revealing a darker side of love if you succumb to possessiveness or jealousy. And an inarguable Mars-Saturn conjunction on **August 15** is a reality check that requires you to face current issues head-on. Ultimately, the Leo New Moon on **August 17** rewards your willingness to enter the unknown darkness by shining light on a previously unseen path to success.

AUGUST 24–26 ★ *lost in the hall of mirrors*

It's tough to know what's real when the Sun and Venus both form disquieting aspects with surreal Neptune on **August 24**. Disappointment can follow if you allow yourself to be distracted by fantasies of sensual enjoyment rather than utilizing your imagination for more creative purposes. Luckily, a Mars-Neptune trine on **August 26** inspires you to apply your passion to spiritual pursuits instead of transient pleasures.

SEPTEMBER

STORMS OF CHANGE

The second of two long-lasting squares this year between revolutionary Uranus and evolutionary Pluto is exact on **September 19**—although you'll feel its impact for much longer—reactivating issues about your long-term goals that surfaced around **June 24** when this potent pair first aligned. Even if you acknowledge that the direction of your life needs remapping, you might not yet realize the magnitude of the changes that are coming your way over the next few years. Fortunately, compelling Pluto receives positive aspects from assertive Mars, communicator Mercury, and maverick Chiron on **September 3–6**, empowering you to make constructive decisions about family matters and work. Your choices may not be what others expect, but it's more important to maintain your integrity than it is to please everyone else. In fact, several annoying quincunxes that occur this month can place satisfaction just out of your reach. Focus on doing the right thing rather than trying to take the easy way out.

The exacting Virgo New Moon on **September 15** invites you to plant a seed of intention in your 4th House of Foundations. Don't force resolution to a domestic problem now, because insistent Mars quincunxes exaggerated Jupiter on the **16th**, tempting you to overextend yourself. Fortunately, the stress can feed your creativity, especially when Mercury enters aesthetic Libra and your 5th House of Self-Expression, also on the **16th**, and forms hard aspects with the Uranus-Pluto square on the **20th**. The Autumn Equinox on **September 22** is marked by the Sun's shift into Libra and your 5th House, adding spontaneity to your artistry. Nevertheless, you may feel the tension ratchet up even more when the Aries Full Moon on **September 29** conjuncts jumpy Uranus and squares obsessive Pluto.

KEEP IN MIND THIS MONTH

It's necessary to think on two levels now. Take care of the most pressing issues while also considering the impact your current actions will have on your future.

KEY DATES

SEPTEMBER 3–5 ★ *all by yourself*

You may feel lost and alone on **September 3** when lovable Venus squares judgmental Saturn. Don't wallow in disappointment; a motivating Mars-Pluto sextile empowers you to do something about your current situation. Thankfully, you can find clarity, because astute Mercury trines incisive Pluto on the **4th** and sextiles straightforward Mars on the **5th**. But your friends might not support your sensible initiative the way you expect when Mars and Mercury make unsettling quincunxes to wayward Uranus in your 11th House of Social Networking on the **4th**.

SEPTEMBER 7–8 ★ *too much of a good thing can hurt*

The Sun squares gigantic Jupiter on **September 7,** infusing your life with joyful optimism, but also pulling you in two directions. Jupiter in multitasking Gemini tempts you to say yes to every opportunity, but the discriminating Virgo Sun affirms that you can't do it all. Rational Mercury also squares Jupiter on **September 8**, increasing the contrast between blind optimism and informed realism. Be wise and exercise self-control or you'll exhaust yourself before you reach your goal.

SEPTEMBER 12–16 ★ *rock and roll star*

It's not easy to keep your desires in check when sensual Venus quincunxes passionate Pluto on **September 12**, and you may want to try something new when Venus trines experimental Uranus on **September 13**. Fortunately, a practical Virgo New Moon on the **15th** can bring you back down to earth, but it might not be enough to snap you out of your mistaken belief that you can do anything you want. Be especially cautious on **September 16**, when a Mars-Jupiter quincunx gives you a false sense of invincibility.

SEPTEMBER 20 ★ *give peace a chance*

The more you talk, the more complicated everything becomes as verbose Mercury in your expressive 5th House opposes shocking Uranus and squares mighty Pluto. Instead of trying to win the debate, stop arguing and allow the sweet Venus-Jupiter sextile to show you how to enjoy yourself in the present moment.

SUPER NOVA DAYS

SEPTEMBER 25–29 ★ *rocky road*

You may be tempted to gamble with your stability in a risky scheme to regain more control of your life. On **September 25–26** uncomfortable aspects from Mars and Venus to the lingering Uranus-Pluto square can reignite a disagreement that you thought was resolved. The pressure to change dysfunctional relationship dynamics continues to mount through **September 29** when the Libra Sun in your 5th House of Romance and the impulsive Aries Full Moon in your 11th House of Dreams and Wishes both stress volcanic Uranus and Pluto.

OCTOBER

CHANGE OF PACE

Take time out from all the pressures for change this month and consider which opportunities merit further exploration. When expansive Jupiter turns retrograde in your sign on **October 4**, it's wise to withdraw from the chaos and noise of your everyday life so you can listen to your own inner voice instead of being distracted by everyone else's opinions. This soulful deepening of your life is punctuated by rational Mercury on **October 5** when it joins somber Saturn as they both enter emotional Scorpio and your 6th House of Self-Improvement. You are less interested now in changing the world than in correcting those things that aren't working optimally in your daily routine. On **October 10**, however, traditional Saturn forms a long-lasting trine with inspirational Neptune in your 10th House of Career—the first in a series of three that culminates on **July 19, 2013**—motivating you to work methodically toward manifesting your professional dreams.

A bit of levity arrives to lighten the mood when the creative Libra New Moon on **October 15** spotlights your 5th House of Fun and Games. A friend or partner may surprise you with unexpected behavior since assertive Mars in your 7th House of Relationships trines unpredictable Uranus. Although you may gain more freedom, an imbalanced sesquisquare between optimistic Jupiter and pessimistic Saturn reveals uncertainty about how to reach your goals. Your resolve intensifies when the Sun enters inflexible Scorpio on **October 22**, yet the Taurus Full Moon in your 12th House of Escapism on **October 29** can be confusing as you seek comfort from your dreams and fantasies.

KEEP IN MIND THIS MONTH

Your newfound vision of the future eases your stress and gives you time to reconsider where you want your life to go.

KEY DATES

OCTOBER 3–7 ★ *the uncertainty principle*

You feel disoriented when lovely Venus opposes foggy Neptune in your 10th House of Status on **October 3** and journeying Jupiter turns retrograde on **October 4**, making it difficult to find direction in your life. Cerebral Mercury runs into solemn Saturn on **October 5**, adding weight to your thoughts. Luckily, a Mercury-Neptune trine encourages dreaming and gives you hope. Although you are drawn to others when ardent Mars enters outgoing Sagittarius and your 7th House of Companions on **October 6**, the misleading Mars-Neptune square on **October 7** reminds you that success will remain elusive as long as you're chasing an unrealizable dream.

SUPER NOVA DAYS

OCTOBER 9–10 ★ *positive vibrations*

You are on top of your game on **October 9**, when the Sun in your 5th House of Fun forms a lovely trine to lucky Jupiter. Romantic Venus trines transformational Pluto in your 8th House of Intimacy to deepen your joy. Messenger Mercury's cooperative sextile to Pluto on the **10th** gives you the words to describe your intense feelings. Additionally, persistent Saturn connects with otherworldly Neptune to open a direct channel between the real world and your imagination. You skillfully blend material and spiritual pursuits now as you look to your future.

OCTOBER 15–16 ★ *over your limit*

You can successfully break out of a rut when impetuous Mars trines electric Uranus just prior to the diplomatic Libra New Moon on **October 15**. You're capable of outsmarting your co-workers when persuasive Mercury sextiles disarming Venus on **October 16**. Unfortunately, stressful aspects to flamboyant Jupiter on both days embolden you to overestimate your resources. Unless you know your limitations and respect other people's boundaries, you could lose all that you stand to gain.

OCTOBER 25 ★ *reality check*

Even if you believe that you're on track with your progress, the Sun's conjunction with stern Saturn in your 6th House of Employment today indicates a temporary setback as you face the facts you tried to avoid. Instead of attempting to work around the issues, learn the lessons they are trying to teach you before moving on.

OCTOBER 28–29 ★ *the power of persistence*

Your enthusiasm knows no bounds when an enthusiastic Mars-Jupiter opposition activates your 7th House of Relationships on **October 28**. Someone might try to steer you off course by misrepresenting the truth as Mercury squares delusional Neptune on the **29th**. However, the stubborn Taurus Full Moon trines unyielding Pluto, so you won't be led astray if you make up your mind and stick to it.

NOVEMBER

HURRY UP AND WAIT

This is a month of delays that you can use to your advantage once you accept that things will take longer than you've planned. You may need to put relationship issues on the front burner when Mercury starts backtracking in your 7th House of Partners on **November 6**. However, your daily routine is affected, too, for mental Mercury reenters your 6th House of Work on **November 14**, remaining there through **December 10**. Although the heavenly messenger turns direct on **November 26**, its sluggish movement through the end of the month means that you could actually lose ground as you review recent mistakes, reconsider your assumptions, redo your calendar, and reinvent your strategy for success. You may grow frustrated with your lack of momentum and attempt to speed things up, but to no avail. Don't think that you have failed if something slips through the cracks. Instead, make a commitment to be patient and dig deeper than ever before to uncover the information that will allow you to improve the quality of your daily life.

Two eclipses—a Solar Eclipse on **November 13** and a Lunar Eclipse on **November 28**—overwhelm you with an abundance of nervous tension. You feel as if you're standing on a precipice and must take exactly the right step to prevent misfortune. The transformational Scorpio New Moon Eclipse on the **13th** is a great time to initiate improvements in your diet and exercise regimen, because it activates your 6th House of Health and Habits. The Gemini Full Moon Eclipse on the **28th** joins propitious Jupiter in your 12th House of Destiny, supporting renewed faith that your hard work will soon be rewarded.

KEEP IN MIND THIS MONTH

If you're just spinning your wheels and getting nowhere fast, back up, catch your breath, reassess your approach, and try again.

KEY DATES

NOVEMBER 1–3 ★ *easy does it*

If you feel blocked by a co-worker on **November 1** when contentious Mars stressfully semisquares bossy Saturn, an angry response isn't your smartest move. Instead, use the unconventional Venus-Uranus opposition to seek a more innovative solution. Surprise others with your uncharacteristic intensity when charismatic Venus squares powerhouse Pluto on **November 3**. But don't go overboard and turn a good thing into a major drama.

NOVEMBER 9–11 ★ *sweet escape*

Flirty Venus in your 5th House of Love and Play forms a delicious trine with opulent Jupiter on **November 9**, replacing problems with pleasure. A fantasy-prone Venus-Neptune alignment further inspires you to believe in your dreams. But a disappointing semisquare between social Mercury and Venus on **November 11** can sour the stew and take the fun out of a delightful conversation if you hold on to unrealistic expectations.

SUPER NOVA DAYS

NOVEMBER 13–17 ★ *out of your element*

Entering unfamiliar territory may not feel comfortable on **November 13** when the enigmatic Scorpio New Moon Eclipse forces you to leave language behind and jump into an emotional abyss. You may feel out of sorts from Mercury's square to spacey Neptune on the **13th** or by Mercury's entry into the shadows of Scorpio on the **14th**. Stable Saturn aligns with forgiving Chiron on the **16th**, offering healing compassion. Although energetic Mars enters persistent Capricorn and your 8th House of Regeneration the same day to push you along on your path, Mars's sextile to metaphysical Neptune on the **17th** favors a spiritual awakening that can catalyze a deep restoration of your well-being.

NOVEMBER 22–24 ★ *lost and found*

You struggle to get an accurate sense of what's happening with your career when hazy Neptune in your 10th House of Public Life squares the Sun and trines Venus on **November 22**. You may be so freaked out with your inability to decide upon a course of action that a volatile Mars-Uranus square on the **23rd** could provoke radical action that you haven't thought out very well. Luckily, a skillful Mars-Saturn sextile the next day helps you to quickly bring some stability back into your life.

NOVEMBER 26–29 ★ *don't look back*

Mercury's direct turn on **November 26**, coupled with the fidgety Gemini Full Moon Eclipse on **November 28**, sets the stage for your next wave of progress. But advancement does not come easily, because the austere Venus-Saturn conjunction on the **26th** forces you to narrow your objectives. Although an aggressive Mars-Pluto conjunction on the **27th** emboldens you to fight for your beliefs, gentler aspects on **November 28–29** allow you to move on without holding on to any unnecessary negativity.

DECEMBER

OVER THE RAINBOW

Now that your key planet, Mercury, is moving direct again, you should begin to notice progress on several fronts. But with jolly Jupiter visiting your sign this year, you can't help but be happily distracted by the holiday hustle and bustle. On **December 2**, the illuminating Sun in uplifting Sagittarius opposes Jupiter from your 7th House of Others, shining a positive light on anyone who brings you opportunities for growth and the potential for adventurous experiences. As long as you don't go overboard blindly seeking a good time, joyful Jupiter is your good-luck charm now. Messenger Mercury becomes even chattier when it enters gregarious Sagittarius and your 7th House on **December 10** and could deliver good news when it opposes Jupiter on **December 17**. Entertaining Venus follows Mercury to join the lively party in your 7th House on **December 15**, and then takes the fun to the next level when she opposes outrageous Jupiter on **December 22**.

The upbeat Sagittarius New Moon on **December 13** confirms this new cycle of optimism, tempting you to agree with your friends and co-workers without doing any critical thinking of your own. Meanwhile, serious Saturn slowly moves toward a supportive sextile with formidable Pluto that's exact on **December 26**. This long-lasting aspect gives you the power to thrive during big changes. But as good as all this sounds, Jupiter forms an unsatisfying quincunx with Pluto on **December 20** and with Saturn on the **22nd**, prompting you to question whether success is even worth the effort. A wave of fear washes in with the worried Cancer Full Moon in your 2nd House of Self-Worth on **December 28**. This lunation opposes relentless Pluto and can remind you of the inevitability of change, which, thankfully, you can handle better than most.

KEEP IN MIND THIS MONTH

It's easy for you to scatter your energy and have nothing to show for your efforts. Enjoying yourself is important, but keep some resources in reserve.

KEY DATES

DECEMBER 1–2 ★ *act as if . . .*

You grow anxious during the nervous Mercury-Uranus aspect on **December 1**, but you should be able to conceal your worries. Animated Mars and alluring Venus both form uncomfortable quincunxes with loud Jupiter, motivating you to overcompensate for any uncertainty by boldly describing your needs and stating how you will fulfill them. But you don't need to prove to anyone else what you can do. If you believe in yourself, then others will jump on the bandwagon as the Sun opposes Jupiter in your 1st House of Self on **December 2**.

DECEMBER 10–14 ★ *into the great wide open*

Your fantasies can stretch the bounds of your creativity when inquisitive Mercury enters inspirational Sagittarius on **December 10** and squares irrational Neptune on **December 11**. Luckily, an innovative quintile between physical Mars and hardworking Saturn on the **12th** restores balance by giving you tools to manifest your vision, however unrealistic it may seem. The extroverted Sagittarius New Moon on the **13th** falls in your 7th House of Partnerships, prompting you to involve someone else in your new project. Mercury's unrestrained trine to progressive Uranus on **December 14** frees your mind, empowering you to take an unproven idea from concept to fulfillment fast enough to make heads spin.

DECEMBER 19–22 ★ *variety is the spice of life*

You want to indulge yourself in a plethora of exciting new activities when insatiable Venus trines restless Uranus on **December 19**. Venus's opposition to extravagant Jupiter on **December 22** continues to offer you more pleasurable options. But the Sun's entry into conservative Capricorn on **December 21** marks the Winter Solstice, a time to rest before cranking up the engines of ambition once more. Unfortunately, complex aspects from uninhibited Jupiter in your 1st House of Personality to Pluto and Saturn on **December 20–22** make it hard to know whether you should push harder or back off. Success depends on finding a middle path that allows steady progress.

SUPER NOVA DAYS

DECEMBER 28–31 ★ *out with a bang!*

You say good-bye to a year full of change with an opportunistic sextile from fiery Mars in your 9th House of Future Vision to wild and crazy Uranus in your 11th House of Friends on **December 31**—and this may be the perfect send-off. Still, the days leading up to New Year's Eve are fraught with emotional traps as the sentimental Cancer Full Moon on **December 28** floods you with memories that may be difficult to express. Keep the communication channels open; the Sun conjuncts intense Pluto in your 8th House of Intimacy on **December 30**, pushing suppressed feelings to the surface. Cleaning up old emotional business permits you to move forward with a clear conscience.

CANCER

JUNE 21–JULY 22

CANCER

2011 SUMMARY

This year overflows for you with the prospect of change, Cancer—and yet even greater transformations wait over the next horizon. Now the time has come to live the life you've chosen for yourself. You need to be careful, though, that your overconfidence doesn't drive you to take on more than you can handle. However, handling issues as they surface is much smarter than waiting for a full-blown crisis next year.

AUGUST—*doing the moonwalk*

Extreme patience is one of your strengths, but don't let your ability to wait for the right moment cause you to miss a rare opportunity.

SEPTEMBER—*hold on to your hat*

The changes that begin to unfold now are part of a much greater cycle that will continue to affect your life into next year and beyond.

OCTOBER—*persistence pays*

You can maintain a positive attitude without slipping into denial if you take time to clarify your vision of the future before starting anything new.

NOVEMBER—*lost and found*

As much as you might try to avoid getting caught in a rut, familiar habits can be reassuring in times of change.

DECEMBER—*we can work it out*

Your feelings aren't always convenient, and they don't always put others at ease. Nevertheless, your nurturing love shines through when you're honest about your emotions.

2011 CALENDAR

AUGUST

MON 1–WED 3 ★ Avoid extremes when making important decisions now

TUE 9–SAT 13 ★ **SUPER NOVA DAYS** Change might not come easily

SUN 21–TUE 23 ★ Gain a clear perspective based on facts instead of illusions

THU 25–SUN 28 ★ Your inner resolve to deal with reality is strengthened

SEPTEMBER

FRI 2 ★ Your positive attitude is like a magnet today

THU 8–FRI 9 ★ Use fewer words and more sincerity to make your point

MON 12–WED 14 ★ The way to win an argument is to know when to stop talking

FRI 23–SUN 25 ★ It's challenging to find your center of gravity now

TUE 27–WED 28 ★ **SUPER NOVA DAYS** Bend with the pressure for change

OCTOBER

SAT 1–MON 3 ★ Consider all the consequences before making a commitment

MON 10–FRI 14 ★ **SUPER NOVA DAYS** Pay more attention to your own needs first

FRI 21–SAT 22 ★ Your sensitivity to nonphysical dimensions is heightened

WED 26–FRI 28 ★ Anything you initiate now has a great chance for success

NOVEMBER

WED 2–SAT 5 ★ You can be quite charming so speak up about what you want

THU 10–SAT 12 ★ Don't rock the boat; stick to your current plans for now

WED 16 ★ You can just as easily lose ground now as gain it

WED 23–FRI 25 ★ **SUPER NOVA DAYS** Ask for the help you need before it's too late

DECEMBER

THU 1–MON 5 ★ Discuss your concerns rationally for the best outcome

SAT 10–TUE 13 ★ You're struggling to gain clarity about the future

TUE 20–SAT 24 ★ **SUPER NOVA DAYS** It's tough to know when to call it quits

THU 29 ★ Let go of your hold on the past; say hello to your future

CANCER OVERVIEW

Friends and colleagues bring an abundance of connections your way in the first half of the year with fortunate Jupiter in your 11th House of Groups until June 11. Having the support of others and aligning yourself with a cause you believe in provide a strong foundation for growth throughout 2012. No matter how idealistic the individual or organization, it's essential that you put practical considerations first. Taking on obligations when you're unclear on goals and procedures can be demanding and exhausting. Steady progress within a solid structure will get you farther than brilliant ideas built on mere hopes and wishes. On June 11, Jupiter skips into flexible Gemini and your spiritual 12th House, where it will cast light on life's deepest mysteries until June 25, 2013. **There is a wealth of soul-nourishing information available to you if you're willing to open up your mind and explore alternative belief systems.** The truths you find most meaningful may not come in one integrated package but as bits and pieces from a variety of sources. Observing the world and your own thoughts without making judgments is a powerful way to enhance your learning and expand your mind.

Expect waves of inspiration and awareness to head your way when imaginative Neptune enters Pisces and your 9th House of Higher Thought on February 3. This transit initiates a period of discovery that encourages you to broaden your perspective by pursuing travel and educational opportunities. If you're touched by the teacher or the subject matter, your soul will grow as much as your mind. But if you're simply striving to polish your résumé, you may be worn out by the struggle. Studying harder won't produce the results that finding meaning and purpose in your educational pursuit will provide. When you really care about the subject, you will absorb information easily. A challenging square between Jupiter and Neptune on June 25 can mark a period of overexpansion when your appetite for travel, learning, or religious experiences is greater than your capacity to absorb it. **It's terrific to be enthusiastic about broadening your horizons, yet avoid spreading yourself so thin that the costs exceed the benefits.**

Saturn, the planet that lays down the law, dictates that keeping order on the home front is vital for you this year. Saturn in Libra occupies your 4th House of Security until October 5, signaling the need for harmony in your surroundings.

You may need to make peace with cohabitants and create a more attractive environment if you hope to establish a constructive atmosphere. **Compromising with relatives isn't always easy, but with patience and maturity you should find ways to overcome any significant differences.** This is also a year when thoughts of starting a new business or a different career could be appealing. Yet if you spend all of your time trying to make your mark in the world, your foundation may become shaky. Don't lose sight of the importance of maintaining a happy home life that will support your ambitions.

FOLLOW YOUR FEELINGS

Your resourcefulness in handling relationship issues will be evident with the Full Moon in your sign on January 9. Mars in efficient Virgo aligns favorably with this lunation, supplying you with the sharpness of mind and focused intentions that can help you clean up a messy situation. Emotions, though, take over when the Scorpio Full Moon on May 5 lights up your 5th House of Romance. Passion can push reason aside, especially with a lunar opposition to boundless Jupiter. Yet there's something positive about totally opening your heart to reveal your true feelings. Desires to go farther with your current partner or to make radical personal changes reach a turning point when the Scorpio New Moon falls in your 5th House on November 13. This is a total Solar Eclipse that can play a major role in your love life. It's understandable that you want to make those you care about happy, given your nurturing nature, but remember that putting a lid on your heart will only reduce your chances for fulfillment or postpone an inevitable change.

A GREAT LEAP FORWARD

Revolutionary Uranus has been stirring up changes in your 10th House of Career since May 2010; it begins a transformative series of squares with potent Pluto on June 24 that returns on September 19 and recurs five more times through 2015. These aspects can deepen your urges for independence and innovation, which can turn your work life in a radically new direction. Power struggles, extreme pressure, or simple boredom and a bright idea are enough to get you moving forward. The enterprising Aries New Moon on March 22 and Full Moon on September 29 are key times when a crisis or sudden awakening provides the impetus to push you into taking action.

TURN LOSS INTO GAIN

On January 23, the progressive Aquarius New Moon occurs in your 8th House of Shared Resources, leading you to reappraise your financial alliances. Untangle yourself from partnerships that inhibit your cash flow or fail to give you a fair return on your investments of time and money. Innovative Aquarius inspires you to look outside the box to discover fresh ways to terminate or repair a floundering economic union or even to find a more rewarding one. A period of uncertainty should end with the proud Leo New Moon in your 2nd House of Income on August 17 bumping up your confidence. Stability and productivity are additional bonuses with solid sextiles from disciplined Saturn and hardworking Mars, supporting your creative ideas for making more money.

VACATION THERAPY

Chiron the Wounded Healer is in your 9th House of Faraway Places, suggesting that you can find comfort and solace when you're able to travel and leave your troubles back at home. The Sagittarius Full Moon on June 4 is a Lunar Eclipse in your 6th House of Health that could challenge you to make adjustments in your daily habits. A close square from hyperactive Mars to the Full Moon amplifies tension on the job, but its primary purpose is to trigger you to change your diet or initiate a new exercise routine. If you're already physically active, however, this may be a cautionary reminder to not push your body too hard.

FINDING BALANCE

Stern Saturn's transit through your 4th House of Roots that began in October 2009 has been demanding that you show more maturity and discipline in order to maintain a harmonious home life. On April 6, the Libra Full Moon illuminates your 4th House, possibly exposing a conflict between public responsibilities and private needs. You may be unable to resolve tension on the home front without making some adjustments in your job to reduce the workload so you can concentrate on personal matters. However, you'll need to stay as objective as possible until October 5, when Saturn finally leaves your domestic 4th House. Circumstances should begin to lighten up at home, which gives you a chance to focus on more creative pursuits.

THE COST OF DREAMS

If you hit the road during the first half of the year, it's essential that you stay comfortable; Jupiter, the traditional ruler of your 9th House of Travel, is snuggling up in cozy and indulgent Taurus until June 11. Your willingness to explore unfamiliar territory grows as Jupiter passes into curious and adaptable Gemini. On June 25, this giant planet's challenging square with mystical Neptune, the planetary ruler of your 9th House, inspires you to take a journey that may lift your spirits but wear out your body or bank account. Striking a balance between a fascinating escape and budgetary and physical limits could be critical.

JOURNEY OF AWAKENING

The Gemini New Moon on May 20 is a Solar Eclipse square Neptune that enriches your intuition. Still, don't let your hunger for uncovering life's mysteries drive you to fall for teachers who don't match their rhetoric with compassion and kindness. Philosophical Jupiter's entry into your 12th House of Spirituality on June 11 initiates a year of metaphysical awareness and soul growth. Recognizing that there are many paths toward enlightenment reduces your tendency to judge yourself and others.

RICK & JEFF'S TIP FOR THE YEAR:
Calm at Your Center

Making peace with yourself and with family members could be the most valuable thing you do all year. It creates a fertile ground of self-love and trust to nourish all your aspirations. The magic that makes this happen is simply being fair to yourself, neither harshly blaming yourself for your mistakes nor overinflating your successes. Your potential to get ahead in the eyes of the world is closely connected to your ability to this harmonious sense of balance within.

JANUARY

STATE YOUR CASE

Relationships are a key issue now with the Sun in your 7th House of Partners until **January 20** and in your 8th House of Intimacy for the rest of the month. Be clear about what you expect from others if you hope to make improvements in your personal and professional alliances. Communicative Mercury marks a significant transition on **January 8** when it leaves optimistic Sagittarius and enters orderly Capricorn, where a lack of planning and commitment may put you under someone else's control. The nurturing Cancer Full Moon in your sign on the **9th** reminds you to consider your own needs first. Making the satisfaction of a lover, friend, or co-worker your top priority is bound to leave you in second place. If you take care of yourself, though, you'll have the emotional and physical strength to also be of service to others.

Paying such close attention to relationships and keeping everyone happy can tire you and leave you dreaming of escape. It's tempting to think about running away from it all when alluring Venus enters your 9th House of Faraway Places on the **14th**. Your imagination opens your mind to foreign lands, where you are free from responsibility and the complications of your current life. Take these impressions as inspiration for future travel, but don't lose touch with the realities of the present. The New Moon in quirky Aquarius falls in your 8th House on **January 23**, attracting unconventional individuals and potential partnerships. If you stretch your boundaries, you'll increase opportunities for love and money. Just don't lose your sense of perspective when expansive Jupiter's square to this Sun-Moon conjunction tempts you with promises too good to be true.

KEEP IN MIND THIS MONTH

You'll earn more respect by saying no with certainty than by compromising simply to maintain the peace.

KEY DATES

JANUARY 8–9 ★ *straight shooter*

There's no room for lazy thinking or careless communication when Mercury the Messenger enters your 7th House of Others on **January 8**. Express yourself with authority or keep your thoughts to yourself. You're going to be held accountable for every word, even offhand remarks. However, you have a more powerful impact on your listeners when you consider issues carefully and plan out what you're going to say. A slick sextile from meticulous Mars in Virgo to the Cancer Full Moon on the **9th** is a gentle nudge to organize your life. Initiating a new health regime is an excellent way to boost your vitality and increase your productivity.

JANUARY 13–14 ★ *get to the heart of the matter*

Discretion is critical on **January 13**, when a punchy conjunction of Mercury and penetrating Pluto in your relational 7th House stimulates deep conversations. Spilling secrets could cause serious damage now. If you're well prepared and stay focused, though, you can cut through the clutter of confusion and make some powerful points. Mental toughness softens on the **14th** when Venus glides into velvety Pisces to touch your emotions. Affectionate feelings and a sense of compassion help you let go of recent conflicts and enjoy pleasurable experiences. Getting away from your usual surroundings is your ticket to magical moments that will open your heart and inspire your dreams.

SUPER NOVA DAYS

JANUARY 19–23 ★ *risky business*

You just might reach a limit with someone when the Sun forms a tense square with sobering Saturn on **January 19**. Recognizing exactly where you stand helps you shore up worthwhile alliances—but can mark the beginning of the end for one where trust has been lost. Your intuition about people and values is accurate on the **20th**, when Venus forms a discerning sextile with perceptive Pluto, enabling you to see if there's something in an investment or a relationship to be salvaged. An adventurous spirit invites a new person into your life or provokes you to seek unusual experiences on **January 21–22**. The courageous Sun's connections with eccentric Uranus and visionary Jupiter make stimulation more important than security. Messages are mixed on the **23rd**: The Aquarius New Moon makes you feel frisky, yet active Mars turns retrograde, reminding you for the next three months to look twice before leaping.

JANUARY 27 ★ *don't give up*

A Mercury-Saturn square makes it hard to obtain the answers that you desire today. Just because you receive a negative response, though, doesn't mean that the discussion is over. Fortunately, Mercury shifts into Aquarius and your 8th House of Deep Sharing, enabling negotiations to resume and, perhaps, ultimately lead to a different outcome.

FEBRUARY

DO YOU BELIEVE IN MAGIC?

Gentle waves of inspiration start lapping at the shore of your life this month when prophetic Neptune returns to idealistic Pisces on **February 3**. The planet of faith, compassion, and imagination is reentering your 9th House of Higher Mind, where it began seeding a field of dreams in its previous visit on **April 4–August 4, 2011**. You'll continue exploring religious and philosophical ideas and interests in faraway cultures until Neptune leaves this visionary part of your chart in **May 2025**. Still, this planet's influence is often subtle, more suggestive than direct in the ways it affects your life. However, reinforcing patterns later this month multiply its impact. First, there's the dramatic Leo Full Moon activating your 2nd House of Income on **February 7** and casting a bright light on financial matters. Penny pinching will not save you cash and, in fact, can inhibit your capacity to earn money. Investing in your creative abilities requires confidence, yet should prove rewarding on many levels.

Mental Mercury shifts into Pisces on **February 13**, followed by the Sun's move into this imaginative sign on **February 19**. Putting your thoughts into words may be impossible—you're flooded with feelings that stretch the boundaries of language. The Sun-Neptune conjunction, also on the **19th**, and its close proximity to the Pisces New Moon on the **21st** float balloons of hope and fantasy. You may find it difficult to keep your feet on the ground and your head out of the clouds, yet if you can maintain contact with reality, an infusion of faith will lead you to a more fulfilling vision of the future.

KEEP IN MIND THIS MONTH

Seek the higher ground of wisdom and meaning, where you can find answers to material and personal questions through spiritual insights.

KEY DATES

FEBRUARY 1 ★ *wordplay*

Your conversation snaps today, bringing edginess to relationships when feisty Mars in your 3rd House of Communication opposes flirtatious Venus. The mood can be sexy and sassy as long as you're willing to be playful with words instead of taking everything that's said too seriously. Connecting with someone in an educational setting can turn a learning experience into a significant social event.

SUPER NOVA DAYS

FEBRUARY 6–9 ★ *all shook up*

You're restless and full of unusual ideas on **February 6**, thanks to hard aspects to Uranus from the Sun and Mercury. Sudden changes of mind or surprising news adds to a sense of uncertainty leading up to the melodramatic Leo Full Moon on **February 7**. Take a long, slow look at the situation before you rush into action or say something you might regret. Responsible Saturn is turning retrograde in your interactive 3rd House, reminding you to rethink your strategy carefully before sharing it with others. Nevertheless, you struggle to obey the speed limit when Venus fires into unstoppable Aries and your 10th House of Career on **February 8**. Frustration with outmoded rules or an inflexible authority figure stirs up your rebellious attitude, especially when artistic Venus joins maverick Uranus on the **9th**. Making business connections or brainstorming fresh ideas related to your work can bring more excitement to your job. Don't jump ship until you've got a sure place to land since it's possible that your ideas may be ahead of their time.

FEBRUARY 14–15 ★ *the true cost of love*

You enjoy romantic thoughts on **February 14**, Valentine's Day, but what you hear and say is probably based more on faith than facts. A whimsical conjunction of Mercury and dreamy Neptune paints the day in pastel colors that keep reality at bay. Enjoying moments of delight with a loved one is fine as long as you don't make promises or buy into any that can't be kept. Be cautious in matters of the heart when loving Venus forms a stressful square with exigent Pluto on **February 15**. The price you'll pay for believing in fantasies can be higher than you expect. Calculating what you're required to give for what you get in return is a good way to assess the value of any alliance.

FEBRUARY 23–25 ★ *war and peace*

You may see an old argument resurface on the **23rd**, when querulous Mercury opposes retrograde Mars in your conversational 3rd House. Be sure that you and the other person are on the same page, because miscommunication can compound your differences. Opening your mind to a broader point of view helps you overcome conflict when the Sun sextiles magnanimous Jupiter on **February 25**.

MARCH

PROFESSIONAL PUSH

Making your mark in the world through your job or another public arena is among your primary goals this month. Planets are popping in your 10th House of Career and Community, offering fresh challenges and new opportunities for getting ahead. Quicksilver Mercury fires into Aries and your 10th House on **March 2**, sparking new ideas and spurring you to pick up the pace at work. The expressive Sun goes next into audacious Aries on **March 20**, the Vernal Equinox, followed by the New Moon, also in the 10th House, on **March 22** that's bound to increase the demands of your public life. Independent Uranus's conjunction with the Aries New Moon brings unexpected changes of status or responsibility. You could be feeling restless and ready to strike out on your own.

If you suddenly realize that a radical shift in your career is what you need, take plenty of time to think it through, because rational Mercury turns retrograde on **March 12** and will backtrack until **April 4**. This is a time to look back at your previous work experiences and reexamine your current choices more thoughtfully. You may reconnect with a colleague from your past whose insights clarify your thinking. If nothing else, redoing recent work is another potential consequence of Mercury's backward cycle. Venus, the planet of values and self-worth, enters earthy Taurus and your 11th House of Groups on **March 5**. There's pleasure to be gained from participating in an organization where others share the workload. The critical Virgo Full Moon on **March 8** occurs in your 3rd House of Information, reminding you to organize your ideas and communicate them more precisely.

KEEP IN MIND THIS MONTH

Holding your position at work takes considerable effort, but looking ahead for something more exciting fires you with fresh resolve.

KEY DATES

MARCH 2–4 ★ *stand up for yourself*

Challenges at home demand your concentration on **March 2**, but you'll eventually achieve the results you seek if you know what you want and commit to seeing it through. The Sun's opposition to assertive Mars on **March 3** stimulates lively discussions that may lead to conflict. Your beliefs might not align with your current circumstances, forcing you to make a practical decision that could compromise your principles. You may have to accept less than you hope for with a tight-fisted

Venus-Saturn opposition on the **4th**. If you're feeling lonely or underappreciated, express your feelings clearly and work for what you want instead of giving in to self-doubt or despair.

SUPER NOVA DAYS

MARCH 13–14 ★ *winning streak*

You can turn an adversary into an ally or revive a faltering relationship on **March 13**, when regenerative Pluto in your 7th House of Others forms a unifying trine with optimistic Jupiter. Playful and generous pals turn an ordinary day into a party on **March 14** as sweet Venus joins Jupiter to complete a supportive Grand Earth Trine with Pluto and Mars. Creative collaboration fills you with energy, while your new enthusiasm increases your ambitions and clears a path to success. The lines between work and play are likely to blur when you're having such an inspiring time with your colleagues.

MARCH 18 ★ *delayed launch*

Your mind says *go-go-go* today, while circumstances require you to act with restraint. Mercury joins Uranus to generate unusual ideas and insights about your professional goals. However, an ungainly quincunx between the Sun and Saturn can sidetrack you from pursuing them. You grow frustrated when your brain's moving so fast in a world moving too slowly. Settle down, there's unfinished business to complete before you can take off on your flights of intellectual fancy.

MARCH 24 ★ *time is on your side*

Your patience may run out with an explosive Sun-Uranus conjunction occurring in your responsible 10th House. You're strongly tempted to escape your obligations and rebel against authority. What you're glimpsing, however, is a more exciting future that will take time to create. Plant your vision in a garden of commitment where you can lovingly and gently guide it from a wild idea into a desirable reality.

MARCH 29 ★ *search your soul*

Today's Sun-Pluto square can undermine your trust in a boss or cost you the confidence of others. Are you on a rewarding professional path that requires increased intensity to take you to the next level, or is this where you want to get off? Look deeply within to connect with your true desires; this is the key to making the best decision.

APRIL

FRESH START

Insightful Pluto turns retrograde on **April 10**, inviting you to look back and review issues about power and desire, but the major trends for this month signal forward movement on two fronts. Intellectual Mercury's shift to direct motion in your 9th House of Journeys on **April 4** encourages you to think about the future, especially as it relates to travel and education. You'll soon be ready to apply philosophical ideas that you've been mulling over in your mind to your daily life. And on **April 13**, Mars, the planet of action and initiative, finally ends a retrograde cycle that began on **January 23**, freeing up energy you've been spending fighting over petty details and wrestling with complicated conversations. Mars's direct turn is a green light for advancing on projects that have been derailed or delayed. Still, be sure to manage them efficiently, especially since popular Venus shifts into flighty Gemini and your 12th House of Escapism on **April 3**, scattering your attention.

On **April 6**, domestic issues take the spotlight when the Full Moon in cooperative Libra falls in your 4th House of Home and Family. You may need to make compromises to maintain harmony or to get out of your own emotional rut. Remember, there's more than one way to look at any situation no matter how personal it is in the moment. Stepping back from your feelings gives you an objective perspective that increases your options at work and at home. The New Moon in Taurus on **April 21** falls in your 11th House of Groups and aligns favorably with Mars in industrious Virgo—an excellent moment for launching projects with friends or colleagues.

KEEP IN MIND THIS MONTH

Letting go of the past is your key to creating a more fulfilling future. Finish what you can and drop whatever you can't improve.

KEY DATES

SUPER NOVA DAYS

APRIL 6–9 ★ *lighten your load*

The Libra Full Moon's intense square with Pluto will reveal secrets or stir up deeply buried emotions on **April 6**. This month's theme is all about moving ahead, and now you are given another opportunity to face an old issue and finally put it behind you. A spicy square between flirty Venus and frisky Mars makes your social life more interesting the next day, especially if you're able to adapt to unexpected changes of plans or tolerate inconsistent people. Staying cool, though, might not be easy as a harsh Sun-Mars aspect on the **8th** fuels impatience or attracts a bully. Fortunately, a clever sextile occurs between Venus and inventive Uranus on **April 9**, opening your eyes to new pleasures and ways to handle relationships that are less confining and, hopefully, more fun.

APRIL 16 ★ *out of sync*

Fast thinking and sluggish people make this a complicated day. Talkative Mercury races into fiery Aries and your 10th House of Career, speeding up communication, especially related to professional matters. Yet pleasure-seeking Venus is bogged down with a clunky sesquisquare from Saturn that can delay gratification and limit recognition. These contrasting events supply common sense and practicality to keep you from wasting time on exciting but unrealistic ideas. Luckily, your innate skill for locating scarce resources helps you afford the ones that will work.

APRIL 21–22 ★ *unexpected epiphany*

Your lunar-ruled sign responds emotionally to the Taurus New Moon in your 11th House of Groups on **April 21**. Taurus is sensual, stubborn, practical, and inherently resistant to change. But this union of the Sun and Moon initiates a fresh cycle of activities with friends and co-workers that could put you in a leadership position within an organization. You could invent a way to bridge the real and the ideal, for this lunation creates positive aspects with Mars in pragmatic Virgo and ethereal Neptune in Pisces. Avoid making a major commitment until you experience the brilliantly original Mercury-Uranus conjunction in Aries on **April 22**. Lightning storms of intuition and restlessness electrify your 10th House of Career with sudden realizations that cause you to rethink your plans and responsibilities.

APRIL 29 ★ *spirit of generosity*

You might reconnect today with someone from the past or rediscover rewards in a fading relationship. That's due to a restorative trine between the heart-centered Sun and passionate Pluto. Your emotions grow bold, too, with the Moon visiting theatrical Leo and your 2nd House of Self-Worth. Giving more of yourself in joyful and generous ways is likely to bring you even more in return.

GET OFF THE FENCE

You shine in group situations through much of the month as the Sun continues to occupy your 11th House of Friends and Associates until **May 20**. Information-rich Mercury joins the party in dependable Taurus on the **9th**, spurring communication, contacts, and ideas when you're part of a team. Yet no matter how busy you are with others, you're also pulled toward privacy—tempted to leave the spotlight and seek out quiet places where less human interaction is required. Venus, the planet of sociability, slows down in your secretive 12th House, turns retrograde on **May 15**, and moves backward until **June 27**. You won't disappear from sight, but you'll appreciate any opportunities you find to step away from daily activities and take a more objective view of your life. Figuring out where you fit in is important as visionary Jupiter forms stressful aspects with Saturn and Pluto on **May 16–17**. You may need to reassess what you want out of relationships and reevaluate your long-range plans.

The Gemini New Moon on **May 20** is a Lunar Eclipse falling in your 12th House and squaring dreamy Neptune, which increases your sensitivity to the point where you may want to run away from it all. Escaping on a well-earned vacation or spiritual retreat is a good way to recharge your batteries and restore your faith. However, it's critical not to space out practical matters—they will become muddled if you let your attention wander too long. In fact, this eclipse signals the need to cut out distractions and focus on a single truth to guide you instead of allowing yourself to be pulled in several spiritual directions.

KEEP IN MIND THIS MONTH

Your usual sources of inspiration may fail you now. Instead, explore your soul and come up with your own answers.

KEY DATES

MAY 5 ★ *actions speak louder than words*

Passion builds with an emotionally intense Scorpio Full Moon in your 5th House of Romance on **May 5**. Your growing need to play and express yourself may provoke you to share your desires more openly. Yet regardless of the strength of your feelings now, you may not be able to describe them in words. A restrictive Mercury-Saturn opposition suggests that it's wise to keep some thoughts to yourself. Still, you can communicate so much with your eyes and actions that explanations aren't necessary.

MAY 12–13 ★ *leader of the pack*

Group dynamics are unpredictable on the **12th**, when restless Uranus makes an itchy semisquare with the Sun in your 11th House of Friends and Associates. Don't back down from a challenge, though, since the Sun joins auspicious Jupiter on **May 13**, infusing you with a renewed sense of purpose. You may finally receive some well-deserved recognition, motivating you to play a more expansive role in changing the world around you.

MAY 16–17 ★ *stay on target*

Beware strong differences of opinions, which could sidetrack your long-term plans right now. The tension is thick in the air due to stressful aspects to judgmental Jupiter from stodgy Saturn on **May 16** and punishing Pluto on the **17th**. Fortunately, a laser-like Mars-Pluto trine on **May 16** should help you to eliminate most distractions and focus on finishing essential tasks. Avoid the temptation to listen to everyone's advice or respond to their needs; don't lose sight of your own priorities.

SUPER NOVA DAYS

MAY 22–23 ★ *reserve judgment*

You understand interpersonal dynamics and receive ongoing support from intelligent allies thanks to a smart Mercury-Jupiter conjunction in Taurus on **May 22**. This union of the planets of little details and big principles sharpens your perceptions. Acute knowledge of your colleagues' talents makes you a better teammate and a skillful motivator. However, excessive compassion could drain you when the Sun squares empathetic Neptune on **May 23**. Believing in someone who is unable to live up to his or her promises costs you precious resources, so soak in the stories you're hearing but don't commit to acting on any of them without further research.

MAY 29–30 ★ *better left unsaid*

Fear and mistrust are lurking about as the Sun tangles with Saturn and Pluto on the **29th**. It's never appropriate to give in to threats, but recognizing who holds the cards will help you play your hand wisely. Patience works better than pushiness now, yet you may find it impossible to suppress your urge to act or speak up. Mouthy Mercury forms an argumentative square with Mars on **May 30** that tempts you to spill secrets, even at your own expense.

JUNE

CREATIVE VISUALIZATION

You clean up unfinished business from the past as this transitional month opens, freeing up time and energy to pursue new interests. On **June 4**, a Sagittarius Full Moon Eclipse in your 6th House of Work is charged with an anxious square from Mars that can bring additional stress to your job, overload you with obligations, and even wear you down physically. Cut out extraneous activities that don't teach you anything; turn your attention to developing skills and exploring hobbies that broaden your horizons. Spiritual growth is encouraged when wise Jupiter moves into multifaceted Gemini and your 12th House of Divinity for a one-year stay starting on **June 11**. The planet of philosophy's presence in this imaginative part of your chart increases your curiosity about the meaning of life, opening your mind to learning from a variety of sources.

Practicality and idealism converge later this month, giving shape to your dreams. Realistic Saturn turns direct in your 4th House of Roots on the **25th**, making it easier to build a solid foundation for your ambitions, while an intuitive square between Jupiter and Neptune excites your mind on the same day. Normally, this hard aspect between astrology's most expansive planets produces more fantasy than functionality, but reliable Saturn's forward shift at the same time provides the substance you need to bring your visions down to earth. Another dose of originality is provided on the **25th** when Mercury moves into Leo and your 2nd House of Resources. Bold thinking can now increase your self-worth—and your income. Venus's direct turn on the **27th** adds momentum to your financial picture.

KEEP IN MIND THIS MONTH

Making space in your busy schedule for daydreaming is not an escape from reality but an excellent way to create a better future.

KEY DATES

JUNE 7–8 ★ *subjective reality*

Your mental clarity sharpens and your ability to articulate your emotions grows when Mercury enters your introspective sign on the **7th**. This intellectual planet swimming in watery Cancer floods facts with feelings to facilitate intimate conversations while also, perhaps, reducing your objectivity and comprehension of abstract ideas. Miscommunication could trigger conflict over petty issues with a quarrelsome Sun-Mars square, yet you could be motivated to take action when led by a skillful teacher. Discussions grow softer and sweeter on the **8th** with a Mercury-Neptune trine that reveals common ground between previously opposing positions.

JUNE 11 ★ *suspicious minds*

Your brain is buzzing as Mercury forms a stressful square with electric Uranus this afternoon and a tense opposition with provocative Pluto at night. Strange thoughts and surprises shake your world, but a flexible attitude can refresh your brain with new and intriguing perspectives. You might feel that someone is manipulating you even when he or she is not. If trust is melting with miscomprehension, it may simply be hypersensitivity to words that makes simple requests sound like commands.

SUPER NOVA DAYS

JUNE 19–20 ★ *starting over*

You are spreading yourself too thin and need to establish some clear priorities to regain control of your life—and the Gemini New Moon on **June 19** marks the beginning of the end. Sweeping out the old is perfect preparation for the Summer Solstice on the **20th**, when the Sun enters sentimental Cancer to begin your astrological year. A smart sextile between retrograde Venus and innovative Uranus gives you a chance to reexamine relationships and resources and uncover unconventional ways to get the most out of them.

JUNE 23–24 ★ *brave new world*

Self-doubt and rejection lead to ruffled feathers thanks to a stingy Venus-Saturn sesquisquare on the afternoon of the **23rd**, but a compassionate Sun-Neptune trine that night smooths things over. On **June 24**, the first revolutionary Uranus-Pluto square in a series that ends in **March 2015** begins to shake the Earth. Your part in this transformational process is to connect with powerful allies who can assist you in changing your professional and public perspectives.

JUNE 29 ★ *creative chaos*

When the Sun slams through a Uranus-Pluto square today, you can expect conflict with people in power over you or—if you're the one in authority—crises with those below you. Fortunately, a thoughtful Mercury-Jupiter sextile enhances communication skills and broadens your frame of reference. You now have the flexibility to maneuver around protracted problems and tactfully suggest solutions. Work to maintain constructive discussions in search of a variety of responses rather than insisting there is only one right answer.

JULY

CURB YOUR ENTHUSIASM

Boundless Jupiter in Gemini in your imaginative 12th House is scattering your energy in more directions than you can possibly go. Challenging aspects from Jupiter to ruthless Pluto and austere Saturn on **July 18–20** begin a pruning process that won't finish until next spring. If you feel as if you've been running around in circles, now's the time to take a strategic view of your plans and establish priorities that will produce tangible results rather than frustration. Don't be afraid to back away from a project while you reconsider its long-term costs and benefits. Mercury's retrograde turn on **July 14** occurs in your 2nd House of Resources, reminding you that additional fine-tuning and adjustments are necessary until this trickster planet turns direct on **August 8**. You may want to boldly push ahead and make an extravagant purchase, but don't let the glitz of the moment cause a lapse in your usually cautious spending patterns.

This month's lunations are significant events that could dramatically affect your life. The Full Moon in Capricorn on **July 3** joins pressurized Pluto in your 7th House of Partners and squares rebellious Uranus, which can intensify desires and sow seeds of uncertainty while stirring up mistrust and fomenting power struggles. The complex emotions and shifting circumstances in personal and professional partnerships may require you to take a stand and restore order around the New Moon in Cancer on the **19th**. Strict Saturn's demanding square to this Sun-Moon conjunction is a clear call for increasing self-discipline that will help you set appropriate boundaries. Fortunately, a breakthrough Jupiter-Uranus sextile on the **22nd** brings exciting opportunities that can present a surprising twist in your path to success.

KEEP IN MIND THIS MONTH

You may not be able to control the world around you, but you can create inner peace by responding to it with maturity and patience.

KEY DATES

SUPER NOVA DAYS

JULY 3–4 ★ *saving grace*

Initiating projects at home and keeping the peace within the family absorb you thanks to Mars's entry into gracious Libra and your 4th House of Roots on **July 3**. You'll need your diplomacy, objectivity, and social expertise with the Capricorn Full Moon illuminating your 7th House of Relationships. Difficult aspects to intense Pluto and explosive Uranus allow you to move through a wall of tension if you're clear about your intentions. However, you can't rely on past patterns to predict future needs. Fortunately, friendly Venus's accommodating sextile with brilliant Uranus can suddenly reveal alternative ways to connect with others on **July 4**.

JULY 13–15 ★ *the man in the mirror*

Check whether your heart and head are in the same place right now, because radical Uranus turns retrograde on **July 13**, as does rational Mercury the following day. Take your time and be sure that what you're thinking corresponds with your emotional needs. The big schemes you proposed thanks to an inflationary Sun-Jupiter semi-square on the **13th** run into a wall of resistance when the Sun squares taskmaster Saturn on the **15th**, quickly showing you what's required to turn your vision into reality.

JULY 19 ★ *from the ground up*

The New Moon in your sign pushes your life in a fresh direction. However, you may be slow getting your plan off the ground, because unyielding Saturn in your 4th House of Foundations harshly squares this lunation. Managing a messy domestic situation or addressing housing issues may delay your plans but will offer you a more solid base of support upon which to build your future.

JULY 24–25 ★ *stroke of genius*

Retrograde Mercury's slick sextile with Jupiter reawakens old aspirations and beliefs on **July 24**. Applying the insights you're receiving, though, may be tricky with a slippery Sun-Neptune quincunx that can drain or distract you. However, a brilliant Mercury-Uranus trine on **July 25** reignites your mind with a unique perspective that helps you leap over doubts and develop shortcuts to achieving your goals.

JULY 31 ★ *claim your future*

Today you can straddle the divide between caution and risk by discovering and applying previously untapped talents and abilities. The creative Sun in your 2nd House of Self-Worth forms a supportive trine with Uranus that encourages you to take chances in your professional life. A financially and socially adept Venus-Saturn trine supplies a material and emotional safety net that balances your desire to escape the limits of your current situation with a realistic assessment of your resources and your relationships.

AUGUST

AIM FOR THE STARS

This should be a very productive month for you since there are three lunations forming favorable aspects with energetic Mars. On **August 1**, the Aquarius Full Moon falls in your 8th House of Deep Sharing. You find it easy to work with unconventional individuals as Mars in amenable Libra and Jupiter in versatile Gemini form a lucky Grand Trine with the Moon. Your ability to adapt to unusual circumstances is also strengthened by progressive Uranus's inventive sextile to the Moon. You're able to see relationships in a different light that opens your mind, overcomes your fear, and helps you to make profitable new connections. The lively Leo New Moon on **August 17** activates your 2nd House of Resources, combining boldness and creativity with efficiency as it sextiles an industrious Mars-Saturn conjunction. This union of two hard-nosed planets in your 4th House of Roots will reward your inner dedication and discipline with the potential for greater income and increasing self-confidence.

The month's second Full Moon—the so-called Blue Moon, which has no special astrological significance—occurs in mystical Pisces and your 9th House of Philosophy on **August 31**. Her trine to Mars in resolute Scorpio and easy sextile with surgical Pluto creates a perfect moment to pluck a dream from your imagination and find the passion it takes to actualize it. This also encourages you to make a commitment to your beliefs by doing charitable work, initiating a spiritual practice, or volunteering for a cause dear to your heart. Idealism and intensity make an unbeatable pair that enables you to let go of the people and expectations that distract you from this higher road to fulfillment.

KEEP IN MIND THIS MONTH

There is too much energy available to you now to use it on anything less important than striving for your highest aspirations.

KEY DATES

AUGUST 2–3 ★ *easy does it*

Use a delicate touch to keep from ruffling feathers with a supersensitive Sun-Venus semisquare on **August 2**. It's advisable to distance yourself from others' critical judgments, which may sting more than usual. An emotional Mars-Neptune aspect on the **3rd** can wear you out with a battle at home—or motivate you, if you're able to channel your frustration into an inspiring project instead.

AUGUST 7–8 ★ *your stock is rising*

Beautiful Venus enters your sign on **August 7** to remind you how sweet life can be when you stop worrying so much. A heightened awareness of your own worth and your desires adds warmth and affection to relationships and increases your value at work. This doesn't necessarily mean others will give you what you want, but simply taking pleasure in yourself and your environment makes you a more desirable partner. Mental Mercury's direct turn on **August 8** slowly frees you to express your wishes in the weeks ahead. Making a pitch to obtain love, approval, or financing is more likely to succeed prior to **September 6**, when magnetic Venus leaves Cancer.

AUGUST 15–17 ★ *cleanup on aisle five*

A fierce face-off between Venus and Pluto shows you exactly where you stand with someone. Flattery doesn't work when you're looking for substantial connections, and manipulation is a major hindrance to trust. Mars joins authoritative Saturn to make it very clear where you can build and when it's time to close up shop. These two hard aspects aren't light and breezy, but they do provide the clarity you need to complete unfinished business before the Leo New Moon on the **17th**.

SUPER NOVA DAYS

AUGUST 22–24 ★ *adrenaline rush*

Your mind is clear and your thinking is incisive on **August 22** thanks to the Sun's entry into analytical Virgo and your chatty 3rd House. Additionally, a Mercury-Jupiter sextile brings finesse to your communication. Your energy continues to deepen and grow when Mars moves into passionate Scorpio and your 5th House of Romance on the **23rd**; your quiet intensity evokes powerful responses from others. Whether you are pursuing pleasure or promoting a creative plan, the force of your will is directed with laser-like focus. Still, a diffusive Sun-Neptune opposition on the **24th** reminds you to ask specific questions to make sure that your words are completely understood.

AUGUST 26 ★ *dare to believe*

You can push others without appearing pushy today if you adopt a gentle approach. You have the sensitivity to handle fragile partnerships and address difficult issues with plenty of compassion and tenderness. Joining up with an ally for a creative project or in pursuit of a mutual dream allows intuition and imagination to contribute to an inspired collaboration.

SEPTEMBER

STICK TO THE FACTS

You enjoy a growing momentum for success this month, by managing data and communicating in a clear and concise manner. September starts with the Sun shining in your 3rd House of Information and Education, which can increase curiosity, facilitate learning, and empower your words with practicality and precision. On **September 15**, the practical Virgo New Moon also highlights your 3rd House, where it's joined by cerebral Mercury. This alignment can cultivate your interest in taking a class to deepen your study of a useful subject. It isn't about exploring abstract ideas or collecting data; it's about developing skills that make you a more knowledgeable and confident speaker. This Sun-Moon conjunction also allows you to step out of the subjectivity of your emotions to recognize habitual patterns of behavior that limit your potential. The point isn't to punish your crimes or put yourself down; it's about adopting a realistic approach to a healthier and more positive lifestyle that will allow you to be at your ultimate best in whatever you do.

Profound Pluto turns direct on **September 18**, followed by its second of seven squares with shocking Uranus on the **19th**. Transits from Mercury, Mars, and Venus on **September 20** and **September 25–26** trigger profound changes, sudden shifts of thinking, and unexpected events. The Sun's entry into likable Libra and your 4th House of Roots on **September 22** marks the Autumn Equinox in the Northern Hemisphere—and a possible tipping point in domestic matters. The impetuous Aries Full Moon in your 10th House of Career on the **29th** propels you to take a fresh look at your responsibilities, both personal and professional, as you may be ready for a radical change of direction.

KEEP IN MIND THIS MONTH

If you can handle the minor details of your daily life more efficiently, you'll free up time, energy, and mindshare for addressing bigger issues.

KEY DATES

SEPTEMBER 3 ★ *no holds barred*

Kind Venus runs into a harsh square with dour Saturn today that can delay rewards, complicate a relationship, or reduce your sense of self-worth. Yet you can still gain love and recognition if you overcome uncertainty and take a stand on your own behalf. An empowering sextile from fearless Mars in your 5th House of Romance to brutally honest Pluto in your 7th House of Partners helps you push past politeness to eliminate who and what you don't want and focus on getting what you need.

SEPTEMBER 6–8 ★ *if the price is right*

You grow extravagant as Venus moves into luxury-loving Leo and your 2nd House of Resources on **September 6**. Purchases that pump up your prestige may be worth the money if a higher status arouses your courage and creativity. Be careful not to go too far, however, when the Sun and Mercury square exorbitant Jupiter on **September 7–8**. Stretching yourself to reach for a higher prize is fine as long as you carefully calculate the costs of fulfilling your dreams.

SEPTEMBER 15–16 ★ *focus on the future*

The Virgo New Moon on the **15th** sharpens your thinking to a razor's edge, but a slippery quincunx between impatient Mars and jocular Jupiter brings plenty of distractions on the **16th**. You may feel pulled in several directions—or, even worse, stuck in a monotonous job that never seems to end. Mercury's move into diplomatic Libra, though, should make you a better negotiator who understands how to meet others halfway without losing sight of your own desires.

SEPTEMBER 25–26 ★ *cool under fire*

Proud Venus in Leo and intense Mars in Scorpio form chaotic aspects with surprising Uranus and complex Pluto on **September 25–26**, creating a climate of volatility and uncertainty. The stress of adapting to shifting circumstances or bossy people can tempt you once again to suddenly pick up and run away. Yet if you're able to avoid any attacks and fine-tune your tactics, you will demonstrate great strength and resourcefulness. A super trine between factual Mercury and philosophical Jupiter on the **26th** attracts guidance from a wise individual or your own intuition that can make sense out of even the most chaotic situation.

SUPER NOVA DAY

SEPTEMBER 29 ★ *better to jump than be pushed*

You're ready for immediate change given electrifying Uranus's conjunction to the Aries Full Moon in your 10th House of Status, evoking a sense of urgency about your professional life. However, domineering Pluto's squares to the Sun, Moon, and Uranus demand that you plan ahead and maintain your deep sense of purpose. If you have the drive and the determination, you can quickly blast yourself into a more exciting career.

OCTOBER

HOME IS WHERE THE HEART IS

Invest your time this month in creating more harmony in your home while the lovely Libra Sun visits your 4th House of Domestic Conditions until **October 22**. Making peace with roommates and family members and beautifying your environment will nourish your soul and enhance your creative abilities. Serious Saturn leaves your foundational 4th House on **October 5**, making it especially important to tie up any loose ends with those closest to you. The ringed planet then moves into unwavering Scorpio and your 5th House of Self-Expression, where discipline and practice strengthen your artistic abilities and help you impress others.

You are appreciated and admired for your willingness to discuss complex issues with humility and grace when congenial Venus enters refined Virgo and your 3rd House of Information on **October 3**. Yet exuberant Jupiter's retrograde turn in chatty Gemini on the **4th** reminds you loudly to be very discreet with what you say and just as discriminating about what you're willing to believe. In fact, Jupiter's challenging aspect with Saturn on **October 15**—which first occurred on **July 20** and will recur **May 20** next year—urges you to focus your efforts on critical matters rather than allowing less important issues to distract you. The Sun's entry into sexy Scorpio and your romantic 5th House on **October 22** helps you channel powerful emotions to elicit the best responses from people. Directing your feelings with a strong sense of purpose can revive a flagging relationship or resurrect an old creative interest. The Full Moon in reliable Taurus highlights your 11th House of Groups on **October 29**, enabling you to find a balance between self-interest and your commitment to others.

KEEP IN MIND THIS MONTH

While it's challenging to understand other people's points of view, doing this work will bring you the freedom to express your own opinions more effectively.

KEY DATES

OCTOBER 5–7 ★ *turn darkness into light*

A Mercury-Saturn conjunction on **October 5** puts you in a serious frame of mind. Although seeing the dark side of things is possible, this is an ideal time to eliminate fantasies that keep you from pursuing achievable goals. Mercury's harmonious trine with Neptune offers inspiration that flourishes with its connection to bountiful Jupiter on the **6th**. Red-hot Mars adds more enthusiasm, probably related to your work, as he enters outgoing Sagittarius. However, this fiery planet's square with Neptune could lead you astray on **October 7** if your actions aren't rooted in reality.

SUPER NOVA DAYS

OCTOBER 9–10 ★ *the force is with you*

You see the value in a relationship when loving Venus trines insightful Pluto in your 7th House of Partners on **October 9**. Mental Mercury's perceptive sextile with Pluto on the **10th** empowers your message as Saturn makes the first of three trines to intuitive Neptune in a series that completes on **July 19, 2013**. This constructive alignment between the planet of realism in your 5th House of Creativity and the planet of fantasy in your 9th House of Adventure sets the stage for making dreams comes true.

OCTOBER 15–16 ★ *fools rush in*

You gain insights and understanding about your past on **October 15** due to the Libra New Moon's eye-opening trine with visionary Jupiter. This newfound clarity mixes well with an innovative Mars-Uranus trine, freeing you to experiment at your job and in your daily routine. Avoid overspending or putting too much faith in an expert's opinion when Venus makes an expansive—and potentially expensive—square with Jupiter on the **16th**.

OCTOBER 23–25 ★ *serious pursuit of pleasure*

You take a ride from boundless expectations to the burdens of responsibility in three short days. The Sun in your 5th House of Love and Play aspects fanciful Neptune and hopeful Jupiter on **October 23** before making a conjunction with dutiful Saturn on the **25th**. This could be a journey from delight to despair if you ignore common sense. Yet if you remember that the goodies you seek will come as a result of hard work and planning, you may actually get what you desire.

OCTOBER 28–29 ★ *it takes a village*

Beware of taking on more than you can handle with a hyperactive Mars-Jupiter opposition and Venus's shift into accommodating Libra on the **28th**. Mercury enters into farseeing Sagittarius and squares illusory Neptune on the **29th**, inspiring you to make grandiose promises that you struggle to keep. The difference between success and failure depends upon the amount of support you receive from your friends and colleagues.

NOVEMBER

RELEASE AND CATCH

There are two eclipses in this transformational month, although the changes they reflect are likely to be gentle rather than traumatic. On **November 13**, the Scorpio New Moon in your 5th House of Love and Creativity is a total Solar Eclipse. While this may indicate letting go of a romantic or artistic dream, the lack of difficult planetary aspects to this Sun-Moon conjunction indicates that you will gain more than you lose. Holding on to a person or plan out of habit or out of fear can cost you an opportunity for an even more rewarding experience. The Full Moon in Gemini on **November 28** is a Lunar Eclipse in your 12th House of Soul Consciousness conjunct boisterous Jupiter. You may be dealing with extraneous spiritual information or an erudite teacher who doesn't resonate with you emotionally. Don't let your mind tell you to follow a path that you don't truly feel in your heart.

Another reason to be leery of clever-sounding concepts is Mercury's twenty-day retrograde cycle this month. This brainy planet turns backward in your 6th House of Systems on **November 6**, reenters your 5th House of Self-Expression on the **14th**, and turns direct on **November 26**. Assimilating new information, no matter how inspirational, can be more difficult than you anticipate during this period. Take your time to test new ideas to see if they work successfully in your real life instead of just accepting them blindly. A persuasive person or your own excitement might tempt you to assume additional duties that stretch your workload beyond the limits of comfort and common sense.

KEEP IN MIND THIS MONTH

Addition by subtraction could be your theme this month. Try simplifying your life to exchange quantity for quality.

KEY DATES

NOVEMBER 1–3 ★ *paradise lost*

Your relationships on the home front may be unstable or even explosive as jealous Venus opposes volatile Uranus on the **1st** and tensely squares manipulative Pluto on the **3rd**. You could feel isolated or surprised by sudden changes that require rapid adjustments. Yet shaking up connections, including those on the job, can force you to take a deeper look at your needs and, perhaps, commit to doing whatever you must to fulfill them.

NOVEMBER 9 ★ *love without limits*

You receive approval from unexpected sources today when lucky Jupiter trines Venus. You might also feel guided by an inner sense of knowing that helps you accurately assess the value of people and products. Venus then slides into a sesquisquare with nebulous Neptune that allows faith to blur facts. Being charitable is a good thing as long as you can afford the price of your kindness.

NOVEMBER 16–17 ★ *heroic efforts*

Mars moves into your 7th House of Partners on **November 16**, bringing new contacts—and fierce competition. This assertive planet may attract domineering individuals, but his higher purpose is for you to take the initiative in relationships. Thankfully, now that Mars is in ambitious Capricorn, knowing where you want to go in a personal or professional alliance, making an action plan, and being tough enough to stick to it enables you to reach your destination.

NOVEMBER 21–22 ★ *tunnel of love*

Signals are mixed on **November 21** when the Sun shoots into optimistic Sagittarius and Venus slinks into skeptical Scorpio. The Sun's month-long visit to your 6th House of Employment reminds you to stretch your boundaries to maintain your enthusiasm at work. Yet the risks you're willing to take may be strategically calculated with Venus's entry into your 5th House of Self-Expression. Nevertheless, it's wise not to be overly cautious. Make the most of a magical Venus-Neptune trine on the **22nd** that infuses romance with fantasy.

SUPER NOVA DAYS

NOVEMBER 26–28 ★ *take control of the wheel*

The air hums with excitement with a Sun-Uranus trine on **November 26**—but you're reluctant to join the party because Venus joining show-stopping Saturn sensitizes you to the possibility of failure. If you're feeling unloved or ill at ease, don't let that keep you on the sidelines. When you focus on your goal, patience and persistence help you get what you want. It's better to set things in motion than to play defense on the **27th**, when a suspicious Mars-Pluto conjunction takes a relationship issue to a dramatic climax. The flirty Gemini Full Moon Eclipse on the **28th**, though, is an instant reminder that you have other options if someone doesn't want to play your game.

DECEMBER

TAKE CHARGE

Relationships are always important but reach a much higher level of significance for you this month. Aggressive Mars continues to push ahead in your 7th House of Partnerships until **December 25**, challenging you to come on stronger to get what you need from others. Another wave of awareness and opportunity in your personal and professional alliances arrives on **December 21** with the Sun's shift into systematic Capricorn and your 7th House, marking the Winter Solstice in the Northern Hemisphere. You need to improve your game when it comes to how you work and play with others. If you don't get onto a more determined track in pursuing your goals, you could wind up being bossed around by someone more willful and stubborn than you.

Fortunately, you're not entering the relationship arena unarmed. The New Moon in visionary Sagittarius on **December 13** is activating your 6th House of Skills, helping you recognize your self-limiting habits and inspiring you to overcome them. Additional job or time management training can fire you up with motivation and greatly expand your options. Mars moves into quirky Aquarius and your 8th House of Intimacy on **December 25** to attract unusual partners and encourage you to explore different ways of interacting with others. Stabilizing Saturn in piercing Scorpio and your 5th House of Romance forms a smart sextile with insightful Pluto in your 7th House on **December 26**. This empowering aspect, recurring on **March 8** and **September 21, 2013**, will clarify your needs and bring you more control in your personal life.

KEEP IN MIND THIS MONTH

Don't worry if others see you as bossy, if that's what it takes to get what you want. It's better than to come across as indecisive and weak.

KEY DATES

DECEMBER 2 ★ *shields up!*

An overblown opposition of the Sun and opinionated Jupiter could draw you into a philosophical discussion today that goes around in circles. There are simply too many ideas floating around to pull them all together. On the other hand, opening your mind is a very good thing as long as you filter what you hear to cut through the clutter of choices and don't fall for a story that sounds too good to be true.

DECEMBER 7 ★ *trust your instincts*

Use your intuition to find the best way to get things done today, even if it defies logic; a slippery Mars-Neptune semisquare can drain your energy if you're following someone else's faulty plan. Mental Mercury in Scorpio conjuncts the Moon's North Node, adding purpose to your words if they rise from your emotions. Still, it's wise to make social adjustments as needed and be open to new forms of fun with an unpredictable Venus-Uranus alignment.

DECEMBER 10–12 ★ *on the wings of love*

You're itching to speak your mind on **December 10**, when Mercury enters outspoken Sagittarius. This could be a good thing if you're motivated by deep desire, but if you are expressing discontent, you might push someone away. A Mercury-Neptune square on the **11th** is ideal for imagination but weak on facts and details. However, on the **12th** a sensual Venus–North Node conjunction in your playful 5th House can turn up the heat on romance and even revive forgotten creative interests.

DECEMBER 21–22 ★ *compassionate leader*

You present yourself and your ambitions to others with a newfound sense of authority and purpose on **December 21**, when the Sun moves into your 7th House of Partnerships and Public Life. Fortunately, a gentle Sun-Neptune sextile on the **22nd** helps you advance your interests in a nonthreatening manner that melts resistance.

SUPER NOVA DAYS

DECEMBER 28–30 ★ *raising the stakes*

The Full Moon in your protective sign on **December 28** is fierce because its opposition to domineering Pluto often engenders power struggles. Don't waste time doing battle; instead, determine whether someone you work with or love is worth the effort it takes to maintain the relationship. The Sun skids off a quincunx with Jupiter on the **29th** that can distract you from the issue at hand. Promises of better times ahead are fine, but performance is what's required now. The Sun's conjunction with Pluto on the **30th** is a critical stage of this transformational process. You must decide if you're willing to commit even more of yourself to a partnership or if it's time to give up and look elsewhere for what you need.

LEO

JULY 23–AUGUST 22

LEO

2011 SUMMARY

Discontent with your current circumstances can drive you to consider making radical changes in your beliefs and your professional life. Yet Saturn in diplomatic Libra asks that you keep an open mind, respect the ideas of others, and listen as much as you talk. Fail to pay attention and you could see a minor matter turn into a major mess. Whether it's mind expansion, a professional leap of faith, or the start of a life of travel, being clear about your intentions with those you trust increases your chances for success.

AUGUST—*in your element*

Creative thinking can help you discover new ways to increase your income, but remember that only a carefully crafted plan can actually make it happen.

SEPTEMBER—*down to business*

Tighten up your ship by finishing old business. Then you can launch your next major project from a reliable and ready vessel.

OCTOBER—*extreme makeover*

Investigating your motives shows you where to stop struggling and where to invest even more time and energy.

NOVEMBER—*mix and mingle*

Maintain emotional balance to avoid being shaken by the extremes of unrealistic expectations and crashing disappointments.

DECEMBER—*the only constant is change*

Managing life's little details requires patience, but the effectiveness and efficiency it brings will serve you for years to come.

2011 CALENDAR

AUGUST

MON 8–THU 11 ★	Don't trust anything until you've double-checked the facts
SAT 13 ★	Demonstrate your interest in others to earn their trust
TUE 16–WED 17 ★	Your overconfidence can appear arrogant and insensitive
SUN 21–TUE 23 ★	**SUPER NOVA DAYS** High hopes encounter the hard ground of reality
SUN 28 ★	Plant the seeds of business ideas and nurture them carefully

SEPTEMBER

FRI 2 ★	Initiate a more ambitious plan for success
SUN 11 ★	Use this time to gain an outsider's perspective
SAT 17–SUN 18 ★	A sudden attraction overrides your sense of good judgment
FRI 23–SUN 25 ★	Avoid pushing your ideas on others even if you are excited
TUE 27–WED 28 ★	**SUPER NOVA DAYS** Valuable information may finally come to light

OCTOBER

SAT 1–MON 3 ★	Don't make big promises that you cannot keep
TUE 11 ★	Your passion for new experiences intensifies
THU 13 ★	Know the facts and state your case clearly
FRI 21–SUN 23 ★	Inspire others with your faith and imagination
WED 26–FRI 28 ★	**SUPER NOVA DAYS** Know when to fight and when to walk away

NOVEMBER

WED 2–THU 3 ★	Blast off with clever ideas and exciting social plans
TUE 8–THU 10 ★	Find a healthy outlet to express your restlessness
SUN 13 ★	Complications are brewing on the home front
SUN 20 ★	Take a break from your obligations
TUE 22–FRI 25 ★	**SUPER NOVA DAYS** Take a second look to find a better solution

DECEMBER

FRI 2–SUN 4 ★	**SUPER NOVA DAYS** Impatience challenges you to concentrate
THU 8–SAT 10 ★	Avoid promising too much or stretching yourself too thin
MON 19–THU 22 ★	Overindulging in pleasure could prove costly
SAT 24 ★	Expect conflict if you're not willing to follow the rules
THU 29 ★	Being honest helps prevent everything from boiling over

LEO OVERVIEW

You have important business to complete this year prior to entering the next phase of your life's journey. Although the potential ahead has been growing by leaps and bounds, stabilizing Saturn's visit to your 3rd House of Communication that began in 2010 will come to a conclusion on October 5, marking a major shift in the tides of your life. You probably had to make serious choices that restricted and focused your development when Saturn was in your sign in 2005–2007. Now there is a fork in the road you chose; you must face decisions that will have significant ramifications as you judge your own success and failure. **The parts of your life that are not meeting your expectations need to be revamped or eliminated, for you are being called to concentrate your ambitions on what could be most productive through the coming years.** There's no time to waste, for Saturn's entry into intense Scorpio and your 4th House of Foundations on October 5 will require you to start building your base for the future rather than looking back to the past.

Be ready to embrace career opportunities that come your way, even if they take longer than you expect to manifest. The world is ready to acknowledge and reward your professional contributions now that prosperous Jupiter in materialist Taurus is visiting your 10th House of Public Life until June 11. But you must be persistent because energetic Mars is retrograde in your 2nd House of Self-Worth from January 23 through April 13, obstructing your progress and possibly even fueling self-doubt. However, it's crucial to maintain a positive attitude during this phase so your efforts continue to bear fruit during propitious Jupiter's one-year stay in your 11th House of Goals, starting on June 11.

Throughout the entire year, your life continues to evolve in ways that you might not expect as irrepressible Uranus in enthusiastic Aries continues its seven-year sojourn through your 9th House of Higher Truth. You become increasingly aware of the high cost of freedom as the long-lasting square between Uranus and unrelenting Pluto heightens stress and the pressure for change. Pluto the Lord of the Underworld symbolizes all that is unknown and unconscious. Its powerful square to Uranus the Awakener shifts the tectonic plates of your mind to birth brilliant ideas and release sudden blasts of suppressed emotions. Pluto's transformational transit through your 6th House of Daily Routine lasts until 2023, yet the cataclysmic squares from Uranus that are exact on June 24 and September 19 initiate a profound process that will ultimately force you to discard unhealthy habits and reinvent your life. But the Uranus-Pluto square recurs five more times through 2015, so **it's wise to pace yourself for the long haul rather than exhausting your reserves too soon.**

VARIETY IS THE SPICE OF LIFE

This year your 11th House of Social Networking plays prominently in matters of the heart. Affectionate Venus usually zips through a sign in a few weeks, but now she spends four months—from April 3 until August 7—in lighthearted Gemini and your 11th House, increasing your intimacy with a casual acquaintance or turning a romantic partner into your best friend. A cohort from the past may return during Venus's retrograde phase May 15–June 27. But all is not easy because the cavalier Sagittarius Lunar Eclipse on June 4 rattles your 5th House of Amour and stresses Venus and Mars. You may experience a disagreement about money or a difference in values. Luckily, you have a chance to expand a friendship or connect with someone on the Internet when opportunistic Jupiter begins its yearlong visit to your 11th House of Friends, Hopes, and Wishes on June 11. The Gemini Lunar Eclipse on November 28 joins Jupiter and opposes the Sun in your romantic 5th House to fire up a new relationship or rekindle an existing one.

WINDOW OF OPPORTUNITY

Bountiful Jupiter is at the top of your chart and remains in your 10th House of Career until June 11, magnifying your public profile and professional good fortune. Be ready to say yes if you're presented with an offer on March 13–14, when valuable Venus conjuncts Jupiter in sensible Taurus to complete a stabilizing Grand Earth Trine with wealthy Pluto and enterprising Mars. If nothing appears to be coming your way, create your own lucky break. But don't rest on your laurels, for Jupiter spends the rest of the year in your 11th House of Dreams. Take the accomplishments of the first half of the year and broaden your vision to include a long-term view of success. Downsize your plans or make adjustments as needed when grandiose Jupiter forms uncomfortable sesquisquares with realistic Saturn on July 20 and October 15.

SECOND CHANCES

Rather than earning money in a new manner, consider another attempt at something you've already tried when action-hero Mars retrogrades in your 2nd House of Income on January 23–April 13. You may need extra time and persistence to achieve positive results. If success still eludes you after Mars turns direct—he remains in your 2nd House until July 3—think about a different approach to financial security. Resourceful Venus's visit to your moneymaking 2nd House on October 3–28 might bring a new income stream, and investments made at the shrewd Venus-Pluto trine on October 9 could be particularly lucrative.

ROOM FOR IMPROVEMENT

Regenerative Pluto's long-term stay in your 6th House of Health holds an important key to your well-being for years to come. A well-balanced trine to this potent planet from benevolent Jupiter on March 13 offers you a chance to do some deep healing to rejuvenate your immune system. High-powered squares from radical Uranus on June 24 and September 19 can speed up your renewal process, especially if you try unconventional forms of health care, such as acupuncture, chiropractic, and homeopathy. But if you are not attending to yourself physically, then the growing stress can produce symptoms that reveal weaknesses in your body. Don't wait for a wake-up call to remind you of the importance of maintaining your health.

SLOW START

You may not have a lot of time for leisure at home, especially while popular Jupiter is in your public 10th House prior to June 11. For six months of the year, a variety of rewarding activities keep you busy and away from home. Your focus turns much more personal from August 23 to October 6, when active Mars visits intense Scorpio and your 4th House of Home and Family. This is a sensible time to put your energy toward domestic projects and to spend more quality time with your family. Your drive to make up for lost time continues as additional domestic responsibilities demand your attention once taskmaster Saturn enters your 4th House on October 5 for a two-year stay.

UP IN THE AIR

Jupiter, the planet of travel, spends the first half of the year in your 10th House of Career and Responsibility; you may be taking some business trips prior to June 11. After that, however, you're more likely to go on an excursion to an exotic place, because journeying Jupiter will be in your 11th House of Dreams and Wishes. Your travel plans may change more than once, particularly throughout the summer when erratic Uranus in impulsive Aries and your 9th House of Faraway Places forms tense squares with mysterious Pluto on June 24 and September 19. Being flexible will surely be your smartest strategy.

BUILDING A MYSTERY

As the pace of your life continues to accelerate this year, you'll be more inclined to search for meaning by journeying within instead of seeking answers in the outer world. Spiritual Neptune is settling in for an extended thirteen-year stay in your 8th House of Transformation. Philosophical Jupiter's magical quintile to Neptune on April 4 can open your eyes to previously hidden realms of your imagination. The disquieting Jupiter-Neptune square on June 25 can muddy your thinking and prompt you to doubt your new metaphysical orientation. But pragmatic Saturn's trine to mystical Neptune on October 10 brings reassurance that your spiritual experiences have tangible ramifications and that you are on the right path.

RICK & JEFF'S TIP FOR THE YEAR:
A Long and Winding Road

The potential for positive change can be so exhilarating that you are tempted to throw caution to the wind and push as hard as you can. Instead of recklessly consuming your resources prematurely, remember that this period of transformation will last several more years.

JANUARY

MONEY IN THE BANK

Consider what you can do to save for a rainy day, because Mars turns retrograde on **January 23**, keeping it in practical Virgo and your 2nd House of Resources until **July 3**. But micromanaging your cash flow isn't a sensible strategy if it prevents you from seeing the bigger picture. Fortunately, you receive reliable assistance now because ambitious Saturn and visionary Neptune align closely in a trine that's not exact until **October 10**, enabling you to devise a sound strategy to make your dreams come true. The sooner you start to shore up your resources, the better—and you can begin when Mercury connects with the Saturn-Neptune trine on **January 7**. The introspective Cancer Full Moon on **January 9** shines in your 12th House of Secrets, reminding you that you don't have to justify your actions to others. Taking care of business is critical, but there's no need to reveal your entire plan.

The middle of the month is an excellent time to push your financial agenda forward by consolidating your bills or taking on an extra job to increase your income. The pressure is on to take care of your fiscal obligations due to enriching Venus's trine to Saturn and conjunction with Neptune on **January 13** following on the heels of the proactive Sun-Mars trine on **January 12**. Acknowledge the truth in what others are telling you, put your shoulder to the wheel, and stay calm during the stressful and chaotic days leading up to the Aquarius New Moon in your 7th House of Relationships on **January 23**. Lunar squares to Jupiter and Saturn can teach you the benefits of being more cooperative while you seek a balance between your values and those of a friend or partner.

KEEP IN MIND THIS MONTH

You may feel as if your year is getting off to a slow start. Still, your current actions will have significant consequences during the following months.

KEY DATES

JANUARY 1 ★ *tiger in your tank*

You are ready to take on the world—and that includes anyone who stands in your way. You're quick with the verbal repartee today as Mercury in opinionated Sagittarius forms a dynamic square from your 5th House of Self-Expression to excitable Mars. In fact, you could provoke an argument without even realizing your role as the instigator. Give yourself permission to take a mental vacation, but choose your words carefully when sharing your thoughts.

JANUARY 7–9 ★ *on a need-to-know basis*

While you're annoyed by circumstances you cannot change right now, shifting your frame of reference can free you from someone else's negativity. Rational Mercury forms supportive sextiles with contemplative Saturn and intuitive Neptune on **January 7**, enabling you to think your way out of an uncomfortable situation. Your logic is sound as Mercury enters orderly Capricorn and makes a free-flowing trine with buoyant Jupiter on the **8th**. But a shocking Mercury-Uranus square can bring up too much information too quickly, as it leads to the hypersensitive Cancer Full Moon on **January 9** that raises your fears about unexpected change.

SUPER NOVA DAYS

JANUARY 12–14 ★ *patience is a virtue*

Hard work produces concrete results on **January 12**, thanks to a powerful trine from the industrious Capricorn Sun in your 6th House of Self-Improvement to action-planet Mars. Fortunately, a sobering Venus-Saturn trine the next day cools your desires so you can wait for gratification. Although you may confuse your fantasies with reality when Venus hooks up with imaginative Neptune, her slick sextile with auspicious Jupiter on the **14th** indicates a positive outcome.

JANUARY 19–23 ★ *less is more*

A reality check is in order on **January 19** when a Sun-Saturn square sets obstacles in your path and slows your progress. You rebound quickly with a little help from a friend, though, when the Sun enters your 7th House of Others on the **20th** and sextiles Uranus the Awakener on the **21st**. You're challenged to maintain a sensible perspective, because squares to the Sun from inflationary Jupiter on **January 22** and the Aquarius New Moon on the **23rd** encourage you to overstep your limits. Nevertheless, Mercury's trine to Mars as it turns retrograde supplies you with enough common sense to save the day.

JANUARY 27–28 ★ *radical solution*

A frustrating Mercury-Saturn square on **January 27** indicates serious resistance to your plans. Still, your optimism is irrepressible; new ideas come to you faster than you can process them when Mercury's aspects to brilliant Uranus and confident Jupiter on the **28th** enable you to turn a problem into an advantage.

FEBRUARY

THE STUFF OF DREAMS

Take the high road in your interactions with others this month. Karmic Saturn in relationship-oriented Libra approaches a flowing trine with inspirational Neptune before backing off when Saturn turns retrograde on **February 7**. You may feel as if you have reached a place of equilibrium and that your dreams are realistic enough to come true. But the individualistic Leo Full Moon, also on the **7th**, reminds you of your unfulfilled needs and encourages you to express your desires.

The spotlight on your personal and professional partnerships intensifies as planets shift from your 7th House of Companions to your 8th House of Intimacy this month. Your relationship expectations grow more idealistic when Neptune makes the transition on **February 3**, but its effects can be quite subtle since it remains in your transformational 8th House for thirteen years. It's easier to face the facts when interactive Mercury trines no-nonsense Saturn and enters your 8th House on **February 13**, but your dreaming continues because Mercury hooks up with otherworldly Neptune on the **14th**. You have a wonderful grasp on both reality and fantasy right now, so use it to your advantage. This pattern of disillusionment followed by re-enchantment is repeated when the willful Sun trines somber Saturn on **February 18** and enters magical Pisces and your 8th House to join ethereal Neptune on the **19th**. The Pisces New Moon on the **21st** is part of a five-planet cluster in your 8th House of Regeneration, giving birth to a new you that is more sensitive and compassionate, while also luring you into unfamiliar emotional waters that can dampen your otherwise fiery nature. Fortunately, cooperative sextiles from the brilliant Sun warm promising Jupiter on the **25th** and impassioned Pluto on the **28th** to bring the acknowledgment and support you seek.

KEEP IN MIND THIS MONTH

Although you might feel unsteady when emotions overtake logic, trust your intuition. You could be given an opportunity to share feelings on a deeper level if you let down your guard.

KEY DATES

FEBRUARY 1 ★ *reconcilable differences*

Tempers could flare over conflicting ideas about money today thanks to a tug-of-war between the cosmic lovers when retrograde Mars in your 2nd House of Self-Worth opposes possessive Venus in your 8th House of Deep Sharing. You might also experience this tension as a battle for control in a personal relationship. Either way, troublemaker Mercury doesn't help, since its annoying aspect to combative Mars can incite verbal warfare over an issue that ultimately proves insignificant. Nevertheless, respect for your opponent can turn a shouting match into good-natured banter that is playful for all involved.

SUPER NOVA DAYS

FEBRUARY 6–9 ★ *truth has consequences*

You speak your mind before thinking about how others might react on **February 6**, when the Sun and communicative Mercury form expressive semi-squares with explosive Uranus. Your partner or workmate will surely give you the other side of the story as the dramatic Leo Full Moon on **February 7** opposes a Sun-Mercury conjunction in your 7th House of Relationships. Additionally, an uncomfortable Venus-Saturn quincunx is like mixing oil and water; conversation doesn't bring you any closer to satisfaction. Nevertheless, taking a risk may pay off for you when creative Venus enters fearless Aries on **February 8** and hooks up with surprising Uranus on the **9th**.

FEBRUARY 15–18 ★ *batten down the hatches*

It's easy for you to overstate your case at work on **February 15** when over-the-top Jupiter in your 10th House of Career aligns with just-do-it Mars. You're convinced there's a lot at stake—an emotionally intense Venus-Pluto square can make you feel as if you're being threatened or abandoned. Luckily, you can overcome your fears thanks to thoughtful Mercury's conjunction to healer Chiron in your 8th House of Transformation and sextile to beneficent Jupiter on the **16th**. Take the extra step to clarify your position and protect your material gains when the Sun forms a solid trine with enduring Saturn on **February 18**.

FEBRUARY 23–25 ★ *sweet surrender*

You seem easygoing now with verbal Mercury in sympathetic Pisces. However, its tense opposition to contentious Mars in your 2nd House of Self-Worth on **February 23** can reveal issues of low self-esteem, causing you to lash out at someone to hide your insecurity. Unfortunately, this behavior won't win you any friends. It's wiser to acknowledge your vulnerability when the Sun conjuncts Chiron the Wounded Healer on the **24th**. Cooperation rather than competition allows you to gain the most benefit from the opportunistic Sun-Jupiter sextile on **February 25**.

MARCH

HURRY UP AND WAIT

Working hard to achieve your goals this month goes a long way toward getting the material support you need for career success. However, you may not see tangible results right away. Mars remains retrograde in your 2nd House of Income, possibly delaying financial rewards. Additionally, quick-witted Mercury in impetuous Aries begins its three-week retrograde period on **March 12**, in your 9th House of Future Vision, revealing weak links in your logic that require you to rethink your long-term strategy. But don't let yourself get discouraged; the obstacles you face now are meant to give you more time to strengthen your plans. Instead of taking on new projects, build on what you've already started. Luckily, acting with integrity will gain you the respect you deserve when Mars backs into a stabilizing Grand Earth Trine with motivational Jupiter, tasteful Venus, and powerful Pluto on **March 13–14**. Don't be afraid to take a stand at work for what you believe is right.

You must make a decision that will affect your long-term finances when the analytical Virgo Full Moon on **March 8** activates your 2nd House of Personal Resources. Even if you want to work with someone in particular, don't let your emotional attachments get in the way of critical thinking. The Vernal Equinox is marked by the Sun's entry into pioneering Aries and your 9th House of Faraway Places on **March 20**, firing up your wanderlust and urging you to go on an adventure. The Aries New Moon on **March 22** is conjunct Mercury and eye-opening Uranus, galvanizing your desire to travel or enroll in a new course of study. The productive Saturn-Pluto quintile on **March 28** helps you bring your plans to fruition.

KEEP IN MIND THIS MONTH

Your current lesson is about patience. Although your need for excitement and adventure grows, you likely won't be able to make your getaway just yet.

KEY DATES

MARCH 2–5 ★ *cool your jets*

Your brain is jumping with fascinating concepts that explode into your awareness. Mental Mercury's leap into restless Aries on **March 2** and its conjunction with electrifying Uranus on **March 5** makes it difficult for you to relax. You struggle to turn your words into action because your mind is so hyperactive that you can't articulate your thoughts. Nevertheless, you want to have your way and tempers may flare as retrograde Mars opposes the Sun on **March 3**. Although your thinking doesn't settle down, a Venus-Saturn opposition on **March 4**, followed by the love planet's entry into easygoing Taurus on the **5th**, helps you take a more grounded approach to interacting with others.

MARCH 12–14 ★ *how to succeed in business*

Mischievous Mercury can interfere with your plans when it turns retrograde in your 9th House of Big Ideas on **March 12**. However, likable Venus's wonderful conjunction with opulent Jupiter on **March 14** in your 10th House of Public Life indicates smooth sailing professionally, including a possible promotion at work. This fabulous hookup also creates easy trines with macho Mars in your 2nd House of Money and unrelenting Pluto in your 6th House of Employment, giving you the stamina to see a job through to completion and all but guaranteeing a positive financial outcome from your investment of time and resources.

SUPER NOVA DAYS

MARCH 22–24 ★ *ready to rumble*

You encounter obstacles on **March 22** thanks to a discouraging opposition between antagonistic Mars and vulnerable Chiron, and your argumentative attitude can make matters even worse. Fortunately, with an exciting Aries New Moon conjunct with Uranus the Awakener activates your 9th House of Future Vision, taking your mind off your recent troubles and psyching you up about what's ahead. Logical Mercury retrogrades back into sensitive Pisces and your 8th House of Regeneration on the **23rd**, softening your outlook and enabling you to better manage your current negativity. On **March 24**, the Sun's conjunction with Uranus suddenly shifts the energy, freeing you from your self-doubt and shaking up all your previous assumptions.

MARCH 28–29 ★ *trust in the process*

Even if you've been short on resources, a transformative quintile between heavyweights Saturn and Pluto on **March 28** helps you make the most of what you have. But the Sun's dynamic square to unyielding Pluto on **March 29** is a test; you must withstand a challenge to your authority before you can take the next step on your journey.

APRIL

DON'T LOOK BACK

The time for reviewing the past is over. If you have reevaluated your core beliefs, put your finances in order, and strengthened your closest relationships, you're ready to move ahead with confidence. But even if you still have unfinished business, this month is a turning point that spins you around and sets you off in a new direction. You can hear the future calling as Mercury the Messenger in your 8th House of Regeneration ends its retrograde phase on **April 4**. A new you is ready to emerge, and all systems should be ready to go by the time Mercury enters unstoppable Aries and your 9th House of Adventure on **April 16**. Meanwhile, energetic Mars—retrograde in your 2nd House of Self-Worth since **January 23**—presented a series of challenges to your self-esteem and possibly your cash flow as well. You begin to regain momentum as you reassert yourself when Mars turns direct on **April 13**.

Although the forward movement of Mercury and Mars does a lot to put your life back on track, there are still complications for you to manage. When the peace-seeking Libra Full Moon on **April 6** illuminates your 3rd House of Communication, you must have a discussion with a family member or loved one. Dynamic aspects between adoring Venus, confusing Neptune, and motivating Mars on **April 5–7** direct conversations toward clearing up a complex relationship misunderstanding. The Sun's entry in dependable Taurus and your 10th House of Career on **April 19**, followed by the New Moon on the **21st**, reaffirms the validity of your professional ambitions and supplies you with the determination to accomplish your goals.

KEEP IN MIND THIS MONTH

No matter how enthusiastic you become when things start to go your way, remember that you must sustain your efforts to realize your dreams.

KEY DATES

APRIL 3–5 ★ *daydream believer*

You're feeling playful with flirty Venus's entry into whimsical Gemini and your 11th House of Friends, Hopes, and Wishes on **April 3**. Usually Venus speeds through a sign in about four weeks, but her retrograde cycle next month keeps her in your sociable 11th House until **August 7**. Nevertheless, this shift in your desires can be disorienting because Venus squares deceptive Neptune on **April 5**, seducing you to confuse your dreams with reality. Meanwhile, Mercury's direct turn on **April 4** opens your thinking as you take stock of what you learned since it turned retrograde on **March 12**. A magical Jupiter-Neptune quintile on the **4th** tilts the scales toward fantasy, encouraging you to embrace the potential of your imagination over the basic facts.

APRIL 13–15 ★ *if you don't at first succeed, try, try again*

It's hard to trust your instincts when Mars turns forward on **April 13** given this warrior planet's near opposition to cloudy Neptune. Fortunately, the skies clear over the coming days as he gains speed and escapes from Neptune's fog, giving you a newfound sense of direction. The next day, a casual conversation becomes emotionally intense due to a complex connection between amicable Venus in witty Gemini and dark Pluto in conservative Capricorn on the **14th**; suddenly a simple social interaction has turned into an awkward encounter. You may feel as if you're fighting a losing battle when restrictive Saturn opposes the creative Aries Sun in your 9th House of Future Vision on **April 15**, but this is no time to give up. Working extra-hard to overcome setbacks builds character, and your persistence could turn disappointment into success.

SUPER NOVA DAYS

APRIL 21–25 ★ *king of the jungle*

Your roar is loud and clear, Leo, when the strong-willed Taurus New Moon activates your 10th House of Status on **April 21**. Your instinctively bold approach is enriched by the New Moon's cooperative sextile to prophetic Neptune. This lunation's trine to superhero Mars gives you so much energy, you're suddenly a force to be reckoned with. Brainy Mercury's conjunction with electric Uranus buzzes your 9th House of Higher Truth on **April 22**, filling your head with unconventional ideas. But Mercury's square to obstinate Pluto on the **25th** suggests that you will have to stand up to someone's posturing to maintain your authority.

APRIL 29 ★ *the force is with you*

You have a deep well of energy to fuel your current ambitions when the Sun in your 10th House of Public Life is revitalized by potent Pluto. Concentrate on your goals and avoid distractions to turn your losses into gains.

THE PAUSE THAT REFRESHES

Your life opens up this month with new options in front of you that offer great potential for growth. But you won't be ready for the future until you have thoroughly considered what you truly want. A series of expansive aspects to boundless Jupiter on **May 4**, **May 7**, and **May 13** shows you the distant horizon and gives you enough confidence to reach it. But the complex Scorpio Full Moon on **May 5** shines a spotlight in your 4th House of Foundations, possibly revealing ghosts from your past that now get in your way. Additionally, thoughtful Mercury's opposition to judgmental Saturn is like a stop sign that prevents your forward progress until you improve the weak parts of your plan. Resistance fades when Mercury enters steady Taurus on **May 9**, and a trio of helpful trines on **May 13–16** fortifies your current position.

Your energy shifts, however, during the retrograde period of loving Venus from **May 15** to **June 27**. This reversal occurs in your 11th House of Social Networking, and is a time to look back at previous relationships to gauge what you lost or gained and, perhaps, even rekindle an old romance. You could question the relevance of your current ambitions when optimistic Jupiter in your 10th House of Career forms unsettling aspects with pessimistic Saturn on **May 16** and with suspicious Pluto on the **17th**. The restless Gemini Solar Eclipse on **May 20** shakes your futuristic 11th House, motivating you to create new friendships that reflect your current interests, rather than maintain old ones that seem to have lost their relevance.

KEEP IN MIND THIS MONTH

Instead of diligently pushing ahead with your agenda, take a strategic time-out to revitalize your body and reignite your enthusiasm.

KEY DATES

MAY 3–7 ★ *the pursuit of happiness*

You can charm your way into nearly anyone's heart on **May 3** when chatty Mercury forms a slick sextile with congenial Venus in your 11th House of Friends. But you might overstep your bounds without realizing it, because a pair of imaginative quintiles on **May 4**—the first between confident Jupiter and maverick Chiron, and the second between the Sun and surreal Neptune—enable you to explore new professional possibilities. However, if you try to circumvent reality, an unforgiving Mercury-Saturn opposition on **May 5** could send you back to the drawing board to remap your strategy. An emotional Scorpio Full Moon the same day can distract you with an intense interaction on the home front. By the time Jupiter forms a mind-expanding semisquare with rebellious Uranus on **May 7**, you're ready to grab on to any good idea that you think has promise.

SUPER NOVA DAYS

MAY 13–16 ★ *great expectations*

An exuberant Sun-Jupiter conjunction on **May 13** floods you with contentment. A Grand Earth Trine through the **16th**—with smart Mercury, courageous Mars, and resolute Pluto—empowers you to follow through on your promises and turn a big idea into an enduring success. But attractive Venus turns retrograde on **May 15**, indicating that your desires may have changed since you began your current course. Move ahead cautiously, for an all-or-nothing Jupiter-Saturn quincunx on the **16th** suggests that your career goals could transform over the coming months.

MAY 20–23 ★ *clean slate*

You feel as if you're starting over on **May 20**, when the Sun and Moon move from stubborn Taurus into freewheeling Gemini to create a New Moon Eclipse in your 11th House of Dreams and Wishes. Your thoughts are all over the map as quick-silver Mercury aspects four planets on **May 20–22**, culminating in a conjunction to philosophical Jupiter that enables you to look beyond the current moment and see unlimited potential everywhere. But you might find yourself climbing too far out on a limb on **May 23** because a fantasy-prone Sun-Neptune square encourages you to put your faith in your dreams rather than in the limitations of reality.

MAY 27–28 ★ *free your mind*

You are exciting—even brilliant—right now, because the Sun's conjunction with cerebral Mercury on **May 27** intensifies all forms of communication. Cooperative sextiles to shocking Uranus on **May 27–28** galvanize your thoughts and shatter the social conventions that normally restrain you. Be careful, though: Unless you are mindful of other people's feelings, your unconventional ideas could create a back-lash that you'll need to handle over the days ahead.

JUNE

THE FUTURE IS CALLING

This is a bellwether month, Leo. Doorways open into your future and reveal what lies ahead. The action starts when the farseeing Sagittarius Full Moon Eclipse on **June 4** polarizes your 5th House of Love, bringing personal change into the moment. This eclipse's connection to romantic Venus and physical Mars can create both dissent and excitement in relationships. Bountiful Jupiter enters flighty Gemini and your 11th House of Long-Term Goals on **June 11**, another sign of your eagerness to leave the past behind. The lighthearted Gemini New Moon on **June 19** allows you to entertain possibilities without being tied to any them.

June 24 marks the beginning of a protracted process of transformation which could alter your life in ways you cannot yet imagine. This is the day when revolutionary Uranus and evolutionary Pluto align for the first of seven profound squares—a series that concludes in 2015. Pay close attention to your diet and exercise program, because Pluto in your 6th House of Health and Work will require you to improve your lifestyle. However, maintaining your well-being is challenging if you're also asked to assume more responsibilities on the job. Unpredictable Uranus in your 9th House of Future Vision indicates your dissatisfaction with the status quo and can precipitate events that wrench you out of your complacency by confronting you with new philosophies, religious beliefs, and political ideas. On **June 11**, fleet-footed Mercury's anxious aspects to the long lasting Uranus-Pluto square trigger you to take a cold hard look at the choices you must make in the coming months and years. The magnitude of the looming changes begins to dawn on you when the Sun uncomfortably reactivates this square on **June 29**.

KEEP IN MIND THIS MONTH

Keep an open mind about modifying your daily routine. Even small improvements can have a positive impact on your health.

KEY DATES

JUNE 3–5 ★ *make love, not war*

You realize how to resolve an uncomfortable relationship dilemma on **June 3**, when a harmonious Mercury-Sun trine blesses you with sound logic. A conflictive Venus-Mars square on **June 4** may heighten the tension of the Lunar Eclipse, but you use your sparkling personality to evade a quarrel as the Sun's conjuncts affable Venus in your 11th House of Friends the next day. Although you probably could justify an argument, the Full Moon Eclipse activates your romantic 5th House of Play, suggesting sweeter ways to resolve the stress between the cosmic lovers, Venus and Mars.

JUNE 11–13 ★ *no pain, no gain*

You can see deeply into the future when farsighted Jupiter enters inquisitive Gemini and your 11th House of Dreams and Wishes on **June 11**. But your intentions have consequences as Mercury in your 12th House of Destiny squares reckless Uranus and opposes unforgiving Pluto. Choose your words carefully to ameliorate an unpleasant situation and ease the struggle between you and a co-worker when Mercury forms a friendly trine to Chiron the Healer on **June 12**. Although the tension is likely to settle down quickly, the Sun's trine to persistent Saturn on the **13th** indicates that this battle is not over for long.

SUPER NOVA DAYS

JUNE 19–21 ★ *actions speak louder than words*

It's time to make your feelings known on **June 19**—even if you're not completely ready—because the New Moon is in changeable Gemini and your 11th House of Groups, indicating a shift in your relationships to friends and associates. Remember that unexpressed emotions can fuel resentment. A hard Mercury-Saturn square on **June 20** makes communication even more strained. However, this is also the Summer Solstice, the day that the Sun enters receptive Cancer and your 12th House of Privacy, giving you permission to take care of your own needs and keep your thoughts to yourself. Although you may not have much to say, your behavior reveals what you are withholding as interactive Mercury forms a collaborative sextile with bold Mars on the **21st**.

JUNE 24–27 ★ *straighten up*

You may incorrectly assume that you can get by without much effort now as indulgent Jupiter squares delusional Neptune on **June 25**, possibly distracting you from focusing on the more important issues raised by the pressing Uranus-Pluto square on **June 24**. Fortunately, you're ready to tackle problems directly when Mercury enters demonstrative Leo and your 1st House of Self on **June 25**, combined with sociable Venus's direct turn in your 11th House of Goals on **June 27**.

JULY

WORK IN PROGRESS

Although the flow of information increases this month, you can handle the noise by quickly integrating what you learn with what you already know. Superhero Mars noticeably kicks up the pace of personal interactions and gives you strong influence over others when he enters charming Libra and your 3rd House of Communication on **July 3**. Also on the **3rd**, the practical Capricorn Full Moon casts its light on your 6th House of Work, drawing your mind away from dreaming about the big picture and inviting you to concentrate on more immediate tasks. Mental Mercury in dramatic Leo is another indication of your heightened need to be in communication with your friends and associates. The Winged Messenger's retrograde turn on **July 14** ushers in a three-week period that can bring delays, missed connections, and miscommunications—all magnified for you because it takes place in your 1st House of Self.

Your life grows more stressful around the emotionally powerful Cancer New Moon on **July 19**, which falls in your 12th House of Privacy. You may want to retreat, yet impetuous Mars forms a struggling square to domineering Pluto on the **17th** and a tension-releasing opposition to rowdy Uranus on the **18th** that could make peace and quiet an unobtainable fantasy. Big issues concerning the overall purpose of your life fill your thoughts as philosophical Jupiter makes four separate aspects on **July 18–24**. Thankfully, a pair of accommodating trines ends the month on an upbeat note, suggesting that a strategic risk will pay off if you are patient enough to wait for your rewards.

KEEP IN MIND THIS MONTH

You're feeling ambitious, but remember that it's not all about getting ahead at work. Take time off and smell the flowers.

KEY DATES

JULY 1–4 ★ *lost and found*

You feel alienated or underappreciated, with satisfaction out of reach, when popular Venus in your 11th House of Friends runs into sobering Saturn's negativity on **July 1**. On **July 3–4**, secretive Pluto forms comfortable quincunxes with innocent Venus and interactive Mercury, revealing previously hidden motives in a relationship that may have an imbalance of power. The calculating Capricorn Full Moon, also on the **3rd**, allows you to contain your emotions and work toward resolving the stress. Additionally, action-planet Mars enters Libra the Scales, restoring equilibrium.

Fortunately, easygoing aspects among Mercury, Venus, and Uranus on the **4th** allow you to quickly process the intensity of these days so you can move on without any lingering hard feelings.

JULY 8 ★ *off the grid*

A fog settles over your life today, obscuring familiar landmarks and making it difficult for you to find your way, as impatient Mars creates an anxious quincunx with drifty Neptune. Having a destination in mind isn't enough if you cannot get your bearings. Your best strategy now is to let the currents carry you along until the mist clears.

SUPER NOVA DAYS

JULY 15–19 ★ *a perfect storm*

You struggle to overcome uncertainty as Jupiter in your 11th House of Goals slowly moves into a hard-to-manage quincunx with manipulative Pluto on **July 18**. A disheartening Sun-Saturn square on **July 15** presents obstacles you must overcome with commitment and hard work. A tough Mars-Pluto square on the **17th** reactivates an ongoing power struggle at work, but an enthusiastic Mars-Jupiter trine enables you to relinquish control in the moment so you can work toward a common goal. An electric Mars-Uranus opposition on **July 18** can cut through the resistance like lightning, shock you with an innovative solution to a problem, and suddenly clear the air of tension. The nurturing Cancer New Moon on the **19th** turns your thoughts toward more personal matters, reminding you to take care of your loved ones.

JULY 22 ★ *all the world's your stage*

You feel like you're on top of the world with the Sun's entry into royal Leo, and it's time to celebrate. An exciting Jupiter-Uranus sextile can unexpectedly throw open the window of opportunity, but it's up to you to take advantage of the potential.

JULY 28–31 ★ *surprise ending*

Mercury crosses over the Sun in lively Leo on **July 28**, aligning your thoughts with your soul's purpose. But the communicator planet is retrograde in motion, making it complicated for you to express what's on your mind. Nevertheless, your actions will tell the story when the Sun trines uncontainable Uranus on **July 31**.

AUGUST

THROUGH THE EYE OF A NEEDLE

You must narrow your focus and postpone extraneous activities in order to reach your goals and feel positive about your life this month. You grow more socially active as the progressive Aquarius Full Moon on **August 1** forms a coordinating trine with expansive Jupiter in your 11th House of Friends. But you may not want to be so outgoing when vulnerable Venus enters passive Cancer and your 12th House of Privacy on **August 7**. Luckily, communicator Mercury turns direct on **August 8** in courageous Leo, encouraging you to say what's on your mind during the upcoming weeks.

You struggle to push your agenda forward through the first half of the month as unstoppable Mars moves closer to a conjunction with immovable Saturn. The Mars-Saturn alignment on **August 15** in your 3rd House of Learning can be a day of reckoning when you become aware of what isn't working in your life. Acknowledging your frustration is a first step to overcoming anger or resentment; otherwise, intense feelings can quickly escalate a seemingly minor difference of taste into an all-out conflict. The Leo New Moon on **August 17** is your own personal New Year's Day, a time to set your intentions for the next six months. Don't scatter your energy in celebration; the Sun's shift into perfectionist Virgo on **August 22** and Mars's move into observant Scorpio on the **23rd** remind you of the importance of concentration and self-discipline. However, the diffusive Pisces Full Moon on **August 31** brightens your 8th House of Transformation, suggesting that it's now time to soften your focus and practice more flexibility when looking ahead.

KEEP IN MIND THIS MONTH

Although your progress can raise expectations about what you might accomplish, don't bite off more than you can chew just to prove you can.

KEY DATES

AUGUST 1–2 ★ *room to move*

A partner is unusually distant and discontent on **August 1**, when the heartfelt Leo Sun is reflected by an emotionally awkward Aquarius Full Moon in your 7th House of Companions. Luckily, the Sun's supportive sextile with buoyant Jupiter on the **2nd** can restore your faith in relationships, enabling you to give those you love the independence they now require.

AUGUST 7–9 ★ *rainbow in the sky*

You can send mixed messages on **August 8** when talkative Mercury ends a retrograde period that began on **July 14**. Although Mercury is in expressive Leo, freeing you to share your plans, demure Venus slips into emotionally protective waters of Cancer on **August 7**, suggesting that you won't tell the whole story. Venus's unifying trine with enchanting Neptune on the **9th** enables you to captivate others with your fantastic imagination. A sweet and tender love connection is possible now, but you must be vigilant about staying honest. Otherwise, disappointment and disillusionment will surface over the coming days.

SUPER NOVA DAYS

AUGUST 15–17 ★ *face your fears*

Unexpressed tensions in both personal and professional relationships are suddenly exposed when Venus in moody Cancer opposes passionate Pluto on **August 15** and squares explosive Uranus on the **16th**. You may feel trapped as hot Mars runs into cold Saturn: You cannot force your way ahead, and you may not be able to gracefully retreat. Minor irritations can turn to anger if you aren't persistent and patient. But the Sun's cooperative sextile with responsible Saturn on the **17th** followed by the resolute Leo New Moon clears the way for you to make decisions as you begin the next phase of your journey.

AUGUST 24–26 ★ *dare to believe*

You're misunderstood on **August 24** when the Sun in your 2nd House of Self-Esteem opposes misty Neptune. The people around you struggle to see your special gifts—perhaps in part due to your own lack of clarity. Thankfully, you can express your dreams more directly when warrior Mars trines Neptune on the **26th**. Whatever you imagine about yourself can now seem real to everyone else.

AUGUST 29 ★ *be your own hero*

You are a force to be reckoned with when the industrious Virgo Sun in your 2nd House of Personal Resources forms a smooth trine with relentless Pluto, supplying apparently inexhaustible power to get nearly any job done. Don't be afraid to defend your ideas; you can win almost any argument as witty Mercury creates a useful sextile with authoritative Saturn, adding weight and humor to your words.

SEPTEMBER

NO TURNING BACK

This month kicks off with a frenzy that can be a thrilling time or an annoying distraction. However, the real action builds to a crescendo when volatile Uranus squares volcanic Pluto on **September 19**—the second in a series of seven squares that began on **June 24** and recurs through 2015. With Pluto in your 6th House of Self-Improvement, this is a chance to look at your routines and eliminate those habits and behavior patterns that don't enhance your life. Of course, it's not easy to alter the rhythm of your daily grind, and the square from unexpected Uranus in your 9th House of Future Vision creates conflict that can provoke you to act suddenly in an unconventional matter.

Impulsive Mars and logical Mercury trigger the Uranus-Pluto square and support your desire for change on **September 3–5**, but not without also increasing your anxiety and inciting you to take unnecessary risks. On **September 12–13**, alluring Venus tempts you with unusual romantic possibilities that can threaten the status quo, especially if you're feeling bored or stifled. The detail-oriented Virgo New Moon on the **15th** falls in your 2nd House of Self-Esteem, encouraging you to step back from the larger issues and take stock: How well are you expressing your true values? It's hard to know what to think when the Uranus-Pluto square is stressed by analytical Mercury on the **20th**. Your feelings are pulled all over the map when Venus and Mars enter the picture on **September 25–26**. The feisty Aries Full Moon on the **29th** can be extremely exciting, yet it's nearly impossible to solidify plans at this time.

KEEP IN MIND THIS MONTH

Sudden insight offers glimpses of your future, yet you still must come back to the present and live your life right now.

KEY DATES

SEPTEMBER 1–5 ★ *down to the core*

You long to see your financial dreams come true when Mercury's opposition to fuzzy Neptune on **September 1** deludes you into believing nearly anything that resonates with your fantasies. But solemn Saturn issues a reality check on **September 3** when it aspects Venus and the Sun. You're ready to leap into action on **September 3–5** as Mars connects with Pluto, Uranus, and Mercury. Concentrating on family matters is a smart way to apply the excess energy of forceful Mars as he now moves through your 4th House of Home.

SEPTEMBER 13–16 ★ *and now for something completely different*

Positive change fills the air on **September 13** when beautiful Venus in theatrical Leo trines unorthodox Uranus. Step out of the box by taking a chance and reinventing your image. But the cautious Virgo New Moon on **September 15** activates your 2nd House of Possessions, shifting your attention from seeking independence to protecting your assets. Being sensible isn't necessarily fun, so your pragmatism quickly morphs into a blind optimism on **September 16**, fueled by an audacious Mars-Jupiter quincunx.

SEPTEMBER 22 ★ *student of life*

The Sun's movement into diplomatic Libra and your 3rd House of Learning proclaims the Autumnal Equinox. Your previously narrowed focus on the world begins to widen, your thirst for knowledge grows, and you get busy responding to new demands on your time.

SEPTEMBER 25–27 ★ *give peace a chance*

When the unexpected happens at home, suppressed feelings are released. It's because irascible Mars in your 4th House of Domestic Conditions forms disquieting aspects with intense Pluto and unstable Uranus on **September 25**. You can lose patience because friendly Venus forms similarly cantankerous aspects with Uranus and Pluto on **September 25–26**. A dynamic Venus-Mars square on the **27th** indicates a lover's quarrel or a friend's betrayal. Fortunately, a rational discussion on **September 26** helps you navigate your way through the chaos as communicator Mercury in compromising Libra forms a unifying trine with generous Jupiter in your 11th House of Friends.

SUPER NOVA DAY

SEPTEMBER 29 ★ *wake up!*

You could lose your temper when Pluto, Lord of the Underworld, squares the Sun in your 3rd House of Communication and the red-hot Aries Full Moon in your 9th House of Big Ideas. Make sure your arguments are factual and stick to the present situation, because Pluto can raise unresolved issues from the subconscious. Additionally, the Full Moon's conjunction to wild Uranus attracts a lightning bolt of awareness that catalyzes a much-needed emotional breakthrough.

OCTOBER

FROM THE GROUND UP

This month your uncertainty gives way to a clearer picture of the future. Your first glimpse of what's ahead arrives on **October 2** when go-getter Mars conjuncts the karmic North Lunar Node in your 4th House of Security. Don't second-guess your intuition now; act with confidence to put your life on track. You probably won't be feeling very playful on **October 5**, because mental Mercury joins serious Saturn just moments before entering enigmatic Scorpio and your soulful 4th House where they emphasize the private side of your personal life. Home and family become a priority as you reconnect with your roots, stabilize your foundation, and engage in deep conversations about the direction of your life. Your dreams play an important role in motivating you to create new goals when Mercury and Saturn trine spiritual Neptune on the **5th** and the **10th**, respectively. Meanwhile, an energetic boost from Mars when it enters thrill-seeking Sagittarius and your 5th House of Spontaneity on **October 6** provokes impulsive action that can be slightly off target because of its troublesome square to irrational Neptune on the **7th**.

On **October 15**, you have a second chance at a previously missed opportunity; you can try a completely different way to maximize your potential. This good fortune is due to a mix of supportive aspects prior to the exciting Mars-Uranus trine and the harmonizing Libra New Moon. The Sun's entry into intensifying Scorpio and your 4th House of Family on **October 22**, followed by its conjunction with hardworking Saturn on the **25th**, adds domestic responsibilities to your agenda that could distract you from your long-term goals. The Taurus Full Moon on **October 29** illuminates your 10th House of Public Life, shifting the focus back to your career.

KEEP IN MIND THIS MONTH

If you take the time to strengthen your family relationships and fulfill your domestic obligations, you will also build an enduring foundation for the years ahead.

KEY DATES

OCTOBER 2–3 ★ *incurable romantic*

You can see through the veneer of your everyday life and reconnect with your soul's purpose when physical Mars crosses the metaphysical North Node of the Moon on **October 2**. Venus's sensible sextile to conservative Saturn helps you scale back your desires to those things that are truly worth waiting for. But this practical perspective doesn't last. Although loving Venus enters efficient Virgo and your

2nd House of Self-Worth on **October 3**, her tense opposition to fanciful Neptune in your 8th House of Intimacy has you chasing unrealistic fantasies instead of the real thing. Balancing your opening heart with common sense will help you avoid disappointment.

SUPER NOVA DAYS

OCTOBER 7–10 ★ *follow the yellow brick road*

Expressive Mars in fun-loving Sagittarius is visiting your 5th House of Romance, but its conflictive square to nebulous Neptune on **October 7** sends confusing signals and you probably don't know which way to go. Your desires may be surprisingly eccentric as Venus connects with weird Uranus on the **8th**, but you should ultimately get what you want because a lucky Sun-Jupiter trine on **October 9** activates your 11th House of Dreams and Wishes. Additionally, Venus forms a sweet trine with provocative Pluto to stimulate deep feelings. You need a plan, because stabilizing Saturn forms a harmonious trine with imaginative Neptune on the **10th**, grounding your fanciful flights in reality and giving you a chance to actually find the elusive pot of gold at the end of the rainbow.

OCTOBER 15–16 ★ *your cup runneth over*

A high-octane Mars-Uranus trine on **October 15** infuses you with energy, yet the even-keeled Libra New Moon in your 3rd House of Communication allows you to maintain objectivity. Nevertheless, it's tough to find a point of balance as an unsettling sesquisquare between expansive Jupiter and contractive Saturn encourages you one minute and discourages you the next. Rational Mercury and emotional Venus both align with joyful Jupiter on the **16th**, emboldening you to err on the side of excess rather than moderation.

OCTOBER 28–29 ★ *stuck in the middle*

Your enthusiasm about a creative project is admirable but could be a bit too much on **October 28**, when incorrigible Mars opposes bombastic Jupiter. However, you may be torn between two sets of desires as Venus shifts into up-in-the-air Libra. You could appear more certain than you actually are when Mercury enters presumptuous Sagittarius and squares vague Neptune on the **29th**. The Full Moon in simplistic Taurus allows you to filter out the distracting noise so you can confidently stand behind your decisions.

NOVEMBER

SO CLOSE, YET SO FAR AWAY

This month's Mercury retrograde period—from **November 6** until the **26th**—can be baffling because it begins in adventurous Sagittarius, where it inspires you to think of the exciting times ahead. You are ready for tomorrow today. Mercury's reversal might be disheartening, however, because it can halt development of your creative and romantic plans until you reconsider your assumptions and, if necessary, revise your tactics. But it's Mercury's reentry into emotional Scorpio and your 4th House of Roots on **November 14** that drives home the realization that you cannot move forward until you have your personal life in order. Meanwhile, the powerful Scorpio Solar Eclipse on **November 13** semisquares ruthless Pluto in your 6th House of Details, acting as a lightning rod to elicit much-needed change to your daily routine.

Although Mercury's retrograde leaves you reticent to take risks, aggressive Mars's entry into strategic Capricorn and your 6th House of Work on **November 16** encourages you to methodically charge ahead. The Sun's shift into fiery Sagittarius and your 5th House of Play on **November 21** brings new opportunities for creative pursuits. The Sun's square to poetic Neptune enables you to draw on your imagination, though it's tough to focus on the immediate tasks at hand. But sweet Venus's entry into your security-conscious 4th House on the **21st**, followed by her conjunction with stern Saturn on the **26th**—the same day as Mercury turns direct—is a strict reminder that you must walk before you run. Nevertheless, the Gemini Full Moon Eclipse on **November 28** conjuncts auspicious Jupiter in your 11th House of Long-Term Goals, announcing that the future has finally arrived.

KEEP IN MIND THIS MONTH

The ebbs and flows of time can be frustrating, especially when your progress is impeded by circumstances that seem beyond your control.

KEY DATES

NOVEMBER 1–3 ★ *finding common ground*

Take care of family responsibilities before you go out and have fun on **November 1**, when a frustrating Mars-Saturn semisquare constrains your urge to play with those obligations at home. Meanwhile charming Venus in your 3rd House of Communication opposes uncontainable Uranus, making it nearly impossible for you to suppress your desires. Making your feelings known seems to clear the air, but Venus's square to formidable Pluto on the **3rd** can raise the resistance you encounter more than you expect. Luckily, Venus in diplomatic Libra empowers you to handle tricky interpersonal tensions if you're willing meet others halfway.

NOVEMBER 9 ★ *when you wish upon a star*
Your dreams can come true when delightful Venus trines lavish Jupiter in your 11th House of Goals. But this isn't a free ticket for the fulfillment of just any fantasy. A conflictive aspect from Venus to elusive Neptune can dangle the bait of an unobtainable goal in front of you, creating disillusionment when you realize you've been hooked. Set your sights on a reachable destination to ensure your happiness.

SUPER NOVA DAYS
NOVEMBER 13–17 ★ *playing for keeps*
An emotionally powerful Scorpio New Moon Eclipse on **November 13** can shake the foundations of your life as it undermines your 4th House of Roots. You may try to bluff your way through a family conflict as retrograde Mercury squares evasive Neptune and then reenters secretive Scorpio and your 4th House on **November 14**. But the stakes of the game may be higher than you realize, because karmic Saturn forms an irresolvable quincunx with irrepressible Uranus on **November 15**. Your current choices will have lasting ramifications. Thankfully, brave Mars in your 6th House of Work sextiles psychic Neptune on the **17th**, enabling you to rely on your intuition, make the best choices, and apply your energy toward getting what you want.

NOVEMBER 26–29 ★ *time is on your side*
Your domestic life is at a turning point when Mercury goes direct on **November 26**. The Sun's trine to lightning-like Uranus in your 9th House of Higher Truth inspires you with brilliant ideas, yet it can also trick you with a sense of urgency. Although a patient Venus-Saturn conjunction helps you realize success won't happen overnight, an intense Mars-Pluto conjunction in your 6th House of Self-Improvement on the **27th** demands extreme dedication. Fortunately, the clever Gemini Lunar Eclipse on **November 28** helps to relieve the pressure by revealing alternative routes to reach your destination. Remember, you can find satisfaction once you realize you don't have to rush the journey.

DECEMBER

COUNT YOUR BLESSINGS

You are looking ahead to the future as the year draws to a close, thanks to broad-minded Jupiter remaining active in your 11th House of Dreams throughout the month. However, there is an uneasy tension between your long-term goals and what's currently happening at home and on the job due to annoying quincunxes to Jupiter from Venus and Mars on the **1st**. You may be so imaginative on **December 10–11** that fantasy overtakes reality when Mercury enters your 5th House of Romance just prior to squaring dreamy Neptune in your 8th House of Intimacy. Although your intentions may be good, you could mislead yourself, your partner, or a love interest as sensual Venus repeats this pattern on **December 15–16**. Nevertheless, the extroverted Sagittarius New Moon on **December 13** also activates your playful 5th House, helping you to get in sync with the holiday spirit.

Fortunately, you can keep your feet on the ground because you receive solid support from loved ones as trustworthy Saturn in your 4th House of Foundations moves toward a collaborative sextile with potent Pluto in your 6th House of Work that's exact on **December 26**. This long-lasting aspect gives you the self-discipline to be highly productive, even with limited resources. Although this is about thriving as much as it's about surviving, both Pluto and Saturn create pesky quincunxes with jovial Jupiter on **December 20–22**, reactivating the disconnect with your life purpose that you experienced at the beginning of the month. Thankfully, the emotionally charged Cancer Full Moon on **December 28** falls in your 12th House of Destiny; its opposition to transformative Pluto gives you a chance to change old habits that continue to limit your growth.

KEEP IN MIND THIS MONTH

An abundance of social activities keep your spirits high. Just make sure that your enthusiasm to spread joy doesn't spread you too thin.

KEY DATES

DECEMBER 1–2 ★ *larger than life*

Good times are just out of reach on **December 1** as an anxious Mercury-Uranus alignment puts your nervous system on edge and Venus and Mars form irritating quincunxes with jolly Jupiter. The outgoing Sagittarius Sun in your 5th House of Spontaneity opposes Jupiter on **December 2**, challenging you to focus on one thing at a time, instead of scattering your energy. You can restore balance to your life if you're willing to be satisfied without reaching the stars.

DECEMBER 10–14 ★ *leap of faith*

Forget practicality when clever Mercury shoots into aspiring Sagittarius on **December 10**. The illogical Mercury-Neptune square on the **11th** has your imagination running wild. Thankfully, on **December 12** forceful Mars in your 6th House of Work magically quintiles concrete Saturn, bringing your unrealistic dreams back into focus. The exuberant Sagittarius New Moon on the **13th** is an energy booster, emboldening you to ride high on the exciting wings of new ideas when messenger Mercury forms a collaborative trine with innovative Uranus on **December 14**.

SUPER NOVA DAYS

DECEMBER 19–22 ★ *let the good times roll*

It's time to reflect on how effectively managing your personal affairs can also move you closer to your life's purpose, when the Sun's entry into traditional Capricorn on **December 21** marks the Winter Solstice. But cultivating self-discipline can be difficult as delicious Venus and jocular Jupiter entice you to explore new ways to enjoy yourself, which can prove satisfying as long as you don't overdo it. Venus trines radical Uranus on **December 19**, putting you in an experimental mood, yet her opposition to Jupiter on the **22nd** makes it almost impossible to know when to stop. Meanwhile, Jupiter's crunchy quincunx to perceptive Pluto on **December 20** and pragmatic Saturn on **December 22** can shift your attention from the current holiday fun to worries about what next year may bring.

DECEMBER 28–31 ★ *back to the future*

The nostalgic Cancer Full Moon on **December 28** illuminates your 12th House of Endings, stirring up deep feelings as you contemplate how you can do better next year. The Sun's conjunction with unrelenting Pluto on the **30th** can be problematic if you get into an argument, for you're not likely to back down. However, it also gives you tremendous firmness when making your New Year's resolutions. A thrilling Mars-Uranus sextile on **December 31** adds an element of surprise to your holiday and assures a high-energy ending to this transformational year.

VIRGO

AUGUST 23–SEPTEMBER 22

VIRGO

2011 SUMMARY

Financial progress—though it may be hard-earned—is also reflective of how you value yourself. Even if your current job isn't aligned with your life purpose, making money goes beyond survival to bring you something more. Being successful enhances your self-esteem and enables you to gather the resources you'll need when you are ready to make your next career move. Your view of life will broaden, whether you begin a course of study in comparative religion or head off on a journey to some distant land. Although you may feel confused by people who aren't what they claim to be, you might also meet a spiritual teacher who reveals the true meaning of mystical love and devotion.

AUGUST—*summertime blues*

If your expectations are too high, reaching them is unlikely. Instead of working harder, take time to reevaluate your aspirations and dreams.

SEPTEMBER—*information overload*

Try as you might to maintain the status quo, the winds of change are picking up. It's wise now to keep all your options open.

OCTOBER—*permission granted*

Your heightened intensity may be great for productivity, but you're more likely to accomplish your goals if you are also sensitive to the needs of others.

NOVEMBER—*ready, set, wait*

Don't allow disappointment to extinguish your dreams. It might just take you longer to reach your goals than you first imagined.

DECEMBER—*love is in the air*

Although you often tend to shy away from too much emotional intensity, right now it provides profound creative inspiration.

2011 CALENDAR

AUGUST

MON 1–WED 3 ★ **SUPER NOVA DAYS** Awakened desires can create an emotional fiasco

MON 8–THU 11 ★ Fuzzy thinking can blur judgment

TUE 16–THU 18 ★ Your creativity is on fire; transform dreams into reality

FRI 26–TUE 30 ★ A fresh start gives you the energy to accomplish your goals

SEPTEMBER

FRI 2 ★ Reach out for a goal beyond your usual limits

SUN 11–WED 14 ★ Your charm goes a long way toward getting what you want

SAT 17–SUN 18 ★ You are unsure of yourself while in an unstable situation

SUN 25–WED 28 ★ **SUPER NOVA DAYS** Don't let down your guard

OCTOBER

THU 6–FRI 7 ★ Fantasy isn't a substitute for getting your facts right

TUE 11–FRI 14 ★ Facing disappointment helps you move through resistance

FRI 21–SUN 23 ★ Relax and enjoy your active imagination

WED 26–FRI 28 ★ **SUPER NOVA DAYS** Be the change you want to see

NOVEMBER

THU 3–SAT 5 ★ Learn from your experience, laugh about it, and move on

MON 7–FRI 11 ★ Loss of motivation brings increased spiritual awareness

TUE 15–WED 16 ★ Your mind can take you nearly anywhere now

TUE 22–FRI 25 ★ **SUPER NOVA DAYS** Releasing hidden tensions makes for a wild week

DECEMBER

THU 1–MON 5 ★ Pursue pleasure with someone you love

SAT 10–TUE 13 ★ Don't promise more than you can manage

SUN 18–THU 22 ★ Kick up your heels while you can and let the good times roll

SAT 24 ★ There is magic if you're willing to explore the shadows

THU 29 ★ **SUPER NOVA DAY** Sweeping changes are transforming your life

VIRGO OVERVIEW

Your skills for solving problems and staying on schedule are well above average, yet as 2012 starts you may be bogged down with complicated issues that require more time to resolve than you expect. Active Mars moves slowly when the year begins as he floats toward his retrograde station in your sign on January 23. The planet of pushing ahead will then move backward into your 1st House of Personality until April 13; it's time for you to tie up loose ends before you take on new challenges. You may be more withdrawn than usual and, perhaps, irritated by delays and fatigued by the extra effort it seems to take to get anything done. **Use this period to step back, reexamine where old habits are no longer useful, and adopt new ways of managing your health and lifestyle.**

Handling money is another key issue this year, with responsible Saturn in your 2nd House of Self-Esteem until October 5. This transit also reminds you to treat yourself kindly and to maintain an emotional balance that acknowledges your strengths as much as your weaknesses. You gain the confidence and status you need to succeed when you're respected and your opinions are listened to. If you're uncomfortable making small talk with strangers or speaking to large groups, investing in a class to improve your communication skills is an excellent idea. Venus, the charming ruler of your 2nd House, retrogrades in your 10th House of Career from May 15 until June 27. On the positive side, this can reconnect you with someone from your past who can benefit you professionally, or revive a talent that's been dormant. However, complex interactions with others can make your job more difficult. **Repairing relationships starts when you demonstrate flexibility and a friendly attitude that's open to new and different points of view.**

Generous Jupiter in Taurus brings gifts of learning that have practical applications as it moves through your 9th House of Higher Education until June 11. One of its fundamental lessons is that simplicity will help you fly higher than burdening your mind with too many details. **Grasping basic principles is your ladder to the stars, rewarding you with a richer sense of meaning and purpose.** Then, on June 11, Jupiter skips into adaptable Gemini and your 10th House for a yearlong stay to multiply options in your professional life. Don't leap at the first opportunity that comes your way—Jupiter's dodgy square with nebulous Neptune on June 25 might seduce you with promises that sound too good to be true, and that's because they probably are. Your natural critical judgment may be skewed, so double-check work-related assumptions before you let hope carry you so high that you leave reason and common sense behind.

AIMING FOR THE STARS

You have an ongoing opportunity this year to powerfully expand your experiences of love and relationships thanks to the long-term transits of transformational Pluto in your 5th House of Romance and spiritual Neptune in your 7th House of Partners. Tender words and a caring conversation show you how good a partnership can be when interactive Mercury joins Neptune on February 14. You're able to sort out details and smooth out misunderstandings when the speedy messenger planet begins a three-week retrograde cycle in your 8th House of Intimacy on March 12. Passion may peak when ardent Mars joins potent Pluto on November 27. This can be a critical moment of choice when you invest more deeply in a relationship, make significant changes, or seriously consider cutting it off completely.

ONE THING AT A TIME

For the second year in a row, two eclipses in your 10th House of Career allow you to make big changes in your work life. A tense square from squishy Neptune to the Solar Eclipse in Gemini on May 20 could put you on slippery ground. Spreading yourself too thin by taking on too many tasks is bound to reduce your efficiency. But taking time away from professional responsibilities to recharge your batteries and find new inspiration and purpose could aim you in a more fulfilling direction. The November 28 Lunar Eclipse falling in clever Gemini and conjuncting opportunistic Jupiter seems promising enough to make you smile. Yet stressful aspects to the Moon from demanding Mars, Saturn, and Pluto put the focus on performance. Your job could grow more difficult if you don't maintain your usual high standards.

PLAY IT SAFE

This year it's more important that you maintain financial stability than make as much money as you can. Reliable Saturn's presence in your 2nd House of Income until October 5 rewards you for being moderate in your spending and consistent in what you earn. Mercury's retrograde turn in your 8th House of Shared Resources on March 12 nudges you to reevaluate any working partnerships or potential investments. Do some careful research instead of allowing someone else's impatience push you into a hasty decision. The Libra Full Moon on April 6 in your 2nd House underscores this point, reminding you to not give in to pressure when you need more time to make up your mind. The Libra New Moon on October 15 forms a favorable trine with enterprising Jupiter that may coax you into adding new skills to your professional repertoire, take on a second job, or start a part-time business.

WELLNESS MADE SIMPLE

Your interest in diet and nutrition comes in handy when active Mars is retrograde in your 1st House of Physicality from January 23 until April 13. What you do during this period can set the tone for the rest of the year. If you encounter an old health issue, don't despair. This is your chance to finally address its root cause and make changes that will enhance your overall well-being. But you don't need to become obsessive about finding the perfect way to eat or exercise; severely limiting your options makes it more difficult to stick to a healthy plan.

HOME IMPROVEMENT

Sparks fly on the home front on June 4, when the Sagittarius Full Moon is a Lunar Eclipse in your 4th House of Family and combative Mars squares both the Sun and Moon. If you can turn irritation into positive action, you'll reduce the intensity of conflict and redirect your passion constructively. If you're feeling cramped, this is a signal to brighten up your environment or think about moving to a larger place. Mercury's retrograde in your 4th House on November 6–26 is a good time for maintenance and repairs where you live. It's also an opportunity to untangle misunderstandings with those closest to you.

GREAT EXPLORATIONS

Mix business with pleasure while Jupiter is in your 9th House of Faraway Places, until June 11. This fortunate planet's presence in economy-minded Taurus helps you get the most bang for your buck when you hit the road. In fact, Jupiter's harmonious trine to penny-pinching Pluto on March 13 is especially good for squeezing an incredible experience out of a journey, especially one to a familiar place. The New Moon in Taurus in your 9th House on April 21 motivates you to pursue your dreams. It is favorably aspected by imaginative Neptune and motivational Mars, which turned direct on April 13, increasing your desire to expand your horizons both physically and mentally. Jupiter's entry into your 10th House of Career on June 11 indicates more work-related travel through the rest of the year.

THE FIRE WITHIN

Summer is a rich time for spiritual exploration this year. Your ruling planet, Mercury's, retrograde in your 12th House of Divinity on July 14–August 8 can turn your mind away from everyday affairs as you seek solace for your soul. The New Moon in Leo on August 17, also activating your 12th House, warms your insides with hope and reminds you of the infinite creative capacity that's available beyond the limits of your own ego. Sturdy Saturn's harmonious alignment with this Sun-Moon conjunction suggests that sharing a devotional practice with a partner makes it easier to maintain than doing it alone.

RICK & JEFF'S TIP FOR THE YEAR:
Help Yourself to the Happiness Buffet

You don't have to complete everything that you start this year. It's wiser to recognize when you've done enough and move on instead of seeking perfection in each activity or task. That's because you may have more opportunities than usual, tempting you to exhaust yourself by taking on too many of them. Give yourself permission to test the waters of a new experience instead of committing yourself to finishing it no matter what the cost. If you think of life as a tray of appetizers where you get to take little bites instead of settling down for a full meal, you could find yourself quite satisfied.

JANUARY

PRUDENT PLAY

Although the year starts with the Capricorn Sun in your 5th House of Fun and Games, you have good reason to apply some self-restraint. Be careful about initiating creative projects and romantic entanglements while the Sun travels through this conservative sign through **January 20**. Energetic Mars's retrograde turn in methodical Virgo on **January 23** is not a stop sign, but should definitely be seen as a yellow caution flag. Rather than giving in to every impulse, analyze new projects or activities to weed out those that will require more effort than you anticipate. Look for emotional support from friends and colleagues around the Full Moon in Cancer on **January 9**, which lights up your 11th House of Groups and forms a helpful sextile with Mars. Instead of forging ahead on your own or just struggling to maintain your current position, turn to dependable allies who can make these challenges more manageable.

A streak of sweetness warms up your relationships in the middle of the month. Romantic Venus floats into imaginative Pisces and your 7th House of Partners on **January 14**, aligning favorably with lucky Jupiter. However, work issues move into the foreground when the Sun enters your 6th House of Employment on the **20th**. Then, on **January 23**, the futuristic Aquarius New Moon seeds your professional life with innovative ideas to make your current job more interesting or to inspire you to consider a radical shift in your career path. Brainy Mercury, your ruling planet, follows the Sun into your 6th House on **January 27**, giving substance to burgeoning ideas that can fill your days with excitement and complexity.

KEEP IN MIND THIS MONTH

Think twice before taking on any new projects. Even the simplest ones can grow into complicated tasks that test your patience.

KEY DATES

JANUARY 1 ★ *watch your mouth*

You should be relaxing on a holiday, but a tense square between verbose Mercury and contentious Mars is more likely to keep you on your toes. A battle with a family member may arise when words are tossed like firebombs, provoking strong and immediate reactions. Even the most casual statements can set off anger, so speak gently and respond slowly unless you want to create verbal fireworks. Expressing the truth, even when it comes from your heart, can be tricky business unless you can soften your delivery.

JANUARY 7–8 ★ *genius at work*

Your mind is a brilliant instrument on **January 7**, when Mercury sextiles Saturn and Neptune. These favorable aspects combine intellect, order, and imagination, enabling you to express your dreams in realistic terms and to communicate with both clarity and compassion. Intellectual leaps follow on the **8th**, when cerebral Mercury trines philosophical Jupiter and squares unconventional Uranus. Your vision extends to horizons you haven't even imagined before; reaching the high peaks you're seeing will not happen overnight.

JANUARY 12–13 ★ *the force is with you*

You have an ideal balance of enthusiasm and practicality on **January 12**, when energetic Mars and the Sun form a trine in pragmatic earth signs. You can easily find effective ways to tackle big tasks, especially when an intense Mercury-Pluto conjunction deepens your perceptions and empowers your communications on the **13th**. You may be privy to information that gives you an edge, yet abusing the power it delivers could undermine trust. A supersensitive Venus-Neptune conjunction in your 6th House of Skills brings artistry to your work but can also make simple comments feel like harsh criticism.

SUPER NOVA DAYS

JANUARY 22–23 ★ *greener pastures*

An optimistic Sun-Jupiter square amplifies your ambitions on **January 22**. Aiming higher and seeking more meaning in life are worthy goals, of course, but don't forget that if you raise the bar too high, hope can quickly dissolve into despair. The Aquarius New Moon on the **23rd** is squared by Jupiter and Saturn, sending mixed signals about how far to reach in work-related matters. Telling off a boss, colleague, or customer can be a costly mistake unless you're standing on solid professional ground. If you have an itch to make your job more fulfilling, starting with a hobby is a way to scratch it without risking your livelihood.

JANUARY 27–28 ★ *into the great wide open*

You're vulnerable to doubts on the **27th** thanks to a naysaying Mercury-Saturn square. Confidence returns the next day, however, when the messenger planet's connections with Jupiter and Uranus lift your mind above immediate obstacles. The bigger strategic perspective you now see can help you resolve your problems.

FEBRUARY

ANGELIC ALLIANCES

Take a step back early in February to reassess your positions at work and in partnerships before moving forward later in the month. A subtle but significant shift occurs on the **3rd**, when limitless Neptune reenters Pisces and your 7th House of Relationships where it will reside until **2025**. This long transit softens critical edges that keep love from flowing freely. Your willingness to overlook minor imperfections enables you to appreciate the essence of those closest to you and sweetens your personal and professional alliances. The creative Leo Full Moon on **February 7** brightens your 12th House of Soul Consciousness, perhaps stirring up desires or sparking vivid dreams that aren't ready to see the light of day. Clever Mercury in your 6th House of Self-Improvement opposes the Moon to remind you that you may need to develop specific skills to make the magic happen.

On **February 8**, you're eager to take risks in how you connect with others thanks to alluring Venus's move into pioneering Aries and your 8th House of Intimacy, spurring your sense of adventure. The push toward boldly expressing your desires gets another boost from the New Moon in Pisces on **February 21**. The Sun and Moon are joined by Neptune in your 7th House of Companions to flood you with feelings you can't easily explain. There's a strong chance that you might feel drained or exhausted by a needy partner. Yet the considerable upside of this lunation is a sense of divine union that inspires you to pursue your highest aspirations. Old relationship wounds are healed in Pisces's oceanic waters of faith and forgiveness, making way for a romantic renaissance.

KEEP IN MIND THIS MONTH

If you're fixated on superficial flaws in yourself or others, you will miss the point completely. Open your heart and see the perfection that lies within.

KEY DATES

FEBRUARY 1 ★ *joy to your world*

Take time out from attending to business and indulge in some midweek pleasure. Passionate Mars in your active 1st House opposes captivating Venus in your receptive 7th House, making you a prime candidate for having fun. The lines between work and play can blur when you're in such delightful company. Creativity grows in cooperation with imaginative individuals, and amorous feelings are plentiful if you don't bury them under a pile of practical obligations.

FEBRUARY 6–7 ★ *think different*

Your mind is buzzing with strange ideas that could turn out to be brilliant or completely off as the Sun and Mercury form uncomfortable semisquares with electric Uranus on **February 6**. Restlessness and rebellious instincts could provoke you to act impulsively or say something you might regret. The Sun's conjunction with Mercury on the **7th** aligns ego and intellect, sharpening your thinking and giving you the words to explain complex issues. There could be tension in the air, though, with the dramatic Leo Full Moon shining its light into your 12th House of Secrets while orderly Saturn turns retrograde in your 2nd House of Resources. Tie up unfinished financial matters before you make any new expenditures.

SUPER NOVA DAYS

FEBRUARY 13–14 ★ *two as one*

Savvy Mercury's supportive trine with solid Saturn on **February 13** roots you in reality just hours before the messenger planet drifts into dreamy Pisces and your 7th House of Others. Mercury's conjunction with mystical Neptune on the **14th** dissolves cynicism and softens your analytical perspective with images and feelings you can't easily explain. While it's true that you could be deceived by a misleading individual or fall prey to your own fantasies, you may reach sublime heights of communication that melt usual boundaries to give you a real soul connection.

FEBRUARY 19 ★ *walls come tumbling down*

Compassion flows to you and from you today if it's not blocked by doubt or fear. The Sun floats into intuitive Pisces and your 7th House where it, too, joins boundless Neptune. What your mind envisioned with Mercury's transit on **February 14** is now connecting to your heart. Softness becomes your strength, when you take the lead and open up to individuals you can trust. Relationships are fueled by faith in yourself and your inspiration to initiate projects with others. A meaningful collaboration is more rewarding now than success on your own.

FEBRUARY 23 ★ *hot topic*

A spicy Mercury-Mars opposition could provoke you to make snippy comments and snap judgments. If you find yourself entangled in a frustrating debate, don't try to force a conclusion. Change the subject or the tone to cool a conflict that's not getting you anywhere. However, a respectful debate will produce a fruitful exchange of ideas.

MARCH

TIME IS ON YOUR SIDE

Pushy partners, both personal and professional, and a crisis-driven atmosphere motivate you to move faster this month. An uncharacteristic impulse to leap before you look may arise when your curious ruling planet, Mercury, zips into impetuous Aries on **March 2**. However, analytical Mercury turns retrograde on **March 12** and continues moving backward until **April 4**, marking a period when you'd be wise to adopt a more leisurely pace. Errors tend to pile up during this period, as do complications with details and communications. Carefully tying up loose ends and tightening up inefficient systems will make you more productive in the long run rather than going into overdrive now. Strong emotions surface with the Full Moon in your normally logical sign on **March 8**. Warrior Mars's proximity to the Moon may propel you to take on new tasks or even explode with anger. Yet before you impulsively embark on a fresh project or boil over with frustration, reflect on your past experiences; you will probably find a solution to your problem.

You find new resources of power and creativity to support your ambitions when expansive Jupiter trines perceptive Pluto on the **13th**. This enterprising alignment, which previously occurred on **July 7** and **October 28, 2010**, is now part of a Grand Earth Trine with active Mars in your sign, bringing patience and persuasiveness to help you reach your goals. The Sun's entry into Aries on the **20th** is the Spring Equinox, which initiates a fresh cycle of enthusiasm in your 8th House of Deep Sharing. On the **22nd**, the Aries New Moon conjunct shocking Uranus could shake up your relationships with radical ideas and unexpected events.

KEEP IN MIND THIS MONTH

The bolder your plan, the more measured you need to be. Crises become opportunities when you are able to maintain your composure.

KEY DATES

MARCH 3–5 ★ *the price is right*

An aggressive Sun-Mars opposition on **March 3** adds an edge to interpersonal interactions while attraction and aggression intertwine to heat up and confuse relationships. Feelings of rejection are common with an opposition between sensitive Venus and stingy Saturn on the **4th**. Yet the gift of this aspect is that it helps you define your needs and clarify where you stand with others. An honest but gentle assessment of what you have to offer can help you make better deals for yourself. The value of money or love is easier to measure when Venus enters earthy Taurus on **March 5**, while an electric Mercury-Uranus opposition sparks unusual conversations and intellectual breakthroughs.

SUPER NOVA DAYS

MARCH 13–14 ★ *adult entertainment*

You handle delicate matters gracefully when an insightful Venus-Pluto trine on **March 13** facilitates deep conversations and the capacity to heal damaged alliances. You then get to reap the rewards of your passion and persistence on the **14th** as sexy Venus joins exuberant Jupiter and both make supportive trines to dynamic Mars. An almost perfect balance of playfulness and practicality is a great setup for a creative project, a party, or an intimate dinner for two.

MARCH 18 ★ *jumping jack flash*

Retrograde Mercury backs over unstable Uranus, igniting explosive discussions and spinning off crazy ideas. Restlessness and nervous energy make it hard for you to concentrate or to stop yourself from saying the first thing that pops into your head. Yet your ability to see things from a completely original perspective puts partnerships in a new light. Still, if you're feeling misunderstood, it's only because you may be struggling to find the words to describe the strange thoughts shooting through your mind. Take a deep breath and try again.

MARCH 24 ★ *call of the wild*

Don't even bother trying to keep a lid on rapidly shifting circumstances today. A volcanic Sun-Uranus conjunction in your 8th House of Intimacy and Transformation is a wake-up call to bring your partnerships up to date instead of relying on the old rules that kept them together. A provocative person pushing your buttons or your own itch for freedom can leave you feeling uncertain. If you're willing to innovate, however, you can reinvigorate a present union—or find an exciting new one.

MARCH 29 ★ *handle with care*

Your relationships continue to rumble with change as the progressive Aries Sun squares relentless Pluto in your 5th House of Romance. This combination often triggers power struggles and trust issues as you encounter a manipulative person or are accused of pulling strings yourself. Fortunately, a smart Mercury-Venus sextile provides sensitivity and diplomacy that can transform a potential loss into a major gain.

APRIL

FORWARD MARCH

You're ready for a fresh start this month as two key planets turn direct. Communicative Mercury makes its forward shift in your 7th House of Partners on **April 4**, helping you accelerate negotiations, initiate new contacts, and present your ideas with panache. Enthusiastic Mars recommences direct motion in your sign on the **13th** to pump you up with adrenaline and infuse you with extra energy. This cosmic boost tells you to be more physically active and assertive in pursuing your goals. Yet even before this happens, you may find yourself in the spotlight when magnetic Venus enters your 10th House of Career and Responsibility on **April 3**. This charming planet's presence in multitasking Gemini can scatter your attention in several directions, making it difficult to set priorities. It is possible, though, to add new interests and skills to your professional life, as long as you have the flexibility to work on several projects at the same time.

Money concerns may surface with the indecisive Libra Full Moon on **April 6** activating your 2nd House of Resources. Uncertainty about a financial decision could keep you on the fence, but it's probably best to bide your time and think things through a bit longer before you jump into action. Don't let an impatient person push you to make a commitment before you're ready. Mercury zips back into excitable Aries and your 8th House of Deep Sharing on the **16th** to attract fast talkers who can make ordinary events sound like emergencies. The Sun's entry into stable Taurus on the **19th** is another reminder to trust your instincts and advance at your own pace.

KEEP IN MIND THIS MONTH

Be kind to yourself. Rewards and recognition will continue to motivate you long after criticism has lost its usefulness and turned self-defeating.

KEY DATES

APRIL 5–7 ★ *precious illusions*

Don't let your soft heart obscure your good judgment about people and money when sweet Venus squares squishy Neptune on **April 5**. Falling in love with someone or something feels delicious, but it's wise to start with a taste before you sign up for the full meal. Idealistic Neptune's aspects to the Sun and the lovely Libra Full Moon on the **6th** continue this romantic theme, which readily erodes your reason. If kindness to others or the pursuit of pleasure leads you too far astray, you may have to pay the price on **April 7** when Venus squares Mars. This sexy and sassy alignment continues to pique your interest in having fun, perhaps with a former partner, but a sharper edge of awareness forces you to be completely honest about how you play the game.

APRIL 12–13 ★ *sort it out*

Getting what you want from others, including simple courtesy and fair treatment, isn't easy on **April 12**, but an insecure Mercury-Saturn quincunx suggests that you might interpret even good news as bad. This could make you nervous, especially when Mars turns direct in hardworking Virgo on the **13th**. There are knots of miscommunication that you must untangle before you feel free enough to move forward. However, your willingness to engage in complicated negotiations could do the trick.

SUPER NOVA DAYS
APRIL 19–22 ★ *clear sailing ahead*

The Sun's entry into reliable Taurus and your 9th House of Big Ideas on **April 19** lays down a solid foundation for your future plans. Investing in education and travel enriches your mind with a wider perspective that helps you grow both personally and professionally. But you may struggle to put together all the pieces when fact-based Mercury clashes with restless Mars on **April 20**, tempting you to take on peripheral issues instead of concentrating on essential concerns. Happily, a healing trine between Mercury and the integrating North Node of the Moon on the **21st** reduces friction and gets information flowing more easily. Additionally, a well-aspected Taurus New Moon inspires your thinking and reenergizes your ambitions. On **April 22**, a brilliant Mercury-Uranus conjunction excites you with original insights that hasten your desire to make your next move.

APRIL 25 ★ *the truth will set you free*

You may have to face the costs and consequences of acting on your latest inspiration when high-strung Mercury in Aries crosses paths with pressure-packed Pluto. Arguing with a potential ally is only helpful if it causes you to rethink your position. If you can avoid personality clashes and dig deeply to focus on facts, the struggle will be worth the effort. Tearing down a concept could lead to rebuilding it in a much more efficient form.

MAY

ADJUSTING YOUR SIGHTS

Reconsidering professional goals should be a top priority for you this month. On **May 15**, Venus, the planet of self-worth, begins her six-week retrograde cycle in your 10th House of Career. Working relationships may become more complicated and financial rewards reduced, motivating you to think about changing jobs. On **May 20**, the New Moon in restless Gemini is a Solar Eclipse in your 10th House, reinforcing your discontent at your place of employment. Borderless Neptune's tense square to this Sun-Moon conjunction could leave you exhausted by too many tasks or disenchanted by a lack of ethics in your current position. However, you might become so inspired by dreams of a more fulfilling occupation that you lose focus on the tasks at hand.

Three harsh aspects involving auspicious Jupiter this month also indicate possible radical shifts in your thinking. A partner or associate can spring surprising news when Jupiter forms a stressful semisquare with reckless Uranus on **May 7**. While this might knock you off course, it could also free you to pursue other interests. On **May 16**, Jupiter aligns in an ungainly quincunx with Saturn that makes it difficult to reconcile future hopes with present realities. You will have two more chances to iron out these differences when this aspect recurs on **December 22** and **March 23, 2013**. Lastly, Jupiter's anxious sesquisquare with purging Pluto on **May 17** can squeeze out one project to make room for a more important one. However, interactive Mercury's move into your 10th House on **May 24** facilitates communication and enhances connections that could offer you more professional opportunities than you can accept at this time.

KEEP IN MIND THIS MONTH

Keeping your eye on your long-term goals helps you make course adjustments that increase your chances of reaching your destination.

KEY DATES

MAY 5 ★ *trust in the process*

You can expect weighty conversations today, because a profound Scorpio Full Moon is illuminating your 3rd House of Communication while talkative Mercury opposes heavy Saturn. While you could get stuck with negative thoughts and messages, the point is to respond to fears with a constructive attitude. No, this isn't about putting happy-face stickers on overdue bills; it's about working toward solutions no matter how long it takes.

MAY 10 ★ *seek higher ground*

This is an excellent day for untangling knots of disagreement with friends and colleagues by looking past differences over details and recognizing the bigger principles you have in common. With a slinky sextile between cerebral Mercury and cloudy Neptune adding subtlety to your thoughts and speech, gentle persuasion and poetic words are more effective now than limiting yourself to logic and reason.

SUPER NOVA DAYS

MAY 13–16 ★ *heroic efforts*

You're ready for risks on May 13 thanks to a magnanimous Sun-Jupiter conjunction, while a lively Mercury-Mars trine spurs you to action. Yet all four planets are in practical earth signs that support your pragmatic side; your feet are solidly on the ground even as you reach for the stars. Mercury's trine to mysterious Pluto on the **14th** is like X-ray vision that permits you to see below the surface and read others' intentions. You may be delayed by a shortage of resources on the **15th** when Mars is tangled up with slow-moving Saturn. But that's not going to stop you for long; macho Mars trines perspicacious Pluto on **May 16** to lead you to exactly what you need.

MAY 20–22 ★ *question authority*

The Gemini New Moon Solar Eclipse on **May 20** encourages you to make long-term professional changes—but Mercury's semisquare to Uranus gets your mind racing right now. Unconventional ideas shake your view of things before tough aspects from Mercury to somber Saturn and Pluto reduce your options on **May 21**. You'd normally be frustrated by this sudden shift from the excitement of discovery to the demands of duty—yet if that happens now, it won't last long. A joyous Jupiter-Mercury conjunction on the **22nd** brings good news, encouragement from others, and a realistic plan for future travel or education to lift your spirits.

MAY 27–28 ★ *prove yourself*

The conjunction of intellectual Mercury and the willful Sun on **May 27** clarifies your thinking and empowers your words while original ideas are cultivated with an ingenious Mercury-Uranus sextile. But then, on the **28th**, obstacles arise when the messenger planet's hard aspects to tight-fisted Saturn and Pluto reveal limits of time and money or attract pressure from powerful people that continue to test your resolve.

JUNE

REBUILD FROM THE GROUND UP

The Sagittarius Full Moon in your 4th House of Roots on **June 4** is a Lunar Eclipse that can shake up family dynamics for the rest of the year. Lunar eclipses are usually reminders to end old habits and shut the door to the past. This one, though, is aligned in a stressful square with aggressive Mars in critical Virgo, which can inflame any differences with those closest to you. Before you get bogged down in a bruising battle that no one is likely to win, think about applying this passion to improve your living space or advance your professional life. Optimistic Jupiter moves into your 10th House of Career on **June 11** to open a twelve-month window of growth, which is another reason to invest time and energy on your public life to reach your goals.

On **June 19**, the multifaceted Gemini New Moon spreads seeds of fresh possibilities in your professional 10th House. But feisty Mars is square this lunation just as it was during the **June 4** Full Moon Eclipse, pressuring you to handle more and more tasks that could irritate you or wear you down. But this time there is help from a constructive trine to the Sun and Moon from strategic Saturn that can reduce your stress if you plan well. On the **20th**, the Sun enters nurturing Cancer and your 11th House of Groups, marking the Summer Solstice, which can attract a little help from your friends. Travel, education, or your career may be affected when wheels of more dramatic change start turning with the transformational Uranus-Pluto square on **June 24**, the first of seven aspects in a series that culminates on **March 16, 2015**.

KEEP IN MIND THIS MONTH

Your chances for greater success in your occupation largely depend on your ability to create a healthier environment at home.

KEY DATES

JUNE 3–5 ★ *after the deluge*

You are cool under pressure with a trine between rational Mercury and responsible Saturn on **June 3**. Solid thinking and straight talking allow you to make your points without pressuring anyone. This can help you to earn trust before the pugnacious Full Moon Eclipse in Sagittarius on the **4th** that's also heated up by retrograde Venus's square to spicy Mars. This tense aspect can revive previous attractions and expose mismatches in taste that rile up relationships. Happily, peace and pleasure roll in with a cuddly Sun-Venus conjunction on **June 5**. This personally pleasing transit occurs in your 10th House of Status, where turning on the charm can produce professional benefits.

JUNE 7 ★ *soft around the edges*

Your intellect is softened by sentiment when your ruling planet, Mercury, enters watery Cancer. While this may reduce your objectivity, especially about co-workers, pals, and groups, communication grows more intimate when you express your feelings with tenderness. However, a harsh Sun-Mars square increases aggression that you're best off channeling into creativity or a friendly competition.

JUNE 11 ★ *communication breakdown*

Conversations crackle with quicksilver Mercury's square to electric Uranus and opposition to volcanic Pluto. One simple statement could trigger an explosion of excitement or anger that's suppressed with silence or amplified to extremes. A more helpful approach is to acknowledge that ordinary language is insufficient to express your ideas or to make sense of what others are saying. Avoid overreacting and take whatever time you need to understand what you hear and to clarify what you want to say.

JUNE 20–21 ★ *fruitful negotiations*

The Sun moves into your 11th House of Groups on **June 20**, and this will eventually help you gather more support in team activities. But a doubting Mercury-Saturn square could make you mistrust others now, perhaps for good reason. Even though a proficient Mercury-Mars sextile on the **21st** is excellent for resolving immediate conflicts or disagreeing in a reasonable manner, you must still work out some deeper issues about power and control before you can ensure cooperative collaboration.

SUPER NOVA DAYS

JUNE 27–29 ★ *brave new world*

Evaluative Venus ends its retrograde period in your 10th House of Public Responsibility on **June 27**, indicating that you're about ready to turn professional relationships in a new direction. A smart Mercury-Jupiter sextile on the **29th** normally aligns current perceptions with long-range goals to help you articulate your vision of the future. Yet the Sun forms disruptive aspects with revolutionary Uranus and reactionary Pluto that can rock your world and open your mind to radically different ideas about your true life's purpose.

JULY

CLEANING CLOSETS

Your ability to maintain privacy and manage details may be tested often this month when your ruling planet, Mercury, turns retrograde on **July 14**. Long-hidden issues return to the surface, since communicative Mercury's three-week backward period starts in the deep recesses of your 12th House of Secrets. It's better to out yourself by discreetly sharing delicate truths than to keep them to yourself. Strengthening relationships by building trust can have a positive impact on your finances when assertive Mars enters accommodating Libra and your 2nd House of Resources on **July 3**. The Full Moon in ambitious Capricorn on the **3rd** lights up your expressive 5th House, underscoring the importance of creating new alliances or reinforcing old ones. Regenerative Pluto's conjunction to the Full Moon could bring back a lover from your past or revive a creative interest or talent that's fallen by the wayside.

Commitments to friends and colleagues weigh heavily on your heart with the caring Cancer New Moon in your 11th House of Groups on **July 19**. Frugal Saturn in your income-related 2nd House makes a stressful square to this Sun-Moon conjunction, challenging you to compromise your feelings in the interest of economic stability. But this is not about shutting your mouth and meekly acquiescing to others; it's about having serious discussions of values and goals to make sure that you and your teammates are pulling in the same direction. Innovation is encouraged by effusive Jupiter's smart sextile with brilliant Uranus on **July 22**, yet its tense aspect to methodical Saturn on the **20th** suggests that it may take months to turn that vision into reality.

KEEP IN MIND THIS MONTH

The truth is a precious commodity that is valuable when shared selectively—but can cause trouble when it's broadcast too widely.

KEY DATES

JULY 3–4 ★ *cut your losses*

Awkward angles to Pluto from sociable Venus and chatty Mercury knock relationships off balance when this potent planet joins the traditional Capricorn Full Moon on **July 3**. Yet so-called mistakes may be exactly what you need to recognize that you're not getting the satisfaction you desire. Measuring the joy you receive against the effort you put into pleasing others may cause you to alter your behavior and, perhaps, eliminate someone from your personal life. Fortunately, a smooth sextile between Mercury and Venus on the **4th** provides the finesse you need to make changes in the least disruptive manner. A Mercury-Uranus trine also enhances originality, helping you to come up with new solutions for old problems.

JULY 8 ★ *lost and found*

Be sensitive to how your actions affect others today, because a slippery Mars-Neptune quincunx indicates wasted effort or money. Even if you do wander off course, however, an inventive quintile between Mercury and Saturn cleverly allows you to find your way back to more efficient ways of spending your energy.

SUPER NOVA DAYS

JULY 14–15 ★ *life in the slow lane*

You get a clear picture of a relationship or resource issue when perceptive Mercury sextiles value-conscious Venus on **July 14**. This normally fast-moving aspect lingers because this is the day that Mercury stops in its tracks to turn retrograde. Therefore, it may take a few weeks before you can communicate your understanding to others. Delays are also signaled by the Sun's square to showstopping Saturn on the **15th**. You could be burdened with obligations or slowed by friends who can't match your pace. Practicing patience produces better results now than being pushy.

JULY 22 ★ *spiritual retreat*

The Sun strolls into Leo and your 12th House on **July 22**, which could leave you feeling invisible. But you won't suffer from the loss of attention; instead, this is a time when discreet behind-the-scenes activities will have great impact on your life. Your creativity and connection to spirituality grow when you're less distracted by public events and have the time to meditate on metaphysical matters. Stepping away from the spotlight for now is, therefore, the best way to gain inner confidence that can earn you greater recognition later.

JULY 28 ★ *in sync*

You are able to align your purpose and perspective today, creating harmony between your head and your heart, for retrograde Mercury's conjunction with the Sun marks a powerful day of self-reflection. However, avoid using this sharp lens to fixate on flaws and failures. Your natural intelligence is capable of finding workable solutions.

AUGUST

STARTING OVER

Your life gets back on track this month as you are finally ready to move from fixing the past to creating the future. This change begins when your ruling planet, Mercury, turns direct on **August 8**, freeing up mindshare to consider new ideas and projects. On **August 22**, the Sun enters Virgo, warming your sign with confidence and courage for the next thirty days. Managing your job and physical well-being could be key areas for breakthroughs with the progressive Aquarius Full Moon on **August 1** brightening your 6th House of Health and Work. However, the push toward innovation is partially countered by lovable Venus's entry into cautious Cancer and your 11th House of Groups on **August 7**. This can bring you comfort from friends and colleagues, but your need for security and a strong sense of loyalty may stop you from taking chances or making dramatic changes.

A rising force of enthusiasm rushes in with the New Moon in proud Leo on **August 17**. This lunation occurs in your 12th House of Spiritual Mystery, so you might feel the growing wave of energy before you understand where it's heading. This powerful Sun-Moon conjunction is supported by sextiles to productive Mars and Saturn, ensuring that you can translate whatever inspiration you find into decisive action. On **August 23**, you get another shot of energy when dynamic Mars dives into emotionally driven Scorpio and your 3rd House of Information, reinforcing the impetus you get from the Sun in Virgo and helping you eliminate obstacles and frivolous tasks so you can focus on your most important goals. A magical Pisces Full Moon joins ethereal Neptune in your 7th House of Partners on the **31st**, inspiring relationship dreams or illusions.

KEEP IN MIND THIS MONTH

You don't need to know every step you'll be taking to begin a successful journey that can enrich your life.

KEY DATES

AUGUST 1 ★ *the sky's the limit*

The quirky Aquarius Full Moon brings an impressive array of insights about your job, health, and daily routine. Harmonious aspects from visionary Jupiter, unconventional Uranus, and pioneering Mars motivate you to reach for the stars. Developing new skills and interests helps you break old habits to revitalize yourself physically and revive enthusiasm about your work.

AUGUST 8–9 ★ *don't look back*

Inquisitive Mercury's direct turn in Leo on **August 8** lifts a burden from your mind. Whether you've completed old tasks or not, you feel a rising sense of optimism inspired by flashes of intuition. However, the winged messenger will slowly be building up speed for the next couple of weeks, reminding you to take time to carefully consider new ideas before putting them into motion. Feelings are more important than facts on the **9th**, when sweet Venus makes beautiful music with empathic Neptune. Friends can introduce you to delightful experiences and relationships grow warmer as forgiveness helps you forget old grievances and enjoy the pleasures of the moment.

AUGUST 15 ★ *overcoming adversity*

Don't be shortsighted when a demanding Mars-Saturn conjunction in your 2nd House of Income confronts you with a tough financial decision. Instead of simply reining in expenses, make a smart investment that will produce long-term benefits. It's understandable if you're low on trust; a stressful opposition of valuable Venus and manipulative Pluto emphasizes the potential for loss more than gain. However, the point is to dig below the surface to uncover hidden resources and deeper desires that can lead you to material and emotional recovery.

SUPER NOVA DAYS

AUGUST 22–24 ★ *into the mystic*

The Sun's ingress into Virgo on **August 22** pulls you out of the shadows of doubt and brightens your mood with a new light of hope. A highly intelligent Mercury-Jupiter sextile aligns immediate perceptions with future goals, which makes you an effective planner and a more skillful communicator. Yet your logic and reason could dissipate when the Sun opposes intuitive Neptune in your 7th House of Others on **August 24**. Compassion for an ungrounded individual or simple gullibility can cloud your judgment, although relationship wounds may be healed if you can overlook petty differences.

AUGUST 29 ★ *phoenix rising*

The Sun's creative trine with formidable Pluto is ideal for putting a positive spin on a negative situation. Where some might see failure, you recognize opportunities for success. Rediscovering forgotten talents empowers you to overcome creative challenges and inspires others to make the most of their gifts, too.

SEPTEMBER

ORGANIZED CHAOS

You have a strong sense of purpose and a cohesive plan to reach your goals as the month begins. The willful Sun in your sign until **September 22** empowers you to act more boldly and creatively, while meticulous Mercury in Virgo focuses your mind to fill in the details and refine systems that support your ambitions. This intense concentration can narrow your thinking and blur your perception of the big picture. When surprises happen—and they will—it's important to look up from your little piece of the puzzle to adapt to the bigger changes in the world around you. The Virgo New Moon on **September 15** is joined with Mercury in your 1st House of Physicality, reminding you to maintain a healthy diet and exercise program. But this lunation also can spur you to take the initiative in relationships and to launch new projects. However, it's essential to be open to alternative points of view once Mercury moves into diplomatic Libra and your 6th House of Work on the **16th**. Making compromises to meet others halfway during this period is more useful than rigidly adhering to your own ideas.

The second of seven life-altering Uranus-Pluto squares occurs on **September 19**. The shocks represented by this long-term pattern, occurring intermittently until **March 16, 2015**, are triggered on **September 20–29** by fast-moving planets that make you acutely aware of what's holding you back. Difficult aspects from Mercury, Mars, Venus, and the Sun can spark sudden shifts in your mood and surprising changes in the current circumstances. Relationships are on shaky ground on the **29th** when the reckless Aries Full Moon squares ruthless Pluto and joins unpredictable Uranus in your 8th House of Intimacy.

KEEP IN MIND THIS MONTH

Being mentally flexible enables you to adjust your thinking, shift your priorities, and adapt your methods to handle unanticipated events effectively.

KEY DATES

SEPTEMBER 1 ★ *loose logic*

Your ruling planet Mercury's opposition to delusional Neptune temporarily messes with your mind and muddles messages with misunderstanding. Supposed facts range from slightly fuzzy to outright fantasies, which can lead you to incorrect conclusions. Exploring your imagination and whispering sweet nothings, though, are desirable applications of this intellectually dreamy aspect.

SEPTEMBER 7–10 ★ *just the facts*

You might raise expectations beyond reason or take on more than you can handle when the Virgo Sun squares boundless Jupiter on the **7th**. This behavior continues on the **8th**, when a Mercury-Jupiter square invites exaggeration and can overload you with information. Stretching your thinking is helpful if you are grounded with a good dose of common sense. Mercury's conjunction with the Sun on the **10th** is an excellent time to weed out useless data, gather your thoughts, and communicate with persuasive precision.

SUPER NOVA DAYS

SEPTEMBER 20–22 ★ *give peace a chance*

Conversations grow convoluted and strange ideas can erupt on **September 20**, when messenger Mercury seeks harmony in pleasure-seeking Libra during its opposition to eccentric Uranus and square to dark Pluto. Words can explode with emotion that reveals uncomfortable truths or unexpressed desires. Luckily, a sweet sextile between loving Venus and generous Jupiter softens stress with humor, playfulness, or a forgiving spirit. The Sun's entry in amicable Libra and your 6th House of Daily Routines marks the Autumnal Equinox on the **22nd** as you consciously choose to be more sociable and improve relationships at work.

SEPTEMBER 25–26 ★ *stranger than fiction*

On **September 25–26**, daring Mars and sultry Venus create hard aspects with Uranus and Pluto that can provoke extreme behavior and stimulate unusual tastes. You can be whipsawed between repulsion and attraction, making it tricky to know where you stand with others. It's also difficult to cooperate when your hunger for freedom and resistance to outside pressure are so strong. Clearly, this isn't the best time to make major decisions about relationships or resources. However, Mercury's trine with wise Jupiter on the **26th** helps you assess the situation and ask the questions that will eventually lead to the answers you seek.

SEPTEMBER 29 ★ *exit strategy*

It's understandable if you want to run away from responsibilities that feel suffocating right now, because the weirdness of the Sun's opposition to Uranus and square to Pluto is intensified by the Aries Full Moon. Yet making an impetuous move is less likely to help than seeking a more creative escape plan that's both safe and stimulating.

OCTOBER

BEAUTY AND THE BOTTOM LINE

Your willingness to make tough decisions now will make your life easier in the future. If you've been wavering about financial matters, this is the right time to tune in to your gut feelings, get off the fence, and take decisive action. The Sun illuminates your 2nd House of Resources until **October 22**, providing you with ample opportunities to weigh your budgetary options. It helps if your choices are rooted in self-confidence, which thankfully receives a boost when attractive Venus enters Virgo on **October 3**. Your charming personality, creative approach, and sense of style should turn heads in your direction with this alluring transit. Yet the refined qualities of Venus in Virgo are contrasted with an adventurous spirit when courageous Mars enters Sagittarius and your 4th House of Roots on **October 6**. While you keep up appearances of commitment to your current situation, Mars at the bottom of your chart can incite conflict at home if you're feeling hemmed in or bored.

On **October 10**, the first beneficial trine of pragmatic Saturn and whimsical Neptune occurs. You can combine your thoughtful analyses with romantic impulses, solidifying an inspiring partnership. These aspects return on **June 11** and **July 19, 2013**, to manifest the dreams that are now taking shape. The Sun's dive into Scorpio on the **22nd** takes your thinking to another level, inviting profound conversations and serious research. The pressure of the Sun's conjunction to restrictive Saturn on the **25th** can temporarily block the flow of communication and sow seeds of doubt. Happily, lovely Venus restores your sense of self-worth on the **28th** with her entry into sociable Libra and your resourceful 2nd House.

KEEP IN MIND THIS MONTH

Taking an objective look at what you've accomplished in life will show you how to get more money, respect, and pleasure from your work.

KEY DATES

OCTOBER 5–7 ★ *down the rabbit hole*

Words take on extra significance as verbal Mercury joins karmic Saturn just before both planets enter intense Scorpio on **October 5**. It's not easy to avoid negative thinking, especially when others seem unwilling to listen to you. Yet this conjunction is ideal for deep thought and observation. You can express yourself indirectly with poetic images thanks to an imaginative Mercury-Neptune trine. The need to limit yourself to logic diminishes with a Mercury-Jupiter aspect and Mars's entry into storytelling Sagittarius on the **6th** and his square with escapist Neptune on **October 7**.

OCTOBER 15 ★ *banking on yourself*

You feel the urge to splurge with extravagant Jupiter's trine to the Libra New Moon in your 2nd House of Money. Yet upping your income to support a spending spree is going to take time. Jupiter's challenging sesquisquare to restraining Saturn reminds you that only a long-term strategy will increase your bank account or raise the value of your work. Investing in developing your marketable abilities is wiser than wasting money on frivolous purchases.

OCTOBER 20–21 ★ *lost in translation*

Mercury bounces from a tense angle with Uranus on **October 20** to another one with Pluto on the **21st**, provoking strange perceptions and complex communications. Exercise all your self-discipline to avoid overreacting to what others say—or to keep from shocking them with your own radical ideas. Ordinary language may be inadequate to express what you're thinking so don't stress if you can't put your thoughts into words.

SUPER NOVA DAY

OCTOBER 25 ★ *keep it real*

The Sun's conjunction with stifling Saturn in your chatty 3rd House casts a shadow of doubt on today's conversations. Withholding information can undermine trust; however, you can express yourself with authority if you're properly prepared. Mercury's union with the integrative North Lunar Node in Scorpio reveals the value of tackling difficult subjects directly rather than watering down what you say.

OCTOBER 28–29 ★ *curb your enthusiasm*

You take on more than you can manage on **October 28**, thanks to an overly optimistic Mars-Jupiter opposition. Expanding the scope of your activities can be healthy as long as you're realistic about your energy level and your schedule. Small differences of opinion can expand into major disagreements, especially when Mercury enters outspoken Sagittarius on the **29th**. The communication planet's square to Neptune promotes exaggeration as feelings are presented as facts. Yet you're able to keep your head in the clouds and your feet on the ground as the Taurus Full Moon in your 9th House of Big Ideas trines efficient Pluto.

NOVEMBER

USEFUL U-TURN

You're better off taking a few steps back this month than forging straight ahead. Your ruling planet, Mercury, turns retrograde on **November 6** and continues in reverse until the **26th**. This cycle starts in outgoing Sagittarius and your domestic 4th House and ends in introspective Scorpio in your 3rd House of Information. Review and revise big plans and expectations, especially related to home and family; you may have overlooked data that's critical to your success. It can be frustrating to reassess and, perhaps, rebuild, but this extra effort will ultimately streamline your thinking and reduce complications. Two eclipses in November also remind you to let go if you want to grow.

The New Moon in Scorpio on **November 13** is a Solar Eclipse in your 3rd House of Immediate Environment. Normally, the monthly conjunction of the Sun and Moon is a launching pad—in this case for learning, research, and communication. However, this eclipse also tells you to simplify data, eliminate superfluous ideas, and concentrate on key people and points instead of overloading yourself with input. The momentum starts to shift with the Sun's entry into adventurous Sagittarius on the **21st** and Mercury's forward turn on the **26th**. Then, on **November 28**, the jittery Gemini Full Moon is a Lunar Eclipse activating your 10th House of Career. Prosperous Jupiter's conjunction to the Moon and a square from fantasy-prone Neptune inspire professional dreams with promises that stretch the bounds of credibility. Avoid chasing an illusion by questioning your assumptions and those of people offering something that sounds too good to be true.

KEEP IN MIND THIS MONTH

Eliminating the clutter that fills your day, your calendar, and your mind's bandwidth frees you from distractions that take more from you than they give.

KEY DATES

NOVEMBER 1–3 ★ *reversal of fortune*

Finances take a sudden turn as Venus in your 2nd House of Resources opposes volatile Uranus on **November 1**. A previously reliable partner can behave erratically, or a new one might motivate you with a brilliant moneymaking idea. Either way, the hidden costs of an economic or romantic connection come into play on the **3rd** when Venus squares unwavering Pluto and it's time to pay the piper.

NOVEMBER 11–13 ★ *margins of reality*

You're alert to the slightest hint of criticism when Mercury forms a tense semi-square with Venus on the **11th**. Being more sensitive invites tender communications, but also makes it easy for you to overreact to casual comments. A Mercury-Neptune square on the **13th**, the same day as the New Moon Solar Eclipse in mysterious Scorpio, favors imagination over common sense. Conversations may wander into fantasyland; avoid paranoia by keeping your beliefs grounded in reality.

NOVEMBER 16–17 ★ *cut to the chase*

Action-hero Mars moves into well-organized Capricorn and your creative 5th House of Love and Play on the **16th**, helping you regain a sense of control over your life. Retrograde Mercury joins the Sun and the Moon's karmically connected North Node on the **17th**. Its gifts are sharper thinking and a precise understanding of where you must push with passion and where you need to let go. This is an ideal time for ending unproductive activities to concentrate on those that have the most impact.

NOVEMBER 22–24 ★ *ironing out the kinks*

You may be taken by surprise on **November 22** when cognitive Mercury forms anxious aspects with irrepressible Uranus and impatient Mars. You'll enjoy spontaneous and original thinking—but restless feelings and tense conversations can rattle your nerves. Mars's square with Uranus on the **23rd** could be a call to rebellion if you choose to invent your own ways of working instead of following standard procedures. There is a risk of conflict, but a smooth sextile from stabilizing Saturn to militant Mars on the **24th** is better for strategic planning than causing a ruckus.

SUPER NOVA DAYS

NOVEMBER 26–28 ★ *honorable intentions*

You may not immediately see the benefits of Mercury's direct turn on **November 26**, since it's accompanied by a stern Venus-Saturn conjunction that weighs communications down with blame. Harsh judgment demands strong action with a potent Mars-Pluto conjunction on the **27th**. Don't waste this force with a fight; focus on your own creative activities. The pressure applied by Pluto and Saturn can help you concentrate attention where it will do the most good. A selective Venus-Pluto sextile on **November 28** helps you recognize the best ways to invest your energy, income, and emotions.

DECEMBER

SPREAD YOUR WINGS AND FLY

Family matters take on deep significance this holiday season, especially with several planets moving through your 4th House of Roots. Loquacious Mercury arrives on **December 10**, spurring frank speech and strong opinions. The ebullient Sagittarius New Moon on **December 13** is also in your 4th House and can inspire a fresh start, compelling you to enlarge your space or consider a move to a larger place. Its higher purpose, though, is to motivate you to look beyond the limits of your current surroundings to imagine a more enlivening personal or professional life. The forward turn of revolutionary Uranus in your 6th House of Work on the same day underscores your need to get more stimulation from your job. Vivacious Venus dances into Sagittarius and your 4th House on the **15th**. This joyous planet sweetens your experiences by helping you look beyond the limitations of the present to visualize a more rewarding future.

Generous Jupiter's quincunxes to shrewd Pluto on the **20th** and stingy Saturn on the **22nd** remind you that every gain comes at a price. Although the final bills will not be due until these aspects finish on **March 23–29, 2013**, potential new resources will soon be available to you. On **December 21**, the Winter Solstice is marked by the Sun's entry into industrious Capricorn and your 5th House of Creativity, where you can reorganize and apply your talents more effectively. Active Mars's move into inventive Aquarius and your 6th House of Skills on the **25th** pushes you to update your techniques or develop new ones. On **December 26**, a savvy Saturn-Pluto sextile, returning on **March 8** and **September 21, 2013**, helps you to apply your force with precision and purpose.

KEEP IN MIND THIS MONTH

You don't have to settle for less in life. Open your mind and think about the many alternatives beyond the limits of your current situation.

KEY DATES

DECEMBER 1–2 ★ *unleashed expectations*

On **December 1**, a scintillating Mercury-Uranus sesquisquare puts you on high alert. While this intellectual odd couple can trigger bright new ideas, your reactions can come so fast, you say something you might regret. You're likely to go too far or expect too much on the **2nd**, when the Sun opposes excessive Jupiter. Yet this might also bring the promise of a promotion or another kind of professional opportunity that piles more responsibilities on your plate.

DECEMBER 10–12 ★ *trust your instincts*

Mercury's launch into visionary Sagittarius on **December 10** lifts your sights above the minutiae of daily life. However, reality can slip completely out of the picture when Mercury squares ephemeral Neptune on the **11th**. Your imagination soars as communications grow confusing. Yet even then, if your grasp of the facts weakens, your instinctive ability to evaluate people, objects, and activities remains sharp with a Venus–North Node conjunction in your perceptive 3rd House on the **12th**.

DECEMBER 16–17 ★ *intellectual adventures*

Expect angry words on **December 16**, when Mercury semisquares demanding Mars. Yet the strong messages conflict with hypersensitivity due to a vulnerable square between Venus and Neptune. Nevertheless, it's hard to stifle yourself as talkative Mercury opposes boisterous Jupiter on the **17th**. You'll encounter exaggerations and outrageous comments, but expanding your mind enlightens you with a leap of awareness or a communication breakthrough.

DECEMBER 21–22 ★ *fun and games*

Your confidence grows with the Sun's entry into your 5th House of Self-Expression on **December 21**. This month-long transit is an appropriate time for you to take the lead in romantic matters. However, your appetite for pleasure and recognition could grow excessive when indulgent Venus opposes giant Jupiter on **December 22**. It could turn out to be a delicious day if you're able to give generously, play without keeping score, and avoid overpaying for what you buy.

SUPER NOVA DAYS

DECEMBER 28–30 ★ *purpose, power, and passion*

The Full Moon in Cancer on **December 28** is a powerful, potentially transformational event in your team-oriented 11th House. Potent Pluto intensifies emotions as it opposes the Moon, while nervous energy and uncertainty are spawned by electrifying Uranus's lunar square. The Sun joins Pluto on the **30th**, ratcheting up tension or empowering you with a surge of creativity that arises from the depths of your being. You may go to extremes of self-expression, but sometimes it's necessary to peel away layers of politeness to get at the heart of desire. Knowing what you're willing to do in order to obtain what you want gives you the fierce spirit you need to succeed.

LIBRA

SEPTEMBER 23–OCTOBER 22

LIBRA

2011 SUMMARY

Discipline and patience in pursuit of your dreams are keys to getting the most out of this formative transit, which has the potential to enhance your self-image and boost your confidence.

AUGUST—*play first, work later*

Carefully walking the fine line between work and play will let you have plenty of fun without creating any difficulties on the job.

SEPTEMBER—*crossing the threshold*

Being a good person doesn't mean that you have to be accessible to everyone. Be selective about whom you invite into your world so you also have time for yourself.

OCTOBER—*a change will do you good*

Aligning yourself with independent people allows you to focus on your own needs instead of trying to carry someone else's load.

NOVEMBER—*pay as you go*

Demonstrate your commitment to future success by your patience and competence in managing your present tasks.

DECEMBER—*to thine own self be true*

When you put yourself first, it gives you the inner strength you need to support the other people in your life.

2011 CALENDAR

AUGUST

MON 1 ★	Be prepared to give up something old to get something new
FRI 12–SAT 13 ★	**SUPER NOVA DAYS** Your heart may skip a beat as emotions rise
TUE 16–WED 17 ★	Others are quick to agree with what you propose
WED 24–THU 25 ★	You have a chance to prove yourself as a resourceful leader
TUE 30 ★	Don't look a gift horse in the mouth; jump on it and ride

SEPTEMBER

THU 8 ★	What you hear is only a rough approximation of the truth
SUN 11–MON 12 ★	High hopes could leave someone disappointed
WED 14–SUN 18 ★	Relationships of all kinds are up for sudden changes
THU 22–FRI 23 ★	Tackle problems in new and different ways
TUE 27–THU 29 ★	**SUPER NOVA DAYS** Meet challenges with power and passion

OCTOBER

THU 6–FRI 7 ★	Measure your words carefully and speak purposefully
TUE 11–FRI 14 ★	**SUPER NOVA DAYS** Don't let anyone push you if you're not ready
FRI 21–SAT 22 ★	Use your imagination to create a sense of magic
TUE 25–WED 26 ★	It's time to grow by letting go
MON 31 ★	Common sense is hard to come by today

NOVEMBER

WED 2–THU 3 ★	Amuse yourself and others with your wit and charm
TUE 8–THU 10 ★	Stay calm in a crisis and focus on simple steps
TUE 15–WED 16 ★	Don't let success make you feel invincible
TUE 22–THU 24 ★	**SUPER NOVA DAYS** Your self-awareness opens to a new sense of freedom
SAT 26–SUN 27 ★	Don't hold on to mixed messages and inconsistent moods

DECEMBER

THU 1–FRI 2 ★	There's no room for indecision as you must make a choice
MON 5–WED 7 ★	Combine competence and charm to make your points
SUN 11 ★	Your good taste allows you to break rules with impunity
SUN 18–WED 21 ★	Self-control lets you bring order back to a relationship
SAT 24 ★	**SUPER NOVA DAY** Overcome your inner contradictions

LIBRA OVERVIEW

Your road hasn't been easy since Saturn the Taskmaster entered your sign on October 29, 2009. You may have already run into your share of setbacks—and there could be more difficulties ahead—but your sincerity and consistent hard work should pay off, because karmic Saturn gives you what you earn. **There's no time to waste complaining or feeling sorry for yourself.** Instead, push through any negativity by meeting challenges and fulfilling your responsibilities. Although Saturn can reveal where you have failed or areas of your life that need serious attention, it also demonstrates where you are on the right track and fully rewards your efforts. Since sobering Saturn remains in social Libra and your 1st House of Personality until October 5, you may be less likely to fritter away your time by playing the role of the host or hostess, unless taking care of others also brings you tangible benefits. **In the long run, it's better for those you love if you organize your life now in a way that will allow you to give of yourself more freely over the years to come.** Saturn's entry into possessive Scorpio and your 2nd House of Personal Resources on October 5 will thankfully relieve the pressure. Hold on to what is most important to you and let go of the rest. Shift gears and build on what you've already started to better establish yourself in the world.

Your ruling planet, Venus, usually runs through each sign in less than a month, but this year her retrograde period keeps her in easygoing Gemini and your 9th House of Higher Mind from April 3 until August 7. This extended transit activates your idealism, encourages you to think big, and motivates you to learn more about the world through education or travel. While Venus is retrograde on May 15–June 27, you may find yourself back in contact with an old sweetheart; or you might become interested in finishing a creative project that you had set aside. **One way or the other, unfinished business from your past is recycled and brought into your current experience.**

Meanwhile, Uranus the Awakener continues a seven-year visit to your 7th House of Companions. Unusual characters enter your life while you find freedom from controlling partners or stagnant relationships. Other people and shifting circumstances may have already begun to shake up your life, because unpredictable Uranus has been in your 7th House since March 11, 2011. However, it's likely that your attraction to the avant-garde will continue to grow as a result of your desire to break out of established patterns. **When you take more risks and live closer to the edge of unconventionality, you can actually reduce the likelihood of unexpected surprises.** Nevertheless, profound changes in the way you interact with others will make an indelible mark on your personal world as Uranus forms dynamic squares with evolutionary Pluto in your 4th House of Roots on June 24 and September 19 in a series of aspects that recur five more times through March 2015.

UP IN THE AIR

You have a real opportunity to get what you want when Venus the Lover hooks up with generous Jupiter in your 8th House of Intimacy on March 14. This propitious conjunction forms a stabilizing Grand Earth Trine with passionate Pluto and physical Mars on March 13–14, offering you a taste of a delicious romance. However, with inventive Uranus in your 7th House of Relationships until 2018, you are bound to be in a long-term process of redefining your most important partnerships. A sudden attraction can awaken your desires on April 9, June 20, and July 4 when Venus forms sweet sextiles to shocking Uranus. Venus's retrograde on May 15–June 27 has you looking back and comparing your relationship history with where you are now so you can learn from your past mistakes. Other people can't help but notice an additional sparkle to your personality when charming Venus visits your sign on October 28–November 21. But it's the larger shift in your thinking caused by long-lasting Uranus-Pluto squares that demands a reevaluation of what you want from relationships.

STREAMLINE YOUR EFFORTS

You are at the beginning of a professional journey; the ladder of success extends from this year into your future. Ambitious Saturn's two-year visit to your sign ends on October 5, so you'll want to make critical decisions about your long-term plans before then. An intense amount of concentration and hard work may be required to finish old business and set new goals, but it will be well worth it in the long run. But this is also time to let go of unrealistic expectations, abandon projects that no longer make sense, and crystallize your vision for what lies ahead.

SAVE FOR A RAINY DAY

Expansive Jupiter in materialistic Taurus and your 8th House of Investments and Shared Resources from June 4, 2011 through June 11, 2012 brings financial opportunities through alliances with generous people who can play an instrumental role in your success. Lucky aspects to Jupiter from valuable Venus on January 14 and March 14 could present you with a sweet deal as long as you don't get greedy and expect too much too soon. When constrictive Saturn arrives in calculating Scorpio and your 2nd House on October 5 for a two-year stay, financial growth slows; it's time for you to take a more responsible approach to money management. The Scorpio Lunar Eclipse on November 13 falls in your 2nd House, indicating a possible change of fortune. Saving your pennies when you have abundance will ease the pressure when the Sun and Venus join stingy Saturn on October 25 and November 26, respectively.

BODY-MIND CONNECTION

Physical issues continue to confront you with your own mortality thanks to Chiron the Wounded Healer's seven-year visit to your 6th House of Health. Spiritual Neptune enters your 6th House on February 3 for a thirteen-year stay, increasing the importance of the mind-body connection in your ongoing healing process. Retrograde Mars opposes Chiron on March 22, and your frustration could also stir up health concerns. Improvements to your diet should have a positive impact on your immune system when regenerative Pluto sextiles Chiron on May 12 and September 6. Stabilizing trines from Saturn to Neptune on October 10 and to Chiron on November 16 are excellent for initiating any kind of healthy lifestyle changes, especially those that utilize the power of the metaphysical over the physical.

EMBRACE CHANGE

Sudden developments on the home front set long-lasting patterns into motion when transformational Pluto in your 4th House of Domestic Conditions is accentuated by volatile squares from surprising Uranus on June 24 and September 19. Watch your temper on July 17–18, when stressful aspects to Pluto from Mars and Jupiter can reveal strong differences of opinions.

Fortunately, supportive aspects to Pluto from the Sun on August 29, the Pisces Full Moon on August 31, Mars on September 3, and Mercury on September 4 are much-needed lubricants to the squeaky wheels of progress.

PACK YOUR BAGS

You start dreaming of adventures on May 20, when the restless Gemini Solar Eclipse falls in your 9th House. Then journeying Jupiter begins its yearlong visit to your 9th House of Voyages on June 11, expanding your vistas and luring you to faraway places. Whether you go somewhere exotic, or enroll in an educational course so you can travel within your mind, you have something to learn by extending your boundaries. Consider scaling back your holiday travel plans; the Gemini Lunar Eclipse on November 28 conjuncts Jupiter and may tempt you to squeeze too much into one vacation.

SPIRITUAL QUEST

Courageous Mars in analytical Virgo retrogrades on January 23–April 13 in your 12th House of Soul Consciousness, motivating you to take a mental journey back in time to reconnect with your higher purpose. Make the most of your inner process by seeing a spiritual adviser or psychotherapist, doing past-life regression work, or developing a meditation routine. Forceful Mars pushes you along this path until he leaves your 12th House on July 3. The Sun's entry into your divine 12th House and opposition to Neptune on August 22–24 initiates the next phase of your exploration, which reaches fruition when Saturn trines Neptune on October 10, putting spiritual ideas into practice.

RICK & JEFF'S TIP FOR THE YEAR:
Procrastination Courts Disaster

There is absolutely no good reason for putting off the hard work that you must do this year—and the sooner you begin, the easier it will be in the long run. You can expect less disruption during the next few years if you face problems directly now. Instead of fearfully retreating into the safety of your past, embracing change empowers you to co-create a future that is more aligned with your soul's true purpose.

JANUARY

FANTASY ISLAND

You may begin the year with heightened expectations about love; your ruling planet, Venus, in your 5th House of Romance aligns with Mars in your 12th House of Destiny on **January 1**. But bridging the gap between what you want and what you have can be tricky business when Venus and Mars, the cosmic lovers, form an ill-adjusted quincunx on **January 7**. Demands at work can put stress on domestic conditions when the security-conscious Cancer Full Moon spotlights your 10th House of Public Responsibility on **January 9**. Thankfully, balancing your dreams with reality is within reach on **January 13** as Venus forms a harmonious trine with stable Saturn and hooks up with ethereal Neptune. This hopeful transit triggers a constructive Saturn-Neptune trine that's exact on **October 10**, yet you must work extra-hard now to get the results you desire. Fortunately, the potential rewards are well worth the wait.

Venus enters psychic Pisces and your 6th House of Self-Improvement on **January 14th**, helping you figure out what you must do to get your needs met. However, her conjunction with Chiron the Wounded Healer on the **16th** can remind you of a hurtful situation from your past, increasing your vulnerability now. But the quirky Aquarius New Moon on **January 23** falls in your 5th House of Fun and Frivolity, tempting you to indulge your playful fantasies and avoid your obligations. Although Venus's alignment to naysaying Saturn on **January 25** may raise doubts or fears about a personal or business relationship, her anxious aspect to buoyant Jupiter on the **28th** encourages you to overcompensate and say yes to just about everything.

KEEP IN MIND THIS MONTH

Although you may be afraid that your illusions won't last when confronted by reality, letting go of impossible dreams makes way for true satisfaction.

KEY DATES

JANUARY 1 ★ *take a deep breath*

Someone's well-aimed criticism can hit you where it hurts today, because messenger Mercury in your 3rd House of Communication forms a conflictive square with warrior Mars in precise Virgo. Instead of losing your temper, slowly count to ten. You can easily turn things around if you respond lovingly, since you have a creative Venus-Mars biquintile on your side.

JANUARY 7–8 ★ *talk it out*

You just can't see an amicable resolution to a lovers' quarrel on **January 7**, when contentious Mars forms a crunchy quincunx to affectionate Venus. Your best bet is an objective discussion, which can lessen the tension because talkative Mercury forms synergetic sextiles to matter-of-fact Saturn and inspirational Neptune. Staying open to new perspectives is easy when Mercury smoothly trines broad-minded Jupiter and squares unconventional Uranus on the **8th**.

SUPER NOVA DAYS

JANUARY 12–13 ★ *dream catcher*

You are blessed with enough energy to realize your goals on **January 12**, when the willful Sun in ambitious Capricorn trines action-hero Mars. You may blur the lines between current circumstances and your romantic fantasies on the **13th** when your planetary ruler, Venus, conjuncts otherworldly Neptune in your 5th House of Love, allowing dreams to overflow into your waking life. Thankfully, artistic Venus also harmoniously trines businesslike Saturn, enabling you to turn the most sensible parts of your idealistic vision into reality.

JANUARY 19–23 ★ *singing the blues*

Although the Sun's entry into Aquarius and your 5th House of Self-Expression brightens your life on the **20th**, you must first pass through a reality checkpoint when the Sun squares authoritative Saturn on the **19th**. This transit reveals whether your current path makes sense and if you have the strength to stay the course despite resistance, obstacles, or setbacks. A solid connection with your heart can kindle a deep passion for your work. Be open to new opportunities that appear on **January 21–22** when the Sun aspects unexpected Uranus and auspicious Jupiter. You grow frustrated with your lack of progress when Mars begins his nearly three-month retrograde period on the **23rd**, the same day as the futuristic Aquarius New Moon begins a fresh cycle and has you looking ahead.

JANUARY 28 ★ *just say maybe*

Permissive Venus-Jupiter semisquare on the **28th** entices you with promises of pleasure. Meanwhile, Mercury in your playful 5th House aspects wild Uranus and permissive Jupiter, making it tricky to stay on the straight and narrow. You don't need to bypass all the fun; just avoid burning your candle at both ends.

FEBRUARY

MAKE IT WORK

You may be pulled between artistic pursuits and more mundane tasks as planets that begin the month in your 5th House of Creativity transition into your 6th House of Employment. On **February 3**, dreamy Neptune is the first to make the move, but its immediate impact is subtle because it stays in surreal Pisces and your 6th House for thirteen years. The proud Leo Full Moon on the **7th** shines in your 11th House of Friends and Wishes, enabling you to put your best foot forward in social situations and show off your generous heart. Fortunately, this reflection of the Sun and eloquent Mercury in your 5th House of Self-Expression gives you just the right words to describe your hopes for the future. Meanwhile, lovable Venus prompts you to find ways to create peace and harmony in your work environment while she travels through your 6th House of Service until the **8th**. Venus's dance into uninhibited Aries and your 7th House of Partners changes the atmosphere completely as you focus on getting along with others, yet her hookup with wild Uranus on the **9th** can excite you with the temptation of freedom and spontaneity in relationships.

You notice the shift from inspiration to necessity when Mercury moves into the methodical world of your 6th House on **February 13**, followed by the Sun on the **19th**, turning your attention toward routine tasks and encouraging you to be more practical. Nevertheless, your best ideas may come from daydreams or fantasies, because Mercury and the Sun each connect with intuitive Neptune as they enter Pisces. The introspective Pisces New Moon on the **21st** falls in your detail-oriented 6th House, hitting the restart button to your creative process and requiring a more pragmatic approach to your life.

KEEP IN MIND THIS MONTH

You're great at making your environment more attractive; your challenge is to also use your creativity to work smarter and be more efficient.

KEY DATES

FEBRUARY 1 ★ *war and peace*

Job-related stress spills over into your relationships when Venus in your 6th House of Work opposes Mars. You are tempted to placate a disgruntled co-worker or partner, yet remember that unexpressed anger can fuel negativity since the warrior planet is retrograde in your 12th House of Secrets.

FEBRUARY 7–9 ★ *your way or the highway*

Beware unreasonable demands from an authority figure when bossy Saturn forms a grumpy quincunx to accommodating Venus in your 6th House of Daily Routines on **February 7**, just hours prior to the flashy Leo Full Moon. You know you should do what you're told, but Venus's dash into restless Aries on the **8th** and her conjunction with reckless Uranus on the **9th** trigger your desire for excitement, prompting you to break free from old habits and routines.

SUPER NOVA DAYS

FEBRUARY 14–18 ★ *playing for keeps*

You may be lost in a romantic fantasy on Valentine's Day, **February 14**, when thoughtful Mercury joins wistful Neptune and a rainbow-chasing Jupiter-Chiron sextile raises your hopes even higher. You could enjoy an intensely intimate connection—but sensual Venus dynamically squares demanding Pluto on the **15th**, raising uncomfortable feelings of obsession, control, and jealousy. However, an intelligent Mercury-Jupiter sextile on the **16th** helps you and your partner transform these darker emotions into a clearer understanding of each other. Thankfully, the Sun's trine to deliberate Saturn on **February 18** indicates that your persistent efforts toward resolving differences can build a healthy foundation for an enduring relationship.

FEBRUARY 22–23 ★ *hot under the collar*

Retrograde Mars in critical Virgo can stir up trouble if others aren't being upfront with their concerns. Its disquieting quincunx to possessive Venus in your 7th House of Relationships on the **22nd** can put you in an argumentative frame of mind. Your tendency now is to shoot off at the mouth and think about what you said later with loquacious Mercury opposing militant Mars on the **23rd**, making this an excellent time to work on your diplomacy skills.

FEBRUARY 28 ★ *natural-born leader*

There's no need to pussyfoot around today, wondering what anyone else thinks. You can get away with doing things your way as the Sun creates a cooperative sextile with unyielding Pluto. Impressing others is easy; you can extend your influence by simply giving a task your very best effort.

MARCH

NOT A MOMENT TO WASTE

This month presents you with significant opportunities, but you must take the initiative, and maybe even risk loss, to make the most of them. Decisive action is required, but you may not see the results of your efforts until later in the year. Action-planet Mars in skillful Virgo continues to backtrack in your 12th House of Secrets, enabling you to act behind the scenes effectively without requiring recognition from others. Communicator Mercury blasts into enthusiastic Aries on **March 2**, but then slows down for its retrograde period on **March 12–April 4**—a time when your words can become tangled, your explanations misunderstood, and solutions unraveled. You may also be hitting the brakes in relationships on **March 4** when eager Venus in impatient Aries opposes restraining Saturn. Venus's entry into slow moving Taurus on the **5th** could impede your immediate progress, yet it gives you the determination to achieve what you want in the long run. The Virgo Full Moon on **March 8** illuminates your 12th House of Spirituality as you try to put together the fragments of faith that can get you moving in the right direction again.

Thankfully, a collaborative trine between resourceful Venus and forceful Mars on **March 14** helps you capitalize on a significant and long-lasting wave of opportunity that rolls into your life when giant Jupiter trines potent Pluto on the **13th**. This is an excellent time to make decisions about your future, take action on an idea that has been germinating, or reaffirm your commitment to your current path. The enterprising Aries New Moon on the **22nd** gives you an energetic boost through a friend or co-worker who supports your efforts and helps you take your project to the next level.

KEEP IN MIND THIS MONTH

Don't worry if your personal and professional progress seems delayed by circumstances beyond your control; your extra efforts will eventually be rewarded.

KEY DATES

MARCH 3–6 ★ *fight for what you want*

Relationships challenge you when feisty Mars opposes the Sun on **March 3** and sexy Venus opposes stern Saturn on the **4th**. You may become angry if a close friend or intimate partner puts up boundaries or avoids your overtures. Don't retreat just because you're afraid of a direct confrontation or hurting someone's feelings. It may be difficult to hear the truth, but it's better to know where you stand than to avoid the issue completely. Anyway, you may end up being happily surprised by what you learn when messenger Mercury joins erratic Uranus on **March 5**. Thankfully, Venus the Lover enters dependable Taurus and your 8th House of Deep Sharing on the **5th** and forms a slick sextile with magical Neptune on the **6th**, empowering you to catch that elusive dream.

SUPER NOVA DAYS

MARCH 13–14 ★ *the power of now*

Mercury and Mars are both retrograde, and your current efforts may be thwarted. But know that what you do now has the cosmic blessings of a solid Grand Earth Trine that indicates success, even if you must be patient until it arrives. Your planetary ruler, Venus—symbolizing money and love—places a pleasant perspective on these days as she trines mighty Pluto and motivating Mars and conjuncts magnanimous Jupiter. The propitious Venus-Jupiter conjunction on **March 14** is like your own personal lucky star that shines in your 8th House of Intimacy and Shared Resources, and its sweet trine to Pluto in your 4th House of Foundations on the **13th** all but guarantees the enduring significance of whatever you choose to undertake at this time.

MARCH 20–22 ★ *dare to be different*

Involve an enthusiastic person in a new venture when the Sun enters pioneering Aries and your 7th House of Partners on **March 20**. This is the Spring Equinox, a natural time to begin a project or a relationship, and anything you start now receives a second infusion of adrenaline from the Aries New Moon on the **22nd**. Revolutionary Uranus conjuncts this lunation, urging you to break free from an old relationship pattern and try something new.

MARCH 28–29 ★ *no pain, no gain*

A creative quintile between no-nonsense Saturn and obsessive Pluto on **March 28** gives you the determination and energy to transform an impossible task into a job well done. But the Sun's square to Pluto on the **29th** suggests that you must overcome strong resistance or unnecessary fear. Although you will likely prevail, your struggle exacts a cost and could leave you wondering if it was worth it.

APRIL

CUTTING THROUGH THE FOG

You are able to reestablish your confidence and forge a new path forward this month as energetic Mars turns direct in your 12th House of Destiny on **April 13**. You might have experienced a loss of direction during Mars's retrograde, which began on **January 23**, yet the spiritual lessons that you have learned instilled a new sense of purpose and now reveal the inner strength you gained. But confusion reigns through the first half of the month as Mars slowly backtracks toward a near opposition to vague Neptune in your 6th House of Habits, making it even tougher to know which way to turn and what to do on a day-to-day basis. If you feel defeated or are tired without knowing why, don't give up. Your energy and clarity will return as Mars distances himself from diffusive Neptune and speeds up throughout the second half of the month.

It's time to rectify a difficult situation at work, improve your health, or handle a variety of details that may have complicated your life during Mercury's retrograde on **March 12–April 4**. Nevertheless, unrealistic yearnings can create disappointment in love and muddle your actions as covetous Venus in curious Gemini squares Neptune and Mars on **April 5–7**. You are challenged to maintain objectivity when the Libra Full Moon on **April 6** forms unsettling aspects with Neptune, Venus, and Mars. Disillusionment can teach you hard lessons about relationships on **April 15** when the Sun in your 7th House of Others tensely opposes strict Saturn. The Sun's entry into down-to-earth Taurus on **April 19**, followed by the reliable Taurus New Moon falling in your 8th House of Regeneration on the **21st**, helps to clear the air and gives you a solid foundation on which to set your new course.

KEEP IN MIND THIS MONTH

It's difficult to make up your mind when you cannot trust the information you have at hand. Double-check your facts before you choose what to do next.

KEY DATES

SUPER NOVA DAYS

APRIL 3–7 ★ *rainbows and unicorns*

You can tell that something is different when your key planet, Venus, enters multifaceted Gemini and your 9th House of Getaways on **April 3**, tempting your curiosity with a variety of interests. Cerebral Mercury's direct turn in your 6th House of Daily Routines on the **4th** allows you to fill in the details of your escape plan, while an imaginative Jupiter-Neptune quintile draws you farther into your fantasies. However, the Cinderella Libra Full Moon on **April 6** can fool you into believing that your dreams are real, especially as lovely Venus aspects four planets, including delusional Neptune on **April 5–7**. Exercise caution; you cannot have everything you want, even if it appears that you're very close to reaching satisfaction.

APRIL 12–16 ★ *mind over matter*

Although you get the green light when Mars turns direct on **April 13**, it will take several days before you see any real progress. Communication at work may be nearly nonexistent when fleet-footed Mercury runs into Saturn's wall on **April 12**. Venus, usually congenial, forms several unfriendly aspects, making it tough for you to feel comfortable. Meanwhile, the inhibiting Sun-Saturn opposition in your relationship houses on **April 15** presents obstacles that require you to get serious in order to handle a difficult situation. If you are sincere, work hard, and don't take any shortcuts, you can overcome nearly any resistance. Messenger Mercury's flight into independent Aries on the **16th** is finally your notice that all is clear; you may let go of recent doubts and move with confidence into the future.

APRIL 21–23 ★ *it takes two to tango*

Someone acts as a catalyst to accelerate the pace of change, bringing excitement, innovation, and instability into your life. While the steady Taurus New Moon on **April 21** usually emphasizes dependability over speed, a conjunction of quicksilver Mercury and shocking Uranus in your 7th House of Others on the **22nd** has an electrifying effect. Thankfully, you are fully motivated and have the energy to rise to the occasion and meet any challenge when macho Mars trines the Sun on the **23rd**.

APRIL 29 ★ *honor the process*

Cleaning house to eliminate unneeded possessions or emotional baggage makes sense today. Yes, sometimes such change is difficult, but the Sun's collaborative trine to evolutionary Pluto in your 4th House of Roots energizes a deep transformation that can alter the very ground upon which you stand. However, your patience and persistence are required, for the work that begins now could take a while to unfold.

MAY

FLYING IN CIRCLES

You are happily freed from delays and obstacles that have blocked your progress this year—but you may still need to overcome your own lack of motivation. Both mental Mercury and physical Mars turned direct last month, and now that they have regained their normal speeds, you're finally able to act on your thoughts. But, ironically, your ruling planet, Venus—in inquisitive Gemini and your 9th House of Adventure—slows to a standstill through the first half of the month. The planet of love turns retrograde on **May 15**, focusing your desires on recapturing the past instead of anticipating the variety of pleasures that await you in the future. Fortunately, this period—until Venus turns direct on **June 27**—can stabilize your love life and give you the chance to solidify long-term plans for travel or education later in the year, because Venus syncs up in a near trine to realistic Saturn throughout the entire month.

Meanwhile, the complicated Scorpio Full Moon on **May 5** highlights your 2nd House of Personal Resources, possibly revealing financial problems that negatively impact a relationship. An opposition from candid Mercury in your 7th House of Partnerships to frugal Saturn indicates that serious discussions can lead you to a more mature way of handling your money. But your fiscal condition is likely tied to jointly held possessions and maybe even an emotional entanglement, because Jupiter in your 8th House of Intimacy and Shared Resources is pressured by Saturn and Pluto on **May 16–17**. The changeable Gemini New Moon Eclipse on **May 20** excites your 9th House of Big Ideas, shifting your focus away from recent financial and relationship concerns and instilling you with hope for your future.

KEEP IN MIND THIS MONTH

Finding satisfaction in the present moment can be a real challenge if you're always thinking about the possibilities of what you can do tomorrow.

KEY DATES

MAY 5–8 ★ *bent out of shape*

Normally, you play well with others, but outspoken Mercury's tense opposition with judgmental Saturn on **May 5** forces you to take a stand if someone is overly critical of your ideas. It's crucial to think about what you're going to say before you open your mouth. The powerful Scorpio Full Moon pushes you to emotional extremes that could reduce the effectiveness of your argument if your feelings get in the way of coolheaded logic. There is a lot riding on this struggle, with overblown Jupiter forming an anxious semisquare to volatile Uranus on **May 7**. If you aren't achieving your desired results, consider backing off instead of escalating the battle. Aggressive Mars tangles with unruly Uranus on **May 8**, making it difficult to control your temper. Remember, patience is the most effective way to reach your objectives.

MAY 13–16 ★ *believe in yourself*

You are feeling optimistic about a recent shift in the energy at home and your potential for future success when the Sun joins benevolent Jupiter in your 8th House of Transformation on **May 13**. Thankfully, fundamental change is grounded in necessity and should prove to have lasting value in your personal life because it's supported by a practical Grand Earth Trine on **May 13–16**. Nevertheless, you must find a way to manage this growth phase, for vulnerable Venus's retrograde turn on **May 15** and an ill-adjusted Jupiter-Saturn quincunx on **May 16** could raise self-doubt about your ability to meet the challenges ahead.

SUPER NOVA DAYS

MAY 20–23 ★ *window of opportunity*

Your brain buzzes with innovation on **May 20** thanks to chatty Mercury's stressful semisquare to brilliant Uranus, while a breezy Gemini Solar Eclipse clears the air of negativity. At first, you may wonder if your ideas are actually worthy of pursuit, but Mercury's conjunction with confident Jupiter on the **22nd** falls in your 8th House of Deep Sharing, inspiring you to take a risk and share your plans. Make sure that you stick to the facts, because Jupiter encourages you to exaggerate while a fantasy-prone Sun-Neptune square on **May 23** tempts you to tell a tall tale to impress someone special.

MAY 27–30 ★ *let yourself go*

Exciting new ideas about an upcoming adventure fill your imagination when brainy Mercury and the illuminating Sun in your 9th House of Future Vision form sextiles to ingenious Uranus on **May 27–28**. Delicious Venus retrogrades back into a wildly creative quintile with Uranus on the **30th**, enticing you with unconventional ideas about pleasure that may be better left unexpressed.

JUNE

THE DARK SIDE OF THE MOON

Patience is your key to success this month as waves of change grow stronger and stronger. Valuable Venus in your 9th House of Big Ideas continues her retrograde period through **June 27**, advising you to reconsider your goals and create a new strategy to satisfy your desires. A casual conversation reveals emotional unrest as the Sagittarius Full Moon Eclipse on **June 4** shakes up your 3rd House of Communication. You are tempted to withdraw from an uncomfortable discussion, because this Lunar Eclipse squares angry Mars in your 12th House of Secrets. But your frustration can fuel resolution when the Sun moves closer to squaring superhero Mars on **June 7**, pushing you into action. Global Jupiter's entry into versatile Gemini and your 9th House on **June 11** excites you with the amazing array of alternatives ahead of you. The jumpy Gemini New Moon on **June 19** increases your restlessness, reminding you that it may be too soon to commit to one single path as Jupiter slowly moves toward a square with spacey Neptune on **June 25**.

Your fair-minded approach to conflict is put to good use as you handle disagreements about family affairs when secretive Pluto in your 4th House of Domestic Conditions squares explosive Uranus in your 7th House of Partners on **June 24**. But stress at work could put additional pressure on you at home as early as **June 11**, when intellectual Mercury triggers the looming Uranus-Pluto square. The Sun reheats this ongoing struggle when it opposes Pluto and squares Uranus on **June 29**. Although these unpredictable transits may turn your life upside down, they also can embolden you to consider making a radical positive change.

KEEP IN MIND THIS MONTH

Although a personal relationship may be the designated battlefield, the real issues are your need for independence and your reluctance to reveal what you truly want.

KEY DATES

JUNE 3–5 ★ *say what you mean*

You must act with full honesty and integrity to navigate the smoothly flowing trine between trickster Mercury and karmic Saturn on **June 3**, even if the Lunar Eclipse in grandiloquent Sagittarius on the **4th** encourages you to embellish the truth with your hopes. The Sun, Venus, and Mercury are all visiting your 9th House of Future Vision, but you are yanked back into the present moment by the friction of warrior

Mars squaring beautiful Venus. Flowery language comes easily to you as the Sun illuminates enchanting Venus in flirty Gemini on **June 5**, but don't try to skirt an important issue by turning on your charm. You'll only cause further irritation by attempting to avoid conflict when a straightforward approach is best.

JUNE 11–13 ★ *all over the map*

You're bursting with enthusiasm on **June 11** when exuberant Jupiter enters airy Gemini for a one-year stay. It's hard not to spread yourself too thin. Quarrelsome Mercury in your 10th House of Public Life forms a square with restless Uranus and an opposition with ruthless Pluto, heightening intensity at work. But Mercury's harmonizing trine with healer Chiron in your 6th House of Self-Improvement on **June 12** offers a smoother path to success if you can concentrate on routine tasks instead of being distracted by one too many unrealistic possibilities. Fortunately, on the **13th** the Sun's sustaining trine to responsible Saturn delivers the wisdom and maturity that you need to keep your focus.

JUNE 19–20 ★ *off you go*

The impatient Gemini New Moon on **June 19** activates your 9th House of Travel and Education, turns your attention from making plans into taking action. But you needn't rush the next step now, because the Sun's entry into cautious Cancer on **June 20** is the Summer Solstice—a time to pause before responding to the inevitable changes. Nevertheless, you won't sit still for long, because a thrilling Venus-Uranus sextile has you wired with anticipation as you think about the possible fun times ahead.

SUPER NOVA DAYS

JUNE 24–25 ★ *future shock*

Two powerful cycles now converge, upping the intensity of everything that happens. The demanding Uranus-Pluto square on **June 24** leaves you agitated and uneasy over unfolding relationship transformations. However, a dreamy Jupiter-Neptune square on **June 25** makes it nearly impossible to focus and lures you into fantasizing about escaping your current obligations. Additionally, strategic Saturn turns direct and smart Mercury steps into expressive Leo and your 10th House of Career to help you shift your concentration back to more immediate concerns.

JULY

FULL STEAM AHEAD

Impulsive Mars blasts into reactive Libra on **July 3**, firing you up with a fresh burst of energy. You may feel more competitive with Mars in your 1st House of Self until **August 23**, but you are also motivated to work in concert with others because you realize that cooperation enables you to accomplish more than working alone. With the Sun in watery Cancer and your 10th House of Career until **July 22**, your emotions play a significant role in your career decisions. However, the dutiful Capricorn Full Moon in your 4th House of Domestic Conditions on **July 3** reminds you that family responsibilities might conflict with your professional ambitions. Meanwhile, graceful Venus dances her way through whimsical Gemini and your 9th House of Adventure, attracting you to an endless parade of interesting people and events.

You may begin to wonder if the revolving door of fascinating experiences is merely a noisy distraction when interactive Mercury turns retrograde in your 11th House of Friends and Wishes on **July 14**. Still, you aren't willing to give up your active social life, because irrepressible Mars and four other planets align with indulgent Jupiter on **July 17–24**. If you are overextended, a volcanic square from red-hot Mars to domineering Pluto on **July 17** and an opposition to volatile Uranus on **July 18** could precipitate a relationship crisis. Luckily, the self-protective Cancer New Moon on the **19th** forms magical aspects with spontaneous Mars and imaginative Neptune, inspiring you to pull a creative solution out of thin air.

KEEP IN MIND THIS MONTH

If you're feeling stressed in a relationship, don't try to change your partner. The real path to harmony is making peace with yourself.

KEY DATES

JULY 3–4 ★ *forward march*

The best way for you to advance during the ambitious Capricorn Full Moon on **July 3** is to find a balance between getting what you want in the outer world and at home. Pushy Mars's entry into peace-loving Libra is a mixed blessing that increases your vitality but can upset the status quo if you don't manage the uncharacteristic aggression that the warrior planet brings. Fortunately, on **July 4** persuasive Venus harmonizes with an innovative Mercury-Uranus trine, enabling you to use your witty charm and talk others into supporting your unconventional plan.

JULY 8 ★ *uncertainty principle*

You don't know how assertive to be as impetuous Mars forms an anxious slippery quincunx with elusive Neptune. People around you seem to be behaving inconsistently, and you're unsure how to respond. However, Mars in your 1st House of Personality suggests that you may be the one who is acting ambiguously. Avoid making significant decisions until the fog dissipates in a day or two and your clarity returns.

SUPER NOVA DAYS

JULY 15–19 ★ *twist of fate*

You question your own wisdom about a career matter when the Sun in your 10th House of Responsibility squares doubting Saturn on **July 15**. An optimistic Mars-Jupiter trine on **July 17** helps you to maintain a positive attitude about your future, even if the present is fraught with struggles as someone tries to undermine your efforts. The trouble indicated by Mars's square to suspicious Pluto on the **17th** probably won't be resolved in the manner you expect, because Mars opposes rebellious Uranus on the **18th**, releasing pent-up tensions and maybe even precipitating a breakup. Fortunately, the caring Cancer New Moon on **July 19** falls in your public 10th House, allowing you to mend hurt feelings among your co-workers and set positive intentions for the days ahead.

JULY 28–31 ★ *unexpected breakthrough*

You enjoy lively discussions about a wide variety of topics on **July 28**, when retrograde Mercury in your 11th House of Friends conjuncts the Sun and backs into an anxious semisquare with amicable Venus. Unfortunately, a simple misunderstanding could quickly change the tone of the conversation. The uncomfortable Sun-Pluto quincunx on the **30th** raises your fears, especially if you believe that someone is trying to control you. Luckily, a stroke of genius suddenly reveals a way for you to break free of an unpleasant situation as the Sun trines progressive Uranus on the **31st**. Happily, a satisfying Venus-Saturn trine indicates that your radical solution will last into the future.

AUGUST

LONG AND WINDING ROAD

The month opens with an urgent reminder to stay true to yourself when the nonconformist Aquarius Full Moon on **August 1** brightens your 5th House of Love and Creativity. A lucky lunar trine to expansive Jupiter in your 9th House of Travel awakens your longings for a thrilling adventure that could turn out to be a life-changing experience. Recognition comes your way when popular Venus trades in her fickle flights of fancy and flies out of airy Gemini to swim into the nurturing waters of Cancer and your public 10th House on **August 7**. You are more eager than ever to engage in clever conversations or flirtatious behavior when effusive Mercury's direct turn in outgoing Leo and your 11th House of Friends on **August 8** motivates you to get your social life back in full swing. However, a few rough days prior to the melodramatic Leo New Moon on **August 17** might find you lost in a new relationship landscape that seems less stable than before. Nevertheless, this lunation forms a supportive sextile with a hardworking Mars-Saturn conjunction, motivating you to go the extra mile, yet also demanding patience as it delays the response to your efforts.

Cosmic messages narrow your thinking and tighten your agenda when the Sun enters perfectionist Virgo on **August 22**, followed by Mars's move into intense Scorpio on the **23rd**. But aspects to nebulous Neptune from the Sun and Mars on **August 24–26** can fuel your imagination—or tempt you with a false sense of security. Meanwhile, the super-sensitive Pisces Full Moon on the **31st** adds its healing powers to the equation, while a collaborative sextile from penetrating Pluto urges you to explore emotional depths beyond your previous experience.

KEEP IN MIND THIS MONTH

Your life is in turn exciting, worrisome, challenging, empowering, frustrating, and satisfying. Instead of focusing on any single event, pay attention to the entire mix.

KEY DATES

AUGUST 1–2 ★ *fun and games*

You're a social butterfly on **August 1**, when the Full Moon in friendly Aquarius reflects the light of the playful Leo Sun in your 11th House of Friends and Associates. Enjoying this upbeat energy grows easier when buoyant Jupiter forms a cheerful sextile with the illuminating Sun on **August 2**. And although your key planet, Venus, in fickle Gemini creates an anxious semisquare to the Sun, a taste of dissatisfaction can feed your sarcasm and wit to make you the life of the party.

AUGUST 7–9 ★ *the power of imagination*

You try to protect yourself by hiding your feelings on **August 7**, when receptive Venus enters moody Cancer. But Venus also lures you into the public spotlight as she moves through your 10th House of Career until **September 6**. Fortunately, a magical Venus-Neptune trine on **August 9** inspires you to see creative and romantic possibilities nearly everywhere you look, but it's still up to you to do the work of turning your fantasies into reality. Sharing your dreams—which is an important part of this process—is easier when communicative Mercury ends its three-week retrograde period on **August 8**.

SUPER NOVA DAYS

AUGUST 15–17 ★ *roll with the punches*

Although a fiery Mars's conjunction with restraining Saturn on **August 15** can throw obstacles in your path, it can also slow you down just enough to focus your attention and increase your efficiency. If you let fear and jealousy overtake your common sense, this process can be a real struggle. Instead of worrying about a co-worker stealing your thunder, use the intensity of Pluto's opposition to diplomatic Venus in your 10th House of Status to build bridges between you and powerful allies. Stay flexible on the **16th** to make the best of an unexpected turn of events when Venus squares unpredictable Uranus in your 7th House of Others. Thankfully, the dramatic Leo New Moon on **August 17** activates your 11th House of Social Networking, gathering group support for your creative impulses.

AUGUST 27–31 ★ *no rest for the weary*

Don't let down your guard just yet, for uneasy Mercury's aspects to Pluto and Uranus on **August 27–28** keep you on edge. Luckily, you gain strength from the willful Sun's harmonious trine to powerful Pluto on the **29th**, allowing you to push away doubts you may be having about work prior to the intuitive Pisces Full Moon in your 6th House of Employment on **August 31**.

SEPTEMBER

CHANGE IS IN THE AIR

Unexpected events keep you hopping this month, yet the sudden shifts have an extremely important function. Surprises are not meant to upset you; rather, their purpose is to reveal places where you need to address suppressed feelings and unresolved issues now so they don't cause too much trouble later. The high-powered square between catalytic Uranus in your 7th House of Others and passionate Pluto in your 4th House of Foundations is exact on **September 19** and sets the tone for the entire month. This is the second in a series of seven occurrences, and it may reactivate domestic stress that previously surfaced around **June 24**. But even if you feel a great sense of urgency to calm an unruly partner or to manage a domineering relative, remember that the current situation is connected to a bigger scenario that doesn't play out until **March 16, 2015**.

You must balance logic and intuition to reach your goals as the analytical Virgo New Moon on **September 15** activates your 12th House of Spiritual Mystery. But ultimately, your greatest attribute is your ability to be fair—and you'll need it when you're called on to mediate a family argument as Mercury in objective Libra triggers the unstable Uranus-Pluto square on **September 20**. Whether or not your act of diplomacy is successful, the Autumn Equinox on the **22nd** is a time of culmination and renewal for you as the Sun enters your sign. Tempers rise at the feisty Aries Full Moon on **September 29**, when this Sun-Moon opposition forms rebellious aspects with Uranus and Pluto. However, this is also a time when a calculated risk could precipitate the changes you've been itching to make.

KEEP IN MIND THIS MONTH

Focus your attention on the present—while also carefully considering the long-term consequences of your current activities.

KEY DATES

SEPTEMBER 1–4 ★ *retreat and regroup*

You may be a bit confused by what you need to accomplish on **September 1** when thoughtful Mercury opposes fuzzy Neptune in your 6th House of Daily Routines. Retreating from the spotlight seems like a sensible option as vulnerable Venus in your 10th House of Public Life squares cautious Saturn on **September 3**. It's a complex cosmic energy, and you'd be smart to tap into it right now to reevaluate your relationships. Aspects to assertive Mars and articulate Mercury on **September 3–4** reinforce your convictions and empower you to clearly communicate your position as long as you make a realistic plan and stick to it.

SEPTEMBER 6–8 ★ *over the top*

You're in a party mood when your key planet, Venus, prances into lively Leo and your 11th House of Friends and Associates on **September 6**, enticing you to spend more time with others. But Venus's aspects with exuberant Jupiter and escapist Neptune on **September 6–7**, combined with an extravagant Sun-Jupiter square on the **7th**, tempt you to take your social activities too far. Don't pretend that everything is okay when fast-talking Mercury squares Jupiter on the **8th**. If you had deadlines you didn't meet or made commitments you now cannot keep, honestly admit it, accept the consequences, and move on.

SEPTEMBER 12–13 ★ *roller coaster of love*

You're challenged to manage all your social interactions on **September 12**, when friendly Venus in your 11th House of Groups forms a disconnecting quincunx to impassioned Pluto. Additionally, Venus trines radical Uranus in your 7th House of Others on the **13th**, attracting you to interesting people who could surprise you. It's not easy to be objective as you grapple with someone's hidden agenda, but the overall experience can be quite thrilling as long as you don't wear yourself out or believe everything you are told.

SUPER NOVA DAYS

SEPTEMBER 25–27 ★ *family feud*

When Venus and Mars, the cosmic lovers, square off on **September 27**, satisfaction will likely elude you—but if you're willing to stick with your pursuit of happiness, you can ultimately improve your personal life. Although the formidable Uranus-Pluto square was exact on **September 19**, contentious Mars and magnetic Venus trigger this profound planetary pattern on **September 25–26** to stimulate stress at home or within your family. Mars in unwavering Scorpio pressures you to fight for what you want while Venus in proud Leo encourages your theatrical behavior, but your immediate needs may be no match for the transformative energies around you. Luckily, a panoramic Mercury-Jupiter trine on the **26th** enables you to see the bigger picture so you're not overwhelmed by the current magnitude of emotions.

OCTOBER

TIME TO SHINE

You've worked hard, Libra, to overcome the hardships that Saturn the Tester has brought into your life since **July 21, 2010**. You've seen major cycles come to an end during the past couple of years, forcing you to revise your general life plan and commit to new goals. If you have used this phase wisely, it's now time to take the next step on your path; taskmaster Saturn leaves logical Libra and enters passionate Scorpio on **October 5** for a two-year visit to your 2nd House of Self-Worth. Start building on the foundations you have established by steadily increasing your authority and assets. Be willing to postpone immediate gratification to achieve greater success. Unfortunately, if you haven't managed your resources well, this can be a period of financial struggle when harsh self-judgment hurts your self-esteem.

A solid trine from rational Saturn to irrational Neptune on **October 10** is the first in a series of three that recurs through **July 19, 2013**, helping you to reconcile your fantasies with what is actually possible. There's no room for self-doubt, so put unwavering faith in your ability to make your dreams come true. The lovely Libra New Moon on **October 15** activates your 1st House of Self. It's like your personal New Year's Day—an excellent time to make a resolution and then plant the seed of your intention. Moneymaking opportunities increase when the Sun leaves ambivalent Libra on **October 22** to warm the emotional waters of Scorpio and illuminate your 2nd House of Finances. The steady Taurus Full Moon on **October 29** highlights your 8th House of Shared Resources, reminding you to team up with responsible people who can help you achieve your vision of success.

KEEP IN MIND THIS MONTH

A weight has been lifted from your shoulders—but instead of just celebrating, contemplate how to use your newfound freedom.

KEY DATES

OCTOBER 2–5 ★ *what dreams are made of*

You're already in a serious frame of mind when Venus forms a collaborative sextile with somber Saturn on **October 2**. And although you want to narrow your options when Venus enters discriminating Virgo on the **3rd**, an opposition to blurry Neptune makes it difficult to focus on what you want. Nevertheless, there are important matters to consider, because analytical Mercury joins orderly Saturn just before both planets cross into Scorpio on **October 5** and their visit to your 2nd House of Personal Resources draws your attention to the material world. Paradoxically, a harmonious Mercury-Neptune trine assures that your imagination will still be vivid despite this shift of your priorities.

SUPER NOVA DAYS

OCTOBER 9–10 ★ *as good as it gets*

You've got cause to celebrate when a wonderful trine from bountiful Jupiter in your 9th House of Higher Mind to the Sun in your 1st House of Personality on **October 9** raises your self-confidence and expands your vision of the future. You're able to satisfy intense desires as sensual Venus trines potent Pluto, but you must settle your thoughts prior to enjoying the richness of the experience. Luckily, practical Saturn trines metaphysical Neptune on the **10th**, creating an equilibrium between mundane events and more spiritual pursuits.

OCTOBER 15–16 ★ *all's well that ends well*

Another person's unpredictable behavior or brilliant idea sweeps you off your feet thanks to a thrilling Mars-Uranus trine on **October 15**. You're challenged to reestablish your balance, too, because a tough aspect between expansive Jupiter and contractive Saturn confuses your picture of where to reach out and where to pull back. Fortunately, the harmonizing influence of the gracious Libra New Moon comes to the rescue. Pleasure overtakes nervous excitement when delicious Venus squares opulent Jupiter on the **16th**, but overindulgence or overestimating someone could prove costly.

OCTOBER 28–30 ★ *keep it simple*

Curbing your enthusiasm can be tricky when uncontainable Mars opposes bombastic Jupiter on **October 28**, allowing your excitement to exceed your common sense. Fortunately, you're especially persuasive with captivating Venus visiting your sign until **November 21**. Unfortunately, your unbridled optimism could fool yourself as well as others, because Venus creates an uneasy quincunx to deceptive Neptune. Your sense of perspective could be warped by logical Mercury's square to Neptune on **October 29**. Thankfully, the down-to-earth Taurus Full Moon on the **29th** opposes realistic Saturn, encouraging you to focus on what's most important.

NOVEMBER

A STITCH IN TIME SAVES NINE

Pay careful attention to your finances this month with the Sun in probing Scorpio and your 2nd House of Self-Worth until **November 21**. Trickster Mercury in carefree Sagittarius turns retrograde in your 3rd House of Communication on **November 6**, creating delays and misunderstandings for the next three weeks, while also giving you a chance to recall recent conversations and resolve any lingering differences. The complex relationship between your self-esteem and your finances is emphasized by the intense Scorpio Solar Eclipse in your 2nd House on **November 13**. This New Moon Eclipse forms a worrisome semisquare with cryptic Pluto in your 4th House of Foundations, possibly revealing information about your fiscal record keeping that now comes back to haunt you. Nevertheless, resource issues remain in the spotlight as Mercury backs into your 2nd House of Income on **November 14**. Your desire for the security that money or possessions offer increases as value-conscious Venus enters this house on **November 21**.

Meanwhile, Saturn is also in your 2nd House of Personal Resources for an extended two-year stay. You may learn of a cash-flow crisis or be forced to reconsider a purchase on the **26th**, when the taskmaster planet conjuncts with Venus. Fortunately, Mercury's direct turn that same day indicates that consistent efforts to manage your income can prevent these issues from getting out of hand. You begin to shift your focus away from current problems and toward the bright future that is beckoning with the curious Gemini Lunar Eclipse in your 9th House of Adventure on the **28th**. This Full Moon Eclipse is conjunct with visionary Jupiter, inspiring you to see the potential that's ahead of you rather than the troubles that are now in the past.

KEEP IN MIND THIS MONTH

The future is not written in stone. Don't just worry about tomorrow's challenges; do something proactive before they manifest.

KEY DATES

NOVEMBER 1–4 ★ *the things we do for love*

You have big ideas about what you want when enterprising Mars forms an imaginative quintile to inspirational Neptune on **November 1**. But a shocking Venus-Uranus opposition destabilizes a restrictive relationship, infuses a healthy one with new energy, or suddenly attracts you to someone new. When innocent Venus squares experienced Pluto on **November 3**, you may be enmeshed in a stressful situation that involves complicated emotions and unexpressed feelings. Although you could be dealing with an intense person, gentle Venus in accommodating Libra gives you a calming touch. Luckily, a Venus-Mars quintile on the **4th** allows you to pursue what you want without appearing overly eager or desperate.

NOVEMBER 9 ★ *the sky's the limit*

Today you're attracted to anything that takes you far from where you are, whether you're traveling via airplane or your mind, with visionary Jupiter visiting your 9th House of Higher Education and Long Journeys. And a Venus-Jupiter trine is a sweet aspect that offers an especially wonderful opportunity while Venus is in harmonious Libra. Don't be afraid to dream big, stretch yourself, and live as if you will assuredly reach the stars.

SUPER NOVA DAYS

NOVEMBER 13–17 ★ *the force is with you*

The impassioned Scorpio Solar Eclipse on **November 13** can be a rude awakening as buried emotions bubble up into awareness. Miscommunication can create an awkward moment when retrograde Mercury squares imprecise Neptune. Someone's sense of freedom can clash with your need for order when irrepressible Uranus forms a disquieting quincunx with structured Saturn on **November 15**. On **November 16**, enthusiastic Mars enters entrepreneurial Capricorn and your 4th House of Foundations, giving you the energy to start a new project from the ground up. Don't be afraid to follow a hunch, for a Mars-Neptune sextile on the **17th** activates your intuition and empowers you to use your dreams as a tool for navigation.

NOVEMBER 26–29 ★ *rebel with a cause*

A partner fills your mind with exciting new visions as the adventurous Sagittarius Sun trines wild Uranus on **November 26**. Your conversations lead to exciting plans as Mercury turns direct. But needy Venus joins restrictive Saturn in your 2nd House of Personal Resources, making you feel as if you don't have enough time or money to do what you would like. Still, the fearless Mars-Pluto conjunction on the **27th** gives you the conviction to fight for what you need. On **November 28**, the Gemini Full Moon Eclipse helps you cut ties from the past and frees you to embark on your future.

DECEMBER

LEAP OF FAITH

Self-confidence is your greatest asset this month, but it could get the best of you if you take it too far. With optimistic Jupiter in inquisitive Gemini and your 9th House of Big Ideas, exploring new avenues can lead you to success. Still, you're challenged to manage all your opportunities—especially on **December 2**, when the Sun in Sagittarius opposes Jupiter from your 3rd House of Communication. You want to say yes to everything, and when Mercury enters Sagittarius on the **10th** and opposes Jupiter on the **17th**, you could promise someone the entire world and actually believe you'll be able to deliver it. Faith in yourself is healthy, but delusions of invincibility are not. This theme is repeated a third time when seductive Venus strides into enthusiastic Sagittarius and your interactive 3rd House on the **15th** to oppose jovial Jupiter on the **22nd**. Although these transits lift your holiday spirits, each can also test your limits by tempting you to overdo, overstate, or overindulge.

The inspirational Sagittarius New Moon on **December 13** stimulates your 3rd House of Siblings. Even if you don't have any brothers or sisters, this is an excellent moment for honest conversations with your closest friends. This lunation anxiously semisquares calculating Saturn, reminding you to honor your commitments. You may believe that your reputation is at stake when the emotionally intense Cancer Full Moon on **December 28** shines in your 10th House of Status. Its opposition to a dynamic Sun-Pluto conjunction that's exact on the **30th** assures you that this year will not end quietly. A power struggle could upset the harmony at home unless you have the wisdom to face the issue without stirring further conflict.

KEEP IN MIND THIS MONTH

You're more likely to sustain the joyful spirit of this season if you set healthy boundaries when it's appropriate.

KEY DATES

DECEMBER 1–2 ★ *a bridge too far*

Your expectations rise so high on **December 1** that you're likely to be disappointed, due to crunchy quincunxes from Venus and Mars to excessive Jupiter in your 9th House of Big Ideas. The Sun in grandiose Sagittarius opposes Jupiter on the **2nd**, making opportunities appear too good to be true. You're more likely to reach your goals if you can balance the unlimited potential that you see with a dash of common sense.

SUPER NOVA DAYS

DECEMBER 10–14 ★ *light at the end of the tunnel*

A tough semisquare from sweet Venus in your 2nd House of Self-Esteem to mysterious Pluto on **December 10** reveals the darker side of love as issues of possession or jealousy rise to the surface. Although Venus's conjunction with the soulful North Lunar Node on the **12th** can put you in touch with what you really want, your desires may be unrealistic because a mesmerizing Mercury-Neptune square on **December 11** crosses the boundaries between fact and fiction. Fortunately, the bold Sagittarius New Moon on the **13th**, followed by an electrifying Mercury-Uranus trine on the **14th**, breaks the spell with a sudden epiphany that can free you from any negativity.

DECEMBER 16–17 ★ *dancing in the street*

A friend or partner catches you off guard with a brilliant move on **December 16** when active Mars forms a creative quintile with ingenious Uranus in your 7th House of Others. Be careful, for you could read too much into what happens as romantic Venus squares starry-eyed Neptune. Although others may enjoy your fun-loving company when mischievous Mercury opposes joyful Jupiter on the **17th**, don't over-extend yourself or you won't be able to play as much through the holidays.

DECEMBER 19–22 ★ *count your blessings*

Direct your thoughts toward your home and family on the **21st**—the Winter Solstice—when the Sun enters traditional Capricorn and your 4th House of Security. Meanwhile, delicious Venus tempts you with pleasures as she trines unexpected Uranus on **December 19** and opposes lavish Jupiter on the **22nd**. Balancing holiday fun with your need for meaning can help you find happiness in the moment.

DECEMBER 28–31 ★ *all together now*

You have a chance to stand up for something that's really important on **December 28**—although difficult aspects to the sentimental Cancer Full Moon can be quite unsettling. Your victory could be hollow if others are hurt by it. Thankfully, a surprising Mars-Uranus sextile on **December 31** mixes up the dynamics, allowing you to include everyone in your celebration.

SCORPIO

OCTOBER 23–NOVEMBER 21

SCORPIO

2011 SUMMARY

As a fixed water sign, Scorpio normally doesn't like unexpected changes. Now, though, it's time to be proactive by shaking up your daily routine, including your diet, your lifestyle, and even your job. Although you may be a natural champion of intensity, you prefer to experience it in the emotional realms. Even when you're under pressure, remember that pushing the river will not speed its arrival to the sea.

AUGUST—*so close yet so far away*

You have an important learning opportunity in front of you now. You're experiencing a practice round for the big game next year, when you'll be playing for keeps.

SEPTEMBER—*extreme makeover*

Riding the wild waves of change is exhausting, but you'll be able to rest again once the energy settles back down.

OCTOBER—*return to power*

Starting a major project may be wise when you're feeling good about yourself, but don't let overconfidence trick you into taking on more than you can handle.

NOVEMBER—*back to basics*

There's magic at work that can create an enduring cycle of prosperity if you're willing to put in extra effort without expecting an immediate payoff.

DECEMBER—*just out of reach*

Pushing too hard for completion or commitment may bring you frustration. Appreciate what you have instead of worrying about what you're missing.

2011 CALENDAR

AUGUST

MON 1–WED 3 ★	**SUPER NOVA DAYS** It's hard to know when to call it quits
MON 8–THU 11 ★	Question the reliability of your assumptions
FRI 12–WED 17 ★	It's challenging to be gracious; overcome your insecurities
WED 24–FRI 26 ★	Watch out, resistance to your efforts surfaces

SEPTEMBER

FRI 2 ★	**SUPER NOVA DAY** Don't wait for a better time to take action
SUN 11–WED 14 ★	Reveal your dreams to someone you trust
FRI 23 ★	Be direct and let others know what you want
TUE 27–THU 29 ★	Emotional equilibrium appears to be elusive now

OCTOBER

SAT 1–MON 3 ★	Own up to your vulnerability to transform your relationships
MON 10–THU 13 ★	**SUPER NOVA DAYS** Stop and consider your own feelings first
FRI 21–SUN 23 ★	Music, meditation, and movies bring you great pleasure now
WED 26–FRI 28 ★	Choose your destination; good fortune is all but assured

NOVEMBER

WED 2–SAT 5 ★	You're inundated with new ideas and ingenious solutions
THU 10–SAT 12 ★	Find the inner strength to transform fear into love
WED 16 ★	Establish healthy boundaries for everyone to honor
WED 23–SUN 27 ★	**SUPER NOVA DAYS** Complex cosmic currents swirl around you

DECEMBER

SUN 4–MON 5 ★	You know exactly what you want to say, but watch your anger
SAT 10 ★	Don't expect to find a quick fix today
TUE 20–SAT 24 ★	**SUPER NOVA DAYS** Step outside your normal tastes
THU 29 ★	Clear the way for a new year of unprecedented growth

SCORPIO OVERVIEW

You cross a significant threshold this year when structuring Saturn leaves your secretive 12th House and enters your sign on October 5. This marks a new stage in your life when discipline, self-respect, and a deep sense of purpose can empower you with greater authority and more control over your environment. Saturn's almost three-year occupation of your 1st House of Personality gives you plenty of opportunities to transform your image by updating your appearance and upgrading your lifestyle. You might want to immediately follow these changes by redefining your relationships—but there is plenty of unfinished business to attend to before this happens, because Saturn moves through your 12th House of Endings until October 5. **Coming to terms with old partnerships by letting go of any remaining anger and resentment can clear the way to smoother sailing ahead.** Identifying yourself as a victim may seem justified based on your prior experiences, yet this view of yourself is dead weight that will only hold you back. If you haven't forgiven those who have wounded or disappointed you by October 5, Saturn's harmonious trines with compassionate Neptune on October 10, and June 11 and July 19, 2013 provide additional chances to let bygones be bygones.

Even if you spend much of 2012 rattling around in the closet of your psyche, unlocking the secrets of your past and preparing for your October takeoff, you still have plenty of opportunities to build alliances that make your life less stressful. For the first half of the year, Jupiter is in your 7th House of Partnerships where its presence in Taurus attracts reliable individuals and shows you that simplicity and directness can work wonders in relationships. Jupiter flips into inconsistent Gemini and your 8th House of Deep Sharing on June 11 for a yearlong stay. **The variety of people, ideas, and experiences you encounter can reinvigorate your interest in a current alliance or excite curiosity about a new person or venture, while simultaneously driving you crazy with distraction.** Optimistic Jupiter's squishy square with dreamy Neptune on June 25, though, elevates hopes beyond reason, so temper inspiration with cool analysis.

Energetic Mars, the traditional ruler of your sign, is retrograde from January 23 until April 13, serving as another reminder to tie up loose ends before you take on any major new challenges. The backward motion of this planet in your 11th House of Groups can stir up enmity among friends or colleagues. But this isn't about settling old scores; Mars is in Virgo, a sign more concerned with productivity than stewing in unresolved emotional juices. The gift of Mars's extended stay in your 11th House until July 3 is to provide you with additional chances to smooth things out with comrades and co-workers so that you're able to work together more harmoniously. Still, **the process of untangling knots of mistrust and confusion requires patience and a willingness to focus on specific tasks instead of personality differences.** Your flexibility goes a long way toward solving complex problems, especially since the dynamic Scorpio Solar Eclipse on November 13 is anxiously semisquare unyielding Pluto.

LOVE WITHOUT LIMITS

Neptune settles in for a thirteen-year stay in your 5th House of Romance on February 3. This long-term transit creates a softer backdrop for love that allows you to give and receive with less concern about the costs of companionship. Jupiter's presence in your 7th House of Relationships from June 4, 2011, to June 11, 2012, should make it easier to establish meaningful connections. Chatty Mercury's retrograde period on March 12–April 4 starts in your 8th House of Intimacy and ends in your 7th House of Others to complicate communications and reopen old issues—or to reunite you with previous partners. Then, when jaunty Jupiter enters breezy Gemini and your 8th House of Intimacy on June 11, a diverse set of people and possibilities show you ways to get closer without losing yourself in the process.

OCCUPATIONAL ITCH

You remain on the move professionally thanks to the seven-year transit of innovative Uranus in your 6th House of Work, lasting until May 15, 2018. Shifting to another organization or entering a different profession could be appealing to you now. Starting your own business, perhaps as a pioneer in a totally new field, is another expression of independent Uranus. Shorter-term issues affecting your job involve two retrograde cycles of communicative Mercury this year. The first, on March 12–April 4, starts in your 6th House of Daily Routines; the second, on July 14–August 8, is in your 10th House of Career. Both serve as cosmic reminders to double-check details, confirm messages, and maintain equipment to avoid time-wasting complications. On the other hand, these periods also give you extra opportunities to improve techniques, receive additional training, and reconnect with old colleagues, customers, and potential employers.

INVEST IN YOURSELF

You'd be wise to adopt a more cautious approach to economic issues this year. A Solar Eclipse in your 8th House of Shared Resources on May 20 can entice you to make spurious investments. Nebulous Neptune's square to this special New Moon could soften your skepticism and make you vulnerable to impractical schemes and financial dreams. A Lunar Eclipse on June 4 falls in your 2nd House of Income and is square to industrious Mars in Virgo. If you're working hard, make sure you'll be fairly compensated. If not, consider putting that energy elsewhere, even if it means quitting a job or project. Mercantile Mercury's retrograde turn in your resource sensitive 2nd House on November 6 could signal some belt tightening. However, this is also a time when you can discover and correct errors that may have cost you money in the past.

TEAM EFFORT

Improving your diet and exercise routine will increase your vitality and make you feel younger at heart when your physical ruling planet Mars is retrograde in health-conscious Virgo and your 11th House of Groups on January 23–April 13. Playing a sport, taking a fitness class, or dancing with pals puts the fun back into exercise. Sobering Saturn's entry into purging Scorpio on October 5 is a good time to consider doing a detoxification program to prepare for the work ahead. The presence of this influential planet in your body-centered 1st House makes it critical to maintain your discipline and commitment to keeping yourself as healthy as possible.

LIGHTNING STRIKES

Deeply held personal or family secrets could suddenly burst into the light of day when Uranus, the ruler of your 4th House of Roots, begins a series of potent squares with ultra-private Pluto on June 24, 2012, that recur on

September 19 and won't finish until March 16, 2015. While this may disrupt your household, it also offers opportunities to shake off shame and rebuild trust among those closest to you. Mars's entry into your 4th House on December 25 can also trigger domestic crises that lead to psychological breakthroughs or meltdowns. However, your willingness to make radical changes will ease the transition from old fears to new possibilities.

HIGHWAY COMPANION

Travel should be more relaxing early in the year as the watery Cancer Full Moon in your 9th House of Faraway Places on January 9 is supported by a sextile with efficient Mars. Education is also favored by this lunation. A summer vacation, though, may be complicated by delays or downsizing when the Cancer New Moon on July 19 falls in your 9th House and squares restrictive Saturn. Tap into the knowledge of a good local guide or an experienced friend to route your trip around potential obstacles.

INFINITE POSSIBILITIES

Learning how to accommodate others without surrendering your own interests is a hard-earned gift available from Saturn in your 12th House of Divinity until October 5. Your soul doesn't grow as quickly when you work solo now, but the process accelerates when partners join you in the search for higher meaning. On October 15, the creative Libra New Moon in your 12th House forms a favorable trine with wise Jupiter in multifaceted Gemini that feeds your mind with inspiring ideas and reveals alternative paths to enlightenment.

RICK & JEFF'S TIP FOR THE YEAR:
Time Is on Your Side

Saturn provides guidance by offering you several options during its stay in balanced Libra. On October 5, as this planet enters your sign, you will be almost ready to make some serious decisions. Only after you've considered all your alternatives can you be sure that you're on the right path. The journey to the next level of personal authority and power is a hard one, so pace yourself.

JANUARY

MASTER OF YOUR DESTINY

Gathering information and making connections are your primary activities for the first part of the month with planets whizzing through your 3rd House of Communication. The ambitious Capricorn Sun lingers here until **January 20**; it can raise your status when you present your thoughts in a well-organized manner. Verbose Mercury speaks with conviction when it enters earthy Capricorn on the **8th** to ground your thinking and clarify your ideas. Be diligent in your pursuit of knowledge and purposeful in what you say. The importance of education is underscored by the Cancer Full Moon's presence in your 9th House of Higher Learning on **January 9**. If you're feeling insecure about a lack of academic accomplishments, don't discount the value of what you've been taught by your life experiences.

The sweet pleasures of love and play entice you when desirable Venus swims into dreamy Pisces and your 5th House of Romance on **January 14**. The magic of attraction happens when you are less focused on a goal and simply open yourself up to enjoy whatever or whoever comes your way. Music, art, dance, and other creative pursuits are delightful expressions of Venus in your playful 5th House. On **January 23**, the New Moon in innovative Aquarius falls in your 4th House of Security, revealing an unconventional perspective on family matters. Its squares to career-defining Jupiter and Saturn could bring challenges that alter your long-term professional plans. However, the retrograde turn of your traditional ruling planet Mars on the **23rd** occurs in your 11th House of Community. It's time to step back and straighten out unresolved issues with friends or colleagues so you can feel free enough to forge ahead when it turns direct on **April 13**.

KEEP IN MIND THIS MONTH

Think and speak slowly to give a seamless presentation that will take your listeners exactly where you want them to go.

KEY DATES

JANUARY 1 ★ *be bright, don't fight*

Be ready to think fast and act quickly on **January 1**, when agile Mercury forms a stressful square with combative Mars. Be careful, for it's all too easy to waste this overheated but intelligent energy on frustration or resentment. Stop talking, get busy, and put your bold ideas into action.

SUPER NOVA DAYS

JANUARY 7–9 ★ *return to the source*

Relationships turn edgy on the **7th** as normally accommodating Venus runs into annoying aspects with impatient Mars and unrelenting Pluto. Your task is to make quick adjustments to work around distractions, and then focus attention where your passion is the greatest. Thankfully, Mercury's shift into traditional Capricorn on the **8th** does not limit your thinking to the practical concerns of this orderly sign, because the messenger planet's contacts with visionary Jupiter and irreverent Uranus spring surprises that take your mind past ordinary logic to conjure up brilliant, unique ideas. The diverse paths of perception come together on the **9th** as the watery Cancer Full Moon blends them with an emotional certainty that allows your feelings to guide your direction.

JANUARY 12–13 ★ *angels and demons*

You are super-productive and extra-efficient on the **12th**, when the life-giving Sun forms a friction-free trine with dynamic Mars. This is an excellent time to demonstrate your leadership abilities by motivating your collaborators with your own hard work. Planetary crosscurrents bring mental intensity and emotional sensitivity on the **13th**. A Mercury-Pluto conjunction deepens your thinking, yet a starry-eyed Venus-Neptune conjunction can skew your judgment. A downside might include paranoid thinking that allows you to misinterpret others' intentions; a plus could be meaningful conversations filled with incredible kindness and compassion.

JANUARY 20 ★ *hungry heart*

While others may be philosophizing about the state of the world today, you're on track to obtain the pleasure that you desire. The Sun's entry into airy Aquarius encourages idealism and abstract ideas—yet you keep your eyes on the prize thanks to a perceptive sextile between Venus and Pluto. Ferret out resources that can make your money go farther or find value that secures a wobbly relationship.

JANUARY 27–28 ★ *a bumpy start*

Rational Mercury flies into freethinking Aquarius just after its square to naysaying Saturn inhibits the flow of communication. Yet even if you can use logic to establish a clear baseline of facts about the present before you rocket off into the future, a stressful Sun-Mars aspect on the **28th** triggers aggression that you should channel into productive activities.

FEBRUARY

LOVE AND LIVELIHOOD

Romantic feelings have warmed your heart since amorous Venus entered your passionately playful 5th House on **January 14**—and opportunities to express those emotions should increase this month. On **February 3**, spiritual Neptune returns to your 5th House, which it first visited from **April 4** until **August 4, 2011**. It's now settling in for a thirteen-year stay that invites you to release suspicion and insecurity and let unconditional love embrace you. Your ability to show affection is enhanced by verbal Mercury's move into the 5th House on **February 13** and empowered when the Sun follows suit on **February 19**. This shift of the Sun into spiritual Pisces combined with its idealistic conjunction to magical Neptune blesses you with the intuitive power you need to enrich your personal life with more creativity and joy. In fact, the magic lingers to enliven your 5th House of Self-Expression when the Pisces New Moon joins otherworldly Neptune on the **21st**.

Work-related issues are on your agenda when the proud Leo Full Moon illuminates your 10th House of Career on **February 7**. You'll produce original ideas with this lunar opposition to brainy Mercury and the Sun in conceptual Aquarius. You may think that you're too smart for your current job, and perhaps you are. However, conservative Saturn turning retrograde on the **7th** reminds you to complete unfinished business and do more research before you make a major professional move. Your itchiness for something new is stimulated when Venus shifts into restless Aries and your 6th House of Habits on **February 8**. Turn down the flame of desire so that your emotional stew can simmer until you're ready for change instead of letting yourself burn out too soon.

KEEP IN MIND THIS MONTH

It's better to be naive and let yourself fall in love than to rule out romance with rational thinking and fear of rejection.

KEY DATES

FEBRUARY 1 ★ *change the rules*

You're inclined to spar with friends and colleagues when Mercury in eccentric Aquarius clashes with cranky Mars in your 11th House of Groups. It's time to alter the ways in which you work with others instead of struggling to stick to outmoded methods. Channel your frustration into devising a fresh collaborative approach that will satisfy everyone's needs.

SUPER NOVA DAYS

FEBRUARY 7–10 ★ *independent streak*

If you have a gnawing sense of uncertainty about someone, it's best to talk about it openly on **February 7**. A sludgy Venus-Saturn quincunx can undermine trust, while the dramatic Leo Full Moon intensifies emotions. Your dislike of being controlled could provoke conflict with an authority figure while Venus moves into freewheeling Aries on the **8th**, underscoring your need for autonomy. Communication clashes are possible when thinking is rigid, yet a brilliant Venus-Uranus conjunction on **February 9** opens your eyes to new ways of being rewarded by your work. Nevertheless, an awkward Sun-Mars quincunx on the **10th** suggests that a delicate approach to introducing fresh ideas will invite more success than springing any sudden surprises.

FEBRUARY 15 ★ *all or nothing*

You go to extremes when loving Venus forms a tense square with dark Pluto. It's an impassioned aspect that provokes intense attraction or instant repulsion. If you're undervalued at work, think about ways to develop your unused talents instead of smoldering in silence. If you're on fire with desire or steaming with jealousy, take a deep breath instead of going overboard. A hyperactive Mars-Jupiter sesquisquare could prompt you to say or do something you will regret, yet if you've calculated your moves carefully, this can be a powerful time to leap into action.

FEBRUARY 19 ★ *field of dreams*

Your dreams are not illusions today; they are outlines of a future that you color in with your actions. There is real magic in the air when the Sun enters your 5th House of Creativity and meets up with ethereal Neptune. Cast your eyes on the distant horizon, where the petty problems of daily life are lost in the mists of what's to come. Take some time out from your routine to motivate yourself with fantasies that you just might turn into reality.

FEBRUARY 22–23 ★ *integrity matters*

February 22 is all about the contrast between doing something right now . . . and doing it right. That's because Venus is in impulsive Aries as she quincunxes Mars in perfectionist Virgo. If you remember that new tasks require time to master, it can help you reduce the stress that might undermine cooperation. A mouthy Mercury-Mars opposition on the **23rd** can cause conflict unless you relay information with kindness.

MARCH

CREATIVITY AT WORK

Expect adjustments in your daily routine this month as planetary currents pull you in several different directions. The Sun continues floating through fanciful Pisces and your 5th House of Love and Creativity until **March 20**, keeping you in a playful mood. Captivating Venus dances into your 7th House of Partners on **March 5** to attract supportive allies who help make your life more enjoyable and easier to manage. However, your comfort in relationships is countered by cerebral Mercury's move into impatient Aries and your 6th House of Work on **March 2**. Developing new skills or responding to emergencies challenges you to get off your cloud and take immediate action, and Mercury's retrograde turn on the **12th** could force you to return to projects that you thought were already finished. It's wise to keep working steadily until Mercury turns direct on **April 4**.

You must perform with greater precision if you hope to work effectively with others on **March 8**, thanks to the Virgo Full Moon conjunct Mars in your 11th House of Groups. Auspicious Jupiter's trine with potent Pluto on **March 13** is the last in a series that previously occurred on **July 7** and **October 28, 2011**. This harmonious alignment can turn losses into gains, uncover resources, and provide motivation that empowers you to pursue your highest ambitions. The Sun enters enterprising Aries and your 6th House of Employment on **March 20**, marking the Vernal Equinox, and is followed by a trailblazing Aries New Moon on the **22nd** that can open your eyes to a radically different perspective about your job.

KEEP IN MIND THIS MONTH

Separating your professional and personal lives keeps the pressures of your work from spoiling your appetite for pleasure.

KEY DATES

MARCH 2–4 ★ *give peace a chance*

Your traditional ruling planet Mars gets tied up in a sluggish semisquare with resistant Saturn on **March 2** that can bog you down with delays and detours or reward you for your patience and concentration. It's hard to keep your cool the next day when the Sun and Venus form aggravating aspects with Mars and Saturn, putting you in a fighting mood—especially if it's for a worthy cause. But if you're feeling underappreciated with the stingy Venus-Saturn opposition on **March 4**, focusing on increasing your self-esteem is better than seeking someone else's approval.

SUPER NOVA DAYS

MARCH 13–14 ★ *irresistible you*

The transformative power of a propitious Jupiter-Pluto trine on **March 13** is supplemented by a Grand Earth Trine involving alluring Venus and physical Mars, attracting individuals who support your goals and appreciate what you have to offer. Your subtle powers of persuasion allow you to make your points with common sense, style, and simplicity. A luscious Venus-Jupiter conjunction in your 7th House of Relationships on the **14th** restores trust with current partners and makes you more desirable to new ones.

MARCH 19–22 ★ *work in progress*

Put more passion into your work when the Sun enters your 6th House of Daily Routines on **March 20**. Making a commitment to improve your health through diet and exercise is also favored, yet a stressful square between Mars and the Lunar Nodes on the **19th** can test your patience if colleagues or family members don't understand your new lifestyle. The Aries New Moon on the **22nd** joins irrepressible Uranus and intelligent Mercury, exciting your mind and your nervous system. Your ability to picture alternative ways of managing tasks or earning a living makes it hard for you to tolerate mundane duties. Nevertheless, what you're visualizing is a glimpse of the future—though you might need additional training before you can make it a reality.

MARCH 26 ★ *soft touch required*

The harder you push today, the farther off track you seem to go thanks to an edgy Sun-Mars quincunx. Quit struggling and try to relax. Gentle coaxing and minor adjustments help you to avoid a frustrating conflict with a friend or co-worker.

MARCH 28–29 ★ *seek higher ground*

Limited resources and manipulative people bring drama to your life when Venus and the Sun form tense aspects with mistrusting Pluto on **March 28–29**. Competent Saturn makes a creative quintile to shrewd Pluto on the **28th**—the second in a series that began on **November 11, 2011**, and ends on **August 19**—that can transform a potential disaster into a long-term win. This clever connection helps you cut through the confusion of conflict to find common points of interest and build a lasting foundation.

APRIL

SHIFTING GEARS

In some ways, you might feel as if your new year is finally starting this month. Your energetic ruling planet Mars turns forward on **April 13** after chugging along in reverse since **January 23**. This has acted as a brake on your progress, especially involving relationships with friends and colleagues. His retrograde cycle in your 11th House of Groups may have reconnected you with old pals and professional allies, but it was a real source of frustration as you tried to get new projects or partnerships off the ground. Another push in a positive direction comes from Mercury, which turns direct in your 5th House of Self-Expression on **April 4**. This communicative planet stopped in your 6th House of Employment on **March 12**, reminding you to reconsider tasks that you might have taken on without serious reflection. Mercury's turnabout in your 5th House helps to inspire creativity that should make your current job more interesting or motivate you to seek another line of work.

Old dreams and vague memories come to life with the observant Libra Full Moon in your 12th House of Secrets on **April 6**. It's as if you're awakened to a new state of consciousness that helps you find inner peace to balance the pressures of your daily life. The Sun's entry into stable, sensual Taurus and your 7th House of Partners on **April 19** opens the way to more collaborative relationships. You are likely to attract reliable individuals and to be more at ease presenting yourself and your ideas to others. The Taurus New Moon on **April 21** underscores the value of simplicity and steadiness as pillars to building enduring alliances.

KEEP IN MIND THIS MONTH

Practical people may not arouse the passion you crave, but they can be essential for your financial and emotional security.

KEY DATES

APRIL 4 ★ *manna from heaven*

Let your imagination flow today, because even the most outlandish ideas can lead to a productive outcome. Illusionary Neptune in your 5th House of Creativity forms a magical quintile with opportunistic Jupiter in your 6th House of Self-Improvement. This can turn an inspiring but seemingly unrealistic concept into an effective tool for enriching your daily routine.

APRIL 7–8 ★ *play ball*

A sexy, sassy square between Venus in flirtatious Gemini and Mars in earthy Virgo adds spice to your personal life on **April 7**—but be careful to distinguish between teasing and a real yearning for intimacy. Aggression can arise on the **8th** with a stressful Sun-Mars sesquisquare. Apply the intensity you feel to a physically invigorating activity rather than getting angry or becoming overly competitive.

APRIL 13–15 ★ *you gotta have faith*

Mars's direct turn on **April 13** puts more fuel in your tank—but it's better to start rolling slowly rather than racing your engine at high speed. An awkward quincunx between loving Venus and punishing Pluto shadows relationships on the **14th**, making it difficult for you to find personal satisfaction. Adjusting values and expectations, though, could deepen a connection or expose untapped resources. Still, constraining Saturn's opposition to the Sun on **April 15** challenges your authority and reduces your sense of power. Practicing meditation, communing with nature, or tuning in to the arts will connect you to your spiritual source and restore balance.

SUPER NOVA DAYS

APRIL 20–23 ★ *dare to be different*

Caustic comments spurred by a Mercury-Mars quincunx on **April 20** add an edge to this normally cuddly Taurus time of year. Yet maybe it's helpful to expose the rough spots of conflicting perspectives so that you can discuss them reasonably, with the support of a healthy trine from Mercury to the Moon's North Node on the **21st**. This is also the day of the Taurus New Moon, which is sweetened with a sensitive sextile from compassionate Neptune. Even if your intentions are good, a high-frequency Mercury-Uranus conjunction on **April 22** throws verbal lightning bolts and illuminates your mind with new ideas. Yet the weirdest concepts may prove useful when the confident Sun-Mars trine brings encouragement and support from capable buddies on the **23rd**.

APRIL 25 ★ *room for improvement*

Your patience for trivia may run short when Mercury forms a hard square with no-nonsense Pluto; you are only interested in investigative research as you brainstorm how to streamline processes and eliminate needless tasks to bring more efficiency to your job. It's tempting to think negatively, but criticism and blunt observations can be constructive when you're committed to finding solutions.

MAY

ON THE FENCE

Relationships keep your head spinning this month as you experience conflicting urges to get closer to and pull away from those around you. Whether it's your fluctuating desires or inconsistent messages from partners, these changes in your personal life will flow more easily if you're flexible. On **May 5**, the Full Moon in passionate Scorpio can bring your emotions to a boil and you may feel forced to make an important decision. The intensity of the Moon in your sign should leave little doubt about your needs, yet even if you know that it's time to cut the cord with someone, exaggerating Jupiter in your 7th House of Partners opposing the Full Moon tempts you to overestimate the value of his or her role in your life. However, perceptive Mercury's entry into back-to-basics Taurus and your 7th House on **May 9** should clarify your thoughts about your personal and professional connections.

Romantic Venus turns retrograde in your intimate 8th House on the **15th** to put another twist into this tale. Your resolve may weaken because you need more time to come to terms with a complicated partnership issue. Magnetic Venus can pull you back into a relationship that you were ready to leave as you review and reconsider your options until the love planet turns direct on **June 27**. You may experience uncharacteristic confusion about alliances with the fickle Gemini Solar Eclipse in your 8th House of Deep Sharing on **May 20**. This powerful New Moon Eclipse forms a tense square with whimsical Neptune, tempting you with fantasies that are belied by facts. Fortunately, this tender alignment may also encourage forgiveness that salves old partnership wounds.

KEEP IN MIND THIS MONTH

Forcing a resolution to an emotional matter may not provide the relief you seek. Let your intuition tell you when it's time to act.

KEY DATES

MAY 5–8 ★ *trust your gut*

Taking a stand gives you back control of your life with the Scorpio Full Moon in your 1st House of Personality on **May 5**. Noticing what you're lacking in yourself or in a relationship leads to constructive action if it's matched with equal recognition of your abilities. The excitement of a new vision for your future can be amplified by a nervous semisquare between philosophical Jupiter and inventive Uranus on **May 7**. Yet if an ally suddenly changes his or her mind, the trust you have in each other may be shaken. Colleagues and friends could also surprise you when brazen Mars in your 11th House of Groups makes an unstable quincunx with unpredictable Uranus on the **8th**, but exploring alternative ways to work together could produce unusual shortcuts.

SUPER NOVA DAYS

MAY 13–16 ★ *persistence pays*

You're able to present big ideas in a practical form that makes them very appealing on **May 13** thanks to an optimistic Sun-Jupiter conjunction in your 7th House. Clever Mercury forms a productive Grand Earth Trine with enthusiastic Mars on the **13th** and incisive Pluto on the **14th**. You can cut to the core of a complex issue, analyze it effectively, and quickly move toward a solution. Still, even the best ideas and intentions can draw resistance when a Sun-Pluto sesquisquare on **May 14** undermines self-confidence and provokes a power struggle. Progress within a group may be slowed when Mars makes an uncooperative aspect with immobile Saturn on the **15th** before your competitive edge is sharpened and your leadership skills shine from the energetic boost you receive from a Mars-Pluto trine on **May 16**.

MAY 21–22 ★ *overcoming doubt*

You're forced into secrecy with messenger Mercury's tough aspect to mysterious Pluto on **May 21**—but it could engender mistrust and suspicion. But faith in yourself and the ability to sell your ideas can be restored with positive feedback and by gathering additional information when Mercury conjuncts outgoing Jupiter in your 7th House of Others on **May 22**.

MAY 28–30 ★ *take the high road*

Your faith in a critical partnership could be compromised as Mercury and the Sun in your 8th House of Shared Resources clash with skeptical Saturn and cryptic Pluto on **May 28–29**. Make sure that messages haven't been misunderstood before you consider changing the nature of an important relationship. If information has been withheld, it's likely to come out into the open when loquacious Mercury squares Mars on **May 30**. This mentally aggressive aspect can turn a simple conversation into an outright argument. State your case with strength and clarity, but season it with kindness to keep the peace.

JUNE

FLEXIBILITY IS KEY

You tend to view glib people who talk too much with justifiable skepticism. Yet instead of closing your mind to these chatty folks, you're likely to learn a great deal from them this month. On **June 11**, wise Jupiter enters verbose Gemini and your 8th House of Transformation where it will spend a year bringing you insights and opportunities from individuals whom you might have once dismissively called lightweights. The Sun's presence in your intimate 8th House until the **20th** and the versatile Gemini New Moon on **June 19** also signify gains in personal and professional partnerships that come with the breezy adaptability of the Twins. Adjusting quickly will take you farther now than anchoring yourself in rigid rules or values.

The Full Moon Lunar Eclipse in daring Sagittarius on **June 4** spurs you to overcome your usual reticence to spend too freely and take some financial risks. However, it's better to trust your instincts now than to rely on the opinions of friends, colleagues, and so-called experts. On **June 20**, the Sun enters Cancer, marking the Summer Solstice in your 9th House of Big Ideas. Dreams of travel and pursuing educational opportunities represent a desire to broaden your life experiences. Still, the road you're on can suddenly take you in surprising directions when restless Uranus begins a series of life-changing squares to your key planet Pluto on **June 24**. Adaptability is an asset as you navigate the twists and turns of these aspects until their completion on **March 16, 2015**. If you're indecisive about love or money, valuable Venus's forward turn in your 8th House of Shared Resources on **June 27** should get you off the fence.

KEEP IN MIND THIS MONTH

Your life this month is like a multiple-choice test that, oddly enough, could have a multitude of correct answers.

KEY DATES

JUNE 4–5 ★ *choose wisely*

It's better to invest in one big object, special event, or important relationship than to spread yourself too thin on **June 4**, when a stressful square between needy Venus and pushy Mars—along with the exuberant Sagittarius Full Moon Lunar Eclipse in your 2nd House of Resources—stimulates self-indulgence and complicates your social life. Happily, a Venus-Sun conjunction the next day in your 8th House of Intimacy is a gift from the planetary gods that attracts a desirable person, earns you approval, or brings a financial opportunity.

JUNE 7 ★ *keep your cool*

You could clash with co-workers or friends or family today, due to a tense square between the willful Sun and forceful Mars. Managing your emotions is a key to maintaining the peace; even if others lose their heads, you don't want to add more fuel to the fire. However, fighting for a just cause or focusing intensely on a single task may produce a breakthrough that's worth the incredible effort required of you.

JUNE 11 ★ *agree to disagree*

Seeking facts and appealing to reason may not be all that advantageous with mental Mercury's challenging aspects to unruly Uranus and provocative Pluto. Conversations grow confrontational with extreme statements and outrageous declarations that leap past the limits of credibility. But think of these claims as mere speculations and you won't feel forced to defend your ideas or attack what others say.

SUPER NOVA DAYS

JUNE 19–21 ★ *new horizons*

You can readily organize an overflow of information spawned by the noisy Gemini New Moon on **June 19**, because a creative trine from responsible Saturn helps you establish your priorities. Listen closely, but don't be afraid to say no with a boundary-setting Mercury-Saturn square on the **20th**. Tough negotiations are necessary to deepen alliances and establish trust with your partners. Slick sextiles between Venus and Uranus and between Mercury and Mars on **June 20–21** open minds to new resources, values, and pleasures that make your struggle to be understood worth it. Don't allow your oversensitivity to what others say end a conversation when no real harm was intended.

JUNE 23–25 ★ *velvet revolution*

The Sun's favorable trine to spiritual Neptune on **June 23** and an inspirational Jupiter-Neptune square on the **25th** provide buffers of faith or escapism around the transformational square of Uranus and Pluto. The tense alignment of this volcanic pair on **June 24** evokes feelings of uncertainty and, perhaps, an impulse to radically change your life. However, Neptune's role is to soften edges enough to access your imagination without getting lost in unattainable fantasies.

JULY

STUDENT OF LIFE

You have a great deal to learn this month, although much of it may seem more like relearning or modifying what you already know. An ambitious Full Moon in Capricorn on **July 3** falls in your 3rd House of Information, where it joins with your co-ruling planet Pluto and stressfully squares surprising Uranus. A new twist on an old idea or fresh evidence comes to light that can blow away assumptions about your work and daily routine, leading to some exciting changes. Intellectual Mercury turns retrograde in your 10th House of Career on **July 14**, sending you back to the drawing board to do further research, complete unfinished projects, and reconnect with colleagues to shore up your professional image. Nevertheless, your most important work may not be obvious to others; energetic Mars enters diplomatic Libra and your 12th House of Behind-the-Scenes Activities on **July 3**, when you could be called upon to rebalance and repair relationships.

You're reminded again that you need to go around obstacles instead of plowing right through them by difficult aspects from Jupiter to Pluto and Saturn on **July 18–20**, sandwiched around the Cancer New Moon on the **19th**. You may see extravagant plans with partners delayed or cut back, and you'll need patience and persistence to bring them to fruition. You can catch some wind in your sails on **July 22** when the Sun strides into bold Leo and your public 10th House, while hopeful Jupiter forms a smart sextile with uncontainable Uranus. Still, letting praise go to your head could encourage you to behave recklessly and take on more obligations than you can handle.

KEEP IN MIND THIS MONTH

Even if you're well versed in a subject, taking another look at it is highly likely to reward you with valuable new insights.

KEY DATES

JULY 3–4 ★ *lucky break*

When evaluative Venus forms a deceptive quincunx with enigmatic Pluto on **July 3**, what you see or hear may not be what you get, but digging deeper could reveal nuggets of gold. Mercury makes the same aspect with Pluto on the **4th**, which often indicates secrecy and manipulative use of language. However, Mercury, Venus, and Uranus align favorably with one another to instigate intellectual breakthroughs and shower you with some pleasurable surprises.

JULY 8–9 ★ *lost and found*

You could come up with a brilliant solution or fake your way through a slippery situation on **July 8**, when a Mars-Neptune quincunx sends you on a wild goose chase. No matter how far off track you wander, a strategic Mercury-Saturn quintile gets your inner GPS working to help you find your way home. Just don't let one small victory overinflate your confidence when the egocentric Sun makes another ungrounded aspect with illusory Neptune on **July 9**.

SUPER NOVA DAYS

JULY 17–19 ★ *wild horses*

Your passion for action may exceed your good judgment when unstoppable Mars forms an exciting trine with Jupiter and an intensifying square with Pluto on **July 17**, along with an explosive opposition to Uranus on the **18th**. Intense effort can be a plus as long as you start with a clear plan and reserve the option to change it when circumstances shift unexpectedly. These transits occur while inflationary Jupiter is making a misaligned quincunx with extremist Pluto, which can provoke reactions out of proportion with the situation. The moody Cancer New Moon on the **19th** falls in your 9th House of Big Ideas, but its square with strict Saturn is a reminder to rein in emotions and apply self-discipline, instead of allowing irrational feelings to dictate your behavior.

JULY 22 ★ *taking care of business*

Retrograde Mercury's sextile with action planet Mars motivates you to reconnect with people from your past and enables you to finish incomplete projects with swift efficiency. The Sun's move into proud Leo illuminates your 10th House of Status, which inspires you to be more assertive and creative in your professional life. There's nothing wrong with wanting recognition for a job well done.

JULY 30–31 ★ *stroke of genius*

The Sun's clunky quincunx with Pluto on **July 30** could enmesh you in an exhausting struggle for control. If you find yourself working hard without getting results, step back and seek another approach. In fact, distancing yourself from a sticky situation opens up a broader perspective that reveals a surprising solution. The Sun's trine to original Uranus on the **31st** rewards you for acting outside the box.

AUGUST

LADDER OF SUCCESS

You must find a comfortable balance between your public responsibilities and private activities this month to give you the sense of personal control you desire. The Sun in demonstrative Leo occupies your 10th House of Career until **August 22**, keeping you in the spotlight and, perhaps, in a position of leadership. However, the intellectual Aquarius Full Moon in your 4th House of Home and Family on **August 1** reflects your reluctance to play such a visible role. Nevertheless, communicative Mercury's direct turn in your 10th House on **August 8** provides encouragement for expressing your ideas with charisma and conviction. Your professional life gets another boost on **August 17** when the creative Leo New Moon, also falling in your 10th House of Status, inspires you to take more risks, perhaps seeking a more prestigious job or even starting a business of your own.

The success story begins on **August 15** when initiating Mars joins structuring Saturn in your 12th House of Destiny. Solidifying relationships through quiet diplomacy, establishing strategies to achieve your long-range goals, and strengthening your commitment to your cause are building blocks to manifesting your dreams. On the **22nd**, the Sun moves into hardworking Virgo and your 11th House of Groups to help you gather support from colleagues and friends. Yet compromise becomes more difficult when independent Mars enters fervent Scorpio on the **23rd**. You can benefit from your sense of urgency and desire to act alone as long as you don't alienate allies in the process. Joyfully, a more playful and personally rewarding period unfolds when the poetic Pisces Full Moon lights up your 5th House of Romance on the **31st**.

KEEP IN MIND THIS MONTH

Setting your own standards of excellence along with a sustainable pace can get you to the top of almost any mountain.

KEY DATES

AUGUST 2–3 ★ *running in circles*

Your hopes and insecurities create a destabilizing mix on the **2nd** that may find you investing your energy foolishly. An expansive Sun-Jupiter sextile widens your professional vision and earns you recognition, although a tender Sun-Venus semisquare has you fretting over the smallest criticism. A squishy Mars-Neptune sesquisquare on **August 3** adds sensitivity and imagination to your actions but could also trick you into wasting time on unrealistic projects.

AUGUST 7–9 ★ *love without limits*
A caring person opens your eyes to opportunities for travel, education, or finding a higher purpose when beautiful Venus enters nurturing Cancer and your 9th House of Faraway Places on **August 7**. Mercury's forward turn on the **8th** gets information flowing more freely, especially in your professional life, while Venus's delicious trine with empathic Neptune on **August 9** fills your heart with compassion and inspires artistic masterpieces.

SUPER NOVA DAYS
AUGUST 14–16 ★ *now or never*
You feel as if you're moving into tight quarters with a series of aspects that narrow your focus and force you to make tough choices. A challenging Sun-Pluto connection on **August 14** exposes the excesses of your ambitions and can incite a battle for control on the job. Innocent Venus's opposition to shrewd Pluto on the **15th** adds tension to relationships and raises financial fears. You may need to reassess a partnership as you become more aware of the high price you're paying just to receive approval. If you can't negotiate more reasonable terms, it may be time to reduce your reliance on someone in whom you're losing trust. Conditions could change suddenly on the **16th** when Venus squares shocking Uranus. This marks a major shift in an alliance, a sudden alteration of values, and an impulse to grab love or pleasure regardless of the risks.

AUGUST 19–20 ★ *strategic planning*
The tactical brilliance of a Saturn-Pluto quintile on **August 19** reveals how to complete a difficult task and establish a framework for greater achievement. The socially sophisticated Sun-Mars sextile on the **20th** energizes you and provides passion for team building. However, an overly optimistic Mars-Jupiter sesquisquare tempts you to overreach or overcommit. Channeling your enthusiasm wisely transforms it into a highly productive force.

AUGUST 29 ★ *leader of the pack*
You're able to motivate others without ruffling feathers today thanks to a friction-free trine between the Sun and unwavering Pluto. Your profound sense of purpose and clear intentions allow you to cut through the clutter of diverse opinions and distractions, concentrating your efforts where they will be most effective.

SEPTEMBER

RIDERS ON THE STORM

This month finds you working diligently to get along with colleagues with the Sun in systematic Virgo and your 11th House of Groups until **September 22**. Yet despite your best intentions to be a team player, discontent may have you thinking about making major changes in your life. The source of this feeling is the long-lasting and potentially disruptive square between radical Uranus and extreme Pluto. It makes its second appearance on **September 19** in a series of seven that started on **June 24** and ends on **March 16, 2015**. Nevertheless, you're able to keep up a cooperative front for most of the month—you may even receive appreciation and admiration for meeting your professional obligations with good cheer when validating Venus enters bright and shiny Leo in your 10th House of Career on the **6th**. If the joy, creativity, and camaraderie you bring to the workplace are genuine, the payoffs of pleasure, recognition, and perhaps even a raise will be satisfying. But if your heart isn't in it, the pressure of pretending will soon wear you out.

Mercury enters accommodating Libra on **September 16** and the Sun follows suit on the **22nd**, marking the Autumn Equinox and engendering a spirit of compromise. Yet because these events occur in your 12th House of Secrets, you may be hiding your unhappiness behind sweet smiles and sappy words. Your true feelings about work can erupt on the **29th**, when the Full Moon in reckless Aries ignites a firestorm in your 6th House of Employment. A lunar conjunction with electrifying Uranus and a tense square with fierce Pluto expose your raw emotions. Chaos and crisis may ensue, yet these can be powerful catalysts that propel you toward a more exciting and fulfilling career.

KEEP IN MIND THIS MONTH

Yes, you must behave politely in front of others, but don't let that keep you from acknowledging the truth you feel in your heart.

KEY DATES

SEPTEMBER 3–5 ★ *tough as nails*

On **September 3**, a restrictive square from Saturn to Venus in your 9th House of Big Ideas throws cold water on your travel plans and educational ambitions. Still, you quickly get back on track when a super-competent Mars-Pluto sextile helps you plow through obstacles and unearth resources to fuel your aspirations. Intelligent Mercury's favorable aspects to Pluto on the **4th** and Mars on the **5th** deepen your perceptions, empower your words, and supply the information needed to prove your point.

SEPTEMBER 11–12 ★ *realigning expectations*

You're easily wounded by harsh words following a sensitive Mercury-Venus semi-square on **September 11**. Disagreement, though, doesn't mean disapproval, so try not to take what you hear personally. Insecurity in relationships could escalate with an aloof Venus-Pluto quincunx on the **12th**. If love or money is lacking, readjust your priorities and maximize the resources you have instead of worrying about what you're missing.

SEPTEMBER 15–17 ★ *system update*

On **September 15**, the New Moon in methodical Virgo invites you to find fresh approaches to working with colleagues and friends. Analyzing these relationships can strengthen the weak links when criticism is aimed at seeking answers more than describing problems. There is a risk, however, in tackling too many tasks or overshooting your target on the **16th** with hyperactive Mars's poorly coordinated quincunx to boundless Jupiter. A sharp Mercury-Mars semisquare on **September 17** could spark angry words, yet may also clarify a cloudy situation with frank talk that leads to a rapid resolution.

SEPTEMBER 20 ★ *take a mental holiday*

Secrets come to light today when gossipy Mercury in your private 12th House opposes volatile Uranus and squares inscrutable Pluto. If your brain is buzzing with too much information or conversations grow uncomfortable, go ahead and indulge yourself. A delicious Venus-Jupiter sextile offers delights for the body and soul to ease your mind.

SUPER NOVA DAYS

SEPTEMBER 25–27 ★ *force of nature*

Persistent Mars in Scorpio tangles with Uranus and Pluto on **September 25** to undermine cooperation. Venus also creates unstable aspects with Uranus and Pluto on the **25th** and **26th** that seem like challenges to your self-worth. This is a volatile period when anger can erupt and damage a relationship. Still, if you can maintain an ounce of objectivity, a smidgen of humor, or a dash of originality, you could turn a potential crisis into an act of liberation and enjoy the chemistry of a sexy Venus-Mars square on **September 27**.

OCTOBER

BLUE SKIES AHEAD

If you've been waiting for the clouds to clear before you make a major decision, this month should bring you the answers you seek. The Sun is floating through your metaphysical 12th House until **October 22**, which could keep you in a relatively docile mood. However, your thoughts are likely to crystallize on **October 5** when Mercury and Saturn join in the last degree of Libra before forging into your sign later that day. The blindfold will be pulled from your eyes and you will see exactly where you stand. Whether the news is good or not, confusion will fade and you'll see what step to take next. Luckily, go-getter Mars, your sign's co-ruling planet, fires into exuberant Sagittarius and your 2nd House of Income on the **6th**, motivating you to think on a bigger scale and consider taking some risks in financial matters.

A spiritual teacher or motivational mentor broadens your perspective when the Libra New Moon in your 12th House of Destiny trines Jupiter on the **15th**. The Sun enters watery Scorpio on the **22nd** to churn up another wave of enthusiasm to enhance your creative capacities, empower your personality, and encourage a stronger desire for physical activity. Venus's shift into harmonious Libra on the **28th** offers you a sense of inner peace by connecting you with nature or the arts. You won't be shy about what you discover, since chatty Mercury is launched into opinionated Sagittarius on the **29th**. Lastly, the dependable Taurus Full Moon on the **29th** illuminates your 7th House of Partnerships to emphasize the obligations and expectations that define your personal and professional relationships.

KEEP IN MIND THIS MONTH

Facts are only the starting point, not the end of a significant question. It's what you do with the information that dictates your future.

KEY DATES

SUPER NOVA DAYS

OCTOBER 5–7 ★ *drawing a line in the sand*

The time for debate is over on the **5th**, and the moment for commitment is here talkative Mercury and stern Saturn dive into tenacious Scorpio. You could receive unpleasant news, but this will only alter your approach; it won't deter you from your true purpose. Your solid grasp of the facts—and of reality—increases your intellectual authority and your power as a communicator.

Besides, optimism is peeking through a faith-filled Mercury-Neptune trine, followed by renewed enthusiasm as the messenger planet connects with cheerful Jupiter on the **6th**. Nevertheless, daring Mars, newly arrived in promising Sagittarius, is softened by a square to diffusive Neptune on the **7th** that could lead you into financial foolishness. Let responsible Saturn enrich you with the persistence and patience you need to gain self-mastery.

OCTOBER 9–10 ★ *eye of the tiger*

You are especially resourceful on **October 9** as a Sun-Jupiter trine expands your vision while a Venus-Pluto trine shows you how to find the money, people, or materials you need to make it real. A magical Saturn-Neptune trine the next day outlines the big picture in a balanced way in the first of their three favorable aspects that will return on **June 11** and **July 19, 2013**. This larger strategic view gets tactical support as a perceptive Mercury-Pluto sextile fills in the details.

OCTOBER 22–23 ★ *the force is with you*

The potent transit of the Sun into Scorpio on the **22nd** motivates you to act with greater independence. However, the Sun's trine with gentle Neptune on the **23rd** tempers this force with a vulnerability that enables you to accept help when it's offered. Let your guard down to allow more love and light to flow through your life.

OCTOBER 25 ★ *work in progress*

The creative Sun's conjunction with sobering Saturn steels you to take on self-defined challenges. These can include developing more self-control and maturity, assuming more responsibility for your physical well-being, improving the quality of your relationships, and reaching a new level of personal achievement.

OCTOBER 29 ★ *partners in crime*

You're tempted to flee reality as Mercury the Winged Messenger flies into adventurous Sagittarius and squares dreamy Neptune on **October 29**. It's a time when what you say and what you hear can be fuzzed by fantasy and weak on facts. Yet a revelatory Full Moon in Taurus in your 7th House of Others slams into an opposition with Saturn that leaves little room for ambiguity. Fortunately, incisive Pluto's trine to the Full Moon clarifies the risk–reward ratio of relationships, increasing your chances of finding fulfilling partnerships.

NOVEMBER

TURNING THE PAGE

This is an incredible month that can change your self-image and spur a new commitment to making the most of your abilities. The key event is the Scorpio New Moon on **November 13**, which is also a total eclipse of the Sun. You may not see its effects immediately, but it marks the threshold between your old life and the future—and what you do with your emotions will make the difference between a leap forward and a lost opportunity. A move that looks illogical to others may be exactly what you need. In fact, interactive Mercury's retrograde turn in your 2nd House of Self-Worth on **November 6** reminds you to take a second look at your talents and the rewards you receive for them. If you're not being fairly compensated, consider a change in direction to gain satisfaction by the time Mercury goes direct on the **26th**.

Your hunger for pleasure and living life to the fullest grows when desirous Venus enters magnetic Scorpio on **November 21**. Yes, this can make you more alluring, especially when you invest effort in your appearance, but the secret to getting what and who you want is to fall in love with yourself. Nourish this critical relationship by celebrating your gifts and committing to work on improving those areas where you fall short of your expectations. You're ready to make a bold financial move when the Sun enters risk-taking Sagittarius and your 2nd House on **November 21**. However, the Gemini Full Moon Lunar Eclipse in your 8th House of Shared Resources on the **28th** may attract partners who don't live up to their promises. Verify credentials before you invest your faith or money.

KEEP IN MIND THIS MONTH

Your truth doesn't have to be describable to have meaning for you. The best answers lie within and can't always be put into words.

KEY DATES

NOVEMBER 3–4 ★ *romantic revival*

You struggle to find trust on **November 3** when manipulative Pluto squares innocent Venus in ambivalent Libra. Secrecy, jealousy, and resentment can undermine relationships and force you to question your commitment. Fortunately, a resourceful Venus-Mars quintile on the **4th** shows you how to repair a weakened alliance and rediscover the joy and passion that make it worthwhile.

SUPER NOVA DAY

NOVEMBER 13 ★ *total eclipse of the heart*

What you see is probably not what you're going to get when retrograde Mercury forms a square with delusional Neptune on **November 13**. Your perceptions are more impressionistic than precise, which is useful for inspiration but dreadful for dealing with facts. The New Moon Solar Eclipse is conjunct the integrative Lunar North Node in intense Scorpio, reminding you that the dark waters of emotion may seem dangerous but are your secret passageway back to yourself. When layers of illusion are washed away, you can connect with deeper desires that will fill your heart instead of dabbling in distractions that leave you hungry. Letting go is the way to grow now.

NOVEMBER 16–17 ★ *lead by example*

You can be tough and tender as macho Mars enters authoritative Capricorn and your 3rd House of Communication on the **16th**. Normally you can appear gruff or ungracious when you push yourself and others to work harder. However, Mars's supportive sextile with forgiving Neptune on the **17th** allows you to forge ahead with sensitivity to others and compassion for yourself. Actions count more than words now.

NOVEMBER 23–24 ★ *rapid recovery*

Your impatience with routine tasks puts you on edge when impulsive Mars forms a volatile square with explosive Uranus on **November 23**. This aspect is useful if you're free to act spontaneously and operate outside the usual rules. But if you're stuck in a boring box of predictability, you could find yourself lashing out at people or facing an unexpected crisis. Order is quickly restored on the **24th** when stabilizing Saturn aligns in a comforting sextile to Mars. Chaos and conflict recede as you put your feet squarely on the ground and get back to work.

NOVEMBER 27–28 ★ *claim your power*

You go to extremes with a provocative Mars-Pluto conjunction on **November 27**. When you're in charge, you can cut through obstacles as if they were butter. But if others lead the way, your resistance to the slightest hint of being controlled could be fierce. The Gemini Full Moon Eclipse on the **28th** urges you to eliminate people and plans that aren't essential to reaching your goals.

DECEMBER

LABOR OF LOVE

Pay more attention to your financial future this month as you seek new opportunities to increase your income in the year ahead. Quicksilver Mercury's entry into farsighted Sagittarius and your 2nd House of Resources on **December 10** gives you a more positive picture of your earning potential. The inspirational Sagittarius New Moon on **December 13** falls in your 2nd House, and the optimism it creates helps you cast aside doubts and dream about bigger rewards ahead. You garner recognition on the **15th** when attractive Venus enters Sagittarius to pump up your self-esteem and reinforce the flow of moneymaking ideas. Your potential for earning more money is connected to the faith you have in yourself and the excitement you feel from your work. Pleasure and profit make an ideal mix because cash will come more easily when you're having a good time.

On **December 20** prosperous Jupiter forms a quincunx with purging Pluto, an aspect that already occurred on **July 18** and will return on **March 29, 2013**. It's one of several reminders to eliminate unprofitable distractions and choose the most productive path for economic success. The Winter Solstice is marked by the Sun's move into prioritizing Capricorn on the **21st** and Jupiter's quincunx with constrictive Saturn on the **22nd**, both reinforcing the importance of concentrating your efforts. On the **28th**, the protective instincts of the Cancer Full Moon encounter an opposition to Pluto and a square with unpredictable Uranus that can throw a monkey wrench into your plans. However, the Moon's supportive trine to Saturn reinforces your sense of commitment, enabling you to make corrections and get right back on track.

KEEP IN MIND THIS MONTH

The limits of your current circumstances only reflect what lies ahead if you don't set your financial imagination free.

KEY DATES

DECEMBER 1–2 ★ *reach for the stars*

Stay on top of your emotions on **December 1**, when aggressive Mars in your 3rd House of Communication forms an indiscreet quincunx with bombastic Jupiter. This cosmic tension can fuel an argument or disperse your energy unless you're watchful. The confident Sun's opposition to Jupiter on the **2nd** makes it nearly impossible for you to focus on the here and now. Luckily, it's fine to dream of more financial gains as long as you take the time to carefully construct your ladder to success.

DECEMBER 12 ★ *hungry heart*

Seductive Venus in sultry Scorpio joins the evolutionary Lunar North Node in your 1st House of Personality to amplify your powers of attraction. Being led by your deepest desires can be dangerous, but knowing what you want now, —even if it's forbidden—adds urgency to your pursuit of happiness.

DECEMBER 16 ★ *sudden epiphany*

You can expect difficulties today as a frustrating semisquare between mobile Mercury and impatient Mars messes with travel plans, provokes harsh language, or complicates minor matters. However, Mars also forms an inventive quintile with brilliant Uranus that prompts a radical new approach to quickly untangle the knots of your day.

DECEMBER 25–26 ★ *question authority*

Your family traditions are challenged on **December 25** when Mars flies into avant-garde Aquarius and your domestic 4th House. The Sun's tense square with unruly Uranus electrifies the atmosphere with rebellious behavior that undermines authority. Still, it's better to break with the past than to allow a breakdown of civility in your household. Knowing how to adapt to change in a mature manner is a gift of the first of three highly competent Saturn-Pluto sextiles on the **26th**. This harmonious alignment returns on **March 8** and **September 21, 2013**, to help you operate at even higher levels of efficiency.

SUPER NOVA DAYS

DECEMBER 28–30 ★ *trust the process*

The Cancer Full Moon on **December 28** brightens your 9th House of Big Ideas to provide a fresh perspective on your long-range plans. The tenderness and protection offered by this sign, however, could be stripped away by its disruptive aspects with stormy Pluto and wild Uranus. Your tendency to rely on the status quo isn't necessarily wise now; there are too many changes happening all around you. Still, support from savvy Saturn in Scorpio shines the spotlight on what's most essential so that you can shift gears without losing direction. The Sun's conjunction with Pluto and smart sextile with Saturn on the **30th** give you a clear sense of purpose as you look to the year ahead.

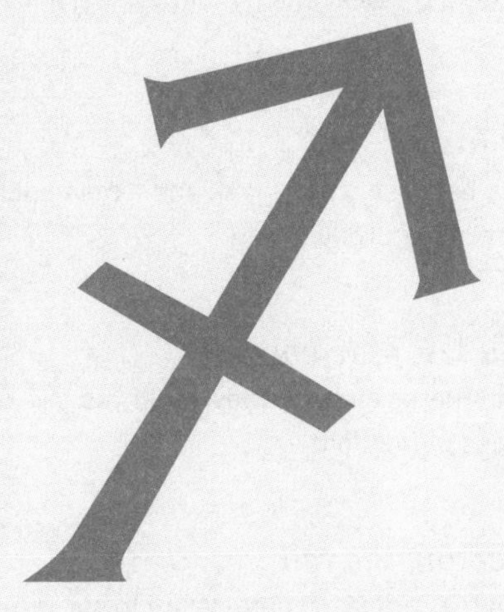

SAGITTARIUS

NOVEMBER 22–DECEMBER 21

SAGITTARIUS

2011 SUMMARY

You're not usually the nostalgic type, but you may have outmoded beliefs about yourself; now you're finally ready to let go of them. Lightening your load frees up mental, emotional, and physical energy that will permit you to fly higher in the future.

AUGUST—*play first*

Knowing the difference between a petty task and a meaningful one will reduce your stress and increase your productivity.

SEPTEMBER—*a test of teamwork*

Gaining the support of others can be a trade-off. If you give up too much, you may regret a certain loss of freedom.

OCTOBER—*piercing the veil*

You are totally safe when a compassionate desire to serve humanity, rather than power, is your primary motivating force.

NOVEMBER—3, 2, 1, *blast off!*

Your head and heart may be urging you to fly, but it's wise to tie up any loose ends before you start a serious venture.

DECEMBER—*claim your power*

Maintaining a sane and solid foundation for yourself now will make it possible for you to become more open with others later on.

2011 CALENDAR

AUGUST

MON 1 ★ Stretch the boundaries but don't ignore reality

FRI 5 ★ Delicious excess may cost you more than you can afford

THU 18 ★ Direct your energy with persistence and purpose

THU 25 ★ Applying too much pressure will only increase resistance

TUE 30 ★ **SUPER NOVA DAY** Rewards at work can be extra sweet

SEPTEMBER

FRI 2 ★ Follow your ambitious idea with a practical plan

SUN 11–WED 14 ★ Tone down your enthusiasm to avoid the dangers of excess

SAT 17–SUN 18 ★ Sudden attractions have hidden costs

THU 22– FRI 23 ★ Expecting too much might leave you disappointed

SUN 25–TUE 27 ★ **SUPER NOVA DAYS** Dramatic change may be necessary

OCTOBER

SAT 1–MON 3 ★ Avoid taking on more than you should

TUE 11 ★ Creative ideas can spice up your love life

FRI 14 ★ Strong desires can also reflect a deep spiritual connection

MON 17 ★ Filter out noise and tune in to the heart of the matter

WED 26–FRI 28 ★ **SUPER NOVA DAYS** Confidentiality can increase intimacy

NOVEMBER

WED 2–THU 3 ★ Free yourself from an outmoded self-image with originality

THU 10 ★ A wake-up call reminds you to make healthy changes

WED 16–FRI 18 ★ It's easy to start quickly now but harder to finish on time

TUE 22–FRI 25 ★ **SUPER NOVA DAYS** Exciting ideas get bogged down by the details

DECEMBER

FRI 2–SUN 4 ★ Channel your emotional intensity into a creative project

SAT 10 ★ Speak your own truth rather than accommodating others

FRI 16 ★ Focusing on what's most important is your challenge now

TUE 20 ★ Separate personal pleasures from professional obligations

THU 22–SUN 25 ★ **SUPER NOVA DAYS** Advance your professional interests

SAGITTARIUS OVERVIEW

This is a year of progress, and what you accomplish during the first half can prepare you for the important people who enter your life during the second. Your key planet, Jupiter, is the magnifying lens of the heavens; you can confidently expect things to grow wherever it is traveling in your chart. Expansive Jupiter is in stable Taurus and your 6th House of Daily Routines until June 11, bringing opportunities at work and success from the little things that you do while managing mundane tasks. **Although you may feel constrained by a regular job, showing up every day and giving it your best now will bring rewards later.** Meanwhile, warrior Mars in your 10th House of Career until July 3 arouses your fighting spirit and will to get ahead. But Mars is in hard-working Virgo, indicating that you can channel your aggressive behavior into carefully constructed strategies instead of blindly pushing forward. However, Mars is retrograde from January 23 until April 13, impeding your progress and forcing you to work even harder to achieve your goals. Recognize what's holding you back, manage your frustration, and keep your eyes on the distant prize, rather than becoming discouraged if success takes longer than expected.

You're less inclined to go it alone once Jupiter shifts into restless Gemini and your 7th House of Partnerships and Public Life on June 11 for a yearlong stay. All types of relationships are favored during this phase, and love can flourish when you share common goals with your partner. It's also easier now to negotiate business arrangements with supportive people who can help you achieve success—as long as you're motivated by mutual benefit and growth, not personal greed. **Instead of pretending that you have all the answers, allow your openness to learning to attract someone who shows you how to go beyond whatever limitations you previously accepted.**

You continue to struggle over when to include others on your journey and when to set out alone as deliberate Saturn continues its visit to objective Libra and your 11th House of Friends and Wishes. **Although you take your obligations to groups or organizations more seriously than ever, you also must learn how to set boundaries as you clarify your long-term goals and recognize where they diverge from everyone else's.** On October 5, Saturn's entry into Scorpio and your 12th House of Endings starts a two-year process of finishing old business, clearing obstacles, and eliminating that which hasn't lived up to your expectations. Saturn forms a harmonious trine with visionary Neptune on October 10, enabling you to creatively balance your ideals with the realities of your current situation. You must show patience and hard work if you hope to be ready for the major new cycle of ambition and accomplishment that begins on December 23, 2014, when karmic Saturn enters your sign.

INEVITABLE EVOLUTION

This year kicks off a long-lasting process of transformation that can turn your love life upside down as your core values change and clash with old assumptions. Your attraction to new experiences, unusual relationships, and eccentric people can be quite thrilling when Uranus the Awakener settles in for an extended visit to your 5th House of Romance. Although revolutionary Uranus remains in independent Aries until 2018, dynamic squares to regenerative Pluto on June 24 and September 19 begin this unstoppable metamorphosis. You feel pressure for change that frustrates your personal life, adds a heightened sense of urgency, and tosses in a few unexpected twists and turns along the way. Meanwhile, Venus the Lover has you looking back to a previous relationship or reconsidering your involvement in a current one when she is retrograde in your 7th House of Partners on May 15–June 27.

THE WAITING IS THE HARDEST PART

You are driven to succeed as motivational Mars—which usually spends about six weeks in each sign—camps out in conscientious Virgo and your 10th House of Status from November 10, 2011, until July 3. Unfortunately, you may feel as if you're losing ground and your career goals are growing more distant during Mars's retrograde period on January 23–April 13. Even if you find success delayed, benevolent Jupiter in your 6th House of Work until June 11 is like a guardian angel that assures positive results. Your undying optimism, combined with a steady work pace despite any setbacks, should pay off later in the year. Recognition and a raise may finally arrive when the Sun moves through your 10th House on August 22–September 22, or perhaps when enriching Venus shows up for a visit on October 3–28.

ABOVEBOARD

You have several opportunities for significant financial gain this year, but unstable Uranus's squares to secretive Pluto in your 2nd House of Money on June 24 and September 19 warn you against any type of scheme that isn't 100 percent honest and forthright. Shady dealings won't escape brilliant Uranus as it brings the truth out into the open. However, a propitious Venus-Jupiter conjunction on March 14 is part of a Grand Earth Trine with dynamic Mars and insightful Pluto that opens a window of opportunity for sensible investments. Another day for smart money management is October 9, when a Venus-Pluto trine brings the potential of success. Your cash flow might be problematic around November 26 when Venus bumps into tightfisted Saturn—but a concentrated effort should turn things around quickly, because assertive Mars conjuncts with Pluto in your 2nd House the next day.

MOVE IT

Though you're tempted to be lazy and overindulgent through June 11 thanks to joyful Jupiter's visit to your 6th House of Health and Habits, this is also a great time to revitalize your body by upgrading your exercise program and improving your diet. The challenge to overcome your own inertia is reinforced on August 29 when the South Node of the Moon shifts into your 6th House, where it remains until February 18, 2014. Holding on to the status quo isn't helpful; instead integrate healthy lifestyle changes into your daily routine.

ON THE THRESHOLD OF A DREAM

On February 3, Neptune the Dreamer enters your 4th House of Domestic Conditions, where it remains for thirteen years, but its immediate effect is to stimulate your fantasies. A creative quintile with happy-go-lucky Jupiter on April 4 encourages you to see the good in every situation, yet disappointment can follow if you're overly unrealistic. Foolish optimism can prompt you to take careless risks when Jupiter squares Neptune on June 25. However, Saturn's stabilizing trine to Neptune on October 10 enables you to turn your abode into the beautiful home of your dreams.

DESTINATION UNKNOWN

During the first half of the year—when journeying Jupiter is in your 6th House of Employment—your travel will tend to be well planned and for specific job-related reasons. But after Jupiter enters flighty Gemini and your 7th House of Companions on June 11, others may tempt you to take a trip on a whim simply for the sake of adventure in going somewhere new. If you must leave home between July 14 and August 8, when Mercury the Winged Messenger is retrograde in your 9th House of Travel, make sure to double-check the details of your itinerary.

GETTING DOWN TO BUSINESS

You have your spiritual work cut out for you this year, and the sooner you start, the easier it will be later on. Powerful Pluto's squares to individualistic Uranus in your 5th House of Self-Expression keeps the pressure for change at a high level all year. The restless Gemini Solar Eclipse on May 20 rattles your 7th House of Partners, revealing hidden anger that can impede your personal growth. The Sagittarius Lunar Eclipse on June 4 falls in your 1st House of Self and is square to contentious Mars, reinforcing the battle lines. But taskmaster Saturn's entry into your 12th House of Soul Consciousness on October 5 puts you on notice that metaphysical studies are no longer just a hobby or passing interest. Taking a more serious approach to spirituality is a significant part of your path ahead.

RICK & JEFF'S TIP FOR THE YEAR:
The Truth Will Set You Free

If you only focus on the brighter side of life, your unflappable optimism can get in your way by preventing you from seeing what's real. This isn't to say that you will benefit from pessimism, but your willingness to engage with the shadow side of your personality enables you to transform negativity into a more useful force for positive change.

JANUARY

AIMING IN THE RIGHT DIRECTION

You have turned a corner and can finally see where you're going. Your key planet, Jupiter, shifted to direct motion on **December 25, 2011**, in your 6th House of Self-Improvement and now clears a path for personal growth in front of you. It may take time before the changes you make in your daily routine produce noticeable results, yet it's crucial to stay focused on what you need to do day by day, even if success still seems far away. Your professional progress may be impeded this month, because physical Mars crawls along at a snail's pace until he starts backpedaling on **January 23**. Mars retrogrades in your 10th House of Career until **April 13**, forcing you to slow down and review recent work, revamp your plans, and re-create your timetable for reaching your goals. Fortunately, you receive significant help from realistic Saturn in your 11th House of Dreams and Wishes as it nears a free-flowing trine with imaginative Neptune this month. This long-lasting aspect isn't exact until **October 10**, yet it reveals a sensible strategy to turn your fantasies into reality if you can be self-disciplined and patient now.

An emotional crisis challenges your common sense when the moody Cancer Full Moon on **January 9** highlights your 8th House of Deep Sharing. Although the Sun's brilliant quintile to electric Uranus can elicit innovative ideas, it doesn't do much to connect you with your feelings. The intelligent Aquarius New Moon on **January 23** activates your 2nd House of Self-Worth, yet its creative squares to optimistic Jupiter and pessimistic Saturn remind you that balance, as elusive as it may be, is attainable with practice.

KEEP IN MIND THIS MONTH

As you begin to fill in the details of the big picture for the year ahead, don't let setbacks or delays create self-doubt.

KEY DATES

JANUARY 1–4 ★ *try, try again*

Watch out lest heated discussions escalate into outright conflict on **January 1**, when outspoken Mercury in irrepressible Sagittarius squares combative Mars. An anxious Venus-Uranus semisquare on **January 2** encourages you to take a risk in your quest for a good time, but does little to settle the tension. Fortunately, continued discussions finally shift the energy and you are able to get what you want on **January 4**, when magnetic Venus creates a magical quintile to magnanimous Jupiter.

JANUARY 7–9 ★ *table for two?*

You may talk about your fantasies on **January 7** as if they're already real, because communicator Mercury in your sign sextiles empirical Saturn and ethereal Neptune. You seem even more serious when Mercury enters conservative Capricorn on the **8th**, yet its aspects to permissive Jupiter and inventive Uranus push beyond the status quo and encourage you to take a chance by sharing your unconventional ideas. It's time to decide if you want to involve someone else in your moneymaking scheme on **January 9**, when the security-conscious Cancer Full Moon in your 8th House of Shared Resources opposes the ambitious Capricorn Sun in your 2nd House of Income.

SUPER NOVA DAYS

JANUARY 12–14 ★ *the force is with you*

You feel invincible on **January 12**, when the Sun in your 2nd House of Self-Esteem trines warrior Mars. Additionally, an illusory Venus-Neptune conjunction on the **13th** infuses you with dreams of a fairy-tale romance, while a steadfast Venus-Saturn trine elicits common sense. Think before speaking, because a Mercury-Pluto conjunction adds intensity to your words. Luckily, you can make the most of any opportunity that comes along when valuable Venus enters your 4th House of Foundations on **January 14** and sextiles auspicious Jupiter. Success is likely with such a propitious aspect as long as you don't have outrageous expectations.

JANUARY 21–23 ★ *cosmic speed bump*

The days leading up to the progressive Aquarius New Moon on **January 23** are filled with anticipation of good times ahead. The Sun's slick sextile to thrilling Uranus on the **21st** and dynamic square to buoyant Jupiter on the **22nd** raise your expectations and increase your self-confidence. Although it seems as if nothing can stop you, Mars's retrograde turn on the **23rd** will set obstacles in your path and delay your journey to success.

JANUARY 28 ★ *heart of gold*

Good news can trick you into promising more than you can deliver today. You may feel as if you've done the work and now the rewards should follow, but difficult aspects from Venus and Mercury to overreaching Jupiter remind you that you can't always please everyone, no matter how hard you try.

FEBRUARY

HOME IMPROVEMENT

This starts off as a very busy month, yet your professional progress may be hampered with so much happening in your personal life. Enterprising Mars continues his extended visit to your 10th House of Career and Community, and activities outside the home increase the demands on your time. But the angry red planet is retrograde until **April 13**, slowing everything down and forcing you to rework your plans in response to the shifting circumstances. Meanwhile, Mercury the Communicator and the Sun are traveling through your 3rd House of Immediate Environment until **February 13** and **February 19**, respectively, drawing your attention closer to home with matters involving siblings, good friends, and the ongoing activities of your everyday life. Spiritual Neptune's entry into sensitive Pisces on **February 3** is a subtle yet significant shift, for it remains in your 4th House of Roots for thirteen years, inviting you to seek solace from the world through your home and family. However, be careful not to confuse your fantasies with what's actually possible when Mercury joins Neptune on **February 14**, followed by the Sun on **February 19**. Keeping your feet on the ground now goes a long way toward minimizing disappointments later on.

The lively Leo Full Moon on **February 7** lights up your 9th House of Higher Thought and Faraway Places, encouraging you to actively pursue your dreams, whether they're about exploring an exotic place or enrolling in a course of study that expands your mind. The compassionate Pisces New Moon on **February 21** joins sympathetic Neptune and healer Chiron in your 4th House of Home and Family, making this an excellent time to forgive a relative, cleanse an old emotional wound, or mend a domestic squabble.

KEEP IN MIND THIS MONTH

It's not enough to imagine that your life will improve. You must also make concrete plans and begin to put them into action.

KEY DATES

FEBRUARY 1 ★ *no more drama*

If someone at work disagrees with your approach, losing your temper isn't the smartest way to handle your frustration. You may think you're being nice, but forceful Mars is retrograde in your 10th House of Public Life, and a challenging aspect from sarcastic Mercury can provoke critical words that hurt rather than help.

Additionally, pleasant Venus opposes Mars from the 4th House of Security, suggesting that you may not have the kind of support from your family that you want. Instead of escalating conflict, channel your emotions to fuel your productivity.

SUPER NOVA DAYS

FEBRUARY 7–11 ★ *off the hook*

You speak with clarity on **February 7**—when the Sun's conjunction with mental Mercury occurs in your 3rd House of Communication—although the dramatic Leo Full Moon tempts you to embellish your message for extra attention. But you may feel underappreciated since lovable Venus forms an irritating quincunx with judgmental Saturn the same day. Luckily, Venus prances into uncontainable Aries and your 5th House of Romance on the **8th**, warming others to your straightforward behavior. An electric Venus-Uranus conjunction on **February 9** fuels your creativity with excitement, encouraging experimentation and innovation. You're challenged to manage your energy, however, because Mercury and the Sun form uneasy aspects with impatient Mars on **February 9–10**. Fortunately, the Sun's creative quintile to goodhearted Jupiter on the **11th** allows your sense of humor to put a positive spin on an awkward situation.

FEBRUARY 15–18 ★ *running down a dream*

You're in the grip of intense emotions—perhaps jealousy or fear—on **February 15**, when possessive Venus in your 5th House of Love dynamically squares passionate Pluto in your 2nd House of Self-Esteem. Confident Jupiter comes to the rescue with enthusiasm, energy, and bright ideas as it aspects active Mars and interactive Mercury on **February 15–16**. Take the opportunity that the giant planet offers and work hard to make it real on the **18th**, when a solid Sun-Saturn trine enables you to crystallize concepts into enduring practical solutions.

FEBRUARY 25–28 ★ *from the ground up*

Although you can tap into a deep well of productivity when the brilliant Sun sextiles abundant Jupiter on **February 25** and potent Pluto on the **28th**, don't waste the potential benefits of these powerful days. Follow your intuition, for the Sun in gentle Pisces in your 4th House of Foundations invites you to spend time in familiar surroundings to revitalize your life and build a solid base for the future.

MARCH

YOU THINK YOU CAN

Lingering tension from recent demands at work and at home adds stress to your relationships when this month begins. Fortunately, the opposition between aggressive Mars in your 10th House of Career and the willful Sun in your 4th House of Family on **March 3** can also expose differences about priorities, which is a good way to start finding solutions. Short tempers could lead to an open conflict, but your good intentions and a willingness to work toward a long-term solution to a current dilemma should be enough to get you through a difficult situation. Thankfully, the instability begins to settle down when graceful Venus enters practical Taurus on **March 5** and forms a cooperative sextile with altruistic Neptune on the **6th**. If you must be critical on **March 8**, when the perfectionist Virgo Full Moon hooks up with expressive Mars, do it constructively rather than saying something hurtful for no reason.

Don't be too disappointed if you fall short of your own expectations, for you'll have another chance to handle those issues that remain unresolved when communicator Mercury turns retrograde in your 5th House of Self-Expression on **March 12**. The Winged Messenger continues its backward flight until **April 4**, giving you plenty of time to review your recent progress and revamp plans as needed. But don't wait until then to take definitive action; Mars backs into stabilizing trines with lovely Venus, opportunistic Jupiter, and incisive Pluto that are all exact on **March 14**. Your strength of conviction enables you to ride a tidal wave of optimism that expands your self-confidence and graces you with the power to accomplish great things. The incorrigible Aries New Moon on **March 22** fires up your creativity and inspires you to express your inner child.

KEEP IN MIND THIS MONTH

You will invite frustration if you expect immediate results from what you initiate this month. However, combining determination with patience should lead to success.

KEY DATES

MARCH 2–5 ★ *no way out*

Your thoughts turn to new forms of play or a new romantic interest when cerebral Mercury enters restless Aries and your 5th House of Love and Creativity on **March 2**. Nevertheless, you may be stymied when you try to turn your ideas into action, because action-planet Mars forms a resistant semisquare with constrictive

Saturn that same day, and opposes the Sun the next. Unfortunately, vulnerable Venus also runs into difficult aspects on **March 3–4**, delaying emotional and physical satisfaction. Nevertheless, you can expect a break from the past when Mercury hooks up with shocking Uranus on **March 5**, triggering radical ideas about love.

SUPER NOVA DAYS

MARCH 13–14 ★ *carpe diem*

Although wordy Mercury and busy Mars are both retrograde, what you start now will likely manifest once these two planets turn direct on **April 4** and **April 13**, respectively. This optimistic outlook comes thanks to a trine from your ruling planet, Jupiter, in your 6th House of Self-Improvement to fierce Pluto in your 2nd House of Self-Worth on **March 13**. Receptive Venus conjuncts propitious Jupiter on the **14th**, combining to form an unshakable Grand Earth Trine, all but assuring your ultimate success. Although this is considered a lucky aspect, it's really about your growing desire for prosperity, your ability to seize an opportunity, and your determination to stick with a commitment until you reach your goals.

MARCH 20–22 ★ *a thrill a minute*

Kick the fun up to a new level on March 20, the Spring Equinox, when the Sun enters into headstrong Aries and your 5th House of Play to mark the beginning of the new astrological year. The spontaneous Aries New Moon on the **22nd** joins clever Mercury and unorthodox Uranus to create an intellectual cosmic party, but it's up to you to bring the heavenly magic down to earth and weave it into your life.

MARCH 26–28 ★ *you're only human*

You are challenged to maintain a healthy perspective on **March 26**, when a magnifying Mercury-Jupiter aspect encourages you to turn every thought into a get-rich-quick scheme or a plan to save the world. But a smart quintile between restrictive Saturn and evolutionary Pluto on **March 28** forces you to realize that you can't do everything. Your own emotional negativity or a shortage of time and money could rain on your parade. However, the lesson here is about setting priorities and eliminating inessentials to help you to achieve your objectives.

APRIL

CHANGE OF HEART

The direct turns of expressive Mercury on **April 4** and enthusiastic Mars on **April 13** set you into motion, allowing you to capitalize on your efforts over the past few months. Mars began his retrograde period on **January 23** and slowed your professional progress with delays and detours as he backpedaled through your 10th House of Career. Mercury's retrograde started on **March 12**, unraveling personal plans as it backed into your 4th House of Family on **March 23**. In both cases, you were given chances to transform the frustration of setbacks into opportunities to gather more information or to utilize what you already knew. Now, with these planets turning direct, you can reassert yourself on the job and put your revised plans into forward gear.

Fortunately, you're greatly inspired by your dreams and are able to integrate them into your daily life when joyous Jupiter in your 6th House of Self-Improvement forms a creative quintile with intuitive Neptune on **April 4**. The objective Libra Full Moon on **April 6** illuminates your 11th House of Friends, Hopes, and Wishes, encouraging you to share your long-term goals with others and to keep an open mind when receiving their feedback. Mercury's shift into irrepressible Aries and your 5th House of Love and Play on **April 16** turns your thoughts to lighter subjects, while the Sun's move into steadfast Taurus and your practical 6th House on the **19th** reminds you that it's still a good idea to keep up your healthy habits. The Taurus New Moon on **April 21** calms your uncertainty about work-related goals as it forms a harmonizing trine to courageous Mars in your public 10th House.

KEEP IN MIND THIS MONTH

Although you're heading in a new direction with fewer obstructions in your path, remember that it can take a while for your momentum to build.

KEY DATES

SUPER NOVA DAYS

APRIL 3–7 ★ *love story*

Affable Venus moves into your 7th House of Others on **April 3** for an extended four-month stay—a great time for you to better understand the needs of your friends and co-workers, balance your desires with the people around you, and express your affections easily. Chatty Mercury's direct turn on the **4th** boosts your eagerness to talk about what you want, but it may be tough to separate your fantasies from reality as Venus squares delusional Neptune on **April 5**. Fortunately, the accommodating Libra Full Moon in your 11th House of Friends on the **6th** supports your efforts to treat others fairly, even if your needs differ from theirs. Nevertheless, sparks could fly when flirty Venus squares feisty Mars on **April 7**, creating a lovers' spat or inviting a sexy interaction with someone special.

APRIL 15–16 ★ *red light, green light*

If you recently initiated action too quickly or reacted to someone without thinking, the Sun's opposition to karmic Saturn in your 11th House of Social Networking on **April 15** can stop you in your tracks, teach you an important lesson about cooperating with others, and, if necessary, make you start all over again. An uncomfortable Saturn-Venus aspect on the **16th** can further isolate you from someone you love. Thankfully, entrepreneurial Mercury blasts its way into fiery Aries and your 5th House of Creativity, rekindling your enthusiasm and enabling you to convey newfound excitement about a current relationship, project, or artistic endeavor.

APRIL 21–23 ★ *the right stuff*

It's back to the healthy basics on **April 21**, when the sensible Taurus New Moon falls in your 6th House of Health. Pay more attention to your physical well-being now, especially in regard to your diet and exercise routine. Still, you can be sidetracked by considering a totally different approach to your healing process on **April 22**, when an erratic Mercury-Uranus conjunction triggers unconventional thoughts. The Sun's collaborative sextile with metaphysical Neptune, also on the **22nd**, reminds you of the importance of mind over matter when dealing with physical issues. Thankfully, the Sun's free-flowing trine with superhero Mars on the **23rd** all but guarantees that you'll have sufficient stamina to accomplish your goals.

APRIL 29 ★ *by the strength of your convictions*

You have extraordinary confidence in your ability to help those who need it today, thanks to a synergetic trine between the Sun in your 6th House of Service and unwavering Pluto in your 2nd House of Self-Esteem. Just remember to be patient; others may struggle to match your level of intensity and can't understand your urgency to get things done.

MAY

IT TAKES TWO

You just can't hide your enthusiasm for relationships with friendly Mercury in excitable Aries and your 5th House of Love and Creativity until **May 9**. Mercury forms a supportive sextile with affectionate Venus in engaging Gemini on **May 3**, inviting someone special to enter your life. The pragmatic Taurus Sun in your 6th House of Details emphasizes discipline and determination, yet small modifications to your lifestyle begin to have a positive impact on your well-being as the Sun moves toward a conjunction with prosperous Jupiter on **May 13**. Meanwhile, the passionate Scorpio Full Moon on **May 5** illuminates your 12th House of Secrets and opposes the Sun in your 6th House, revealing hidden motives that can complicate a liaison at work. Rational Mercury opposes ambitious Saturn on the same day, exposing your doubts and confronting you with an alternative point of view.

A past romantic interest may return, or a current one reignite, when loving Venus retrogrades in your 7th House of Partners on **May 15–June 27**. This is also a time when you may have to wait for pleasure, or find it just out of reach. Fortunately, your common sense leads to a cautious approach to intimacy, increasing the likelihood of satisfaction as long as you keep your expectations realistic. A flighty Gemini New Moon Eclipse on **May 20** brings additional energy to your interactive 7th House, but its square to wistful Neptune can weaken your connection with another person if you confuse fantasies with reality. Mercury's conjunction with extroverted Jupiter on **May 22** and its entry into your already busy 7th House on the **24th** supply you with confidence and clarity, making this a good time to negotiate for what you want.

KEEP IN MIND THIS MONTH

Instead of trying to mold a relationship into something it isn't, gratefully accept the support and love that are offered to you just as they are.

KEY DATES

MAY 3–7 ★ *reversal of fortune*

You may feel irritable on **May 3** if someone challenges your ideas, but a lighthearted Mercury-Venus sextile supplies you with the finesse that lets you turn a problem to your advantage. Unfortunately, your good-natured charm may not carry you through the relationship difficulties that can surface on **May 5**, when conversational Mercury in your 5th House of Love opposes doubting Saturn in your 11th House of

Community. It's hurtful if a close friend or lover cannot hear what you have to say. The brooding Scorpio Full Moon in your 12th House of Endings tempts you to walk away from an awkward situation, but a bolt out of the blue on **May 7** can suddenly reveal a radical solution to the problem as broad-minded Jupiter aspects eclectic Uranus in your spontaneous 5th House.

SUPER NOVA DAYS

MAY 13–16 ★ *as good as it gets*

The Sun's conjunction with your ruling planet, Jupiter, on **May 13** falls in your 6th House of Health, gracing you with a joyful and optimistic attitude. You want to tell others how good you're feeling as Mercury the Messenger harmoniously trines physical Mars. In turn, Mercury and Mars trine resolute Pluto on the **14th** and the **16th**, respectively, forming a practical Grand Earth Trine that empowers you to set goals and create an effective action plan. Don't give up if the finish line appears to recede when Venus turns retrograde on **May 15**. Exercise self-control and stick to your plan when an annoying Jupiter-Saturn quincunx on the **16th** distorts your perspective on the future. The long-term significance of these days is not diminished, even if reaching your destination takes longer than you expect.

MAY 20–22 ★ *fork in the road*

The Sun's entry into dualistic Gemini and a Solar Eclipse on **May 20** could destabilize your relationships if a new opportunity is more interesting than your current path. Take your time before choosing your direction, for Mercury's conjunction with overblown Jupiter on the **22nd** makes nearly any idea sound better than it actually is.

MAY 27–30 ★ *no quick fix*

You are quite convincing when Mercury and the Sun form synergetic sextiles with innovative Uranus on **May 27–28**. But someone's hidden agenda can stir complex crosscurrents when Mercury and the Sun form unmanageable quincunxes with unwavering Pluto on **May 28–29**. If you try to force a resolution to the tension, you'll only make matters worse as mouthy Mercury in your 7th House of Others squares cantankerous Mars on the **30th**. If you can take a light-handed approach, however, the discord will settle on its own.

JUNE

AT THE EDGE OF CHANGE

Your partnerships are less stable—yet also quite exciting—as Venus in fickle Gemini retrogrades through your 7th House of Others. The inspirational Sagittarius Full Moon Eclipse on **June 4** floods your 1st House of Self with big ideas that you want to share with someone special. It's a good idea to talk with your partner or a person you can trust while logical Mercury is in your 7th House until **June 7**. The Sun's presence here—until the Summer Solstice on **June 20**—encourages your proactive involvement in business or personal relationships; it may also motivate you to clarify the purpose of an existing partnership. On **June 11**, your ruling planet, Jupiter, joins the party as it shifts into your interactive 7th House for a yearlong visit, increasing the influence of others on your life. One-on-one encounters of all types can bring new possibilities, but Gemini's diversity can also be distracting. Establishing limits prevents you from scattering your energy and wasting time. The jittery Gemini New Moon on **June 19** amplifies your restlessness, so make sure that change is what you truly desire before you jump into something new.

Your dreams prod you to act when visionary Jupiter moves toward a square to otherworldly Neptune that's exact on **June 25**. It's not enough to have big ideas; your challenge is to manifest them into reality and demonstrate that you're not as impractical as you may seem. You could get caught up in a social movement or the need to make sweeping changes in your love life as unstable Uranus in your 5th House of Self-Expression squares formidable Pluto on **June 24** in the first occurrence of a series that finishes in 2015.

KEEP IN MIND THIS MONTH

Nearly everyone who enters your life at this time has something to teach you, but it's up to you to discover exactly what it is.

KEY DATES

SUPER NOVA DAYS

JUNE 1–5 ★ *we can work it out*

You may find yourself returning to a previously unfinished conversation about your romantic desires when talkative Mercury in your 7th House of Partnerships joins enchanting Venus on **June 1** and forms a magical quintile with surprising Uranus in your 5th House of Love and Creativity on **June 2**. But a sobering Mercury-Saturn trine on the **3rd** turns a lighthearted discussion into a serious one. Your emotions rush to the surface as a Sagittarius Lunar Eclipse on **June 4** sets your needs apart from someone else's. Although the cosmic lovers, Venus and Mars, are in an argumentative square, a Sun-Venus conjunction on the **5th** indicates a happy outcome if you can control your temper.

JUNE 11–13 ★ *give and take*

Someone may try to prove you wrong when the upcoming Uranus-Pluto square is triggered by trickster Mercury on **June 11**. Or you might become obsessed with getting others to agree with your point of view. Either way, the Sun's trine to persistent Saturn on **June 13** reinforces your certainty and makes you less willing to negotiate. With Mercury in your 8th House of Transformation, your resistance to someone else's needs could prevent you from exploring common ground. Unexpected new information can catch you off guard if you're inflexible, but magnanimous Jupiter's entry into your 7th House of Relationships on the **11th** inspires you to open up to different perspectives.

JUNE 19–20 ★ *hurry up and wait*

A mentally buzzing Gemini New Moon on **June 19** can put you in a panic, with your thoughts racing every which way. Communicator Mercury forms a difficult square with severe Saturn on the **20th**, provoking harsh judgments of a poorly conceived plan. Additionally, the Sun's shift into cautious Cancer could force you into temporary retreat. Nevertheless, your need for radical change won't diminish because Venus forms a saucy sextile with unconventional Uranus to keep your desires on edge.

JUNE 27–29 ★ *no turning back*

Relationship plans that have been on hold can now move forward again as resourceful Venus turns direct on **June 27** to untie you from your past. And although you have grand plans with intellectual Mercury in your 9th House of Big Ideas, they are inflated even more by Mercury's slick sextile to exaggerating Jupiter on **June 29**. Unfortunately, you could face steep resistance when the Sun opposes unyielding Pluto. Nevertheless, the Sun's dynamic square to ingenious Uranus indicates that your tenacity could pay off suddenly with an unexpected breakthrough at the last minute.

IT TAKES A VILLAGE

You face a dilemma this month, because warrior Mars moves into peaceful Libra and your 11th House of Community on **July 3**, where he stays until **August 23**. The action of Mars is assertive and individualistic, yet now you must balance your personal ambitions with the goals of others. Your social life should improve, but you may need to tone down your approach so you don't upset the dynamics of your work group or social network. The serious Capricorn Full Moon—also on **July 3**—is conjunct to transformative Pluto in your 2nd House of Money and Resources, highlighting a deep shift that's already beginning to affect your finances. This lunation is also square to unpredictable Uranus in your 5th House of Love, suggesting that a relationship could take an unexpected turn. You can't help but take center stage when witty Mercury enters outgoing Leo, but its retrograde turn on **July 14** begins a three-week backpedaling period in your 9th House of Journeys when plans require revision and travel may be delayed.

Mars heats up your enthusiasm with a superconductive trine to exuberant Jupiter and a stressful square to ruthless Pluto on the **17th**. This can kick off a very intense few days, especially if a power struggle, possibly over money, gets out of hand. Tempers fly on the days leading up to the moody Cancer New Moon on **July 19**. You may feel as if everything is at stake, but don't let your extreme emotional reactions—based on a combination of excitement, anticipation, and fear—tempt you to take a foolish risk you'll later regret. Your energy level settles down toward the end of the month as a stabilizing Venus-Saturn trine on **July 31** shows you that satisfaction is on the way.

KEEP IN MIND THIS MONTH

It's up to you to continue your personal progress, even if you must shift your priorities and go along with the group for now.

KEY DATES

JULY 3–4 ★ *let's make a deal*

Although you're tempted to work within a partnership with amicable Venus in your 7th House, she forms a crunchy quincunx with enigmatic Pluto on **July 3** that makes it difficult for you to trust a controlling person. The calculating Capricorn Full Moon reminds you to proceed slowly and only say yes once you're sure everyone is on the same page. Solid negotiations can lay the foundation for profitable creativity when Venus sextiles innovative Uranus on the **4th**.

JULY 15 ★ *overcoming adversity*

Frustration can turn to conflict today if your progress is blocked by the restrictive Sun-Saturn square. The Sun is visiting your 8th House of Regeneration, indicating that some aspects of your life could fall away in order to morph into something new and different. But this won't happen easily; Saturn's involvement forces you to be patient and put in the necessary work before you're free to move on.

SUPER NOVA DAYS

JULY 17–20 ★ *count to ten*

Push through any lingering resistance when daring Mars forms a free-flowing trine to high-minded Jupiter on **July 17**. Still, your positive attitude isn't enough to get you back on track now, because Mars squares manipulative Pluto, provoking a battle for control that can get out of hand. Mars also opposes volatile Uranus on the **18th**, amplifying your anxiety level. You can derive a tremendous boost of energy from these aspects as long as you don't go too far and lose your temper. With an uncertain Jupiter-Pluto quincunx further complicating the situation, disagreements over allocating limited resources—time, energy, and money—appear to be irresolvable. Fortunately, the introspective Cancer New Moon on the **19th** falls in your 8th House of Shared Resources, reminding you to put up walls to protect your interests. Additionally, an uneasy aspect between wildly enthusiastic Jupiter and sobering Saturn on the **20th** pulls you back from the edge and prevents you from going to extremes.

JULY 30–31 ★ *closer to free*

Though you're inspired by the vibrant Leo Sun in your 9th House of Big Ideas, its awkward quincunx to dark Pluto on **July 30** leaves you uncertain about the value of your actions. Fortunately, you have amazing ideas when the Sun forms a trine to astonishing Uranus on **July 31**, stimulating your 5th House of Self-Expression. A grounded Venus-Saturn trine assures that your plan, however crazy it seems, has the potential to create lasting positive change.

AUGUST

BIG PICTURE SHOW

The freethinking Aquarius Full Moon on **August 1** lights up your 3rd House of Communication to kick off this busy month. A happy trine to beneficent Jupiter in your 7th House of Others brings good news from a friend or colleague. Look beyond your daily routine and make exciting plans for the future as the radiant Leo Sun moves through your 9th House of Adventure until **August 22**. But with Mercury moving backward until **August 8**, it's imperative that you tie up loose ends in existing projects before jumping into what's next. Your belief systems are undergoing a metamorphosis that impacts the way you express yourself. These issues began to surface when transformational Pluto first squared irrepressible Uranus on **June 24**. They're now moving closer together again—their second square is on **September 19**—and magnetic Venus forms stressful aspects to this dynamic duo on **August 15–16**, attracting jealous or controlling people who might try to squelch your desire for independence.

The demonstrative Leo New Moon on **August 17** activates your expansive 9th House, widening your horizons and inspiring you to take bold action to put your big ideas into motion. But just-do-it Mars sneaks into cryptic Scorpio and your 12th House of Secrets on **August 23**, suggesting that you keep your strategy to yourself. Avoid the spotlight while preparing for your next big move, when Mars enters your sign on **October 6**. A second Full Moon this month on **August 31**—this one in dreamy Pisces and your 4th House of Security—draws your attention away from the outer world, invites you to spend more time at home, and revitalizes relationships with your family.

KEEP IN MIND THIS MONTH

Be patient with yourself. Coming up with new ways to add fun and excitement to your life is easier than turning them into reality.

KEY DATES

AUGUST 1–4 ★ *proceed with caution*

Your confidence runs high during the airy Aquarius Full Moon on **August 1**, because it harmoniously aspects jovial Jupiter. The exuberant Sun-Jupiter sextile is exact on the **2nd**, placing a favorable spin on your relationships and allowing you to play easily and work successfully with others. But mixed signals on the home front gnaw away at your optimism and weaken your resolve as confusing Neptune in your 4th House of Domestic Conditions is stressed by pushy Mars on **August 3** and retrograde Mercury on the **4th**. Stick to the facts and choose your words carefully to minimize any misunderstandings that might arise.

SUPER NOVA DAYS

AUGUST 14–17 ★ *navigating the storm*

Your emotions rise to the surface as the illuminating Sun and needy Venus team up to form difficult aspects to the ongoing Uranus-Pluto square on **August 14–16**. Frustration within a relationship could leave you seeking satisfaction through material acquisitions. A disconcerting Mars-Saturn conjunction on the **15th** falls in your 11th House of Social Networking and is indicative of the mixed messages you receive from friends, who tell you yes and no in equal measure. Fortunately, on the **17th** a beneficial Sun-Jupiter quintile reveals a way through the labyrinth while a stabilizing Sun-Saturn sextile enables you to carry out your agenda. The ardent Leo New Moon gives its stamp of approval as you put your plan into motion.

AUGUST 20–24 ★ *no time to waste*

If you don't take on too much, you have the stamina to finish your work when the Sun sextiles action-planet Mars on **August 20**. Be careful, though, because aspects to overconfident Jupiter from Mars on the **20th** and Mercury on the **22nd** encourage you to overestimate yourself. Although the Sun's entry in methodical Virgo on **August 22** helps keep you on point, its opposition to fanciful Neptune on the **24th** lures you away from being practical. Luckily, Mars enters intentional Scorpio on the **23rd**, enabling you to avoid the distractions of idle fantasies and focus on what's most important.

AUGUST 29–31 ★ *trust your instincts*

The Sun in your 10th House of Career trines powerful Pluto on **August 29**, giving you all the necessary resources to reach your goals. However, an erratic Sun-Uranus quincunx on the **30th** can throw you a surprise that requires your immediate attention. Nevertheless, the psychic Pisces Full Moon on **August 31** reveals a solution to your predicament if you can be quiet enough to listen to your inner voice.

SEPTEMBER

NO EASY ESCAPE

Your career takes center stage this month with Mercury and the Sun spotlighting your 10th House of Public Life until **September 16** and **September 22**, respectively. But action-hero Mars in shrewd Scorpio and your 12th House of Privacy until **October 6** has you working behind the scenes. Fortunately, your concentrated effort goes a long way on **September 3–6**, when Mars forms helpful aspects with impressive Pluto, communicative Mercury, and effusive Jupiter. You receive another boost of energy as popular Venus enters fellow fire sign Leo and your expansive 9th House on **September 6**. However, you could promise more than you're able to deliver or underestimate the complexity of a job when the Sun and Mercury square Jupiter on **September 7–8**. The discerning Virgo New Moon on **September 15** activates your ambitious 10th House and is an excellent time to prioritize your tasks. Focus on one specific goal and set aside other, less important aspirations.

Meanwhile, deeper rumblings are shaking your life as radical Uranus in your 5th House of Self-Expression forms the second of seven life-changing squares to relentless Pluto in your 2nd House of Self-Esteem. Although this aspect is exact on **September 19**—the first was on **June 24**, and the series completes on **March 16, 2015**—you could feel the effects more strongly when it's stressed by mischievous Mercury on the **20th**, Mars and Venus on the **25th–26th**, and the impetuous Aries Full Moon on the **29th**. Your patience wears thin as financial pressures and your desire for personal freedom make you aware of the gulf between what you have and what you want.

KEEP IN MIND THIS MONTH

Change is inevitable—but it doesn't have to happen right away. Explore ways to reinvent yourself over time.

KEY DATES

SEPTEMBER 3–5 ★ *take a sad song and make it better*

Loneliness and self-doubts arise when your friends or colleagues don't understand what you need as warm Venus in your 8th House of Deep Sharing squares cold Saturn. Don't let feelings of rejection prevent you from trying to bridge the gulf of misunderstanding when macho Mars in insightful Scorpio sextiles incisive Pluto on **September 3** and analytical Mercury on the **5th**. But do watch your temper while making your case, because Mars and Mercury both form cantankerous quincunxes with explosive Uranus on the **4th**.

SEPTEMBER 7–10 ★ *promises to keep*

It's a difficult time for relationships if you've led your partner to assume that all is well when it isn't, or if your own expectations are overinflated. Either way, you have specific tasks to complete as the Sun and Mercury move toward a conjunction on **September 10** in your 10th House of Public Responsibility. But their squares to promising Jupiter in your 7th House of Others on **September 7–8** enable you to accomplish these goals if you practice a bit of self-discipline.

SEPTEMBER 13–16 ★ *curb your enthusiasm*

Social Venus in theatrical Leo prompts you to let everyone know what you want, especially on **September 13** when her free-flowing trine with unconventional Uranus stirs up irrepressible desires. Making a sensible decision should be easier on **September 15**, when the meticulous Virgo New Moon narrows your field of perception. However, superhero Mars forms an uneasy quincunx with pompous Jupiter on the **16th**. Self-confidence is helpful, but believing that you can do anything leaves you wasting time with little to show for your efforts.

SEPTEMBER 20–22 ★ *weighing your options*

Friends and co-workers question your tactics on **September 20**, when insistent Mercury opposes independent Uranus and squares inflexible Pluto. Luckily, a generous Venus-Jupiter sextile can alleviate some of the tension. Seek more balance in your life, especially around the Fall Equinox on the **22nd**, because the Sun's entry into fair-minded Libra allows you to see a problem from everyone's point of view.

SUPER NOVA DAYS

SEPTEMBER 25–29 ★ *a perfect storm*

You experience a power struggle in a close relationship beginning on **September 25**, due to a series of disruptive aspects from Mars and Venus to the life-changing Uranus-Pluto square. It becomes increasingly apparent that your partner and you have very different goals as Venus squares Mars on the **27th**. Avoid reckless behavior when the rowdy Aries Full Moon on the **29th** highlights your 5th House of Spontaneity, reactivating rebellious Uranus and dangerous Pluto. Instead of gambling on quick fixes, work toward long-term solutions.

OCTOBER

IN THE ZONE

It looks like you're on a roll this month as Mars jumps into extroverted Sagittarius and your 1st House of Personality on **October 6**, motivating you to assert yourself as you push ahead on all fronts. Your physical vitality is strong, yet you could be so enthusiastic about showing others what you can do that you become overbearing. Fortunately, the socially astute Libra Sun in your 11th House of Friends and Associates sensitizes you to others and helps you balance your aggressive approach until the **22nd**. Meanwhile, just prior to the loud arrival of rambunctious Mars in your sign, cerebral Mercury and solemn Saturn enter your 12th House of Spirituality on the **5th** in an ironic move that turns your thoughts inward just as your behavior becomes more highly animated. Although Mercury only stays in Scorpio until the **29th**, Saturn remains in your 12th House of Endings until **December 23, 2014**. This is a long-lasting transit that will require you to retreat from the outer world, redefine your life path, and clear out old emotional baggage. However, it makes sense to get started on these ambitious goals when Saturn harmonizes with visionary Neptune on the **10th** because common sense helps you ground your dreams.

Powerful waves of expansion and contraction are washing over you now as cheerful Jupiter aspects somber Saturn—yet the gracious Libra New Moon on **October 15** falls in your 11th House of Dreams and Wishes, encouraging you seek moderation. The materialistic Taurus Full Moon on the **29th** illuminates your 6th House of Work while thoughtful Mercury enters fun-loving Sagittarius, reminding you that maintaining your daily routine is crucial to keep your life in order and reach your goals.

KEEP IN MIND THIS MONTH

Even if others think they know what you're doing, you have more going on than they realize. There's nothing wrong with keeping some of your plans to yourself.

KEY DATES

OCTOBER 3–5 ★ *practical illusion*

The spotlight of recognition shines on you when crafty Venus enters your 10th House of Status on **October 3**—but if your expectations are too high, her opposition to idealistic Neptune can leave you disappointed. Still, at least you know where you stand when messenger Mercury conjuncts no-nonsense Saturn on the **5th**. Fortunately, Mercury's harmonious trine to Neptune can restore your faith in your dreams while you remain realistic about what you can accomplish.

OCTOBER 9–10 ★ *the power of positive thinking*

The Sun's smooth trine to buoyant Jupiter on **October 9** increases your confidence in your friends and co-workers. Not only do you believe what others tell you, you do so with an unrelenting passion as beautiful Venus trines poignant Pluto. Although you can turn a good offer into a great deal that earns you more respect or money, avoid jumping to conclusions. Carefully think through your plans on the **10th**, when a collaborative Mercury-Pluto sextile sharpens your perceptions. Thankfully, your intuition won't likely lead you astray as pragmatic Saturn trines psychic Neptune to bring elusive truths down to earth.

SUPER NOVA DAYS

OCTOBER 15–16 ★ *fools rush in*

You're all fired up with punchy Mars in your 1st House of Self—so much that you may turn radical and disruptive thanks to the warrior planet's friction-free trine with unruly Uranus on **October 15**. Exercise caution; bombastic Jupiter forms an uneasy sesquisquare with karmic Saturn on the **15th** and an overindulgent square with sensual Venus on the **16th**, bringing unpleasant consequences if you break the rules or ride roughshod over someone else's feelings. Luckily, the peaceable Libra New Moon, also on the **15th**, allows you to be accommodating if you simply consider the needs of others.

OCTOBER 25 ★ *school of hard knocks*

The Sun's annual conjunction with taskmaster Saturn is like trying to take a final exam in a class that you never actually attended. This serious alignment occurs in your 12th House of Endings, indicating that the lessons you must learn are important enough for you to stop and get them right. Don't try to escape the truth; instead, confront it.

OCTOBER 28–29 ★ *rein it in*

Self-discipline eludes you on **October 28**, when just-do-it Mars opposes flamboyant Jupiter. Quicksilver Mercury tricks you to act without thinking when it enters outspoken Sagittarius on the **29th**. Your adrenaline level is high, but you could exhaust yourself if you don't pay attention. Fortunately, the back-to-basics Taurus Full Moon trines shrewd Pluto, helping you contain your energy.

NOVEMBER

GOOD THINGS COME TO THOSE WHO WAIT

This month begins with a bit of excitement as delicious Venus opposes wild Uranus in your 5th House of Love and Creativity on **November 1**. Your vitality is high and your patience is low with impulsive Mars in extroverted Sagittarius until **November 16**. Additionally, you can be hyperactive with inquisitive Mercury also in your sign. But it becomes harder to say what you mean without being misunderstood when the Winged Messenger turns retrograde on **November 6** and backs into enigmatic Scorpio and your 12th House of Secrets on **November 14**. Although Mercury turns direct on **November 26**, releasing you from the past, your thoughts won't be flying free again until it reenters Sagittarius on **December 10**.

You long for emotional connection—or perhaps to eliminate something or someone that's dragging you down—when the Scorpio New Moon Solar Eclipse on **November 13** falls in your 12th House of Destiny. But watch out, because moving too quickly is as bad as doing nothing at all on the **15th** when erratic Uranus forms a quirky quincunx with stable Saturn. Mars's shift into sure-footed Capricorn on the **16th** may slow your progress, but improves your chances for success by encouraging sound methods over rash action. Your popularity increases when the bright Sun enters your 1st House of Personality on the **21st**, giving you extra energy. However, vulnerable Venus slips into your reclusive 12th House, tempting you with the idea of solitude. The Gemini Full Moon Eclipse on the **28th** joins Jupiter in your 7th House of Others, confirming that your waiting period is over and that it's time to move ahead in a relationship.

KEEP IN MIND THIS MONTH

Although you picture yourself as the overconfident hare, you'll be much more successful in the long run if you act like the slow-moving but obstinate tortoise.

KEY DATES

NOVEMBER 1–4 ★ *delicate dance*

Obligations require you to work more than you wish as dynamic Mars runs into stern Saturn's intense demands on **November 1**—the same day that a thrilling Venus-Uranus opposition tantalizes you with the possibility of unexpected pleasure. Although you may be tempted to say yes to an invitation with indulgent Venus in your 11th House of Social Networking, the love planet's stressful square to provocative Pluto on the **3rd** indicates that you may be getting into more trouble than you realize.

Fortunately, magical quintiles from Mars in effervescent Sagittarius to imaginative Neptune on the **1st** and creative Venus on the **4th** enable you to figure out what's happening and gracefully maneuver through an emotional minefield.

NOVEMBER 6–9 ★ *happily ever after*

Your optimism about a current relationship is contagious on **November 6**, when the Sun forms an uncontainable quincunx to flamboyant Jupiter in your 7th House of Others. Normally, this aspect makes things appear bigger and better than they actually are. This time, however, your positive thinking is on track because attractive Venus in your 11th House of Dreams trines auspicious Jupiter on **November 9**, all but assuring that your high expectations will be met.

NOVEMBER 13–15 ★ *wake-up call*

The emotionally powerful Scorpio Solar Eclipse in your 12th House of Spirituality on **November 13** reminds you to feed your soul and not just your need for adventure. Mercury's retrograde shift back into your private 12th House on the **14th** confirms this inner-directed movement. But authentic Saturn—also in your 12th House—forms an irritating quincunx with Uranus in your 5th House of Self-Expression on the **15th**, challenging you to practice your spiritual work while also pursuing your creative interests.

NOVEMBER 23–24 ★ *watch your wallet*

You're tempted to spend without thinking when impetuous Mars in your 2nd House of Finances squares uncontainable Uranus on **November 23**. Nevertheless, a bit of patience pays off; common sense returns when Mars sextiles practical Saturn on the **24th**, allowing you to make a wise decision.

SUPER NOVA DAYS

NOVEMBER 27–29 ★ *give peace a chance*

You could lose your temper if you believe that someone is undermining your efforts on **November 27**, the day of a volcanic Mars-Pluto conjunction. But a close friend or partner helps you see the situation in a more positive light when the Gemini Lunar Eclipse in your 7th House of Relationships conjuncts jolly Jupiter on the **28th**. Additionally, cooperative sextiles from gracious Venus to Pluto and Mars on **November 28–29** allow you to transform any lingering fear or anger into love and acceptance.

DECEMBER

HOME FOR THE HOLIDAYS

This month is all about relationships, because your ruling planet, Jupiter—retrograding in your 7th House of Companions—forms ten separate aspects. Despite the significant role that others play in your life now, it's up to you to take the lead as the radiant Sun moves through your sign, illuminating your 1st House of Self until **December 21**. Your mental acuity helps you to communicate what's important as long as you don't fall prey to exaggerations when gregarious Mercury visits risk-taking Sagittarius on **December 10–31**. You thoroughly enjoy being you—while pleasure-seeking Venus visits your adventurous sign, from **December 15** until **January 8, 2013**. The tension becomes palpable as your desire for independence and exploration pulls one way while enticing opportunities and good fellowship pull the other. This is most noticeable when oppositions to jolly Jupiter are formed by the Sun on the **2nd**, Mercury on the **17th**, and Venus on the **22nd**. It's wise to address unstable dynamics between you and your spouse, friend, or colleague when cosmic heavyweights Pluto and Saturn move into the picture on **December 20–22**, forming uneasy quincunxes with Jupiter.

The cavalier Sagittarius New Moon on **December 13** could make you feel invincible, as if nothing can prevent you from reaching your goals. Although the power of positive thought can propel you far, this lunation's semisquare to prudent Saturn requires you to acknowledge that time and resources are limited. If you're overextended, the nurturing Cancer Full Moon on the **28th** illuminates your 8th House of Regeneration, reflecting your need to revitalize your spirit by spending memorable holiday time with friends and family.

KEEP IN MIND THIS MONTH

As important as others are to you, if you don't take care of your own needs first then you won't have much to give anyone else.

KEY DATES

DECEMBER 1–2 ★ *jumping jack flash*

You're restless without knowing why when trickster Mercury forms an uncomfortable aspect with high-strung Uranus on **December 1**. Unfortunately, you find it difficult to settle down with Venus and Mars both creating cantankerous quincunxes with overbearing Jupiter. Although your optimism grows on **December 2** when the Sagittarius Sun opposes Jupiter in your 7th House of Partners, you can stir resentment if you appear arrogant or overstep your bounds.

SUPER NOVA DAYS

DECEMBER 10–14 ★ *high on life*

You can easily put your enthusiasm and joy into words when loquacious Mercury enters uplifting Sagittarius on **December 10**. Its creative square with surreal Neptune on the **11th** is good for expressing fantasies, but is less useful for sustaining concentration. However, a practical Mars-Saturn quintile on **December 12** grounds your energy and brings organization into your life in preparation for a cycle of manifestation that's initiated by the idealistic Sagittarius New Moon on the **13th**. Mercury's trine to uncanny Uranus in your 5th House of Spontaneity on **December 14** can trigger so much innovative thinking that you can't turn off your brain to get some rest.

DECEMBER 19–22 ★ *life of the party*

You're drawn toward new and different ways of expressing yourself as Venus in your 1st House of Personality trines Uranus on the **19th**. However, the Sun's entry into Capricorn marks the Winter Solstice on the **21st**, which helps to settle your energy. Your casual manner could upset someone as Jupiter in your 7th House of Relationships awkwardly quincunxes Pluto and Saturn on the **20th** and **22nd**.

DECEMBER 25–26 ★ *not what you expect*

This holiday week is super busy, thanks to energetic Mars's shift into high-frequency Aquarius on **December 25**. The unpredictable Sun-Uranus square charges your day with an exciting buzz while promising an unexpected surprise or two. But a serious Saturn-Pluto sextile on the **26th** enables you to immediately put your long-term goals into proper perspective.

DECEMBER 28–31 ★ *out with a bang*

The emotional Cancer Full Moon on **December 28** intensifies family dynamics when she activates a potent Sun-Pluto conjunction that's exact on the **30th**. A power struggle may be exacerbated by the Sun's aspects to expansive Jupiter on the **29th** and contractive Saturn on the **30th**, evoking overconfidence one minute and self-doubt the next. The year ends on a wild note as heroic Mars in your 3rd House of Communication sextiles reckless Uranus on **December 31**, tempting you to make a statement of your individuality, even if it means shocking others.

CAPRICORN

DECEMBER 22–JANUARY 19

CAPRICORN

2011 SUMMARY

You have already experienced a lot of change in the last couple of years, yet you still have quite a bit ahead of you. You can't yet see the end results of this long-term transition from caterpillar into butterfly, but you will instinctively know when it's time to break free from the cocoon. You may become more successful than you expected, which forces you to work harder than ever and can stress your personal life. Accomplishing tangible goals is a significant part of being a Capricorn, but now you can explore areas that make your soul richer and your body healthier, even if there's no apparent practical connection to your life path.

AUGUST—*all's well that ends well*

Misunderstandings and delays can be discouraging, complicating your personal and business affairs. Your task is to balance high expectations with practical considerations.

SEPTEMBER—*occupational hazards*

Don't waste your time and resources during the first half of the month. You'll need both when unexpected changes shake the mountain upon which you climb.

OCTOBER—*extending your reach*

Completing the obstacle course you're currently running is not the ultimate goal. Think of it as training for a greater purpose yet to be revealed.

NOVEMBER—*into the mystic*

Don't be complacent when your life seems to be going along smoothly. These are the times when you should be preparing for the next storm on the horizon.

DECEMBER—*resistance is futile*

Instead of fighting to hold onto structures that no longer support your growth, eliminate what you no longer need. Your future progress will grow much easier.

2011 CALENDAR

AUGUST

FRI 5–SUN 7 ★	Focus on serious matters instead of self-indulgence
TUE 9–SAT 13 ★	**SUPER NOVA DAYS** Expect power struggles within relationships
SUN 21–THU 25 ★	Your fears may be based on fantasy and not reality
SUN 28–TUE 30 ★	Remain patient; the rewards will come gradually

SEPTEMBER

FRI 2 ★	Take a significant risk today
SUN 11–WED 14 ★	You need a creative outlet for your energy
FRI 23–SUN 25 ★	Impatience gives way to risky behavior
TUE 27–THU 29 ★	**SUPER NOVA DAYS** Talk about your frustrations

OCTOBER

SAT 1–MON 3 ★	Consider the work required before saying yes
MON 10–FRI 14 ★	Follow through with your commitments
FRI 21–SUN 23 ★	Take time to prepare for the big week ahead
WED 26–FRI 28 ★	**SUPER NOVA DAYS** Work patiently toward your goals

NOVEMBER

TUE 1–THU 3 ★	Postpone important decisions or business negotiations
TUE 8–FRI 11 ★	Attend to the nuts and bolts of your job
WED 16 ★	Start only what you know you can finish
WED 23–SUN 27 ★	**SUPER NOVA DAYS** Expect delays for the next three weeks

DECEMBER

SAT 3–MON 5 ★	**SUPER NOVA DAYS** Be persistent no matter what
SAT 10–TUE 13 ★	Balance your desires with what's actually good for you
SUN 18–MON 19 ★	Cut back to the bare essentials
THU 22–SAT 24 ★	Letting others take charge adds an element of sweet surprise

CAPRICORN OVERVIEW

This year sees you uproot unhealthy habits and uncover underexploited resources—a process driven by the long, slow march of penetrating Pluto in your sign. This life-changing transit began on November 26, 2008, and will continue its transformational influence until 2023. Your courageous journey of self-discovery is likely to produce surprises when unpredictable Uranus starts a series of formative squares with Pluto on June 24 and September 19, recurring five more times until March 16, 2015. However, the most important changes may not be visible at first as you privately question your place and purpose in the world. **Take time to explore the swirling seas of unfamiliar ideas and emotions that are altering your perception of yourself before you abandon any major commitments or make any new ones.**

A significant turn on your path commences this year on October 5 when your responsible ruling planet, Saturn, leaves gracious Libra and your 10th House of Career to enter passionate Scorpio and your 11th House of Groups. **The weight you've been carrying on your shoulders since Saturn entered your dutiful 10th House on October 29, 2009, may earn you respect and advance your professional ambitions.** However, Saturn's entry into your 11th House emphasizes collaboration and cooperation as the primary keys to success rather than the solo flying you've been doing for the past three years. Saturn the Tester in Scorpio could bring you resistant teammates, co-workers, and friends whose emotional issues complicate your relationships. Nevertheless, this transit can also solidify your position within an organization due to your keen ability to identify the skills of others and apply them more effectively. Reliable Saturn's harmonious trines with idealistic Neptune on October 10 and June 11 and July 19, 2013, align reality with imagination, which can help you to make your dreams come true.

Optimistic Jupiter shifts from your 5th House of Self-Expression to your 6th House of Service on June 11, marking a time to refine techniques and master the skills necessary to give form to your creative impulses. Jupiter's presence in sensual Taurus for the first half of the year emphasizes the importance of pleasure to maintaining your well-being. **Innocent play and childlike self-indulgence remind you of the sweetness of life, which makes all your hard**

work worthwhile. This is not an escape from reality; it's a joyous and necessary celebration of life. Lastly, expansive Jupiter's stressful sesquisquares to prohibitive Saturn on July 20 and October 15 may slow your ambitions and require adjustments to your long-range plans until this aspect's third and final occurrence on May 20, 2013.

LOVE WITHOUT LIMITS

The first half of the year is a favorable time for matters of the heart, with lucky Jupiter in your 5th House of Romance until June 11. The delights of this transit in easygoing Taurus are emphasized when delicious Venus is in Taurus on March 5–April 3 to multiply your pleasure and make you even more desirable. On March 14—when sweet Venus joins promising Jupiter and forms a brilliant grand trine with passionate Mars and potent Pluto—you can take romantic joy to unexplored new heights without losing touch with reality. Loving Venus is in comforting Cancer and your 7th House of Partners from August 7 until September 6—another positive period for enriching an ongoing relationship or initiating a new one. Still, Venus's opposition to obsessive Pluto on August 15 may stir jealousy, mistrust, and a struggle for control that can spur a reevaluation of your partnership status.

ON TOP OF THE WORLD

Your organizationally gifted ruling planet, Saturn, has been reshaping your professional life during a two-year transit of your 10th House of Career since October 29, 2009. You'll be solidifying your position and taking on additional responsibilities until the taskmaster planet leaves this public part of your chart on October 5. Yet you may encounter delays or even have to take a step backward during karmic Saturn's retrograde period from February 7 to June 25. In fact, a Solar Eclipse occurring in your 6th House of Employment on May 20 is square to spacey Neptune, which can lure you into following an unproductive fantasy or deplete you with ill-defined tasks. This energy-shifting event reminds you to be more sensitive to your physical, mental, and emotional limits, instead of driving yourself with relentless disregard of your personal needs.

FISCAL FLEXIBILITY

You're struck by a brand-new moneymaking idea on July 22, when innovative Uranus, the ruling planet of your 2nd House of Income, is supported by a sextile from enthusiastic Jupiter. However, this occurs while mercantile Mercury is retrograde in your 8th House of Shared Resources, complicating business partnerships. If you can maintain an adaptable attitude, though, you can avoid losses and cash in on unexpected opportunities during the long series of squares between Uranus and Pluto starting on June 24, recurring on September 19, and lasting until March 2015.

SEEK DIVERSITY

Mastering your dietary and exercise habits is an ongoing issue this year because Pluto, the planet of metamorphosis, is camping out in your 1st House of Physicality. However, with enterprising Jupiter entering your 6th House of Health for a yearlong stay on June 11, you may find a variety of ways to stay fit. The planet of optimism's presence in multifaceted Gemini presents you with so many choices that sticking to any one system can be difficult. It's fine to sample different nutritional styles and forms of movement until physical Mars's transit returns to your disciplined sign on November 16–December 25. This is the opportune time to establish a consistent health regimen—though you might have trouble maintaining it during the holidays, because susceptible Neptune's tense square to the Lunar Eclipse in your 6th House on November 28 makes it easy to grow lazy with distractions or fatigue. Take a gentler approach to meeting your body's needs, instead of depriving yourself with an overly restrictive diet or torturing yourself with a harsh workout.

PARADIGM SHIFT

Patterns established early in the year can determine the quality of your domestic life for a long time to come. On March 12, Mercury turns retrograde in your 4th House of Home and Family, which can stir up old emotional issues and pangs of isolation. The New Moon conjunct to revolutionary Uranus in pioneering Aries falls in your 4th House on March 22. This could give you a fresh start if you address unresolved feelings from a radically different perspective and make a major break with the past. You will be free to take your life in a whole new direction if your urge for adventure is equal to your desire for security.

TRAVEL WITH A PURPOSE

Work-related trips and training are likely to be major themes this year with active Mars in your 9th House of Travel and Education from November 10, 2011, until July 3. Mars's retrograde period from January 23 to April 13 is excellent for reviewing and updating your skills but could slow your pace as you learn new subjects. Complications when traveling are more likely, too, reminding you to be extra vigilant in managing all the little details of lodging and transportation.

MAKE IT REAL

Bubbles of metaphysical fantasies and fairy-tale illusions may be popped with the Gemini Lunar Eclipse in your 12th House of Divinity on June 4. What you do becomes more important than what you believe as Mars in functional Virgo makes a challenging square to the Moon. If you can't apply your faith in down-to-earth ways, you might question its value. Fortunately, informative Mercury's retrograde turn in your idealistic 12th House on November 6 inspires your soul with a renewed perspective that can restore a sense of spiritual meaning in your life.

RICK & JEFF'S TIP FOR THE YEAR:
No Man Is an Island

The satisfaction you experience this year may be directly connected to the quality of your relationships. Going the extra mile to include others in major decisions may seem like a tiresome process but can build a solid foundation for the future. Strengthening personal and professional alliances involves discussions and compromises that don't always align with your expectations. Yet the sometimes messy process of inclusion establishes a base for limitless growth.

JANUARY

DOWNSHIFTING GEARS

Your new year usually gets off to a fast start with the Sun traveling through ambitious Capricorn. This time, however, take a more cautious approach to reduce wasted effort because Mars, the planet of action, is slowing down prior to turning retrograde on **January 23**. Its period of backward motion will continue until **April 13** in your 9th House of Big Ideas, requiring adjustments and refinements and possibly even a significant shift in your vision of the future. Travel, education, and belief systems are most likely to be affected, so when you think you've nailed down a plan or a point of view, additional information could turn you in another direction. That logical brain of yours, though, kicks into a higher gear of organization when calculating Mercury enters industrious Capricorn on the **8th**. This is a great time for thinking strategically and expressing yourself with clarity and conviction to maintain short-term order until the bigger pieces of your life fall into place.

Relationships grow warmer when the caring Cancer Full Moon illuminates your 7th House of Partners on **January 9**. Lovely Venus begins her dance in sensitive Pisces on **January 14**—another reminder that kindness and compassion take priority over duty and deadlines when it comes to matters of the heart this month. Yet look for a cooler and more original approach to finances when the Sun enters quirky Aquarius and your 2nd House of Income on **January 20**. The Aquarius New Moon on **January 23** seeds fresh ideas for increasing your income with a smart sextile to inventive Uranus. However, a restrictive square from hardworking Saturn in your 10th House of Public Responsibility indicates that current obligations may put your vision on hold for now.

KEEP IN MIND THIS MONTH

Managing the petty details of your life is not a meaningless distraction but a necessary step toward making bigger moves in the future.

KEY DATES

JANUARY 1 ★ *wisdom waits*

A clever quintile between the creative Sun and serious Saturn helps you bring together seemingly disconnected obligations and expectations to paint a more coherent picture of your goals. Still, this is more about establishing a long-term strategy than taking immediate action, so give yourself time to let your ideas germinate before you do anything about them.

JANUARY 8 ★ *free your mind*

Your mind is cooking as trickster planet Mercury moves into your sign, but you're open to much more than conventional thinking and conservative ideas today. Mercury's harmonious trine with Jupiter broadens your perceptions and enriches your communication with a perfect balance of data and big dreams. Later in the day, radical thoughts, impulsive words, and unexpected events can rattle relationships at home as Mercury forms a tense square with Uranus. Take what you see and hear with a grain of salt instead of attempting to process it logically.

SUPER NOVA DAYS

JANUARY 12–14 ★ *in the name of love*

A sturdy Sun-Mars trine on **January 12** provides you with a steady supply of energy and the ability to forge ahead without seeming pushy. Intellectual depth from a conjunction of Mercury and piercing Pluto on the **13th** helps you peel away any illusions you have about yourself. Yet kindness is a key as evaluative Venus joins supersensitive Neptune. Seek a gentler approach to self-assessment and a more delicate way of sharing your thoughts when Venus moves into compassionate Pisces and your 3rd House of Communication on the **14th**. Joyous, even romantic, encounters are likely as the love planet forms a sweet sextile with generous Jupiter in your 5th House of Amour.

JANUARY 19–20 ★ *mining for gold*

Responsibility weighs on you as the Sun forms a square with sobering Saturn on **January 19**. Nevertheless, this is an excellent time to recognize that you must complete a professional task as expeditiously as possible to clear the way for more rewarding endeavors. The Sun enters airy Aquarius and your 2nd House of Income on the **20th**, while a resourceful Venus-Pluto sextile can uncover underused assets and increase your powers of persuasion as long as you take a subtle approach.

JANUARY 25–27 ★ *reality check*

Don't take no as the definitive answer when Venus and Mercury create hard aspects to Saturn on **January 25** and the **27th**. A lack of approval challenges you to reevaluate your expectations on the job or in a relationship. Being clear about your own limits or the inability of others to meet your needs is the first step toward rectifying the situation. Now that you know the whole story, roll up your sleeves and get busy.

FEBRUARY

DREAM WEAVER

Moving beyond the practical limits you tend to place on yourself is your main priority this month. February starts with the Sun in unconventional Aquarius and your 2nd House of Income, suggesting that you'll earn more for ambitious thinking than by cautiously managing what's already on your professional plate. The return of Neptune to its imaginative home sign Pisces on **February 3** picks up the thread that started during its first foray there on **April 4–August 4, 2011**. Ethereal Neptune will occupy your communicative 3rd House until 2025, softening the hard edges of your mind to allow imagination and intuition to flow more easily. Reason is no match for the powerful feelings unleashed by the dramatic Leo Full Moon in your 8th House of Intimacy on **February 7**. An emotionally needy or over-the-top individual may try to sell you something you don't want to buy, yet taking the risk of opening your heart is preferable to turning your back on an opportunity for a more rewarding personal or business relationship.

Logic can also get lost in the fog of fantasy when rational Mercury floats through Pisces's mystical waters on **February 13–March 2**. Facts grow fuzzy as you learn to read subtle clues and to use tone and tempo to send messages beyond the boundaries of mere words. On the **19th**, the Sun follows suit to begin a month-long stay in your 3rd House of Communication. Compassionate conversations can heal wounds and awaken a more spiritual and poetic view of life. The Pisces New Moon conjunction with Neptune on the **21st** is a reminder that magic can occur in the most ordinary settings, reviving your faith with moments of bliss.

KEEP IN MIND THIS MONTH

Following your feelings freely will teach you so much more than clinging to a rigid view of reality that strangles hope in a net of so-called safety.

KEY DATES

FEBRUARY 1 ★ *different strokes*

Watch out today for disagreements that are more about style than substance This tension is due to an opposition of Mars in unpretentious Virgo and your 9th House of Philosophy to Venus in idealistic Pisces in your 3rd House of Learning. Whether you take the practical side of an argument—your generally preferred position—or the creative side, it's best not to be too serious. When humor is present, this face-off turns from fierce to flirtatious.

FEBRUARY 8–10 ★ *call of the wild*

Expect fiery feelings on the home front when romantic Venus rushes into reckless Aries and your 4th House of Roots on **February 8**. Trying to douse the flames of passion or impatience, though, only leads to explosions in other parts of your life. Besides, Venus conjuncts incendiary Uranus on the **9th**, igniting an itch for change that you must scratch. Alterations in your environment or family patterns are meant to encourage personal growth, since standing still is not a viable option now. Be careful; the willful Sun's volatile quincunx with rebellious Uranus and Mercury's semisquare with provocative Pluto on **February 10** could incite harsh words that undermine stability.

FEBRUARY 15–16 ★ *return to reason*

A fear of loss or lack in one area of your life might tempt you to overreach in another on **February 15**. A stressful square of Venus and Pluto can arouse feelings of mistrust or discontent, while an overly expansive Mars-Jupiter connection generates exaggeration, anger, or harsh judgment. Happily, a rational sextile between interactive Mercury in your 3rd House of Communication and benevolent Jupiter in your 5th House of Self-Expression restores a sense of balance to help you patch up differences on the **16th**.

FEBRUARY 18 ★ *time is on your side*

Trust your instincts when it comes to financial matters and resource allocation today. The Sun's favorable trine to calculating Saturn reflects your innate knack for accurately assessing what things are worth. Be patient; your sustained effort helps you complete what you start and get what you want.

SUPER NOVA DAYS

FEBRUARY 21–23 ★ *feeling is believing*

The New Moon in Pisces connects with this sign's spiritual ruling planet Neptune on **February 21.** Psychic channels open for you, allowing you to understand things you might not be able to explain otherwise. The mystical gifts of this lunation come with a skeptical Mercury-Saturn aspect that demands hard evidence and a Venus-Neptune semisquare that's ripe with uncertainty. Nevertheless, go with what you're feeling now even if others doubt you. If you need to make a case for your point of view, a Mercury-Mars opposition on the **23rd** is the time for the truth to be told.

MARCH

RUNNING AGAINST THE WIND

You're ready for a fresh start at home and work this month—but you must complete some unfinished business before you can take the next step. Curious Mercury blasts into uncontainable Aries and your 4th House of Foundations on **March 2**, stirring restless feelings that can provoke domestic conflict if you don't have a constructive outlet to occupy your overactive mind. However, Mercury turns retrograde on **March 12**, slowing your progress with interruptions and backtracking until it goes forward again on **April 4**. Moving at a more leisurely pace enhances the pleasure that comes with Venus's entry into Taurus and your 5th House of Fun and Games on **March 5**. Your creativity and charisma sparkle when you indulge yourself in each moment instead of hurrying to reach a goal. Nevertheless, your tendency to put work before play is kicked up by the methodical Virgo Full Moon on **March 8**. This lunation in your 9th House of Future Vision is useful for long-range planning as long as you don't fret about minor issues that may never arise.

The Sun's entry into trendsetting Aries marks the Spring Equinox in your 4th House of Roots on **March 20**. You won't likely see the full impact of this energizing event until the unstoppable Aries New Moon occurs on **March 22**, however, which can feel like a rocket ship ride into the future. Rowdy Uranus and busy Mercury join the Sun and Moon to stir up wild ideas and resistance to routine activities. Your desire for a more exciting life can precipitate a crisis at home and motivate you to consider radical action to reinvent your career or relocate.

KEEP IN MIND THIS MONTH

Finding the balance between your ambitions and fun can reward you personally and give you the fuel to sustain the long journey to success.

KEY DATES

MARCH 1–4 ★ *keep your cool*

Prepare to carefully decipher unclear messages on **March 1**, when Mercury's awkward quincunx with your orderly ruling planet, Saturn, can complicate conversations and slow the flow of information. Concentration is critical as mobile Mars runs into a restrictive semisquare with Saturn on the **2nd**. You may feel driven to forge ahead, especially when an impulsive Sun-Mars opposition on **March 3** urges you to take immediate action. Yet both the Sun and Venus form hard aspects with exacting Saturn that reward persistence and patience but punish haste. You may be underappreciated during the Venus-Saturn opposition on the **4th**, but you will get the chance to learn where you stand in a relationship.

SUPER NOVA DAYS

MARCH 13–14 ★ *fortune smiles*

Old loves and artistic interests resurface when regenerative Pluto makes its third and final trine to prodigious Jupiter in your 5th House of Romance on **March 13**. This potent aspect previously occurred on **July 7** and **October 28, 2011**, but it's in richer company this time around. Irresistible Venus trines Pluto on **March 13** and conjuncts Jupiter on the **14th**, creating a spicy stew of physical passion and material rewards. Superhero Mars joins the party with a sexy trine to resourceful Venus and a lucky one to auspicious Jupiter, completing a Grand Earth Trine that promises financial and emotional rewards.

MARCH 18 ★ *the long shortcut*

You may get on the wrong side of an authority figure today, or find yourself trying to manage uncooperative people, due to a slippery Sun-Saturn quincunx. Although working your way around obstacles appears overly time-consuming at first, it's likely to reduce further delays and frustration.

MARCH 26 ★ *lost in translation*

Small stuff can derail big plans as retrograde Mercury in your 3rd House of Communication makes stressful aspects to strategic heavyweights Jupiter and Saturn. Doubling back to recheck details can restore credibility that could be lost by making inaccurate statements. A slight alteration of your perspective is also helpful as it allows you to make sense out of concepts that aren't easy to understand.

MARCH 28–29 ★ *less is more*

You have extraordinary problem-solving abilities on **March 28**, powered by the second of constructive Saturn's three brilliant quintiles with provocative Pluto, which will return on **August 19**. It's even more critical to work through issues with difficult associates now than during the first occurrence on **November 11, 2011**. Trust may be reduced and resources limited with tense angles between Venus and Pluto on the **28th** and the Sun and Pluto on the **29th**. It's wiser to eliminate a task or a person than to give in to unreasonable pressure.

APRIL

GET A MOVE ON

You're finally able to close the books on some old business this month and get yourself in gear for new adventures in travel and education. On **April 4**, mutable Mercury in Pisces turns direct in your 3rd House of Communication. Hopefully you've had a chance to patch up some misunderstandings during this chatty planet's three-week retrograde cycle and now are free to open your mind to fresh ideas and information. Adapting to new people and systems at work is a key to getting recognition and enjoying your job with value-conscious Venus entering diverse Gemini and your 6th House of Employment on **April 3**. The socially skilled Full Moon in Libra also addresses professional issues as it lights up your 10th House of Career on **April 6**. This lunar opposition from the sign of compromise to the Sun in independent Aries dramatizes the challenge of accommodating others when you prefer to operate at your own pace.

The wheels of progress gradually start turning on **April 13**, when initiating Mars shifts into forward gear for the first time since **January 23**. The direct motion of the action planet in your 9th House of Faraway Places puts you on track for higher learning or travel for practical purposes. Quicksilver Mercury's return to speedy Aries on the **16th** can get your head moving faster than your body as innovative concepts inspire you to shake things up at home and wake them up where you work. Yet the Sun's entry into comfortable Taurus and your playful 5th House on **April 19** signals you to slow down and smell the roses—a notion that's reinforced with the Taurus New Moon falling in your 5th House of Love and Creativity on the **21st**.

KEEP IN MIND THIS MONTH

No matter how excited you are to be heading in a constructive direction, pushing yourself harder won't get you there any sooner.

KEY DATES

APRIL 7–8 ★ *destination unknown*

You experience a clash of values on **April 7** with a stressful square from friendly Venus in your 6th House of Work and Service to pugnacious Mars in your 9th House of Big Ideas. You may want to stick to a well-defined plan while a partner, colleague, or friend's attention turns in another direction. Negotiating a compromise may not be fully satisfying, but it's preferable to falling into a mood-killing dispute. However, an irritable Sun-Mars sesquisquare on the **8th** incites aggressive tendencies that can make it difficult to give ground. One way through an impasse is to remember that you might find pleasant surprises by relaxing your rules and exploring an unfamiliar experience.

APRIL 12 ★ *acute angles of perception*

Going the extra mile to describe a concept someone doesn't understand or asking for further explanation about an idea you're unsure of is an awkward but necessary way to communicate now. Mental Mercury's slippery quincunx with oppressive Saturn can make even simple statements sound obscure. While the additional effort required to exchange messages might be burdensome, the work can uncover insights you'd otherwise miss.

SUPER NOVA DAYS

APRIL 15–16 ★ *give and take*

The Sun's opposition to your exigent ruling planet, Saturn, on **April 15** could be one of the most important aspects of the year. The contrast between your need for independence and your obligations to others—which was exposed earlier this month during the Libra Full Moon—could come to a head now. But it's not in your best interest to turn this into a showdown, because your success ultimately requires the support of others. A crunchy Venus-Saturn sesquisquare on the **16th** could leave you feeling like you got the short end of the stick if you've made any concessions. Yet if you can appreciate even the smallest gains now, you will be able to build on them to garner more love, money, approval, or pleasure later.

APRIL 22–23 ★ *lightning strikes*

You take a radically different perspective that can free you from the past on **April 22** thanks to an ingenious Mercury-Uranus conjunction in your 4th House of Roots. Describing this vision, though, is neither easy nor necessary; even those closest to you may not understand. Instead, hitch a ride on the rising tide of a powerful Sun-Mars trine on the **23rd** that's more suited to action than explanation. This harmonious alignment in pragmatic earth signs produces concrete results instead of mere promises.

MAY

WORK LESS, PLAY MORE

While your personal relationships are on the upswing this month, alliances at work could become more complex. The warmth of the Sun continues to heat up your 5th House of Love until **May 20**, encouraging you to show the playful and affectionate parts of your personality. Talkative Mercury's move into your creative 5th House on **May 9** allows easier expression of your feelings about art and your heart. Your willingness to be open is reinforced on the **13th**, when the Sun enthusiastically conjuncts gregarious Jupiter. Their union inspires the kind of confidence that makes you a powerful presenter of your ideas, a great performer, and even an inspiration to others. The scrutinizing Scorpio Full Moon on **May 5** falls in your 11th House of Groups, challenging you to streamline collaborative projects to make them more efficient. Changing the ways that you work with others and cutting back on extraneous commitments help you put your priorities in order.

On **May 15** Venus turns retrograde in your 6th House of Employment. Her six-week backward run in dispersive Gemini can otherwise distract your attention with gossip and irritating personnel issues. This is another signal to reexamine your professional alliances and make adjustments needed to stay on top of your job. Yet the Sun's move into Gemini and your 6th House on the **20th** motivates you to expand your skill set or discover alternative ways to improve your health. The Gemini New Moon Eclipse also occurs on **May 20**. Neptune's stressful square to this Solar Eclipse in your busy 6th House might inspire vocational dreams but could wear you out mentally and physically if you don't reduce your workload.

> **KEEP IN MIND THIS MONTH**
>
> *The pleasure you get from your personal life will not only be fun—but it can also provide you with a much-needed breather from job-related stress.*

KEY DATES

MAY 5 ★ *mum's the word*

Keeping quiet or communicating with a very high degree of discretion is called for in spite of the powerful emotions you feel today. The intense Scorpio Full Moon in your team-oriented 11th House may trigger strong reactions from friends or colleagues, but a restrictive opposition of verbal Mercury and stoic Saturn allows little room for loose talk. Stick to facts and simple statements now to establish a solid foundation of trust that will support more fruitful conversations later.

SUPER NOVA DAYS

MAY 13–16 ★ *a long and winding road*

You can now back up your big plans with the data that will to start turning them into reality. The radiant Sun's conjunction with effusive Jupiter on **May 13** fills you with hope and inspires you to make bold promises. Yet the harmonious trine between fact-loving Mercury and energetic Mars in efficient Virgo indicates that you know exactly how to deliver on your commitments. Mercury's trine to insightful Pluto on the **14th** enables you to anticipate problems, helping you make adjustments necessitated by the Sun's challenging aspects to Saturn and Pluto. Your patience and persistence will determine whether you're going to be stopped in your tracks by obstacles on **May 15**, when dynamic Mars clashes with static Saturn. Fortunately, there's no lack of power with a laserlike Mars-Pluto trine on the **16th**, when you also encounter the first of three Jupiter-Saturn quincunxes. These awkward alignments between the planets of expansion and contraction recur on **December 22** and **March 23, 2013**, requiring you to skillfully shift perspectives from an optimistic vision of the future to the ubiquitous demands of the present.

MAY 21–22 ★ *on the rebound*

You could fall into a hole of doubt if Mercury's difficult aspects with Saturn and Pluto on **May 21** bring disappointing news. Thankfully, you're apt to recover very quickly, because the messenger planet's conjunction with buoyant Jupiter on the **22nd** tells a much happier story. Whether one person's *no* leads to another person's *yes* or you're able to regain your balance by seeing these small problems in a larger philosophical context, relief should be rapid.

MAY 28–29 ★ *patience is a virtue*

Heavy conversations may cloud your skies as another round of tough aspects hit somber Saturn and dark Pluto—this time from winged messenger Mercury on **May 28**. If you're blocked moving in one direction, however, an electric Sun-Uranus sextile cooks up bright ideas that empower you to leap over obstacles. Still, the testing connections from the Sun to Saturn and Pluto on the **29th** are likely to remind you that even the most brilliant concept requires time to be executed properly.

JUNE

HEART AND SOUL

You may be spending more time in self-reflection as you contemplate life's complex mysteries and begin to disconnect from old beliefs in search of greater meaning. Fortunately, there are sympathetic and caring individuals who are willing and able to provide you with the support, if not the answers, to make this soulful journey more comfortable. The major cosmic event in this powerful but private process is the philosophical Sagittarius Full Moon Eclipse on **June 4**. This eclipse rattles your 12th House of Metaphysics and could cast shadows of doubt on your faith and sense of higher purpose. Aggressive Mars's tense square to this Sun-Moon opposition can precipitate a spiritual crisis, perhaps when someone turns against you. Thankfully, when the Moon forms a creative trine to brilliant Uranus, you break through to a new level of consciousness that allows you to leapfrog over any loss or betrayal and renew your hope in the future.

Fresh opportunities may arise for you at work when magnanimous Jupiter shifts into Gemini and your 6th House of Employment on **June 11**. The busy Gemini New Moon on the **19th** might find you overburdened by tasks due to a pressuring square from overbearing Mars, but a smooth trine from productive Saturn shows you how to balance the load and be as effective as ever. The Sun's entry into nurturing Cancer marks the Summer Solstice in your 7th House of Partners on **June 20** to remind you that you are not alone. Still, deep rumblings of change are stirred by a square between irreverent Uranus and transformational Pluto on the **24th**—the first in a series of seven that recur through **March 16, 2015**. Your uncanny people skills, patience, and perseverance help you to navigate the waves of change as your responsible ruling planet, Saturn, turns direct on the **25th**, followed by charming Venus's forward shift on the **27th**.

KEEP IN MIND THIS MONTH

Sometimes you have to wander off a dead-end path and seek a different one to complete your journey.

KEY DATES

JUNE 3–5 ★ *whistle while you work*

Solid thinking and clear communication help you manage minor tasks as Mercury in your 6th House of Systems trines strategic Saturn on **June 3**. Yet precision may not be enough to avoid a clash of styles at your job on the **4th**, when Venus in your 6th House squares Mars in perfectionist Virgo on the same day as the Lunar

Eclipse. Any differences are unlikely to be substantial, so focus on common goals instead of conflicting methods. You can smooth out rough spots when an amicable Sun-Venus conjunction on **June 5** creates a joyful work environment.

JUNE 7 ★ *call a friend*

Mercury's entry into consoling Cancer and your 7th House of Partners opens new channels of communication while your compassion enhances alliances in ways that cold hard facts never could. Stay alert to the needs of others to enrich personal and professional relationships with a deeper sense of trust and understanding.

JUNE 11–13 ★ *turn down the noise*

You could find yourself overstimulated intellectually on **June 11**, when Jupiter enters Gemini and Mercury squares Uranus and opposes Pluto. You probably can't make sense of every bit of information that comes your way. Instead, establish your priorities and focus on one task or conversation at a time. Even if your head is spinning with contrary ideas, a grounding trine between the illuminating Sun and orderly Saturn on **June 13** should put your feet back on solid ground.

SUPER NOVA DAYS

JUNE 20–21 ★ *tender moments*

The Sun shifts into nurturing Cancer and your 7th House of Relationships on **June 20**, enabling you to revive ongoing alliances and find your way to new ones. Reaching out to others with a fresh concept, business idea, or desire for close personal contact succeeds when your feelings are genuine. Even if you encounter barriers due to lack of interest, time, or resources, gently pursuing your agenda could eventually work. A slick sextile between sweet-talking Mercury in Cancer and Mars in serviceable Virgo on the **21st** helps you make your case in both emotional and practical terms.

JUNE 29 ★ *eye of the hurricane*

Conflict, chaos, and confusion await you today as the Sun in your 7th House activates the earthshaking Uranus-Pluto square. The best way to handle this craziness is to stay calm while others' insecurities and odd behaviors increase or when someone is pressuring you to change. In fact, a peaceful center allows you to demonstrate your value as a caring and competent lover, friend, or colleague in a time of crisis.

JULY

BREAK FROM THE PAST

You are a hardworking and dedicated individual, but if the energy you're putting out isn't earning you the returns you want, it makes sense to drop some of your obligations this month. On **July 3**, the sobering Capricorn Full Moon can bring you to a critical point where you recognize that major changes are in order. Extreme pressures and powerful emotions are stirred as the Moon conjuncts intense Pluto. Normally, you might keep your feelings to yourself while simmering inside and quietly plotting your next move. However, irrepressible Uranus's tense lunar square breaks through your calm exterior with an urgency to take immediate action. Whether you're facing crises at home or work or need to drastically change your life, standing still or going backward is not your best option.

Mercury turns retrograde in your 8th House of Deep Sharing on the **14th**, opening a three-week window in which to reassess relationships and see if you have the will to reinvest in a personal or financial union or if radical change is inevitable. The Cancer New Moon highlights your 7th House of Partners on **July 19**, broadening your social horizons and offering a fresh start in a current alliance. However, Saturn's tough square to this Sun-Moon conjunction suggests that any gains come at a stiff price. Knowing exactly what you want helps you set the terms instead of finding yourself limited by someone else's rules. Yet once you know where you stand, stop keeping score and open your heart. The Sun enters Leo and your 8th House of Intimacy on **July 22**, inviting generosity and deeply creative connections.

KEEP IN MIND THIS MONTH

Inventing a more vibrant and exciting future is risky but probably less exhausting than trying to hold on to structures that no longer work.

KEY DATES

SUPER NOVA DAY

JULY 3 ★ *remain calm, cool, and collected*

Be kind to yourself as the judgmental Capricorn Full Moon illuminates your 1st House of Personality, because unrelenting Pluto's presence can make your flaws seem greater than they actually are. It's wise to clean up any unhealthy habits as long as you don't go to extremes. The Moon squares unruly Uranus, provoking rebellious feelings and the urge to run from routine, but don't let the emotional intensity force you to act in haste. Fortunately, Mars moves into moderate Libra and your 10th House of Responsibility to help you regain your composure and line up your support team while contemplating major changes.

JULY 8 ★ *asleep at the wheel*

It's challenging for you to follow a plan today, and you could waste valuable time as pointed Mars forms a slippery quincunx with fuzzy Neptune. Maintaining an adaptable attitude and adopting flexible expectations will lower the stress level and give you more room to breathe. Even if your day looks like it's careening out of control, an astute quintile between clever Mercury and capable Saturn provides you with the presence of mind to keep things from flying off the rails.

JULY 15–18 ★ *learning to fly*

The burdens of responsibility you're all too familiar with are evident with an exacting Sun-Saturn square on **July 15**. If others are counting on you to carry the load, be sure to claim the authority that comes with it. Work may be weird, because entrepreneurial Mars in your 10th House of Career is buoyed with vision and belief in what you're doing by a trine with enthusiastic Jupiter on the **17th**, yet restrained by a square from exigent Pluto that clips your wings. A volatile opposition of Mars and Uranus on the **18th** might make you feel like fleeing or fighting the system, yet the first of three quincunxes from Jupiter in flighty Gemini to Pluto in your sign—recurring on **December 20** and **March 29, 2013**—is an ongoing lesson in managing growth.

JULY 20–22 ★ *the hero in you*

Amplifying Jupiter's sesquisquare with limiting Saturn on **July 20** can make it difficult for you to assess the scope of a project or discover the best way to fulfill your ambitions. You'll revisit these issues when the aspects recur on **October 15** and **May 20, 2013**. For now, a brilliant Jupiter-Uranus sextile on **July 22** can show you how to leap over obstacles with a single bound.

JULY 31 ★ *chemistry at work*

Your people skills and good sense of judgment pay off professionally today as sociable Venus in your 6th House of Employment forms a trine with practical Saturn. Working closely with a creative partner when the Sun trines electric Uranus sparks contagious excitement and fascinating ideas, so make sure to record your conversations for future use.

AUGUST

TEAM SPIRIT

Finances are a top priority this month, with plenty of planetary activity occurring in your 8th House of Shared Resources. The avant-garde Aquarius Full Moon shines in your 2nd House of Income on **August 1**, placing money matters in the spotlight. Harmonious aspects to the Moon from enterprising Mars, propitious Jupiter, and surprising Uranus open your eyes to unexpected economic opportunities. It's vital to look outside your usual areas of expertise and invest in new tools and training to get the payoff you desire. A demanding conjunction of mobile Mars and scrupulous Saturn in your 10th House of Career on **August 15** could be a critical point in your professional life. If you've been working hard for a good cause, you finally receive the recognition that you deserve. You might launch a new project or take an existing one to a higher level if you have supportive partners. Yet you could run into resistance or simply run out of gas if you find yourself in the familiar position of doing everything on your own.

The brassy Leo New Moon in your 8th House of Intimacy on **August 17** pushes you to take bold steps forward in both your personal and professional relationships. Collaborative sextiles from workhorses Saturn and Mars to this lunation supply the initiative and dogged determination to build something that lasts. Efforts intensify on team projects, yet you could experience conflict with friends and colleagues when Mars moves into strong-willed Scorpio and your 11th House of Groups on **August 23**. The imaginative Pisces Full Moon in your 3rd House of Communication conjuncts dreamy Neptune on the **31st**, inspiring poetic perceptions and tender conversations. Don't confuse feelings with facts when it's time to make tough decisions.

KEEP IN MIND THIS MONTH

Instead of seeking someone who always agrees with you, find a trustworthy partner who cares enough to tell you the truth—even if it makes you mad—for the sake of success.

KEY DATES

AUGUST 3 ★ *make it work*

While a confusing Mars-Neptune sesquisquare could send you on a wild goose chase, you have an exceptional capacity to turn chaos into order today. The Sun's quintile with Saturn finds reason in the strangest situations and, perhaps, can even help you find a way to transform a vague idea into a constructive one.

AUGUST 7–8 ★ *building bridges*

Gentle Venus moves into kindly Cancer and your 7th House of Partners on the **7th**, bringing caring people who appreciate your softer side. You could make a significant step toward closeness—and a foundation for a meaningful business alliance—by listening to someone's concerns. Messenger Mercury's direct turn in your intimate 8th House on the **8th** can restart stalled negotiations as the pursuit of fortune picks up speed in the days ahead.

SUPER NOVA DAYS

AUGUST 15–17 ★ *seeds of success*

You pay full price to get what you want with a hard-nosed Mars-Saturn conjunction and a frugal Venus-Pluto opposition on **August 15**. However, your acute sense for sniffing out value can help you initiate a work-related project on a very limited budget. Inconsistency can rattle relationships and spur financial surprises with Venus's square to unsettling Uranus on the **16th**. But the theatrical Leo New Moon on the **17th** encourages bold alliances and is backed up by a strategic Sun-Saturn sextile to provide a realistic plan and the right people to help you execute it.

AUGUST 22 ★ *street smarts*

Practical intelligence is a gift of the Sun's entry into technically astute Virgo and your 9th House of Higher Mind. Mapping out the details of a complex journey comes easily with brainy Mercury's favorable aspects to realistic Saturn and farsighted Jupiter. The future is now as you're ready to apply the principles that you hold most dear. You're primed to learn from the best and can be an effective teacher for those who lack your skills and experience.

AUGUST 28–29 ★ *return to reason*

Don't panic if surprising news knocks you off stride on **August 28**. An enervating Mercury-Uranus sesquisquare can put you on edge with weird ideas or illogical information. Fortunately, this mental jolt could spark original thinking that helps you break through an obstacle in a relationship. In any case, thoughts settle and communication makes more sense as a penetrating Sun-Pluto trine gets down to the core of the matter on the **29th**, while a stabilizing Mercury-Saturn sextile restores your sense of order and puts discussions back on track.

SEPTEMBER

A CHANGE IS GONNA COME

One of your greatest strengths is your sure-footedness in the pursuit of your goals. This month, though, the earth may feel less solid under your feet, for both long-term aspirations and immediate circumstances force you to alter your reliable patterns. You've already encountered the main planetary players in this tale; on **September 19**, volatile Uranus and volcanic Pluto make their second of seven stressful squares, which first occurred on **June 24**. These are not one-day events but moments when you can see the tops of glaciers that will continue reshaping your life through **March 16, 2015**. Yet while these transits sometimes pass unnoticed, the fiery Aries New Moon on **September 29** sets off a charge of inner excitement—or an avalanche of unexpected events that could knock you off balance. The Moon's close conjunction to Uranus in your domestic 4th House and square to Pluto in your 1st House of Self shake up your living situation. However, keeping a sense humor and remaining open to change inspires you with fresh insights, while resistance is likely to only increase the pressure.

Gifts of love or money could start to flow when attractive Venus enters generous Leo and your 8th House of Deep Sharing on **September 6**. Sure, you may hear some big plans that stretch credibility, but you have more to gain by engaging your heart and raising your hopes than by stewing in skepticism or hanging back in fear. The detailed Virgo New Moon on the **15th** activates your 9th House of Travel and Education, prompting interest in expanding your mind and exploring faraway places. The Sun's entry into cooperative Libra—the Fall Equinox—and your 10th House of Public Life highlights professional relationships and responsibilities on **September 22**.

KEEP IN MIND THIS MONTH

Uncertainty can be your friend when you give your mind permission to wander. Your imagination can lead you to treasures you wouldn't otherwise find.

KEY DATES

SEPTEMBER 3–5 ★ *rallying the troops*

You may feel underappreciated by a partner when needy Venus in your 7th House of Others squares stingy Saturn on **September 3**. Still, a tight Sun-Saturn semisquare and potent Mars-Pluto sextile show that clearly defined desires and concentrated efforts can produce positive results under less-than-optimal conditions. Cerebral

Mercury's creative trine with incisive Pluto on the **4th** and smart sextile with go-getter Mars on the **5th** deepen your insights and sharpen your words to help you motivate co-workers and friends.

SEPTEMBER 8–10 ★ *cut to the chase*

Too much information can be more dangerous than not enough when data-driven Mercury squares overblown Jupiter on the **8th**. Don't lose sight of essential details in an endless sea of facts. Mercury's union with the Sun in your 9th House of Higher Truth on the **10th** clarifies your thinking as you shut out external noise and ground yourself in your beliefs. Your firm grasp on reality enables you to be an effective communicator and teacher, so make sure to share your insights with others.

SEPTEMBER 16–17 ★ *taking care of business*

Mercantile Mercury's move into your professional 10th House on **September 16** helps you make new contacts, give birth to fresh ideas, and smooth over misunderstandings during the next three weeks. Keeping an open mind and recognizing that there are at least two valid ways to see any situation will make this transit more valuable to you. However, Mercury makes tense aspects with Mars and Neptune on the **17th**, and the harder someone pushes a point of view, the less likely it is to hold up to careful scrutiny. Take what you hear with a grain of salt and don't let the heat of the moment provoke you to say something you might regret.

SEPTEMBER 20 ★ *after the storm*

Watch out for anger, irritability, and mistrust with verbose Mercury's stressful aspects to manipulative Pluto and disruptive Uranus—yet a brilliant idea may appear when the dust settles. Besides, a delicious Venus-Jupiter sextile justifies all the fuss if the negativity clears and you're able to kiss and make up.

SUPER NOVA DAY

SEPTEMBER 29 ★ *break on through to the other side*

Full Moons almost always raise emotional tides. Your feelings swell to extremes that can, at best, lead you to breakthroughs of awareness. Today's trailblazing Aries Full Moon lights a fire in your 4th House of Roots, stirring up restless feelings with a little splash of mischief on the side. However, the lack of stability that you experience at home or the uncertainty you have about your career could be a catalyst that turns your life in an exciting new direction.

OCTOBER

PACE YOURSELF

You might feel an invisible hand on your back pushing you forward this month, but if you go too fast or too far, you'll probably have to turn around and start over again. The drive to go farther than you should originates from motivating Mars's entry into restless Sagittarius and your 12th House of Escapism on **October 6**. This urge to get moving is only helpful when you have a specific direction in mind and a map to guide you on your journey. Right now it's better to be restrained due to the conjunction of mental Mercury and cautious Saturn on **October 5**, just before they both enter emotionally accountable Scorpio. Their move into your 11th House of Groups can burden you with long-term obligations to an organization—but if you rise to the challenge, you could earn the respect from your colleagues that you deserve.

Applying your enthusiasm where it will do you the most good is underscored by the crafty Libra New Moon in your 10th House of Career on the **15th**. Prosperous Jupiter's supportive trine to this lunation offers you opportunities to align with beneficial business partners. However, a strategic sesquisquare between expansive Jupiter and conservative Saturn the same day signals the importance of patience and good judgment to distinguish realistic professional aspirations from seductive-sounding fantasies. The Sun's entry into discerning Scorpio and your 11th House on **October 22** attracts results-oriented associates who have a gift for sniffing out false trails and discovering fruitful ones. Magnetic Venus's shift into your 10th House on the **28th** gifts you with a gracious and diplomatic charm that enriches your career, while love, creativity, and personal pleasure take center stage when the indulgent Taurus Full Moon brightens your 5th House of Love and Play on **October 29**.

KEEP IN MIND THIS MONTH

When you feel the heat of desire rising, slow down and make sure you're on the path to take you where it can be fulfilled.

KEY DATES

OCTOBER 5 ★ *just the facts*

Don't be shy about asking questions if you need more information today, because the conjunction of communicative Mercury and methodical Saturn can slow the flow of data or reveal gaps in your knowledge. Luckily, friends and colleagues are ready to come to the rescue as Mercury and Saturn shift into your team-oriented 11th House. Investing the effort to get on the same page as those you rely on may require tedious discussions, yet the clarity you gain now will more than pay for your time and trouble.

SUPER NOVA DAYS

OCTOBER 9–10 ★ *pick of the litter*

Take a careful look at professional opportunities on **October 9**, because an expansive Sun-Jupiter trine may offer you more choices than you can use. Fortunately, favorable aspects connecting Venus and Mercury to investigative Pluto on the **9th** and **10th** clarify your thinking, empowering you to eliminate wasteful activities to focus on those that bring you the greatest rewards. Your ruling planet Saturn's trine to imaginative Neptune is a great asset for turning dreams into reality, but the final results may not show up until the second or third recurrence on **June 11** and **July 19, 2013**.

OCTOBER 15–17 ★ *timing is everything*

Innovation intensifies the initiative of the 10th House Libra New Moon on **October 15** as pioneering Mars trines radical Uranus. Yet the second of three sesquisquares between visionary Jupiter and uncompromising Saturn—the first was on **July 20** and the last will be on **May 20, 2013**—can frustrate your desire for immediate action. Aim for long-term gains to cool impatience caused by temporary obstacles. A lusty Venus-Jupiter square on the **16th** could make you hungry for more money, love, pleasure, and approval, but Venus's semisquare with Saturn on the **17th** should restrain you with a return to your usual good sense.

OCTOBER 25 ★ *judgment day*

It's time to take a stand with the Sun's conjunction to dutiful Saturn in your collaborative 11th House. If you assume new responsibilities for a group, be certain that you have the support you need to succeed. If your teammates are not up to the task or if you doubt the value of the cause, saying no is probably your best option.

OCTOBER 30 ★ *strong but silent type*

An empowering Sun-Pluto sextile in your sign today infuses you with quiet confidence. Your ability to motivate your peers so effortlessly makes you a natural leader without attracting any extra attention in the process. Your clear sense of priorities shows you where to hold on and where to let go.

NOVEMBER

AGENT OF CHANGE

This is a month of adjustments as loquacious Mercury turns retrograde in your 12th House of Secrets on **November 6**, which can reopen private issues that you thought were behind you. Fortunately, compassionate Neptune's forward shift in your 3rd House of Communication on the **11th** reduces the likelihood of harsh judgment for past mistakes. Conversations start to flow easily again and your social life picks up in general when Mercury goes direct on **November 26** in your 11th House of Groups. The Sun's presence there in emotionally intense Scorpio until **November 21** could create a suspicious atmosphere, although deepening personal and professional relationships are possible benefits. Nevertheless, on **November 13** the New Moon Solar Eclipse in Scorpio may challenge some of your assumptions about teammates and allies. This is a time to reassess your friendships and professional connections, although you may need to reduce someone's role in your life. Kindness is a wonderful quality, but it can become very costly if a supposed friend takes much more than he or she gives.

The Sun's entry into adventurous Sagittarius on **November 21** is more about inner expansion than external experiences as it moves into your 12th House of Divinity. This transit can help you discover answers by exploring spiritual practices that open windows of awareness and increase your sense of connection with nature and the cosmos. The jittery Gemini Full Moon on the **28th** is a Lunar Eclipse in your 6th House of Work. Its conjunction with excessive Jupiter can overload you with opportunities or obligations that lead you to rethink your professional aspirations.

KEEP IN MIND THIS MONTH

Sometimes too much of a good thing is more than even you can handle. Fewer options can make your life easier.

KEY DATES

NOVEMBER 1 ★ *no margin for error*

Pay careful attention to where you're going today because Mars in enthusiastic Sagittarius tends to leap without looking. This energetic planet runs into a rigid semisquare to restrictive Saturn that places roadblocks in your path. If you're going to push hard, make sure that you're in control of your body and emotions to maintain the focus needed to hit your target.

NOVEMBER 9 ★ *hope floats*

Good times can inspire you at work as sweet Venus in your 10th House of Career aligns with astrology's most expansive planets. Venus's favorable trine to lucky Jupiter offers recognition for your efforts and inspiration for new professional opportunities. However, her ungainly sesquisquare with squishy Neptune can blur your usually impeccable judgment if you romanticize a person or a project instead of seeing it for what it really is. Avoid committing to tasks until you're clear about how much time and effort you'll need to complete them.

SUPER NOVA DAYS

NOVEMBER 16–17 ★ *the force is with you*

Dynamic Mars prods you to be more physically active and assertive on **November 16**, when he enters ambitious Capricorn. This powerful transit is excellent for initiating projects. You're motivated to operate at your best, which includes a combination of planning and persistence that almost always produces the outcome you seek. The risk of appearing overly aggressive or pushing yourself past reasonable limits is reduced by an intuitive Mars-Neptune sextile on the **17th**. This unifying alignment of action and imagination shows you that you can be productive while remaining sensitive to your impact on others.

NOVEMBER 22–24 ★ *out of bounds*

Your need for order can melt away on **November 22**, when the Sun and Venus form aspects with idealistic Neptune and unusual ideas are spurred by a Mercury-Uranus sesquisquare. Then a rebellious Mars-Uranus square on the **23rd** that's unwilling to abide by the rules may lead you to behave intemperately. While you may be very inventive and able come up with fresh approaches to resolving issues, it's tempting to explode or to give up and run away if you're bored or frustrated. Fortunately, you will reconnect with the ground beneath your feet when solidifying Mars sextiles Saturn on **November 24**.

NOVEMBER 26–27 ★ *tough as nails*

You might feel underappreciated by associates when valuable Venus joins austere Saturn in your 11th House of Networking on **November 26**. Yet if you know exactly what role you want to play, it's time to work hard to get it. A formidable Mars-Pluto conjunction in Capricorn on the **27th** supplies you with the passion, intensity, and power to go for exactly what you want.

DECEMBER

BEND LIKE A WILLOW

The extra energy and enthusiasm you're feeling this holiday season come courtesy of Mars's visit to your ambitious sign. However, there are some detours that will probably slow down your productivity. While you may chafe at having to deal with delays and distractions, be adaptable instead of forcing yourself to meet unrealistically rigid deadlines. Intellectual Mercury's entry into your 12th House of Escapism on **December 10** can take your mind off your work, as will the inspirational Sagittarius New Moon on the **13th** and beautiful Venus's entry into this house on the **15th**. These planetary tides can pull you off your schedule—and maybe even off the grid entirely. Instead of fighting these forces, give yourself time to escape to explore unfamiliar places and metaphysical dimensions. Furthermore, overreaching Jupiter's off-kilter quincunx with naysaying Saturn on **December 22** can alter your course. Adjustments you made when this aspect first occurred on **May 16** might need to be revisited now and repeated again during their third and final alignment on **March 23, 2013**.

Energetic Mars's shift into experimental Aquarius and your 2nd House of Resources on **December 25** reminds you that there are many ways to prove your worth and earn a living. A potent and pragmatic Saturn-Pluto sextile on the **26th** shows you how to turn a stressful situation into a productive one and will recur to provide similar support on **March 8** and **September 21, 2013**. On **December 28**, the hypersensitive Cancer Full Moon in your interpersonal 7th House brings surprises in relationships. A tense lunar square with shocking Uranus and an opposition to unwavering Pluto could force a showdown that radically reshapes a meaningful alliance.

KEEP IN MIND THIS MONTH

The greatest strength you have now is the ability to adjust your approach to shifting situations instead of trying to resist the winds of change.

KEY DATES

DECEMBER 7 ★ *try before you buy*

It pays to take another look before you speak or act today as contemplative Mercury joins the integrative Lunar North Node in probing Scorpio. You may be anxious to try something new, for a difficult aspect between Venus and Uranus makes you itchy for unusual experiences and a spacey Mars-Neptune semisquare tempts you to behave in a relatively careless manner. There's nothing wrong with a social experiment, as long as you don't go too far too fast.

DECEMBER 12–14 ★ *be prepared*

A clever Mars-Saturn quintile on **December 12** is like having a Swiss Army knife that can handle almost any task that arises. Just be certain that your tools are sharp when unpredictable Uranus turns direct in your 4th House of Roots and the risk-taking Sagittarius New Moon lands in your mystical 12th House on the **13th**. If you feel lost in unfamiliar physical or psychological territory, the brilliance of a Mercury-Uranus trine and the gravitas of a Sun-Saturn semisquare on the **14th** will supply the smarts you need to find your way home.

SUPER NOVA DAYS
DECEMBER 21–22 ★ *ahead of the curve*

The Sun's entry into competitive Capricorn on **December 21** is the Winter Solstice—the beginning of your personal astrological New Year. Normally, this is a time to review the past and make resolutions for the coming twelve months. You also receive a generous dose of faith and imagination with a Sun-Neptune sextile and an extravagantly hopeful Venus-Jupiter opposition on the **22nd**. However, a number of surprises just around the corner are likely to change your plans, while a constraining Jupiter-Saturn quincunx reminds you that your shortest route to the future may not be a straight line.

DECEMBER 25 ★ *surprise package*

Tradition goes out the window when the Sun squares unorthodox Uranus today. Trying to keep your ducks in a row can be a difficult chore—your own restlessness or the unpredictable behavior of others messes up your plans. However, your gift is to recognize that you aren't as bound up by your identity as you thought, inviting you to break patterns as you discover exciting new aspects of yourself.

DECEMBER 30 ★ *letting go to grow*

Today you face strong feelings of resentment, mistrust, and a tendency to tear yourself down with harsh criticism thanks to the Sun's conjunction with ruthless Pluto. Yet a wise Sun-Saturn sextile gives you plenty of ways to build yourself up again if you can shed the negative baggage of the past.

AQUARIUS

JANUARY 20–FEBRUARY 18

AQUARIUS

2011 SUMMARY

Enlightening conversations and amazing new ideas are certain to excite your curious mind. You may have to compromise your plans or slow down to accommodate people who don't move at your pace. Speaking the simple truths of your physical needs is a powerful means for fulfilling your desire for closeness and comfort.

AUGUST—*a slice of heaven*

Being innocent and openhearted invites love and recognition—which can fade in a flash unless you maintain care and attention.

SEPTEMBER—*the cost of freedom*

It's easier to stay afloat in choppy waters when you're willing to adjust your course at any moment.

OCTOBER—*climb to the top*

Playing your cards close to the vest puts you in a stronger position to win than revealing every move you're going to make in advance.

NOVEMBER—*a little help from your friends*

Being right doesn't mean that you'll be heard. Pick your words and situations carefully when conveying important messages.

DECEMBER—*surprise ending*

If you're willing to make minor adjustments as needed, you won't have to make radical changes at the last minute.

2011 CALENDAR

AUGUST

MON 1 ★ You may be ready to jump into a new experience

MON 8–THU 11 ★ Imaginative individuals could catch your interest

TUE 16 ★ This is a great time to make an important presentation

MON 22–THU 25 ★ **SUPER NOVA DAYS** A reality check can be painful

SAT 27–SUN 28 ★ Shifting circumstances or unstable moods should settle

SEPTEMBER

FRI 2 ★ Think big but act prudently

SUN 11–MON 12 ★ It's easy to lose control

SAT 17–SUN 18 ★ An urgent need for change intensifies

FRI 23–SUN 25 ★ **SUPER NOVA DAYS** A world of options is available

WED 28 ★ An enthusiastic ally turns darkness into light

OCTOBER

MON 3 ★ Recognize when a challenge is beyond your reach

MON 10–FRI 14 ★ **SUPER NOVA DAYS** You aren't in the mood to play by the rules

MON 17 ★ A hint of arrogance will turn off your audience

SUN 23–TUE 25 ★ Prepare to meet others halfway

FRI 28 ★ Reignite your passion and power

NOVEMBER

WED 2–THU 3 ★ Demonstrate your brilliance and originality

TUE 8–THU 10 ★ Impulsive behavior could backfire

SAT 12 ★ Seek alternative ways to deal with your anger

TUE 22–WED 23 ★ **SUPER NOVA DAYS** Inspire others with your vision

THU 24–SUN 27 ★ Take a step backward until you can restore order

DECEMBER

THU 1–FRI 2 ★ It's not your job to solve everyone's problems

SAT 3–MON 5 ★ Careless words can spark a conflict

SAT 10–SUN 11 ★ Uncover new sources of delight

TUE 20–THU 22 ★ **SUPER NOVA DAYS** Act boldly in pursuit of your dreams

THU 29 ★ Weigh your motivation and resources against your quest

AQUARIUS OVERVIEW

You've been stewing in a mix of symbols that flow into your imagination from the hidden realms of your dreams. Your vision of the future began to clear last year when enchanting Neptune left your sign for a trial visit into compassionate Pisces on April 4–August 4, 2011, before retrograding back into your 1st House of Self. However, Neptune's fourteen-year visit to Aquarius ends on February 3, when it reenters Pisces and your 2nd House of Self-Worth, where it will remain until 2025. The spiritual nature of Neptune can conflict with the materialistic 2nd House, creating problems if you're too attached to what you own or to the idea of making more money. **An overhaul of your finances and a reevaluation of how you produce income will be gradual** but, thankfully, hardworking Saturn, your traditional planetary ruler, plays an important role this year in bringing you much-needed patience and practicality.

Saturn the Tester first entered your 9th House of Big Ideas on October 29, 2009, restraining your growth just enough for you to learn some important lessons about life. Your pragmatic approach to education has given you the self-discipline to tackle complex subjects such as philosophy, religion, or politics. But what you discover about the world through study or travel will become even more important when karmic Saturn enters your 10th House of Career on October 5 for a two-year stay. Saturn's visit to passionate Scorpio and your 10th House is a time of increased professional responsibilities. **You get what you deserve—and if you've defined your goals and worked hard to achieve them, this can be the payoff.** But in areas of your life where you've let things slip, you'll be laboring extra hard to put them right. On October 10, sobering Saturn's harmonious trine to idealistic Neptune—the first in a series of three that last until July 19, 2013—balances your dreams of material success with common sense and persistence to bring your ideas into reality.

It feels as if nothing's been quite the same—and your everyday life will never return to normal—since electrifying Uranus entered fiery Aries and your 3rd House of Immediate Environment on May 27, 2010, for a seven-year stay. You should be thrilled with the buzz and excitement as new ideas, unconventional people, and spontaneous events become part of your daily routine, yet on occasion you may also long for a return to more peaceful times. However, a series of dynamic squares from transformational Pluto to radical Uranus that occur on June 24 and September 19—and recur five more times through March 2015—force you to leave nostalgia behind and see your life through a new lens. Although you may be progressive in your thinking, Aquarius is a fixed sign, and you don't always handle change easily. Unfortunately, the more you seek security by grasping the status quo, the more sudden and shocking the changes will be. Above all, **remember that during these hectic times, flexibility is your friend**.

LOVE IS A MANY-SPLENDORED THING

Expect the unexpected in relationships this year. Three eclipses—a Solar Eclipse on May 20 and Lunar Eclipses on June 4 and November 28—rattle your 5th House of Love and Romance, creating reverberations that last all year long. Aquarius is an intellectual air sign, and although you often prefer cool logic to heated passion, romance is still likely to come knocking on your door when alluring Venus visits your 5th House of Love on April 3–August 7. An old flame may reenter your life, or the sparks of a flagging relationship might be rekindled, during Venus's retrograde period on May 15–June 27. But the South Node of the Moon is in your expressive 5th House until August 29, pulling you back into familiar relationship patterns that may no longer be useful. Fortunately, auspicious Jupiter enters flirty Gemini on June 11 for a yearlong visit to your 5th House, giving you multiple opportunities to let your love light shine.

ROOM AT THE TOP

Take an organized approach to looking ahead this year as your traditional ruling planet, Saturn, is visiting your 9th House of Future Vision. Ambitious Saturn forms skillful quintiles with powerful Pluto on March 28 and August 19, inspiring you to get serious about achieving your long-term aspirations. On October 5, conscientious Saturn moves into your 10th House of Public Responsibility, demanding that you to step up to the plate and work harder than ever before. Fortunately, this can be the culmination of many years of striving toward professional goals, which are now within reach. If you fall short, however, you'll need to make critical decisions about whether to continue struggling along the same path or to think about a change of direction.

PATIENCE PAYS

Learning to be less self-critical can actually boost your earning potential this year as Chiron the Wounded Healer and Neptune the Dreamer both settle in for extended visits to your 2nd House of Finances. Luckily, Jupiter in your 4th House of Domestic Conditions forms magical quintiles with Neptune and Chiron on April 4 and May 4, respectively, creating the possibility that you might work from home or in a field that resonates with your spiritual path. Be cautious; opportunities can look better than they actually are. The devil is in the details when Mercury backs into your 2nd House on March 23–April 16, so read the fine print to avoid costly errors. Your persistence will be rewarded when Saturn harmoniously trines Neptune on October 10 and Chiron on November 16, revealing a concrete path to fulfill your dreams for financial success.

MIND YOUR BODY

You may be more susceptible to stress this year, because your nervous system is taxed by profound changes when your key planet, Uranus, squares ruthless Pluto on June 24 and September 19. Fortunately, you can increase your vitality if you learn to manage anxiety and eliminate unhealthy habits. You excel when it comes to intellectual matters, yet you're tempted to ignore the detrimental effects of suppressing your feelings. Physical Mars is in your 8th House of Intimacy and Transformation until July 3, possibly manifesting symptoms that are linked to unexpressed emotions. Finding ways to release this bottled-up energy is crucial during Mars's frustrating retrograde period on January 23–April 13. Exercise, psychotherapy, acupuncture, and meditation can help to remove the blocks between your mind and body to increase your sense of well-being.

FAMILY AFFAIR

Your personal life is likely a source of contentment, but even difficult issues can be handled more easily as generous Jupiter graces your 4th House of Home and Family during a one-year visit that began on June 4, 2011. Although you may invest in real estate or make improvements to your place of residence, lasting security comes from a sense of inner peace, not something external from your environment. Jupiter's move into your 5th House of Spontaneity on

June 11 can shift your personal focus toward children and creative activities. On August 29, the Lunar South Node moves into your 4th House for a year-and-a-half visit that can resurrect childhood memories and replay old family issue you thought were already handled.

WAITING FOR TAKEOFF

You need a practical reason to justify your travel this year, Aquarius, and traveling for pleasure continues to be nearly nonexistent. It's because serious Saturn is finishing up a two-year stay in your 9th House of Journeys. Nevertheless, just-do-it Mars passes through your adventurous 9th House on July 3– August 23, firing up your wanderlust, which can prompt a last-minute trip or leave you frustrated sitting at home. Thankfully, restraints are relaxed and your passport is once again approved for recreational use on October 5 when prohibitive Saturn finally leaves your 9th House for the more public arena of your 10th House of Career.

TRUST THE PROCESS

Rather than placing your faith in any one system, deity, or dogma, remember that spiritual growth comes when you stay engaged in the process of transformation. Pluto, the planet of gradual metamorphosis, is camped out in your 12th House of Soul Consciousness until March 2023. But Uranus, the planet of sudden change, squares evolutionary Pluto on June 24 and September 19 to punctuate your intuitive development with lightning bolts of instantaneous awareness. However, it's not about any one metaphysical truth that trumps all the rest. The journey itself ultimately teaches you what you need to know.

RICK & JEFF'S TIP FOR THE YEAR:
Cultivate a Beginner's Mind

An enormous amount of change is being thrust upon you, and the smartest strategy is to keep learning as much as you possibly can. When you think you already know the truth, it becomes harder to take in new data. Approaching new situations as a student rather than a teacher will help you navigate even the trickiest of circumstances.

JANUARY

INCH BY INCH, IT'S A CINCH

The New Year brings prospects of big changes, yet you're wise to start slowly and be realistic about how long it will take to reach your goals. You still have some old business to complete with the Sun in dutiful Capricorn and your 12th House of Endings until **January 20**. Communicator Mercury keeps your thoughts anchored to reality when it, too, visits earthy Capricorn on **January 8–27**. Bold Mars is currently energizing your 8th House of Transformation, yet his presence in finicky Virgo demands that you move ahead one small step at a time. Additionally, your progress can be mired in red tape and delays as active Mars slows to turn retrograde on **January 23**. Practice flexibility and let your schedule slip when required; remember that pushing harder will only bring frustration.

Mercury's dynamic square to revolutionary Uranus on **January 8** and conjunction with extremist Pluto on the **13th** foreshadow a major shift in your life path or, at a minimum, in your everyday activities. These changes will become obvious as the Uranus-Pluto square becomes exact on **June 24** and **September 19**. Now, however, restlessness stimulates your thinking and planning. The self-protective Cancer Full Moon on **January 9** shines in your 6th House of Work, reminding you of the security you gain from performing your job well and maintaining regularity in your daily routine. The Sun's move into your sign on **January 20**, followed by the freethinking Aquarius New Moon on the **23rd**, is the true beginning of your yearly cycle, although the retrograde turn of Mars admonishes you to be patient and allow extra time to reach your destination.

KEEP IN MIND THIS MONTH

If your expectations are unrealistically high, you can only be disappointed. Setting attainable goals will help you succeed in the long run.

KEY DATES

JANUARY 1–2 ★ *ready to rumble*

You come across as argumentative on **January 1**, when verbose Mercury in cavalier Sagittarius squares contentious Mars. You might be cheering for your favorite football team or discussing your political views and not even realize that your words sound angry until you've provoked an argument. Luckily, amicable Venus in your sign forms a magical biquintile to Mars in your 8th House of Deep Sharing, enabling you to smoothly charm your way out of the uncomfortable situation you created and even endear yourself to the other person in the process. Although you may need to head back to your job on **January 2**, you won't be very serious; an electric Venus-Uranus aspect draws you toward excitement and fun rather than discipline.

SUPER NOVA DAYS

JANUARY 9–13 ★ *hidden agenda*

Your quiet manner on the job leads others to assume that you're a pushover—yet the strong-but-silent Cancer Moon on the **9th** tells a completely different story. You might think you'll have more freedom if no one is paying attention to you. This passive strategy won't last, though, because the Moon enters demonstrative Leo later in the day, pushing your feelings to the surface. A unifying Sun-Mars trine on **January 12** has you bristling with enthusiasm. Venus's trine to persistent Saturn on the **13th** gives you the endurance you need to finish what you start and the willingness to patiently wait for satisfaction. However, your life is complicated by an enigmatic Mercury-Pluto conjunction in your 12th House of Secrets, making what you don't say more important than what you share. Meanwhile, an illusory Venus-Neptune conjunction helps you masterfully bend the truth.

JANUARY 19–23 ★ *alternating currents*

The Sun's square to judgmental Saturn on **January 19** can rain on your parade, but you'll also experience forward movement due to the Sun's entry into futuristic Aquarius on the **20th** and a supportive sextile with edgy Uranus on the **21st**. Additional encouragement comes from the Sun's square to exuberant Jupiter on the **22nd**, while the Aquarius New Moon on **January 23** clears you for takeoff. Nevertheless, motivating Mars turns retrograde, so you won't progress as quickly as you expect. Be thankful for small gains while taking setbacks in stride.

JANUARY 27–28 ★ *red light, green light*

A rational Mercury-Saturn square on **January 27** tells you *no,* yet a philosophically expansive Mercury-Jupiter square on the **28th** says *yes*. Additionally, perceptive Mercury's collaborative sextile with unconventional Uranus in your 3rd House of Information fills your head with one brilliant thought after another, encouraging you to act even if it takes time for your best ideas to produce tangible results.

FEBRUARY

JUST OUT OF REACH

It's all about you as the Sun in brilliant Aquarius illuminates your 1st House of Self until **February 19**. Your perceptions are keen and you're able to easily put your thoughts into words while prolific Mercury is also traveling through your sign until **February 13**. However, the Leo Full Moon on **February 7** shines in your 7th House of Partners to remind you that there are others, too, whose needs you must also consider. And it's not enough for you to think you know what someone else wants; Mercury's alignment with this Sun-Moon opposition requires you to be fully involved in the give-and-take of dialogue as you balance your desires with another person's needs. This is accentuated by the ongoing retrograde of assertive Mars in your 8th House of Intimacy this month.

Your dreams of happiness and material abundance are highlighted on the **3rd** when fanciful Neptune floats into imaginative Pisces and your 2nd House of Self-Worth. However, goals that have seemed close start to slowly recede into the distance when karmic Saturn turns retrograde on the **7th**, just prior to reaching a trine with Neptune. Don't be concerned; there's plenty to do before the Saturn-Neptune trine is exact on **October 10** to make your fantasies come true. Although you may experience financial uncertainty when Mercury and the Sun conjunct confusing Neptune in your 2nd House of Resources on the **14th** and the **19th**, your attention to money matters should help clear things up. The supersensitive Pisces New Moon on **February 21** joins spacey Neptune, so don't waste energy feeling sorry for yourself if resolution takes longer than you wish.

KEEP IN MIND THIS MONTH

If your actual experiences don't live up to your expectations, remember that the purpose of your dreams is to spur you to something greater.

KEY DATES

FEBRUARY 1 ★ *cleanup in aisle two*

Make a phone call or write a letter about a financial matter that should have already been handled when mercantile Mercury aspects a tense Venus-Mars opposition that activates your money houses. The problem might not be of your making; contentious Mars is retrograde in your 8th House of Shared Resources, suggesting that someone else's failure to follow through complicated the situation. Nevertheless, it's now up to you to untangle a mess that's putting stress on your relationship.

SUPER NOVA DAYS

FEBRUARY 7–9 ★ *spills and thrills*

Wit and wisdom slip off your tongue on **February 7** as the Sun and expressive Mercury meet up in your 1st House of Personality. You'll enjoy animated conversations, because the lively Leo Full Moon occurs on the same day. However, you could be so eager to please someone you like when charming Venus prances into spontaneous Aries on the **8th** that you speak before considering the effects of your words. Awkward apologies or unconscious pushiness create social discomfort when Mercury forms an ill-adjusted quincunx to aggressive Mars on **February 9**. But a thrilling Venus-Uranus conjunction in your 3rd House of Communication indicates that intellectual or romantic excitement is yours if you're willing to be vulnerable and take a risk with your heart.

FEBRUARY 14–17 ★ *have faith*

You see a murky financial picture right now, but this lack of clarity might be more about self-doubt than it is about the money. Mental Mercury's conjunction with nebulous Neptune on **February 14** is what's clouding your 2nd House of Money, obscuring the truth, yet your imagination can also inspire positive action if you don't get discouraged. Fortunately, optimistic Jupiter forms a useful sextile with Chiron the Wounded Healer, allowing you to forgive yourself for a recent mistake and move on. Still, intense emotions may come to the surface and you won't be able to escape the consequences of your actions when needy Venus in incorrigible Aries squares potent Pluto on the **15th**. Thankfully, an overconfident Mercury-Jupiter sextile on **February 16** should alleviate a tough situation as long as you don't take the easy way out.

FEBRUARY 25–28 ★ *live long and prosper*

You take extra time to appreciate your home and family on **February 25** when the affectionate Pisces Sun sextiles lavish Jupiter in your 4th House of Domestic Conditions. However, an anxious Mercury-Jupiter aspect raises concerns about losing what you have or not getting what you want now. There's no need to worry; just make a new plan, for a shrewd Sun-Pluto sextile on the **28th** encourages you to dream big as long as you're not selfish.

MARCH

FOOLS RUSH IN

Money issues are on your plate this month with the Sun in your 2nd House of Personal Resources—and its opposition to insistent Mars in your 8th House of Shared Resources on **March 3** means that others are involved in your financial picture, too. Mars in introspective Virgo is retrograde, turning your energy inward as you seek solutions through logical analysis rather than overt action. The cautious Virgo Full Moon is conjunct to action-planet Mars on **March 8** in your regenerative 8th House, but even if you know your next move, you might not be able to put your plan into motion yet. Someone comes to your rescue or you receive sound advice on **March 13–14** when Mars forms a practical Grand Earth Trine with sweet Venus, magnanimous Jupiter, and insightful Pluto. But everything takes longer than you wish since your everyday life is so busy, with mischievous Mercury turning retrograde in your 3rd House of Immediate Environment on **March 12**. Because of its backward turn, the trickster planet's conjunction to erratic Uranus on **March 5** is repeated on **March 18**, bringing detours and unexpected distractions that can surprise and even shock you with their suddenness.

Your life grows hectic on the Spring Equinox, **March 20**—the day that the Sun shifts into impetuous Aries and your busy 3rd House. You can find yourself running around in circles without getting a lot done. The excitable Aries New Moon on the **22nd** conjuncts cerebral Mercury and high-strung Uranus in your 3rd House of Communication, generating radical ideas that can take you on a wild goose chase unless you remember to think before you act.

KEEP IN MIND THIS MONTH

There's so much coming at you from many directions that it's important to find time to relax and soothe your overactive nerves.

KEY DATES

MARCH 1–5 ★ *bouncing off the walls*

This is a thrilling but tricky time. You're all fired up when insistent Mercury enters enthusiastic Aries on **March 2** and the Sun opposes feisty Mars on **March 3**. But a restrictive Mercury-Saturn quincunx on **March 1** and a sobering Venus-Saturn opposition on the **4th** can rain on your parade. Although Venus saunters into sensual Taurus on the **5th**, bringing comfort and pleasure, Mercury's conjunction with wild and crazy Uranus sends sparks of excitement that once again set you on edge.

MARCH 13–14 ★ *the force is with you*

Opportunistic Jupiter rolls into a unifying trine with formidable Pluto on **March 13**, urging you to take control of your life. Your goal should be to build a strong foundation for the next phase of your life, with Jupiter hanging out in your 4th House of Security. Valuable Venus trines Pluto on the **13th** and conjuncts Jupiter the next day, possibly bringing a financial windfall or other good news. Expressive Mars enters the picture on the **14th** to complete a Grand Earth Trine that is an additional harbinger of success. But with both Mercury and Mars now retrograde, don't expect too much right away. Instead, use these days to develop your strategy, build up your strength, and cultivate patience.

SUPER NOVA DAYS

MARCH 20–24 ★ *simple twist of fate*

The restless Aries New Moon on **March 22** is a turning point—though you're already eager to hit the road and try something new on the **20th**, when the Sun enters bold Aries and your 3rd House of Short Trips. This is less about altering the direction of your life than it is about making the most of the moment, even if that involves taking a risk. Communicative Mercury backs into intuitive Pisces on the **23rd**, confusing your interactions, because words no longer convey the subtleties of current events. The Sun's conjunction with surprising Uranus on **March 24** indicates that an unexpected break in your routine can turn out to be quite the memorable experience.

MARCH 28–31 ★ *give it time*

Don't let the transformative Saturn-Pluto quintile on **March 28** slip by unnoticed. Use this creative moment to shape your future by taking stock of your current resources and skills and then setting clear intentions for what you want. An intense Sun-Pluto square on the **29th** requires you to overcome resistance—either someone working against you or just your own fears playing tricks on you. Nevertheless, it's hard to know how forceful you should be in your approach because macho Mars forms an uncertain quincunx to unruly Uranus on the **31st**. Instead of pushing for final resolution now, stay on your toes but allow events to unfold naturally.

APRIL

ON THE MOVE

Obstacles fall by the wayside this month as you break free from whatever limitations have been holding you back. If you've been stuck in a boring routine, the pace of events in your personal life picks up nicely on **April 3**, when flirty Venus dances into interactive Gemini and quicksilver Mercury turns direct on **April 4**. A second energetic boost arrives when enterprising Mars—who's been retrograde in your 8th House of Transformation since **January 23**—also commences moving forward on **April 13**. Changes that began last year and then were put on the back burner for one reason or another now take center stage as your recent efforts to deepen relationships finally start to bring results. The busyness of your daily schedule is further emphasized by the Sun, which is in go-getter Aries and your 3rd House of Communication until **April 19**; then it moves into placid Taurus and your 4th House of Home and Family. You won't have much time to relax, however, since loquacious Mercury shifts into pioneering Aries and your noisy 3rd House on **April 16** to assure that you continue pushing into new territory.

You're ready for an adventure or to expand your mind through a new course of learning when the relationship-oriented Libra Full Moon on **April 6** brightens your 9th House of Travel and Education. However, several uncomfortable aspects to the Full Moon suggest that without conscious restraint, your big ideas may be so ungrounded that disgruntled disappointment can quickly replace your overeager optimism. Thankfully, the pragmatic Taurus New Moon on **April 21** activates your 4th House of Foundations and is just what you need to help you get back in the groove. It forms a stabilizing Grand Earth Trine with action-planet Mars and incisive Pluto, providing you with enough stamina and fortitude to follow through on what you've already begun.

KEEP IN MIND THIS MONTH

No matter how chaotic your life grows, let yourself feel anticipation for the wonderful experiences around the corner.

KEY DATES

APRIL 4–7 ★ *the trouble with love*

You struggle to focus your attention on specific details when Mercury's direct turn in Pisces stimulates your dreams on **April 4**. Jupiter's metaphysical quintile with Neptune adds to the surreal quality of the day. Romantic fantasies can be alluring but disorienting as Venus in your 5th House of Love and Play forms a confusing square to Neptune on the **5th**. It's not easy to balance your needs with your partner's wishes on **April 6**, when the Libra Full Moon floods your 8th House of Deep Sharing with emotions that don't fit into your current relationship dynamics. A scrappy Venus-Mars square on **April 7** may create conflict or sparks as your sassy approach differs in style from someone close to you.

APRIL 9 ★ *can't hurt to ask*

You're reminded of how different your needs are from the social norm today when frisky Venus in your 5th House of Fun and Frivolity creates a collaborative sextile with unorthodox Uranus. Fortunately, your current desire for independence and other eccentricities won't necessarily stand in the way of satisfaction as long as you're willing to engage in an honest discussion about what you want.

APRIL 13–16 ★ *not so fast*

You may be eager to push ahead with your plans when impulsive Mars turns direct on **April 13**, but the speedy Aries Sun slams into an immovable wall as it opposes unyielding Saturn in your 9th House of Big Ideas on **April 15**. If you slow down and learn the lesson that's being taught, messenger Mercury's shift into trailblazing Aries on the **16th** can ignite your mind with exciting new ideas. If you take a shortcut, however, your path may be fraught with frustrating setbacks.

SUPER NOVA DAYS

APRIL 21–25 ★ *stick to the plan*

Your goals seem quite reachable on **April 21** thanks to the Taurus New Moon, yet an erratic Mercury-Uranus conjunction in your 3rd House of Information on the **22nd** has you jumping to conclusions. Following your plans is a dependable strategy with the Sun's trine to Mars in Virgo on the **23rd**. However, changing your course midstream could provoke intense resistance from Mercury's square to unwavering Pluto on **April 25**.

APRIL 29 ★ *against all odds*

You may feel invincible, even if you've had to face difficult challenges. And if you remain focused today, you have the power and stability you need to complete a tough job when the Sun in your 4th House of Roots trines resolute Pluto in your 12th House of Endings.

MAY

TROUBLE ON EASY STREET

Although your feet are on the ground and you're confident about achieving success this month, step back and reconsider what you want most or you might end up heading in the wrong direction. The Sun is in solid Taurus until **May 20**, activating your 4th House of Foundations. Meanwhile, the insightful Scorpio Full Moon on **May 5** illuminates your 10th House of Status, revealing complexities in professional and social relationships that affect your progress at work and in the community. But the Sun's conjunction with prosperous Jupiter on **May 13** fills you with such a strong sense of well-being that you're tempted to set your goals too high and then try to pursue them anyhow. Fortunately, a steadying Grand Earth Trine with energizing Mars and compelling Pluto on **May 13–16** is anchored by thoughtful Mercury in your personal 4th House, demanding that you contemplate the consequences of your actions prior to starting something you won't be able to finish.

On **May 15**, you start to reevaluate the path you're on when crafty Venus turns retrograde in curious Gemini. The love planet backpedals through your 5th House of Love and Play until **June 27**, unleashing your quirky creativity, scattering your attention, and distracting you from your primary obligations. You can make a clean break from the past on **May 20** when the Gemini New Moon Solar Eclipse rattles your spontaneous 5th House to illuminate the differences between your serious ambitions and how you're currently spending your time. Thankfully, you can catch a wave of positive change on **May 27–28** when Mercury and the Sun conspire with futuristic Uranus.

KEEP IN MIND THIS MONTH

Pay attention to what's happening when everything is copasetic—that's exactly when you're most likely to make a bad judgment call.

KEY DATES

MAY 5–8 ★ *instant karma*

It's not fun being told no, but sometimes this is exactly what's necessary to grab your attention. Trickster Mercury in impatient Aries opposes authoritative Saturn on **May 5**, requiring you to have your ducks in a row before moving ahead with your plans. Being flexible is a smart idea because you can get hooked on an obsessive idea with the fixed Scorpio Full Moon, also on the **5th**. Fortunately, a brilliant solution to your dilemma is within reach as philosophical Jupiter forms a dynamic semisquare to your key planet Uranus the Awakener on **May 7**. Just don't take any unnecessary risks, because reckless Mars makes a slippery quincunx to unstable Uranus on the **8th**.

SUPER NOVA DAYS

MAY 12–16 ★ *overcoming adversity*

You're sure that things are spinning out of control on **May 12**, when the Sun forms an anxious semisquare with unpredictable Uranus. On the **15th**, pleasure-seeking Venus begins her retrograde period in restless Gemini, tempting you to repeat a recent mistake as you try to fulfill your desires. Meanwhile, communicator Mercury's trines with Mars and Pluto on **May 13–14** enable you to talk about very difficult issues without panicking. Additionally, a unifying Mars-Pluto trine on the **16th** blesses you with a deep well of physical stamina and spiritual energy, empowering you to pick yourself up, handle the complex circumstances, and move on.

MAY 20–22 ★ *zip it*

This is an exciting yet disruptive time for you, given the Sun's shift into lighthearted Gemini and your 5th House of Fun and Games, followed by a liberating New Moon Solar Eclipse on **May 20**. A restraining Mercury-Saturn quincunx on the **21st** could mean that communication is frustrating if you aren't willing to lay a proper foundation before trying to make your point. Your intellect is evident, but you could easily get carried away with your ideas or with the sound of your own voice as chatty Mercury conjuncts inexhaustible Jupiter on **May 22**.

MAY 27–29 ★ *squeaky wheel gets the grease*

The Sun-Mercury conjunction in your playful 5th House on **May 27** encourages you to express something personal, whether it's the latest leanings of your heart or what you want to do for fun. Wild Uranus's supportive sextile to Mercury on the **27th** and to the Sun on the **28th** can awaken your inner child. However, a Sun-Pluto quincunx on **May 29** suggests that you shouldn't try to force your agenda on or discuss a topic with anyone who doesn't share your passion.

JUNE

SHUFFLING PRIORITIES

Your challenge this month is to balance your desire for fun in the moment with the need to keep a watchful eye on the future. A cluster of planets in your 5th House of Play can tempt you with immediate gratification, but the Sagittarius Full Moon Eclipse on **June 4** galvanizes your aspirations in your 11th House of Long-Term Goals. Its opposition to sweet-hearted Venus—retrograde in flirtatious Gemini until **June 27**—reveals what may be lacking in the romance department. The eclipse's square to warrior Mars in nitpicky Virgo provokes you to argue with others to make your position known. But you're likely to change your mind, especially when permissive Jupiter enters fickle Gemini and your spontaneous 5th House on **June 11** for a one-year visit.

Meanwhile, you grow increasingly frustrated as the demands of your daily routine interfere with what you really want to do in your life thanks to a long-lasting and intensifying square between unsettling Uranus and unrelenting Pluto. The first of seven Uranus-Pluto squares occurs on **June 24** in a series that lasts until 2015, but its arrival is heralded on **June 11** when Mercury squares Uranus and opposes Pluto. Nevertheless, the indecisive Gemini New Moon on **June 19** indicates that you might not be quite ready to face the large-scale changes ahead., On **June 25,** a square between the two most expansive planets, Jupiter and Neptune, widens your horizons and amplifies your imagination, which could confuse you about where you should be focusing your energy. Harnessing your creativity isn't easy, but if you can discipline your craft you could produce worthwhile results.

KEEP IN MIND THIS MONTH

There's nothing wrong with having a good time. Just make sure you're not avoiding serious issues that you should address now rather than later.

KEY DATES

JUNE 3–7 ★ *look before you leap*

A stabilizing Mercury-Saturn trine on **June 3** helps you strengthen your plans for the stressful days ahead. Still, emotions run hot when sensual Venus squares impetuous Mars on **June 4** and they both form harsh aspects with the Lunar Eclipse in risk-taking Sagittarius. Think before you act or the Sun's square to brash Mars in your 8th House of Deep Sharing on **June 7** could trigger a temper tantrum over a heated issue that's ultimately not as critical as it seems in the moment.

JUNE 11–13 ★ *stand up for your rights*

You vacillate among multiple choices on **June 11**, when giant Jupiter shifts into dualistic Gemini and makes it hard for you to reach a definitive decision. However, rational Mercury in your 6th House of Details forms a compelling square with lightning-like Uranus, allowing you to cut through ambiguity and find an answer. Mercury's tense opposition with domineering Pluto could put you face-to-face with a powerful opponent who disagrees with your ideas. Thankfully, the willful Sun's unifying trine to industrious Saturn on the **13th** gives you the determination and persistence to hold your ground.

JUNE 19–20 ★ *work in progress*

Your position is fragile on **June 19**, with the New Moon in changeable Gemini. You can't go on expressing yourself in the same old way; it's time to pay more attention to improving your life than just accepting the status quo. The Summer Solstice on **June 20**—marked by the Sun's entry into self-protective Cancer and your 6th House of Daily Routines—motivates you to cultivate a healthier lifestyle. Yet you may not feel up to the task, for a doubting Mercury-Saturn square on the **20th** reminds you of all the things you haven't finished. Fortunately, you're not ready to admit defeat and could even have some unconventional ideas up your sleeve as sly Venus sextiles brilliant Uranus in your 3rd House of Information.

SUPER NOVA DAYS

JUNE 24–29 ★ *the power of now*

If you feel like you've been running in place at work or stuck in an old relationship pattern, now is the time to get yourself back on a productive path. The Uranus-Pluto square on **June 24** and the Jupiter-Neptune square on **June 25** both stir the waters of change; then the direct turns of Saturn on the **25th** and Venus on the **27th** set you into forward motion. However, you may need to fight to advance your interests if your agenda conflicts with someone else's plans on **June 29**, when the Sun opposes evolutionary Pluto and squares catalytic Uranus.

JULY

BACK UP TO GET AHEAD

You must turn around and retrace your steps in relationships this month as messenger Mercury retrogrades in your 7th House of Partners on **July 14**. This event signals the importance of reconsidering and, where necessary, renegotiating your agreements with others. Additionally, your ruling planet Uranus turns backward in your 3rd House of Communication on **July 13**, reinforcing the necessity of double-checking expectations that come to light during conversations with those close to you. Fortunately, you receive assistance as you redress relationship imbalances on **July 3** when Mars enters cooperative Libra, facilitating your ability to compromise. You'll need to use reason as the normally orderly Capricorn Full Moon, also on the **3rd**, lights up your 12th House of Privacy, triggering revelations from your subconscious and exposing secrets. The Moon conjuncts obsessive Pluto, squares rebellious Uranus, and aspects reactive Mercury, producing a volatile cocktail of mistrust, anger, and suspicion that can rock your world. It's difficult to remain detached if you feel betrayed by others or disappointed by your own failure, but punishment only prolongs the pain without providing any answers.

Establishing healthy routines at home and work may not sound exciting, but it'll earn you peace of mind you're unlikely to find any other way. An electrifying Mars-Uranus opposition on **July 18** sparks unusual behavior, yet the tenacious Cancer New Moon on the **19th** is stressed by a square with cautious Saturn that rewards patience and makes haste especially costly. Happily, an eye-opening Jupiter-Uranus sextile and the Sun's entry into theatrical Leo on **July 22** are bound to get your creative juices flowing again.

KEEP IN MIND THIS MONTH

Changing the rules in a relationship is neither irresponsible nor weak when it's an authentic response to your needs.

KEY DATES

JULY 3–4 ★ *out of the shadows*

You could easily become entangled in a dangerous intrigue or swallowed up by negative emotions during the somber Capricorn Full Moon of **July 3**. It's wise to mind your own business, which is likely to be more than enough for you to handle. Fortunately, you can quickly rise from despair as flirty Venus and friendly Mercury create positive aspects with inventive Uranus on the **4th**. This rapidly refreshes your thinking with a new perspective and rejuvenates your social life with fresh forms of fun.

JULY 14 ★ *stretching the truth*

Mercury's retrograde turn can complicate communications during the next three weeks, but this chatty planet's reversal is rich with charm as it aligns with a sweet sextile to seductive Venus today. Easygoing banter and captivating conversations makes whatever you say more believable and what you hear more attractive. Be sure to add a dash of skepticism so you don't fall for a line that's too good to be true.

JULY 17–19 ★ *opposites attract*

You're in for a wild ride on **July 17**, when dynamic Mars in your 9th House of Faraway Places forms a freewheeling trine with effusive Jupiter that encourages endless adventures. Yet before the day is over, Mars crosses swords with pressurized Pluto in a squeezing square that requires you to narrow your perspective and concentrate your forces where they're most vital. Your ability to mesh contrary views is served by a creative Sun-Mars quintile on the **18th** that weaves together the contradictory threads of a radical Mars-Uranus opposition and the conservative Cancer New Moon on the **19th**.

SUPER NOVA DAYS

JULY 22–25 ★ *get smart*

Your genius jells on **July 22** when the Sun enters animated Leo and an experimental Jupiter-Uranus sextile opens your mind to visionary people and fascinating ideas. Factual Mercury fills in details and facilitates getting your messages across when it forms easy connections to Jupiter and Uranus on the **July 24–25**. The messenger planet's retrograde period makes this an ideal time to resurrect interesting old ideas, repackage them, and present them to others in provocatively new and entertaining forms.

JULY 31 ★ *one of a kind*

You take giant leaps over stubborn problems today as the confident Sun makes a generous trine with revolutionary Uranus. When you put your heart and mind into a cause, the obstacles you encounter are no match for your conviction. You can attract intelligent allies, demonstrate your loyalty without losing your freedom, and awaken others with your unique insights.

AUGUST

DO WHAT YOU LOVE, LOVE WHAT YOU DO

The month gets off to an auspicious start. A deliciously playful Full Moon in quirky Aquarius on **August 1** ignites an explosion of joy as bountiful Jupiter trines the Moon from your 5th House of Romance. If you've been feeling at odds in your personal and professional relationships, you should find your footing when communicative Mercury turns forward in your 7th House of Others on **August 8**. The audacious Leo New Moon on the **17th** brings another wave of self-confidence, goodwill, and supportive friends and co-workers. The extravagant ideas of your allies and the boldness of your own proposals gain credibility from a smart sextile to solid Saturn that provides the common sense and follow-through to turn your plans into reality.

Connecting with reliable people can strengthen the practical foundations on which your partnerships are built when the Sun enters loyal Virgo and your 8th House of Shared Resources on **August 22**. However, you could also feel nitpicked by petty thinkers or nagged by a worried lover or business associate. Rather than ignoring their concerns and complicating the situation by acting defensively, it's wiser to dig in and do the hard work of maintaining trust and developing more efficient teamwork. Active Mars's shift into intense Scorpio and your 10th House of Career on the **23rd** also calls you down from the clouds to concentrate your efforts where they're most needed. Financial uncertainties may come to light when the vulnerable Pisces Full Moon illuminates your 2nd House of Resources on **August 31**. Fortunately, a supportive sextile from perceptive Pluto shows you how to turn losses into gains and revive a creative interest for profit and pleasure.

KEEP IN MIND THIS MONTH

Hard work is child's play when you do it for a cause or project you fully believe in.

KEY DATES

SUPER NOVA DAYS

AUGUST 1–2 ★ *in your element*

The Aquarius Full Moon on **August 1** dramatizes your emotions and puts you in the spotlight. Your newfound confidence and enterprising spirit bloom with a Grand Air Trine among the Moon, outgoing Jupiter in inquisitive Gemini, and energetic Mars in collaborative Libra. Lining up support for your most idealistic and innovative concepts should be easy given your contagious enthusiasm.

The Sun's sextile to Jupiter on the **2nd** keeps you flying on a cloud of self-confidence, but don't let your ego run roughshod over other people's feelings. A vulnerable Sun-Venus semisquare can surprise you with a sense of rejection if you don't get the high praise you expect.

AUGUST 9 ★ *vision of success*

Your vivid imagination and sincere compassion for others can increase your income and enhance your self-worth. Resourceful Venus's trine from your 6th House of Work to magical Neptune in your 2nd House of Money today produces payoffs when you bring an extra dose of creativity and a heartfelt commitment to your job.

AUGUST 15–18 ★ *stairway to heaven*

There's no room for nonsense on **August 15**, when stern Saturn conjuncts persistent Mars in your 9th House of Higher Truth. Keeping your goals modest and sticking to your commitments won't take you very far just now, but should provide the stability you need to climb to the highest peak later on. Impulsive appetites may cause you to act with haste when desirous Venus squares spontaneous Uranus on the **16th**. Fortunately, realistic and reliable associates show you how to keep passion flowing without burning out on **August 17** when the New Moon in courageous Leo activates your 7th House of Partners, aligning favorably with calculating Saturn. Creative colleagues invite your original thoughts with brainy Mercury's trine to ingenious Uranus on the **18th**.

AUGUST 20–22 ★ *trial and error*

Finding the right pace may be difficult on **August 20** as an energy-efficient Sun-Mars sextile gives you plenty of fuel, tempting you to put the pedal to the metal with an overly adventurous Mars-Jupiter sesquisquare. Reason is restored with the acute judgment of a smart sextile between logical Mercury and farsighted Jupiter, along with the Sun's entry into refined Virgo, on the **22nd**. If you've gone too far and rubbed others the wrong way, you can find the right words now to restore harmonious channels of communication.

AUGUST 28 ★ *ahead of the curve*

Your thinking could be so far out on the edge today that people believe that you're losing touch with reality. It may simply be that your ideas are too far ahead of their time as intellectual Mercury forms a stressful sesquisquare with futuristic Uranus. Slow down and simplify things so others can understand.

SEPTEMBER

COMPLICATED CONNECTIONS

The complexities of relationships are key issues for much of the month with the analytical Virgo Sun in your 8th House of Deep Sharing until the Autumn Equinox on **September 22**. You may feel crowded in personal and professional partnerships that hem you in with rules and expectations, infringing on your precious freedom. You face hard work ahead to untangle knots of misunderstanding and create more harmonious relationships. Don't despair if situations seem irresolvable; the Sun's entry into objective Libra on the **22nd** illuminates your 9th House of Higher Principles, broadening perspectives, enabling compromises, and showing you light at the end of the tunnel. Thankfully, enticing Venus enters generous Leo and your 7th House of Others on **September 6**, which should attract enthusiastic allies. Enjoying the attention and encouragement of your peers can be exhilarating, yet promises may exceed performance, so restrain your expectations until someone has truly earned your trust.

The Virgo New Moon in your 8th House on **September 15** plants seeds of partnership possibilities—but if you want them to grow, you must be clear about your goals and willing to plan meticulously. The second explosive Uranus-Pluto square occurs on the **19th**—the first was on **June 24**—to help you give voice to your unexpressed desires. The thoughts and feelings exposed now raise complex questions that you might not resolve until the final Uranus-Pluto square on **March 16, 2015**. The tectonic shifts promised by this pair might also initiate crises during the Full Moon in Aries on the **29th** as you struggle to maintain your independence without shattering relationships. Uranus's conjunction and Pluto's square to the impulsive Aries Full Moon incite sharp words but can also thrill you with radical new ideas.

KEEP IN MIND THIS MONTH

Minor adjustments may save a relationship, even if you think that drastic changes are the only way to keep it from falling apart.

KEY DATES

SEPTEMBER 6–7 ★ *let the good times roll*

An abundance of pleasure can be sweet on **September 6** but watch out for a tendency to overpay, overindulge, or expect too much given romantic Venus's entry into extravagant Leo and her aspect to excessive Jupiter. It's tempting to let fantasy overcome reason on the **7th** with a boundless Sun-Jupiter square and a sketchy

Venus-Neptune quincunx. If you must set reality aside to have some fun, remember not to lose touch with your common sense.

SEPTEMBER 13 ★ *dare to be different*

Relationships relax today, and you find new forms of enjoyment with an easygoing trine from playful Venus to experimental Uranus. Your light touch helps you to work around the resistance of strong-willed partners and collaborate on innovative projects. Putting your heart and plenty of charm into a presentation makes your unconventional ideas more attractive to others and earns you praise for your originality.

SEPTEMBER 20 ★ *short fuse*

A few poorly chosen words may be all it takes to start an argument. Stressful aspects from talkative Mercury in your 8th House of Shared Resources to shocking Uranus and blunt Pluto supercharge conversations, put everyone on edge. If you can maintain a modicum of civility, however, brilliant concepts can emerge from the storm of clashing ideas. A calming sextile from sociable Venus to broad-minded Jupiter keeps windows of hope open and provides a dash of good humor that could transform a volatile situation into an engine for partnership growth.

SUPER NOVA DAYS

SEPTEMBER 25–26 ★ *conflict resolution*

Your reluctance to follow the rules may increase tension at work on the **25th**, when Mars clashes with Uranus and Pluto. You may try to enforce order in a chaotic situation if you're in a position of authority. Venus adds fuel to the fire as she collides with Uranus on the **25th** and Pluto on the **26th**. Relief comes through the wise and skillful communication offered by a harmonious trine between verbal Mercury and philosophical Jupiter on the **26th**, supplying cool reason to resolve a stressful situation.

SEPTEMBER 29 ★ *exit strategy*

The headstrong Aries Full Moon lights up your 3rd House of Short Trips, disrupting your day and hijacking your schedule. You can't sit still with the Moon's conjunction to restless Uranus and square to intense Pluto as you search for an alternative route. If you find a way to escape, make a quick getaway before anyone notices you are gone.

OCTOBER

BALANCING ACT

This month is all about the relationship between your ideals and the execution of your strategy. October starts with the Sun in your 9th House of Big Ideas and finishes with it shining in your 10th House of Public Responsibility. The entry of agreeable Venus into pragmatic Virgo and your 8th House of Shared Resources on **October 3** puts a priority on efficiency, yet dashing Mars's move into theoretical Sagittarius and your 11th House of Community on the **6th** tends to value adherence to a cause above practicality. A similar contradiction is illustrated on the **5th** when mental Mercury joins dependable Saturn in the last degree of Libra in your 9th House before both planets move into Scorpio in your 10th House later that day. You may be able to articulate a perfect plan for bringing peace and justice into your life but then encounter limits imposed by your duties.

Fortunately, you can span the gap between your highest hopes and current realities thanks to a creative trine between earthbound Saturn and heavenly Neptune on **October 10**. This favorable alignment, which recurs on **June 11** and **July 13, 2013**, widens your picture of reality until you find room for these seemingly opposing perspectives. On the **15th**, the diplomatic instincts that the Libra New Moon gives you are enriched with a trine to promising Jupiter. The Sun's entry into scrutinizing Scorpio on **October 22** and the Taurus Full Moon in your 4th House of Home and Family on the **29th** reveal the gulf between your personal and professional lives. The Sun's conjunction with strict Saturn on the **25th** requires you to set clear priorities, maintain a singular focus, and develop the patience of a saint.

KEEP IN MIND THIS MONTH

You can balance utopian dreams with earthbound necessities if you develop the flexibility to adjust your behavior.

KEY DATES

OCTOBER 5–7 ★ *stay on track*

Mastery of information is critical when studious Mercury joins ambitious Saturn in your 9th House of Higher Learning on **October 5**. If you know your stuff, this is the right time to make a presentation; however, if you don't have all the facts, the holes in your plan could be glaringly obvious. You can succeed with the help of colleagues and with a boost of your own enthusiasm when activating Mars enters upbeat Sagittarius and your 11th House of Groups on the **6th**. Still, noble as it is to battle for a cause, you might be wiser to measure your efforts since Mars's square with diffusive Neptune on the **7th** can send you on a wild goose chase that dissipates your energy and wastes your time.

SUPER NOVA DAYS

OCTOBER 9–10 ★ *the sky's the limit*

You're able to look beyond short-term issues and see long-range opportunities on **October 9**, when a visionary Sun-Jupiter trine fills your mind with a cornucopia of ideas. Others, though, may not catch on as quickly as you might like, provoking an impatience that can turn them off to your plans. Inviting questions is necessary to gain support. You can mix authority with compassion on the **10th**, when bossy Saturn is softened by a trine to altruistic Neptune. Dreams supported by discipline can be brought gently down to earth.

OCTOBER 15 ★ *technical wizardry*

Your genius for coming up with original solutions and methods is evident with a trine between active Mars and bright Uranus. The peace-seeking Libra New Moon plants seeds for initiating alliances, yet a sticky sesquisquare between expansive Jupiter and contractive Saturn reminds you to move cautiously and consolidate gains before you push on to the next level.

OCTOBER 20–21 ★ *agent of change*

Your fears about your job take center stage with Mercury in perceptive Scorpio in your 10th House of Career. Still, the messenger planet's stressful aspects to wayward Uranus on **October 20** and inscrutable Pluto on the **21st** can make them difficult to explain. If you're feeling frazzled and overwhelmed by unnecessary complications, step back, cut yourself some slack, and try a simpler approach.

OCTOBER 28–29 ★ *a bird in the hand*

You may be driven by pure adrenaline on the **28th** with an overamped opposition of Mars and Jupiter and a nervous Sun-Uranus quincunx. If you go too far or too fast, you're likely to hit a wall of resistance when the steady Taurus Full Moon opposes immovable Saturn on the **29th**. Stay calm, narrow your focus, and commit to your most useful idea instead of draining yourself by chasing every rainbow in sight.

NOVEMBER

LISTEN TO YOUR HEART

Your mind may be wrapped around professional issues for much of this month, but it's really your heart that could win out in the end. The emotionally powerful Scorpio Sun in your 10th House of Career stresses you out at work until **November 21**. Managing those below you or dealing with control from those above provokes you to look more deeply at your current position. The Scorpio New Moon on the **13th** is a Solar Eclipse that reminds you to invest more of yourself where you are—or look elsewhere for fulfillment on the job. You can't continue to drive yourself ahead on sheer will unless your inner commitment matches your external obligations. The dominance of intellect may also recede when cerebral Mercury is retrograde on **November 6–26**. The communication planet begins this period of reevaluation in your team-oriented 11th House and ends it in your individually responsible 10th House, which could reveal those areas where a lack of support from colleagues increases the burden on you.

You enjoy some much-needed relief from professional pressures when delightful Venus in Libra creates a sweet trine with indulgent Jupiter in Gemini on **November 9**. This harmonious connection between two social planets can brighten relationships and inspire romance. While you're likely to have a good time—even if reality falls short of your expectations—a joyous vision can also lift your spirits. On **November 28**, the Gemini Full Moon Lunar Eclipse in your 5th House of Love challenges you to stop playing around the edges of desire and finally make a choice that should be worth much more than you have to give up in return.

KEEP IN MIND THIS MONTH

Persistence is only useful if it's moving you toward a better place. Don't just hold on out of habit or fear.

KEY DATES

NOVEMBER 1–3 ★ *out of the box*

Tantalizing Venus's opposition to your exciting ruling planet Uranus triggers sudden changes of taste on **November 1**. An unexpected, instantaneous attraction—or explosion—shakes up your personal life on **November 1**. Whether this is a passing thunderstorm or the beginning of a more significant change could be revealed on the **3rd**, when magnetic Venus forms a defining square with mysterious Pluto.

NOVEMBER 9–11 ★ *the call of the wild*

A trine from attractive Venus in your 9th House of Faraway Places to adventurous Jupiter broadens your romantic horizons on **November 9**. There is a spirit of open-mindedness that embraces intimate feelings in spite of any differences of opinion. The need to reassert your independence, though, arises with an edgy Sun-Uranus aspect on the **11th** that can arouse conflict with authority figures. Nevertheless, innovation and originality may help you blast through barriers or boredom or inefficiency.

NOVEMBER 15 ★ *learning to fly*

Your desire to break free is bogged down today by inescapable obligations. It's because conservative Saturn and progressive Uranus—the traditional and modern ruling planets of your sign—form the first of three awkward quincunxes that recur on **April 12** and **October 5, 2013**. You can avoid frustration by remembering that you earn your freedom one small step at a time. It's tempting to express your frustration now, but don't waste your energy fighting against external forces holding you back. It's up to you to steadily develop the skills you need to create a more exciting future.

SUPER NOVA DAYS

NOVEMBER 22–23 ★ *paradise lost*

There's a distinct energetic shift during these two days as **November 22** is dominated by the sweet sensitivity, imagination, and compassion of Neptune. This dreamy planet's square to the Sun in your 11th House of Groups can evoke promises from friends or colleagues that are based more on hope than reality. However, an enchanting Venus-Neptune trine distracts you with visions of pleasure beyond measure. If you're charmed into pursuing an illusion, you're likely to wake with a start on **November 23** when combative Mars crashes into a volatile square with uncooperative Uranus. The open acceptance you felt yesterday gives way to impatience and anger. These feelings may appear destructive, but they give you the impetus you need to clear the air.

NOVEMBER 26 ★ *genius at work*

You're ready to carve out a unique new path when a brilliantly creative Sun-Uranus trine motivates you to express your originality. This wake-up call releases you from doubt and drudgery, opening the way for others to follow in your pioneering footsteps.

DECEMBER

BURIED TREASURE

Secrecy, power, and spiritual transformation lead you to the depths of your soul this month. You may experience moments of unpleasantness as you face hidden issues about trust and ethics. However, you have untapped resources that require a journey to the shadows of your psyche for extraction so you can bring them into the light. Cryptic Pluto, the mythological Lord of the Underworld, is stirring in the lair of your 12th House of Soul Consciousness to awaken desires and expose fears with several aspects to strategy-making outer planets. On **December 20**, visionary Jupiter makes its second quincunx to Pluto—the first was **July 18** and the last is on **March 29, 2013**—forcing you to edit your expectations. It's wise to make minor adjustments now to avoid major losses later. Fortunately, reliable Saturn forms a competent sextile with incisive Pluto on **December 26** to concentrate your focus and get you back on course for the New Year.

Eliminating unrewarding projects and patterns frees you to open yourself to the fresh ideas inspired by capricious Uranus's forward shift on **December 13**. Your sights are also raised by the inspirational Sagittarius New Moon in your 11th House of Hopes and Wishes. Empowering Mars provides further momentum for change when he moves into nonconformist Aquarius on the **25th**. Still, ambition is best managed prudently as the Sun enters traditional Capricorn, marking the Winter Solstice on **December 21**. Work-related matters may be dramatized by the security-conscious Cancer Full Moon in your 6th House of Employment on the **28th**. The Moon's opposition to provocative Pluto and square with irrepressible Uranus foments restlessness, perhaps even chaos. Nevertheless, the Full Moon trines stable Saturn, supplying a balance of reason to keep things from going completely off the rails.

KEEP IN MIND THIS MONTH

Looking into your heart of darkness is not a ticket to despair, but rather a passport to a brighter future where you can put your talents to use.

KEY DATES

DECEMBER 1–2 ★ *diamond in the rough*

Your brain is tightly wired with fast-moving ideas as clever Mercury forms an electric sesquisquare with innovative Uranus on **December 1**. Nervous energy is high, and if you talk too fast or act without reflection you could skip over a critical point or confound listeners with your outrageous ideas. The confident Sun's opposition to inflammatory Jupiter on the **2nd** adds strong opinions and the potential for overstatement to the mix, even though your enthusiasm could be contagious.

DECEMBER 7 ★ *sudden chemistry*

Your threshold of boredom is very low today—and your desire for new forms of pleasure high—as indulgent Venus in passionate Scorpio aspects unorthodox Uranus. Attraction to an unusual individual or activity can be risky, but you find it hard to resist. Adding spice to your relationship life by doing something completely new is one way to keep things fresh.

DECEMBER 14–16 ★ *stroke of genius*

A creative Mercury-Uranus trine on **December 14** sparks unique questions, exciting conversations, and unconventional answers. Your advanced ideas, which are often ahead of their time, can become reality with a magical quintile between physical Mars and radical Uranus on the **16th**. The rules that limit what others can do may be suspended for you as you experiment with new techniques, allowing you to leap over conventional methods of getting things done.

DECEMBER 19 ★ *alternative lifestyles*

You can have your cake and eat it, too, as today's harmonious trine between delicious Venus and maverick Uranus allows you to make constructive connections without losing your sense of independence. Freethinking friends and colleagues make perfect allies in projects that can advance your ideals and energize a group dynamic. Regrets are easily left behind as you are released from previous agreements and have the liberty to work and play in less predictable ways.

SUPER NOVA DAYS

DECEMBER 25–26 ★ *rebel with a cause*

Sparkplug Mars enters independent Aquarius on **December 25** to prod you into action. Keep it cool and kind, though, because an anti-authoritarian Sun-Uranus square can set off a charge of rebellion in you that shocks other people. It's appropriate to start new traditions as long as you don't suddenly cast all the old ones away. Helpfully, sturdy Saturn's savvy sextile with regenerative Pluto on the **26th** is effective for deep healing and transformation. This empowering aspect recurs on **March 8** and **September 21, 2013**, giving you time to firm up your resolve and develop the resources you need to achieve your goals.

PISCES

FEBRUARY 19–MARCH 20

PISCES

2011 SUMMARY

By now, the foundations upon which you built your life have been radically changed. This year you have a chance to put things back together in a manner that integrates these recent changes. Your charge is to assimilate your new sense of purpose into the fabric of your life. Your relationship with the material world begins to shift this year as you become excited about different ways to earn money. Neptune's fourteen-year swim through your watery world will surely increase your intuition, deepen your spirituality, and blur the barriers between reality and illusion.

AUGUST—*stormy weather*

The stress you are facing is not a test; it's a chance to prepare for the big changes coming your way next year.

SEPTEMBER—*midcourse corrections*

Sink into the depths of your feelings and watch the metamorphosis happen. Don't be impatient; everything will unfold on time.

OCTOBER—*uphill battle*

You are on the threshold of major transformation . . . yet you cannot rush the process. Aim high, work hard, and be patient.

NOVEMBER—*over the rainbow*

Your heart and mind may be racing toward tomorrow, yet it's the careful steps you take today that ensure a successful journey.

DECEMBER—*onward and upward*

It's not about reaching the mountaintop. It's about seeing it clearly in your mind's eye, putting intent into your vision, and creating a strategy to get there.

2011 CALENDAR

AUGUST

MON 1–WED 3 ★ It's impossible for you to concentrate now

MON 8–THU 11 ★ **SUPER NOVA DAYS** Play for keeps

SAT 13 ★ Seek to understand hidden mysteries

SUN 21–THU 25 ★ Temper your actions with kindness

SUN 28–TUE 30 ★ Love may be right at your doorstep now

SEPTEMBER

FRI 2 ★ Do something that will be memorable

THU 8–FRI 9 ★ Find your way back to reality

MON 12–WED 14 ★ **SUPER NOVA DAYS** Act with common sense

SAT 17–SUN 18 ★ Seek a compromise, whatever the cost

SUN 25–WED 28 ★ Be careful of overplaying your hand

OCTOBER

SAT 1–MON 3 ★ Practice moderation to prevent a serious headache

THU 6 –FRI 7 ★ Back up what you say with irrefutable facts

TUE 11–THU 13 ★ Enter the hidden realm of emotions

TUE 25–FRI 28 ★ **SUPER NOVA DAYS** You are hopeful for what's ahead

NOVEMBER

TUE 1–WED 2 ★ Facts get fuzzy and conversations grow tender

MON 7–THU 10 ★ **SUPER NOVA DAYS** Sharpen your skills and tighten up your act

TUE 15 –WED 16 ★ Pleasure appears where you least expect it

SUN 20 ★ Let a competent person take the lead today

SUN 27 ★ Demonstrate your affection now

DECEMBER

THU 1–MON 5 ★ It's easy to stir up passion, possessiveness, and jealousy

SAT 10–TUE 13 ★ Do what's best for someone you love

TUE 20–SAT 24 ★ **SUPER NOVA DAYS** Express your positive feelings

THU 29 ★ Dreaming of your future is a key ingredient in creating it

PISCES OVERVIEW

Simply just getting by isn't enough for you, Pisces; you need a more meaningful life. Your sensitive sign is the bridge between the realms of matter and spirit, which sometimes carries you toward the divine and sometimes leaves you disappointed with the crudeness of this world. For the first part of this year, though, **the gap between the real and the ideal may shrink as you find ways to infuse your daily routine with faith and imagination that restore your belief in humanity and in your own higher potential**. Wise Jupiter, the traditional ruler of your sign, begins 2012 in earthy Taurus and your 3rd House of Immediate Environment. The giant planet's broad vision reveals significance in the most mundane activities, instilling even the simplest acts with a deeper sense of purpose. You'll discover precious nuggets of truth in everyday conversations as your intuition takes you past the words to pick up deeper messages. Then, on June 11, Jupiter enters adaptable Gemini and your 4th House of Roots to open up new perspectives on family patterns and memories that can free you from the past. Options arise in this liberating environment, allowing you to step beyond old conditioning to play new roles at home and in your career.

Strategic Saturn entered your 8th House of Shared Resources on October 29, 2009, challenging you to negotiate with others to establish goals and boundaries that bring fairness and open communication to your relationships. The taskmaster planet shifts into your 9th House of Higher Thought and Faraway Places on October 5, beginning a two-year period of initiation that requires you to consolidate your big ideas and distill their essence to guide your journey and share what you've learned with others. On October 10, Saturn forms harmonious trines with your modern ruling planet Neptune in a series that completes on July 19, 2013. **This favorable alignment between earthbound Saturn and metaphysical Neptune gives shape to your dreams, showing you what it takes to bring your idea of heaven down to earth.** Your ability to skillfully navigate the paths between reality and fantasy allows you to patiently build your stairway to the stars. But this isn't just about satisfying your own desires; your personal success is a contribution to the collective well-being of the universe.

It's helpful to be flexible early in the year, because energetic Mars is retrograde from January 23 until April 13. This reversal occurs in your 7th House of Others, possibly delaying projects due to minor issues with partners. Carefully iron out kinks and attend to pesky details given the action planet's extended stay in conscientious Virgo. **Focus on resolving one issue at a time to keep from getting entangled in convoluted situations that take you farther from your goals.** And of course, make sure that you're working with individuals who are as committed as you to the task at hand.

OPEN YOUR HEART

Early in the year, the nitpicky issues that complicate relationships are more about bothersome material concerns than the bigger principles that govern intimacy as Mars retrogrades in your 7th House of Partners on January 23–April 13. However, you've already been addressing those deeper concerns during serious Saturn's two-year transit of your 8th House, which ends on October 5. Your frustration level hits the roof when the Virgo Full Moon joins Mars in your 7th House on March 8, but don't let one incident determine the future of a meaningful alliance. Saturn's role is to keep your mind on the bigger picture with an honest assessment of your needs and the chances of getting them satisfied in your present union. If you see the long-term value of a current connection, don't let little flaws tear apart the delicate fabric that binds you together. The small stuff is fixable if your hearts and financial interests are aligned. If you're single, reviewing your relationship history during Mars's retrograde will help you recognize how to alter your approach so you can establish more fulfilling alliances in the future.

SLOW ASCENT

Your professional life hits a turning point on June 4 with a risk-taking Sagittarius Lunar Eclipse in your 10th House of Career. Contentious Mars in critical Virgo tensely squares the Sun and Moon, stirring up conflict with colleagues or motivating you to shake things up at work. Raising your skills to a higher level is an excellent response but will probably require additional training. You get a subtle job-related boost when opportunistic Jupiter enters your foundation-building 4th House on June 11, starting a six-year climb toward greater public recognition as it moves toward the top of your chart. It helps to be patient, because delays on the job are inevitable when communicative Mercury retrogrades in your 6th House of Employment on July 14–August 8. You may spend the better part of this period completing unfinished tasks, repairing relationships, and reevaluating creative projects before you get back on track.

PATIENCE PAYS OFF

It's time for a financial reorganization and a reassessment of resources when assertive Mars, the ruler of your 2nd House of Money, turns retrograde on January 23. The action planet's reversal lasts until April 13, giving you plenty of time to tighten budgets, adjust expenses, and consider alternative paths to increase your income. However, the capricious Aries New Moon on March 22 joins excitable Uranus in your 2nd House to trigger new ideas that urge you toward immediate action. It makes sense that you long to flee your current situation in search of more stimulating ways to make a living. Still, no matter how brilliant your economic insights are—and you will have plenty of them this year—moving too quickly reduces their likelihood of success.

TENDER LOVING CARE

The ongoing transits of sensitive Neptune and compassionate Chiron occurring in your physical 1st House are gentle reminders to treat yourself tenderly. Relying on natural medicines and noncompetitive exercise such as yoga or t'ai chi helps you tap into your intuition to understand your body's needs. Retrograde Mercury backs into your sign on March 23, which could reactivate symptoms related to previous health issues. Yet this time around, you can find alternative means of addressing them to ensure your well-being. Stabilizing Saturn's supportive trine to your ruling planet Neptune on October 10 is favorable for long-term physical maintenance as you find sustainable ways to take care of yourself without worrying about petty details.

FREEDOM OF CHOICE

A restless Gemini Solar Eclipse in your 4th House of Home and Family can create domestic confusion on May 20. Foggy Neptune's tense square with this Sun-Moon conjunction blurs boundaries, making it hard to see where you stand with those closest to you. Forgiveness, inspiration, and spiritual insights are upsides of this important lunation. Generous Jupiter's entry into your 4th House on June 11 opens the way to conversations that expand your view of the past, helping you leave undesirable aspects of it behind and pursue a more rewarding living situation.

EARN WHILE YOU LEARN

You're eager to hit the road and broaden your horizons, especially during the Scorpio Full Moon in your 9th House of Adventure on May 5. Visionary Jupiter in sensible Taurus opposes the Moon, indicating great potential for turning your ideas into a profitable experience. Travel and education take on a more serious tone when stern Saturn enters your 9th House on October 5. Additionally, retrograde Mercury in this house on November 14–26 means that double-checking minor details can make major differences.

FAITH IN ACTION

Your spiritual beliefs may not align with your real-life conditions on January 23, when the Aquarius New Moon in your 12th House of Divinity forms stressful squares with worldly Jupiter and Saturn. It's time to either reassess your core philosophy or start applying your highest ideals in more down-to-earth ways. A long series of squares between Uranus the Awakener, the ruler of your 12th House, and transformative Pluto beginning on June 24 and ending on March 16, 2015, marks a period of profound soul searching spotted with spontaneous moments of doubt and revelation.

RICK & JEFF'S TIP FOR THE YEAR:
A Bouquet of Choices

While it's true that certainty rests weary minds, settling for simple answers now is more likely to limit you than contribute to your happiness. Evaluative Venus's retrograde period in your 4th House of Roots on May 15–June 27 converges with wise Jupiter's entry into this house on June 11. These transits of astrology's traditional benefics in multifaceted Gemini indicate that a wider range of views will not overload you with too much information but can carry you toward your desired destination.

JANUARY

LOVE AND LOGIC

The debate between your head and heart heats up with this month's stark contrast between romantic ideals and relationship realities. Reason's role, played by the Sun in pragmatic Capricorn, takes center stage when cerebral Mercury enters this earthbound sign on **January 8**. Yet feelings flow freely when the sentimental Cancer Full Moon on **January 9** lights up your 5th House of Love and Creativity, bringing hopes for romance to fruition. Waves of emotion and your need for affection can erode the walls of logic that help you maintain order in your life. In principle, the Full Moon's supportive sextile to active Mars in practical Virgo should help you keep at least one foot on the ground, yet it's a weak anchor against the winds of amour—which will soon blow even stronger. On **January 14**, Venus, the planet of attraction, dances into poetic Pisces to further arouse your interest in intimacy. This transit tends to make you more desirable, too, inviting attention from others while encouraging your pursuit of pleasure. There can be a self-indulgent side to Venus, which isn't necessarily a bad thing; putting a priority on your personal interests can balance your tendency to make too many sacrifices for others.

Keeping partners happy can become more difficult when Mars turns retrograde in your 7th House of Relationships on **January 23**. This backward turn of the aggression planet in persnickety Virgo lasts until **April 13**, requiring extra time and attention to keep alliances from unraveling. Nevertheless, repairing unions and rebuilding trust can be wise investments. Still, the independent Aquarius New Moon on the **23rd**, falling in your 12th House of Privacy, activates your need for breathing space, tempting you to run away from your responsibilities.

KEEP IN MIND THIS MONTH

Use your common sense to manage your time efficiently and to establish the guidelines that allow you to safely experience intense emotions.

KEY DATES

JANUARY 4 ★ *don't press your luck*

You can work your way through an awkward social situation or find methods to stretch your budget today as value-conscious Venus forms a creative quintile with your expansive co-ruling planet Jupiter. Just don't let good fortune overinflate your self-confidence; a slippery Sun-Neptune semisquare makes it easy for you to miscalculate your power and influence.

JANUARY 8 ★ *paradigm shift*

Conversations with friends and colleagues are rich with useful ideas as Mercury enters your 11th House of Groups and forms a favorable trine with Jupiter. Your ability to express and understand complex concepts benefits from this integration of fact and philosophy in reliable earth signs. However, a Mercury-Uranus square prompts provocative remarks and takes discussions in unexpected directions.

SUPER NOVA DAYS

JANUARY 13–14 ★ *love without limits*

Amorous and artistic Venus joins magical and dreamy Neptune on **January 13** to wash away inhibitions and stimulate your already vivid imagination. Your images of love, peace, romance, and beauty may exceed the limits of the material world, but instead of becoming lost in fantasy, let these discoveries inspire you to bring bits of heaven down to earth. Venus moves into mystical Pisces on the **14th**, continuing this deliciously inspiring theme. While it might not be the best time for objective analysis of practical matters, you could find yourself in an exceptional state of grace. Venus's slick sextile with benevolent Jupiter garners approval and offers respect from your peers—yet sensual delights may be its greatest reward.

JANUARY 22–23 ★ *audacity of hope*

Expectations and promises may stretch credibility with an overly optimistic square between the Sun and Jupiter on **January 22**. It is appropriate to expand your vision of what life could bring you, yet the payoff is unlikely to come quickly. Be leery of those whose faith is bound up with moralistic judgment. The Aquarius New Moon on the **23rd** paints pictures of a more perfect world and, perhaps, a more meaningful career, but with dynamic Mars turning retrograde, you have more groundwork to do with others before you're free to pursue your dreams.

JANUARY 28 ★ *consider your audience*

There's nothing wrong with seeking new experiences and speaking frankly. However, you must express even the brightest ideas carefully if you want them to get the reception they deserve. Mental Mercury's sextile to electric Uranus sparks brilliant concepts, but the messenger planet's square to overeager Jupiter is a reminder to avoid saying too much too soon.

FEBRUARY

DIVINE INTERVENTION

You're tempted to think about avoiding the challenges of daily life now, because the Sun in your 12th House of Spirituality until **February 19** tends to distract your attention from mundane activities. But instead of escaping into a fantasy world, you're meant to transmit images and dreams that inspire everyone around you. Still, your attraction to environments without rules and other states of consciousness is strengthened when your modern ruling planet Neptune returns to psychic Pisces on **February 3**. Its previous visit to your sign on **April 4–August 4, 2011**, was a preview of a transit that will last until 2025. Clearly, you can't stand on the sidelines that long, and you may not want to live in an ashram, convent, or monastery, either. Nevertheless, your dual existence between the worlds of fact and faith is likely to become even more important in the years to come.

The expressive Leo Full Moon brightens your 6th House of Work on **February 7**, generating bold ideas about your career. Finding the courage to make a significant change is wonderful as long as you combine it with logic to ground your strategy in reality. New ways to earn money can be kindled when resourceful Venus dashes into trailblazing Aries and your 2nd House of Income on **February 8**. The lure of creativity calls again when Mercury moves into watery Pisces on the **13th**, followed there by the Sun on the **19th**. The real magic happens, though, during the Pisces New Moon on **February 21**, as it is connected with spiritual Neptune. Dreams are being seeded; when you nourish them with compassion, forgiveness, and faith, they can grow into enduring expressions of your highest ideals.

KEEP IN MIND THIS MONTH

You have access to everything you need to be happy when you set aside your doubts and follow the flow of your positive feelings.

KEY DATES

FEBRUARY 1 ★ *give and take*

The line between flirting and fighting is very thin today as sexy Venus in your 1st House of Personality opposes feisty Mars in your 7th House of Partners. Chatty Mercury chimes in with a tense aspect to Mars that provokes snappy comments and conflict if you don't soften sharp verbal edges with a bit of kindness and a dash of humor.

FEBRUARY 7–9 ★ *spice up your life*

You long to go to extremes on **February 7**, but this will probably produce frustration rather than fulfillment. Affectionate Venus's ungainly quincunx with austere Saturn requires restraint that day despite the powerful emotions arising from the dramatic Leo Full Moon. On **February 8**, however, Venus fires into pioneering Aries, where she joins ingenious Uranus on the **9th**. This is a hot time for moneymaking ideas and spontaneous leaps of desire. Updating your image or investing in new equipment and training is bound to make your life more exciting.

FEBRUARY 13–16 ★ *down the rabbit hole*

Intellectual Mercury's slide into your empathic sign increases your intuitive awareness on **February 13**. But what you see can be very difficult to explain, especially when Mercury joins surreal Neptune on the **14th**. Poetic pictures of reality should inspire your artistic side but can make ordinary conversations a little fuzzy. Misunderstandings might undermine trust when Venus forms a tense square with suspicious Pluto on **February 15**. It's easy to be resentful and for tempers to flare, because irritable Mars also clashes with overblown Jupiter. Fortunately, letting off steam probably won't burn relationships to the ground as long as you use the clever communication skills of an articulate Mercury-Jupiter sextile on the **16th** to heal wounds rather than lay blame.

SUPER NOVA DAYS

FEBRUARY 19–21 ★ *star of the show*

The Sun's annual return to shape-shifting Pisces is a special event this year as it immediately joins your sign's modern ruling planet Neptune on **February 19**. The difference between inspiration and illusion may elude you in this dreamy environment. Venus's squishy semisquare with Neptune on **February 21** feeds the fires of fantasy with romantic feelings that are not necessarily rooted in reality. However, the Pisces New Moon, also on the **21st,** is a reminder that you can reinvent your sense of self and add more magic to your life. Imagine that you're an actor who gets to write his or her own part. Playing it with conviction turns it from fiction to a model of the new you. But if you're insincere in your new role, an exacting Mercury-Saturn sesquisquare will show you the false notes and point you back in the right direction.

MARCH

WORTH THE WAIT

Your natural tendency is to be trusting and open-minded, but it's important not to let others influence you to make decisions that go against your instincts. On **March 8**, the Full Moon in Virgo highlights your 7th House of Partners, which can connect you with authoritative individuals who provide you with valuable information. But these facts don't necessarily resonate with your deeper feelings and needs, so take your time before acting on them. Mercury turns retrograde in your 2nd House of Self-Worth on **March 12**, reenters Pisces on the **23rd**, and turns direct on **April 4**, which means this an ideal period for reflection and reconsideration before you make any significant choices. It's often difficult to explain your thoughts with mental Mercury in reverse—especially in your impressionistic sign—but that's not reason enough to surrender the power of making up your own mind.

Finances become a key issue when the Sun enters bold Aries and your 2nd House of Income on **March 20**, marking the Spring Equinox. The season is turning, and you may be driven by a sense of urgency with the impulsive Aries New Moon on the **22nd**. This Sun-Moon conjunction is closely joined with spontaneous Uranus and retrograde Mercury, which could ignite magnificent-sounding ideas about making money. Your desire to take immediate action is understandable but not necessarily wise. A more prudent and profitable approach is to wait and see if emerging economic revelations still sound good after Mercury turns direct on **April 4**. Leaving a job without giving sufficient notice or investing significant resources before doing your research is likely to prove more costly than clever.

KEEP IN MIND THIS MONTH

Always respect brilliant ideas, but remember that even the best of them can go up in smoke if you're in such a hurry that you leave common sense behind.

KEY DATES

SUPER NOVA DAYS

MARCH 3–6 ★ *change of heart*

You could run the emotional gamut from conflict to contentment during this intense period. It starts with the stress of an opposition between the willful Sun in Pisces and impatient Mars in Virgo on **March 3**. Normally, this combination has as much potential for playful passion as contentious combat, but harsh aspects now from vulnerable Venus to Mars and from the Sun to doubting Saturn make this a hard time to relax and trust others. Venus's opposition to Saturn on the **4th** can put a chill on relationships and leave you feeling underappreciated. You can state your needs and prove your worth more convincingly when Venus moves into her earthy home sign Taurus on the **5th**, yet a volatile Mercury-Uranus conjunction makes it hard for you to find stability. Animated speech and amazing ideas add excitement along with a tension that should subside on the **6th** when Venus sextiles Neptune to erase differences and invite shared moments of pleasure and delight.

MARCH 11 ★ *leader of the pack*

A creative quintile from the Pisces Sun to potent Pluto in Capricorn in your 11th House of Groups helps you transform chaos into order. Your ability to remove distractions allows you to reset your priorities and discover different ways to be an effective leader in your personal or professional life.

MARCH 13–14 ★ *irresistible you*

Passion motivates you to express your beliefs powerfully and pursue them with calculated concentration. Your strong conviction is due to Jupiter's third and final trine to profound Pluto on **March 13**, which repeats a regenerative pattern that occurred previously on **July 7** and **October 28, 2011**. Alluring Venus's trine to Pluto on the **13th** and conjunction with Jupiter on the **14th** add a delicious dose of pleasure and savvy social skills to help you achieve your aims or amuse you with entertaining friends and colleagues. Assertive Mars trines Venus, Jupiter, and Pluto to complete a stabilizing Grand Earth Trine, aligning you with powerful allies, and making you a compellingly attractive and competent figure.

MARCH 23–24 ★ *rebel with a cause*

Talkative Mercury backs into dreamy Pisces on **March 23**, muddling your thoughts with illusions or inspiring your words with imagery. A jumpy semisquare between stylish Venus and avant-garde Uranus brings surprises to your personal life that could entice you to explore unusual experiences. However, the Sun's conjunction with Uranus on the **24th** reveals your capacity to shock others, perhaps as a conscious agent of change or simply due to a sudden shift of attitude. Your generally compliant personality can grow more innovative, independent, and irreverent as you're less inclined to stick to the usual script.

APRIL

BACK TO BUSINESS

If you've been spinning your wheels without making any progress lately, you're ripe for change this month. Information should begin to flow more freely when interactive Mercury turns direct in your sign on **April 4**. Important conversations put on hold and unfinished work that was postponed are now set to resume as the messenger planet picks up speed in the days ahead. An imaginative quintile between your co-ruling planets, Jupiter and Neptune, on the **4th** reveals ways that you can meet practical considerations while also living up to your ideals. Making the most out of your relationships, both personal and financial, becomes top priority with the Libra Full Moon illuminating your 8th House of Shared Resources on **April 6**. Fairness is a concern meant to cut both ways, so make sure that you're being treated equitably instead of being the one to make all the compromises.

You receive a second wave of energy when dynamic Mars turns direct in your 7th House of Relationships on **April 13**. This is excellent for initiating professional projects, presenting new concepts to potential allies, and starting fresh in current partnerships. If you're single and looking, this is your cue to take the lead instead of waiting for someone you desire to make the first move. On **April 19**, the Sun enters sensual Taurus and your 3rd House of Communication to simplify your ideas so that you can easily explain your vision to others. You may also find more pleasure and comfort without going far from home with the Sun in this neighborly part of your chart. The Taurus New Moon on the **21st** forms a constructive sextile with magical Neptune that inspires you to take tangible steps toward living your dreams.

KEEP IN MIND THIS MONTH

You can find all the information you need to live a more fulfilling life with quiet contemplation and through insightful conversations with individuals you trust.

KEY DATES

SUPER NOVA DAYS

APRIL 5–7 ★ *precious illusions*

A heart-opening Venus-Neptune square on **April 5** stimulates your imagination—yet it could also skew your judgment about people and money. Stretching your financial and emotional limits in search of adventure is fine as long as you don't spend more than you can afford to lose or love someone who can't love you back. Your desire to escape a dull routine is understandable, especially with the Sun's semisquare to enchanting Neptune on the **6th**. The emotional fireworks should be strongest on the **7th** when the planetary lovers, Venus and Mars, clash in an explosive square that provokes exciting but risky behavior or simply complicates a current relationship.

APRIL 9–10 ★ *clean slate*

You discover new forms of play and pleasure on **April 9** with a slick sextile between flirty Venus in Gemini and unconventional Uranus. However, Venus's conjunction with the karmic Lunar South Node in your 4th House of Roots on the **10th** can pull you into a situation that may compromise your principles. It's better to let go and move on than to make allowances for someone who isn't worthy of your attention.

APRIL 15–16 ★ *hold your ground*

Your willingness to take less than you deserve avoids conflict but can set a bad precedent in an important relationship. The Sun and Venus run into tough aspects with immovable Saturn on **April 15–16** that can make it harder to get what you want from others. Patiently working for what you desire and learning to say no requires persistence and a strong commitment to yourself—which is, after all, the best place to put your trust.

APRIL 19 ★ *less is more*

Factual Mercury runs into a stressful semisquare with excessive Jupiter today, and you're left with an overload of information. Talking too much, exaggerating your story, or believing someone else's tall tales could prove costly. Expanding your perspective to consider other moneymaking opportunities is useful as long as you don't jump in without doing more research first.

APRIL 22–23 ★ *make it real*

You are imaginative, sensitive, and smart as the Sun aligns favorably with psychic Neptune and perceptive Mercury joins inventive Uranus in your 2nd House of Income on **April 22**. The brilliant moneymaking ideas you generate could involve a radical change of direction in your career. Yet no matter how unusual a concept you concoct, an energetic and realistic Sun-Mars trine in reliable earth signs on the **23rd** should give you every chance to launch your plan on a solid foundation.

WINDOW OF OPPORTUNITY

Solid plans and values quake like tectonic plates this month when your visionary ruling planet Jupiter forms stressful aspects with three outer planets. On **May 7**, a semisquare to electrifying Uranus can shock you with unexpected news, a sudden shift of circumstances, or a brilliant breakthrough that drastically alters your view of the future. Unfortunately, you'll run into obstacles turning this newfound perspective into reality as Jupiter makes the first of three cranky quincunxes with stodgy Saturn in your 8th House of Deep Sharing on the **16th**. Delays due to uncertain partners may be repeated when this aspect recurs on **December 22** and **March 23, 2013**, giving you more chances to get your allies on board. Lastly, Jupiter's ungainly sesquisquare with purging Pluto on **May 17** challenges you to intensify your commitments or cut some of them loose.

The intense Scorpio Full Moon on **May 5** in your 9th House of Big Ideas underscores the trend of stretching boundaries and seeking answers. Your natural desire to hold on to the past is overcome by the Moon's opposition to optimistic Jupiter. Thoughtful Mercury visits simplistic Taurus on the **9th**, supplying a desirable dose of common sense. However, family matters grow complicated when loving Venus turns retrograde in your 4th House of Roots on the **15th**. Reviewing and repairing domestic issues continue until amenable Venus turns direct on **June 27**. The Sun and Moon both enter curious Gemini and your 4th House on **May 20** to join in a New Moon Solar Eclipse that squares spacey Neptune to inspire dreams and sow confusion on the home front.

> **KEEP IN MIND THIS MONTH**
>
> *You can see so far into the future, it's hard to pay attention to the present. Nevertheless, it's today's small steps that can take you to your dream destination.*

KEY DATES

MAY 1 ★ *the price is not right*

You're enchanted with creative ideas as logical Mercury in your 2nd House of Resources forms a dynamic semisquare with illogical Neptune. However, misleading information could provoke a fanciful purchase or a verbal faux pas that turns out to be more expensive than expected.

SUPER NOVA DAYS

MAY 5–8 ★ *born to be wild*

You're hungry for adventure on **May 5**, thanks to a sexy Scorpio Full Moon in your 9th House of Faraway Place. Its opposition to boundless Jupiter expands your desire to escape the predictability of your daily routine, especially because trickster Mercury's opposition to stonewalling Saturn can make your world look so narrow. Energetic Jupiter and Mars form unsettling hard aspects with rebellious Uranus on the **7th** and **8th** that keep these restless feelings bubbling. It's healthier to experiment by trying new and different activities than to vent your emotions in outbursts of anger. In fact, if you push hard against someone, he or she may push back even harder—so pick your battles carefully or, even better, sidestep them entirely.

MAY 13–14 ★ *claim your power*

A joyous Sun-Jupiter conjunction in your 3rd House of Information broadens your mind and increases your powers of persuasion on **May 13**. The details of this big-picture perspective are filled in by a keenly observant Mercury-Mars trine. Just don't be too forceful with your ideas, since a sensitive Mercury-Venus aspect encourages you to interpret even innocent comments as harsh criticism. But you're likely to push on in your pursuit of knowledge and to make your points with an unwavering Mercury-Pluto trine on the **14th.** You feel little tolerance for weakness now that a pair of tense solar aspects to Saturn and Pluto demands your concentrated effort.

MAY 23 ★ *daydream believer*

Water can wear down the hardest rock when dissolving Neptune squares the willful Sun. This soft approach—which is about avoiding confrontation—is less than direct but corresponds to the day's cosmic weather. Leave room for your mind to wander instead of forcing yourself to follow a map that you don't want to read.

MAY 25–27 ★ *inconvenient truth*

Rationality may be derailed when perceptive Mercury squares deceptive Neptune on **May 25**. It's tempting to buy into stories that lack substance or to say anything that comes to mind if that's what it takes to placate others. Little lies, though, can add up to big problems, particularly when Mercury joins the Sun in verbose Gemini on the **27th**. It's better to stick to the facts or say nothing at all than to communicate carelessly now.

JUNE

UNEASY RIDER

It's hard to know exactly where you stand this month; planetary activity in your 4th House of Home and Family and 10th House of Career suggests significant movement in these key areas. On **June 4**, the thrill-seeking Sagittarius Full Moon is also a Lunar Eclipse in your 10th House that could get you itching for something different professionally. A challenging square to this eclipse from impulsive Mars could indicate conflict with a colleague, yet the upside is that it adds something new to your working environment. On **June 11**, your traditional ruling planet Jupiter enters multifaceted Gemini and your domestic 4th House, starting a year of self-discovery and a reexamination of the foundation upon which you build your life. Fresh ideas keep pouring in with the inquisitive Gemini New Moon on **June 19**, while a combative square from Mars could force you to defend them against an aggressive individual. Fortunately, stabilizing Saturn's harmonious trine to the New Moon grants you patience and reason to help navigate through choppy waters.

The Sun enters emotional Cancer on **June 20**, marking the Summer Solstice and turning up the heat in your 5th House of Romance and Play. This is a perfect time for working with children, engaging in creative activities, and opening up your heart. Still, security-seeking Cancer reminds you to step cautiously into new areas of self-expression to ensure your comfort and safety along the way. A series of seven transformational squares between Uranus and Pluto that can affect teamwork and money starts on **June 24** and intermittently reappears until **March 16, 2015**. Ripples of uncertainty, though, may be smoothed by an inspiring and imaginative square between your co-ruling planets, Jupiter and Neptune, on **June 25**.

KEEP IN MIND THIS MONTH

Avoid responding too quickly to apparent crises. Conditions are changing so fast, many will resolve themselves without any effort on your part.

KEY DATES

SUPER NOVA DAYS

JUNE 4–5 ★ *all you need is love*

Stay light on your feet and flexible in your head as you go with the flow of the adventurous Sagittarius Full Moon Eclipse on **June 4**. Your modern ruling planet Neptune turns retrograde, adding a layer of confusion. But the key to managing in the midst of shifting moods and circumstances is to maintain harmonious relationships. The stressful square between retrograde Venus in your 4th House of Foundations and reckless Mars reveals stark differences of values and methods. However, beautiful Venus joins the Sun on the **5th**, blessing you with charm and a greater sense of self-worth that can calm troubled waters.

JUNE 8 ★ *sixth sense*

Your imagination and faith are lifted by a hopeful trine between Mercury and Neptune. This easy alignment of intellect and intuition plugs you into higher truths, even if you can't find the words to clearly express what you're thinking. This is more about gentle epiphanies than hard facts, so swim in the warm waters of understanding and inspiration without worrying about what others think.

JUNE 16–17 ★ *stranded on fantasy island*

Mercury's semisquare with giant Jupiter on **June 16** makes small things appear big and details seem more overwhelming. Exaggeration colors statements to prove a point that could be misleading. Avoid overselling your ideas or buying what others say until you have a strong grasp of the facts. Mercury's sesquisquare with Neptune on the **17th** continues this pattern of mixing up wishes with reality. Luckily, you have the freedom now to be creative and follow your dreams.

JUNE 23–25 ★ *hansel and gretel*

The Sun's sensible trine to Neptune gives form to fantasies on **June 23**, helping you to produce magic in your personal life. An air of romance pervades your atmosphere, enabling you to relax, release your previous expectations, and let yourself go. The surreal Jupiter-Neptune square on the **25th** can put you on very thin ice if oversensitive emotions or alluring illusions carry you away from reality. Exploring the outer limits of imagination is a worthy journey as long as you drop enough bread crumbs to eventually find your way back home.

JUNE 27–29 ★ *the art of persuasion*

You find solid ground beneath your feet on **June 27** with valuable Venus's direct turn in your 4th House of Security. Power struggles can ensue, however, due to a competitive Sun-Pluto opposition on the **29th**. Happily, a charming Mercury-Jupiter sextile should help you think fast and talk your way out of any difficult situation.

JULY

THE THINGS WE DO FOR LOVE

You feel a growing desire to express your feelings and deepen your emotional connections this month with the Sun shining brightly in your 5th House of Romance until **July 22**. Yet opening your heart without using your head is unlikely to produce the results you seek. Enterprising Mars enters diplomatic Libra and your 8th House of Intimacy on **July 3**, pointing out the importance of coolly assessing situations to avoid giving too much for what you get in return. Polite persistence in pursuing your interests is needed to keep relationships in balance. This also pertains to your associations with friends and workmates on the **3rd**, when the steadfast Capricorn Full Moon illuminates your 11th House of Groups. A lunar conjunction with powerful Pluto and square to unstable Uranus can shake up the rules, leaving you unclear about your status with others. However, this unpredictability factor also excites you with a fresh perspective that frees you from the limits of your old alliances.

Mercury's retrograde turn in your 6th House of Employment on **July 14** initiates a three-week period that's excellent for reviewing how you work with others and reassessing your skills and techniques to make improvements where you can. The Cancer New Moon on the **19th** plants seeds of creativity and playfulness in your expressive 5th House. However, a stressful square to this Sun-Moon conjunction from Saturn can frustrate you with delays or disapproval. Don't duck the challenges you're facing; your commitment to overcoming obstacles and your consistent effort is what matters. The Sun moves into Leo and your 6th House on **July 22**, dramatizing work-related issues and enlivening your daily routine. Your newfound confidence enables you to overcome a lack of recognition by being more assertive and standing up to pushy people.

KEEP IN MIND THIS MONTH

Even if complex issues are very clear to you, it may prove difficult to explain them to others. Think through your concerns before discussing them with anyone else.

KEY DATES

JULY 2 ★ *information overload*

Minor complications at home could spiral out of control today—or you may simply spread yourself too thin—as boisterous Jupiter joins the Moon's karmic South Node in diverse Gemini and your 4th House of Roots. A little insight is a wonderful thing, but discussing matters endlessly won't change anything until you make a decision and take appropriate action.

JULY 8–9 ★ *save your energy*
Applying a soft touch will get more done than pushing hard when macho Mars and the Sun form slippery aspects with blurry Neptune on **July 8–9**. This is no time for a show of strength; instead, your ability to adapt will help you skirt a conflict. Be gentle with yourself, as physical exertion can be more tiring than usual now. If you have the chance, rejuvenate your spirit by quietly tuning into nature, the arts, or spirituality. You will feel much better for the experience.

JULY 13 ★ *great expectations*
Revolutionary Uranus turns retrograde in your 2nd House of Income, delaying radical financial moves that need more time for review. Nevertheless, holding your ground may not be very interesting with the Sun's semisquare to auspicious Jupiter. Your desire to take personal risks can provoke a bold move toward pleasure. Enjoying the moment makes sense as long as you don't make promises you can't keep.

SUPER NOVA DAYS
JULY 17–18 ★ *reckless abandon*
You're feeling unbridled enthusiasm or uncontrollable restlessness, fueled by a high-octane trine between loud Jupiter and hyper Mars on **July 17**. You're tempted to go to extremes when a Mars-Pluto square increases the intensity. If you can focus the powerful forces you're feeling, almost nothing can stop you. It is possible, though, to waste that passion on a battle with an unsupportive ally. Yet the real issue is your fluctuation between boundless faith and bottomless fear with a Jupiter-Pluto quincunx on the **18th**. This aspect returns on **December 20** and **March 29, 2013**, giving you additional opportunities to find harmony with this unlikely couple. Still, an explosive Mars-Uranus opposition in the financial and self-worth houses of your chart can confront you with an irrational individual or cause you to erupt if you're fed up with a stagnant situation.

JULY 24 ★ *psychic self-defense*
Your willingness to take on a thankless task and your dedication to duty are admirable traits, but self-sacrifice could cost more than you expect. A misty Sun-Neptune quincunx dissolves boundaries, leaving you vulnerable physically and emotionally if you don't consciously set limits to protect yourself.

AUGUST

OSCAR-WINNING PERFORMANCE

This unique month is rich with opportunities for spiritual and emotional growth. The first of two Full Moons occurs on **August 1** in your 12th House of Divinity, and it features an exact trine to visionary Jupiter that tunes up your intuition and floods you with insights. This socially responsible Aquarius Full Moon is also harmoniously aligned with irrepressible Mars and innovative Uranus, giving you the impetus to break with the past and apply your vision to a higher cause. A more personal transit is magnetic Venus's move into nurturing Cancer and your 5th House of Romance on **August 7**, which coaxes you to express your feelings more openly. A combination of tenderness and lust makes you a very desirable partner in love.

Messenger Mercury's direct turn on the **8th** gets information flowing more easily, especially when related to work, health, and school. Then on **August 17**, the creative Leo New Moon in your 6th House forms efficient sextiles with Mars and Saturn that are perfect for sharpening your skills and becoming more effective at work. The Sun's entry into service-oriented Virgo and your 7th House of Partners on the **22nd** puts relationships on the front burner. Fortunately, Mars's move into formidable Scorpio and your 9th House of Philosophy on **August 23** provides the punch you need to fight for your beliefs and stimulate your interest in travel and higher education. On **August 31**, the whimsical Pisces Full Moon joins your modern ruling planet Neptune in your 1st House of Personality. This is a time of make-believe when you can alter your image to fulfill your fantasies. Just don't get so lost in your role that you can't tell when the play is over.

KEEP IN MIND THIS MONTH

The purpose of dreaming is to take what floats to the surface of your subconscious mind and creatively integrate it into your everyday life.

KEY DATES

AUGUST 3–4 ★ *dancing in the dark*

Pushy Mars in your 8th House of Intimacy makes a tense aspect with spacey Neptune on **August 3**, which can distract you or diffuse your efforts. A romantic escape can be fun as long as you're not looking for something more lasting. Examine even the best-sounding ideas with skepticism when retrograde Mercury skids off a quincunx with murky Neptune on the **4th**. There's no need to struggle to clarify your point unless you're sure that the other person is really committed to the process.

AUGUST 15 ★ *safety first*

It's time to draw a line when it comes to relationships due to a super-serious Mars-Saturn conjunction in your 8th House of Deep Sharing. A possessive Venus-Pluto opposition can raise desires to the boiling point, but it's vital to know what the ground rules are before giving into your passion. Arguing with someone needlessly or withholding vital information can threaten financial partnerships. Take the time to build trust and study the matter in detail before moving forward.

AUGUST 20–22 ★ *collaborative effort*

You can advance your agenda with another person on **August 20** if you don't come on too strong. A Sun-Mars sextile provides motivation, though the warrior planet's irregular sesquisquare with bloated Jupiter pushes optimism beyond the bounds of reason. Logic returns and you align yourself with trustworthy people on the **22nd**, when the Sun enters analytical Virgo and your 7th House of Relationships. You also have the benefit of a witty Mercury-Jupiter sextile that empowers your words and enhances your comprehension.

AUGUST 24–26 ★ *the magic touch*

You are inspired to look past the limits of reality as the expressive Sun and desirable Venus form difficult aspects with otherworldly Neptune on **August 24**. Your judgment may not be very practical—but don't close the door to your imagination. Even the most outlandish dreams are worthy of serious consideration on the **26th**, when persistent Mars in Scorpio forms a creative trine with magical Neptune that gives you the gift of making miracles happen.

SUPER NOVA DAY

AUGUST 31 ★ *hope floats*

The Full Moon in colorful Pisces opposes the Sun in pragmatic Virgo, while phantasmagoric Neptune's conjunction with the Moon favors spirit and faith over materialism and mere facts. You can be enchanted by ideas and feelings that lift the weight of the world off your shoulders. Forgiving yourself for past mistakes removes barriers to self-acceptance and opens the way to attracting competent allies to help you turn your vision into reality.

SEPTEMBER

TALK IT OUT

Delving into the details of relationships can be a tedious process, yet it's essential work for you this month. While it's true that love and cooperation sometimes flow in the magic of silent understanding, words are the means to establishing deep connections now. This emphasis on communication began on **August 31**, when thoughtful Mercury entered your 7th House of Partners and discriminating Virgo, where every little syllable counts. The risk is that you can become overly critical or subject to excessive criticism by others, even over trivial matters. The value is not in pointing out flaws but in fixing them. When you and those who are supposed to be on your side think positively, you will find solutions, not just problems. Mercury's conjunction with the Sun on **September 10** is an important date for clear communication as whatever's said has the power to make a permanent impression. On the **15th**, the New Moon in trustworthy Virgo clears the way for a fresh start in personal and professional unions. Knowing what you want, instead of accepting whatever's given, will help you build mutually beneficial alliances.

Your ability to discuss delicate matters goes even farther when Mercury enters negotiating Libra and your 8th House of Shared Resources on **September 16**. Although this transit might put you in the middle of some sticky situations, a cool head and sense of fair play should bring peace and cooperation. Relationships are strengthened when the Sun enters harmonious Libra and your 8th House on the **22nd**, marking the Autumn Equinox. On **September 29**, the incorrigible Aries Full Moon connects with unorthodox Uranus in your 2nd House of Income, shocking you with unexpected expenses or intriguing moneymaking ideas.

KEEP IN MIND THIS MONTH

You don't need brilliant partners to be successful, but you do require individuals ready to work hard to make the most of your relationships.

KEY DATES

SEPTEMBER 1 ★ *sound check*

Sweet talk is the upside of chatty Mercury's opposition to dreamy Neptune. However, confusion is also possible if you don't double-check your impressions to make sure that everyone's on the same page. Don't naively assume that your interpretation matches anyone else's until you're able to validate this instinct.

SUPER NOVA DAYS

SEPTEMBER 5–8 ★ *connect the dots*

A smart Mercury-Mars sextile on **September 5** is excellent for figuring out how to untangle a misunderstanding or become more productive with a partner. But unnecessary pride and outrageous promises could set you up for disappointment at work on the **6th** when Venus strides into theatrical Leo and makes an unbalanced semisquare with overly confident Jupiter. Grand gestures can attract attention, but expecting too much or offering more than you can deliver is risky. Facts rule on the **7th**, when analytical Mercury connects with realistic Saturn even as a Sun-Jupiter square could have you dreaming about bigger and better days ahead. Pushing the intellectual envelope when Mercury squares promising Jupiter on **September 8** can eventually assist your career if you do the research necessary to fill in the details of your impressive plans.

SEPTEMBER 16–17 ★ *bite your tongue*

A little push provokes a big reaction when excitable Mars in your 8th House of Deep Sharing skids off a quincunx with loud Jupiter on the **16th**. Adjust your approach if you sense that you're making someone uncomfortable. But if you're on the receiving side of undesirable pressure, do what you can to skirt the issue until you've had a chance to consider the best response. Mercury's semisquare to Mars and quincunx with imaginative Neptune on the **17th** spur some very creative thinking, yet also can stir up conflict based on a misunderstanding.

SEPTEMBER 20 ★ *grace under fire*

Staying cool under pressure earns you positive recognition at work with a pleasing sextile between graceful Venus and bighearted Jupiter. However, Mercury's tense aspects to unpredictable Uranus and dark Pluto can test your patience with a friend who seems to have gone off the deep end. Your support can mean the world to someone in need.

SEPTEMBER 25–27 ★ *start making sense*

Don't take the bait and engage in battle or rush to meet someone's unrealistic expectations on the **25th**, when Mars hits the Uranus-Pluto square with stressful aspects to both complex planets. Venus joins the fray with a surprising aspect to Uranus on the **25th** and entangling engagements with Pluto and Mars on **September 26–27** that rattle relationship dynamics. Luckily, Mercury's trine to know-it-all Jupiter gives you the wisdom to manage the chaos.

OCTOBER

HONESTY IS THE BEST POLICY

Your compassionate nature can sometimes leave you struggling to speak your mind. However, a union of expressive Mercury and authentic Saturn on **October 5** demands honesty even in delicate situations. This conjunction occurs in your 8th House of Intimacy just before both planets move into passionate Scorpio and your 9th House of Higher Truth, where being honest is as important as being kind. Exuberant Mars fires into courageous Sagittarius and your 10th House of Career on the **6th**, which rewards you for boldly expressing yourself. Sure, you might rub someone the wrong way, but it's better than keeping silent or agreeing to activities that go against your beliefs. Fortunately, a harmonious trine between strict Saturn and gentle Neptune on the **10th**—the first in a series that concludes on **July 19, 2013**—provides a perfect balance between necessity and empathy so you can still take care of business without losing touch with your heart.

The equitable Libra New Moon in your 8th House of Deep Sharing also favors frankness over pleasantries on **October 15**. Normally, the sign of the Scales is willing to waffle to avoid unpleasantness, yet a trine to this Sun-Moon conjunction from open-minded Jupiter in lighthearted Gemini allows you to take even difficult messages in stride. The Sun's entry into resolute Scorpio on the **22nd** reinforces the 9th House theme of living up to your word and your principles regardless of the cost. On **October 29**, the Taurus Full Moon in your 3rd House of Immediate Environment trines incisive Pluto, forcing you to recognize what habits to let go of so that you can concentrate your efforts where they have the most impact.

KEEP IN MIND THIS MONTH

Confidence in the value of what you have to say will give you the authority to broach difficult subjects without arousing resistance.

KEY DATES

OCTOBER 3–5 ★ *dream lover*

You're more alluring than ever on **October 3**, when captivating Venus enters loyal Virgo and your 7th House of Relationships. Being clear about what you want is a good idea, yet the love planet also opposes illusionary Neptune, which may obscure facts with fantasy. A magical connection stirs romantic feelings, but you'll need to test it over time to see if it's real. Jupiter's retrograde turn on the **4th** reminds you to seek answers within rather than relying on others as your guides. Still, the sobering Mercury-Saturn conjunction on **October 5** squeezes out illusions and demands intellectual accountability.

SUPER NOVA DAYS

OCTOBER 9–10 ★ *the force is with you*

You're ready to take action instead of dwelling on your thoughts on **October 9**, when a lucky Sun-Jupiter trine blesses you with hope. You can rely on your mental acuity as Mercury sextiles penetrating Pluto on the **10th**, the day of the Saturn-Neptune trine. You're able to focus on key issues and communicate with power to establish strategies for achieving lofty goals. When you believe in your work, you can line up the support you need and will benefit from the resources that others contribute to your ultimate success.

OCTOBER 15–16 ★ *with open arms*

Look for financial partners or soul mates when the 8th House Libra New Moon trines magnanimous Jupiter on **October 15**. Jupiter's stressful sesquisquare with Saturn, though, is a reminder to consolidate gains, as was the case with their first aspect on **July 20** and will be with their last on **May 20, 2013**. A healthy dash of skepticism will help you avoid paying or expecting too much on the **16th**, when gabby Mercury and indulgent Venus create hard aspects to exaggerating Jupiter.

OCTOBER 23 ★ *a bridge too far*

A solar trine to ethereal Neptune infiltrates your imagination and increases your faith. However, the Sun's stressful aspect to Jupiter might have you leaping to get your rewards before they're ready. Lie back and let the goodies come to you instead of pursuing something you might not be able to catch.

OCTOBER 28–29 ★ *in the zone*

You're itching for action with restless Mars opposite adventurous Jupiter. This is excellent for firing up a new enterprise, promoting an idea, or stretching your muscles. Just avoid overdoing things by setting a reasonable goal and stopping once you reach it. Although rational Mercury's square to irrational Neptune on the **29th** can muddle your thinking, its entry into enthusiastic Sagittarius and the determined Taurus Full Moon keep you moving forward with your plans.

NOVEMBER

PROFESSIONAL REORIENTATION

Stepping back from long-range plans to reset your priorities may slow you down this month, but it'll ultimately save you considerable time and energy. Mercury, the information planet, turns retrograde in your 10th House of Career on **November 6** to bring unfinished business into the foreground. Tying up loose ends and clarifying communications at work can be frustrating, but it's the only way you can maintain a reasonable level of comfort. Mercury returns to your 9th House of Adventure on the **14th**, urging you to examine the relationship between your current reality and your ideals. When the Messenger turns direct on **November 26**, you can begin moving forward with a greater sense of purpose. On **November 13**, the provocative Scorpio New Moon Solar Eclipse activates your 9th House, reminding you of unfulfilled promises you made to yourself. If you're hungering for travel, learning, or other experiences beyond your work and daily duties, it may be time to commit to fulfilling those desires—or perhaps to cut those dreams loose and move on with your life.

You'll experience healthy competition with colleagues on **November 16**, when hardworking Mars enters ambitious Capricorn and your 11th House of Groups. If you can raise the level of your game, however, you'll earn respect and support to advance your interests in the future. The Sun's entry into exuberant Sagittarius and your professional 10th House on the **21st** is another signal to be more assertive at work. Still, the changeable Gemini Full Moon Eclipse on **November 28** lights up your 4th House of Roots, stirring up a variety of issues at home. Stressful lunar aspects from hyperactive Mars and restrictive Saturn reflect the importance of completing current obligations before you take on anything more.

KEEP IN MIND THIS MONTH

Look into the bottom of your heart where your deepest desires lie, for that's where you can find the passion and power to achieve success.

KEY DATES

NOVEMBER 6 ★ *big appetite*

What you can see is much bigger than what you can digest as the Sun forms an irregular quincunx with famished Jupiter. It's great to stretch your mind, but today's hopes and promises may exceed your reach. Mercury's retrograde turn is another reminder to finish what's already on your plate before adding more to it.

NOVEMBER 9 ★ *generous to a fault*

You feel like a lottery winner with a rewarding trine between delightful Venus and bountiful Jupiter. Just don't give away your winnings too quickly; this lucky transit is followed by a delusional Venus-Neptune aspect that makes it easy to forget how hard you've worked for the respect, money, or pleasure that you're receiving. Make sure the recipient of your largesse—whether it's material or emotional—is worthy of your affection and attention.

SUPER NOVA DAYS

NOVEMBER 13–14 ★ *process of elimination*

The truth may be staring right back at you on **November 13**, yet you still find it extremely hard to see. The transformational Scorpio New Moon in your 9th House of Journeys can arouse feelings you don't readily understand, especially while retrograde Mercury forms a fact-fuzzy square with diffusive Neptune. This lunation, a total Solar Eclipse, can expose unfilled needs that may be too painful to face. However, you'll clear space for more achievable aspirations once you recognize which unrealistic goals need to be deleted from your list. A contentious Sun-Pluto semisquare on the **14th** might trigger a power struggle, but it also backs up the idea that letting go is the way to grow.

NOVEMBER 21–22 ★ *the stuff of dreams*

Contrasting planetary patterns raise your hopes and your suspicions when the Sun moves into sunny Sagittarius and Venus enters skeptical Scorpio on **November 21**. Both planets form aspects with diaphanous Neptune on the **22nd** that increase your tendency to favor fantasy over reality. Still, if your inspiration is more than a fleeting idea or feeling, and you back it up with a serious assessment of what it takes to bring it down to earth, you could be on your way to making magic.

NOVEMBER 26–27 ★ *rise to the challenge*

A sobering Venus-Saturn conjunction on **November 26** can cause you to question your worth. However, don't let stingy people determine your value. This aspect rewards you for patience and commitment, but also reminds you to recall earlier accomplishments that built a foundation for future growth. An intense conjunction of combative Mars and ruthless Pluto on the **27th** could make you feel like you're fighting for scraps. Still, if your drive and determination are strong, you can blast through almost any obstacle.

DECEMBER

ADJUST AND ADVANCE

There may be aspects of your professional life that are difficult to accept this month but don't let that get in the way of tasting the personal pleasures that are also available. Planets flying into farseeing Sagittarius and your 10th House of Career and Responsibility will motivate you if you love your work—or make you restless if you don't. Messenger Mercury leads the parade on **December 10**, followed by the cheerful Sagittarius New Moon on the **13th**, and sociable Venus on the **15th**. Sagittarius is ruled by your key planet Jupiter, sharing your taste for expansion, but it's a fire sign that lacks the sensitivity of Pisces. You may be called upon to do some hard selling or to maintain enthusiasm whether you feel like it or not. It's reasonable, though, to have some doubts about what you're doing; your principled ruling planet Jupiter forms edgy quincunxes with tough guys Pluto and Saturn on **December 20–22** that could raise ethical questions. These aspects recur on **March 23–29, 2013**, when you'll be better prepared to make a definitive decision about your job.

The pressure diminishes for you—thanks to supportive friends and colleagues—on **December 21** with the Sun's entry into competent Capricorn and your 11th House of Teamwork. This is the Winter Solstice, marking a seasonal change that encourages you to step away from the past and turn your life in a new direction. The caring Cancer Full Moon on the **28th** lights up your 5th House of Romance to open your heart to deeper delights. Then the Moon's square with disruptive Uranus and opposition to extreme Pluto intensify your emotions, rattle your personal life, and give you a taste of the year ahead.

KEEP IN MIND THIS MONTH

It's hard to trust your progress when unexpected obstacles arise, but keep plugging. You'll find your way around before you know it.

KEY DATES

DECEMBER 2 ★ *sneak peek*

The Sun's opposition to propitious Jupiter blesses you with a philosophical perspective today that allows you to overlook immediate problems and see future possibilities. There is, however, a long road between where you are and where you want to be. What you're getting is a rough outline; you'll need to fill it in with serious thinking and planning before the picture comes completely clear.

DECEMBER 10–12 ★ *study buddy*

The Winged Messenger's launch into excitable Sagittarius on **December 10** could produce misdirected rockets of enthusiasm. Then, on the **11th**, its square to cloudy Neptune is awesome for creative thinking and spiritual experiences but not so strong on facts or objectivity. Still, even if you go off track, guidance arrives on the **12th** from a super-capable quintile between active Mars and disciplined Saturn to correct your course and put you in a more productive mode. An uplifting conjunction of Venus and the Moon's North Node in your 9th House of Big Ideas can connect you with a passionate partner in the pursuit of knowledge.

SUPER NOVA DAYS

DECEMBER 16–18 ★ *a world beyond*

Your heart and head are wide open as Venus squares Neptune on the **16th**, and Mercury opposes Jupiter on the **17th**. This combination isn't great for self-restraint and common sense. In fact, you're able to justify the most impractical actions and may prefer to leave reality behind as you float through a romantic dreamscape. It's your job not only to find inspiration, but also to encourage others to recognize the metaphysics and magic behind the facade of the material world. Physical Mars's dynamic aspect with jovial Jupiter on the **18th** also lifts your enthusiasm, yet beware taking on more than your fair share of responsibility in a group.

DECEMBER 22 ★ *reconcilable differences*

Sweet Venus's opposition to Jupiter can make you generous to a fault, yet its real purpose is to recognize how good you can be to those nearest and dearest to you. Yes, it's possible to love without limits and still notice other people's flaws, but accepting someone's essence doesn't mean that you have to approve of every aspect of his or her behavior.

DECEMBER 28 ★ *feelings without borders*

Emotions may erupt at the moody Cancer Full Moon in your 5th House of Self-Expression. A lunar opposition to Pluto can attract a manipulative partner, while a square to Uranus fires up your urge for freedom. Clearly, this is a complicated time—but a favorable trine to the Moon from mature Saturn helps you create calm in the middle of the storm.